# Global Norms with a Local Face

To what extent are global rule-of-law norms, which external actors promote in post-conflict states, localized? Who decides whether global standards or local particularities prevail? This book offers a new approach to the debate about how the dilemma between the diffusion of global norms and their localization is dealt with in global politics. Studying the promotion of children's rights, access to public information and an international commission against impunity in Guatemala, Lisbeth Zimmermann demonstrates that rule-of-law promotion triggers domestic contestation, and thereby changes the approach taken by external actors and ultimately the manner in which global norms are translated. However, the leeway in local translation is determined by the precision of global norms. Based on an innovative theoretical approach and in-depth study of rule-of-law translation, she argues for a shift in norm promotion from context sensitivity to democratic appropriation, speaking to international relations, peacebuilding, democratization studies, international law and political theory.

LISBETH ZIMMERMANN is a senior researcher at the Peace Research Institute Frankfurt. She is an external lecturer at Goethe University Frankfurt and affiliated with the university's Cluster of Excellence 'Formation of Normative Orders'.

# Cambridge Studies in International Relations: 143

## Global Norms with a Local Face

*Cambridge Studies in International Relations* is a joint initiative of Cambridge University Press and the British International Studies Association (BISA). The series aims to publish the best new scholarship in international studies, irrespective of subject matter, methodological approach or theoretical perspective. The series seeks to bring the latest theoretical work in International Relations to bear on the most important problems and issues in global politics.

# Cambridge Studies in International Relations

*Series list continues after index*

# Global Norms with a Local Face

## Rule-of-Law Promotion and Norm-Translation

LISBETH ZIMMERMANN
*Peace Research Institute Frankfurt*

# CAMBRIDGE
UNIVERSITY PRESS

University Printing House, Cambridge CB2 8BS, United Kingdom

One Liberty Plaza, 20th Floor, New York, NY 10006, USA

477 Williamstown Road, Port Melbourne, VIC 3207, Australia

4843/24, 2nd Floor, Ansari Road, Daryaganj, Delhi – 110002, India

79 Anson Road, #06–04/06, Singapore 079906

Cambridge University Press is part of the University of Cambridge.

It furthers the University's mission by disseminating knowledge in the pursuit of education, learning, and research at the highest international levels of excellence.

www.cambridge.org
Information on this title: www.cambridge.org/9781107172043
DOI: 10.1017/9781316771341

First published 2017

Printed in the United Kingdom by Clays, St Ives plc

*A catalogue record for this publication is available from the British Library.*

*Library of Congress Cataloging-in-Publication Data*
Names: Zimmermann, Lisbeth, author.
Title: Global norms with a local face : rule-of-law promotion and norm-translation / Lisbeth Zimmermann.
Description: Cambridge, United Kingdom ; New York, NY : Cambridge University Press, 2017. | Series: Cambridge studies in international relations
Identifiers: LCCN 2016056472 | ISBN 9781107172043 (hardback)
Subjects: LCSH: Rule of law. | International law. | Convention on the Rights of the Child (1989 November 20) | Children's rights. | Freedom of information. | Rule of law – Guatemala. | BISAC: POLITICAL SCIENCE / International Relations / General.
Classification: LCC K3171 .Z56 2017 | DDC 340/.11–dc23
LC record available at https://lccn.loc.gov/2016056472

ISBN 978-1-107-17204-3 Hardback

# Contents

# *Figures*

# Tables

# Abbreviations

| | | |
|---|---|---|
| ANAM | Asociación Nacional de Municipalidades de la República de Guatemala | National Association of Guatemalan Municipalities |
| ATI | access to information | |
| CACIF | Comité Coordinador de Asociaciones Agrícolas, Comerciales, Industriales y Financieras | Committee of Agricultural, Commercial, Industrial and Financial Associations |
| CALDH | Centro para la Acción Legal en Derechos Humanos | Centre for Legal Action on Human Rights |
| CCOIPINGUA | Comité Consultivo de Organismos Internacionales para la Protección Integral de la Niñez Guatemalteca | Guatemalan Consultative Committee of International Organizations for Child Protection |
| CEH | Comisión para el Esclarecimiento Histórico | Commission for Historical Clarification |
| CIA | Central Intelligence Agency | |
| CIACS | Cuerpos Ilegales y Aparatos Clandestinos de Seguridad | Illegal Groups and Clandestine Security Structures |
| CICIACS | Comisión de Investigación de Cuerpos Ilegales y Aparatos Clandestinos de Seguridad | Commission for the Investigation of Illegal Groups and Clandestine Security Structures |
| CICIG | Comisión Internacional contra la Impunidad en Guatemala | International Commission against Impunity in Guatemala |
| CLAI | Conferencia Latinoamericana de Iglesias | Latin American Conference of Churches |
| CNJ | Código de la Niñez y la Juventud | Children and Youth Code |

*(cont.)*

| CRC | Convention on the Rights of the Child | |
|---|---|---|
| DOSES | Asociación desarollo, organización, servicios y estudios socioculturales | Association for Development, Organization, Services and Socio-cultural Studies |
| DR-CAFTA | Dominican Republic–Central America–United States Free Trade Agreement | |
| EU | European Union | |
| FDNG | Frente Democrático Nueva Guatemala | New Guatemalan Democratic Front |
| FMLN | Frente Farabundo Martí para la Liberación Nacional | Farabundo Martí National Liberation Front |
| FOSS | Proyecto de Fortalecimiento de Organizaciones Sociales en Temas de Seguridad | Project to Strengthen Social Organizations in the Area of Security |
| FRG | Frente Republicano Guatemalteco | Guatemalan Republican Front |
| FSLN | Frente Sandinista de Liberación Nacional | Sandinista National Liberation Front |
| GAM | Grupo de Apoyo Mutuo | Mutual Support Group |
| GANA | Gran Alianza Nacional | Grand National Alliance |
| GDP | Gross Domestic Product | |
| GIZ | Gesellschaft für Internationale Zusammenarbeit | German government development agency |
| IACHR | Inter-American Commission on Human Rights | |
| IFAI | Instituto Federal de Acceso a la Información | Federal Institute for Access to Public Information |
| IR | International Relations | |
| Ley PINA | Ley de Protección Integral de la Niñez y Adolescencia | Comprehensive Child and Adolescent Protection Code |
| MINUGUA | United Nations Verification Mission in Guatemala | |

(*cont.*)

| | | |
|---|---|---|
| NGO | non-governmental organization | |
| OAS | Organization of American States | |
| ODHAG | Oficina de Derechos Humanos del Arzobispado de Guatemala | Human Rights Office of the Archbishop of Guatemala |
| PAN | Partido de Avanzada Nacional | National Advancement Party |
| PP | Partido Patriota | Patriotic Party |
| PRODEN | Comisión Pro-Convención sobre los Derechos del Niño | Commission in Favour of the Convention on the Rights of the Child |
| SEDEM | Seguridad en Democracia | Security in Democracy Association |
| SEGEPLAN | Secretaría de Planificación y Programación de la Presidencia | Secretariat of Planning and Programming of the Presidency |
| TAN | transnational advocacy network | |
| UN | United Nations | |
| UNDP | United Nations Development Programme | |
| UNE | Unidad Nacional de la Esperanza | National Union for Hope |
| UNICEF | United Nations Children's Fund | |
| UNIIIC | United Nations International Independent Investigation Commission | |
| URNG | Unidad Revolucionaria Nacional Guatemala | Guatemalan National Revolutionary Unity |
| USAID | United States Agency for International Development | |
| WOLA | Washington Office on Latin America | |

# Acknowledgements

A book's journey to production is a long one. However often this observation may crop up in acknowledgements, I have not ceased to be surprised by the twists and turns the present project has taken and the number of people who have influenced the book's final form. To all who lent a collaborative hand, I offer heartfelt thanks.

The book is based on a doctoral dissertation presented at the Technische Universität (TU) Darmstadt in 2012. My first intellectual 'home base' was the 'Formation of Normative Orders' Cluster of Excellence, a rather rare interdisciplinary commingling of international relations (IR) researchers and political theorists working out of Goethe University Frankfurt and TU Darmstadt. The discussions I took part in here helped shape my thinking on the normative implications of tensions between global norms and local translations. At the Peace Research Institute Frankfurt (PRIF), which became my second base, I benefited enormously from the dual focus on global governance and the dynamics of local conflict. Terms like 'localization', 'contestation' and 'translation' may seem very much *en vogue* in IR research today, but eight years ago scholarly interest in them was minimal and the diverse expertise of PRIF colleagues was therefore key in helping me to shape my approach to these topics.

Before acknowledging the input of individual academic and editorial colleagues, I must remind the reader that what lies at the core of this study is the time I spent conducting research in Guatemala City and Washington, D.C., between 2009 and 2011. Countless individuals not specifically named in the study provided me with invaluable help during these visits, taking time to share their knowledge and opinions and helping me establish further contacts.

The situation of many politically active individuals in Guatemala is a frustrating one. The constant scrutiny to which they are subjected by researchers (and foreign donors) appears to them to bring few direct results in terms of their overall political aim – making Guatemala a more just and democratic country. I hope that this book, besides being of academic value, may help bring about further change in the practices employed to promote democracy and the rule of law. I hope also that it conveys, and acknowledges, the everyday conflicts of Guatemalan politics.

I owe special thanks to the local office of the German development agency GIZ – and in particular to Bernhard Dohle and Natascha Solis – and to Tjark Eggenhof of the Adenauer Foundation for helping me to establish my first contacts in Guatemala City. Although he may not realize it, my conversation with Oscar Chavarría flagged up many of the key routes along which the book's main argument eventually developed. Besides generously giving of their expertise, Leonardo Castilho, Sergio Pivaral and Claudia Reyes provided me with a number of interesting contacts. Special thanks must also go to the staff of the Biblioteca Nacional de Guatemala for their friendliness and the interest they showed during the many days I spent in the library's newspaper archive.

Guatemala City is not the easiest of locations in which to do research. My warmest thanks go to Luis Eric Gudiel and Maria Georgina Quiñones, and to Natascha Solis, for making me feel so welcome, comfortable and safe during my visits to Guatemala. I would also like to thank my friend Kezia McKeague in Washington, D.C., particularly for introducing me to her network of first-rate contacts in the field of Latin American politics.

A great many people have been involved in the actual writing of this book, particularly the drafting of the original dissertation and its translation into book form. I would like to thank in particular my dissertation supervisors Klaus Dieter Wolf, whose talent for breaking down seemingly intractable problems into practical research steps proved invaluable, and Nicole Deitelhoff, who helped hone the various versions of the text with countless helpful suggestions. I am grateful to them both for the time they devoted to the project at each of its many stages.

Thanks are also due to all those who, at different stages and in different contexts, commented on the manuscript itself or on the key arguments presented in it. This includes Amitav Acharya, Tanja Börzel, Lothar Brock, David Chandler, Stephan Engelkamp, Katharina Glaab, Amichai Magen, Harald Müller, Kathryn Sikkink, Richard Price, Thomas Risse, Susan Sell, Chris Reus-Smit and Antje

Wiener. Amongst my colleagues at PRIF, Jonas Wolff was unstinting in his advice and Melanie Coni-Zimmer, Anne Flohr, Svenja Gertheiss, Steffi Herr and Eva Ottendörfer were a source of great support, as were the members of PRIF's colloquium of doctoral students. I also drew considerable inspiration from my discussions with Friedrich Arndt, Angela Marciniak and Peter Niesen at TU Darmstadt, and numerous excellent ideas for improving the text were provided by members of our research colloquium at Goethe University, including, amongst many others, Christopher Daase, Thorsten Thiel, Ben Kamis and Julian Junk.

I was fortunate to be offered scholarly sanctuary in a number of exceptional academic locations. Thanks to Susan Sell, during spring 2011 I had the opportunity to work as a research fellow at the Institute for Global and International Studies, located within the Elliott School of International Affairs at George Washington University. Likewise, in autumn 2010, Tanja Börzel and Thomas Risse provided me with a desk and an inspiring research setting in their group on 'The Transformative Power of Europe' at the Freie Universität Berlin.

Transforming a dissertation into a readable book is always a challenge, involving as it does a lengthy process of rethinking, rewriting and synthesizing. I am grateful to Anne Reiff, Anna Ferl, Michael Pollok and Lydia Both for helping me to update the manuscript and get to grips with citation managers. Invaluable native-speaker input was provided by Margaret Clarke, who helped polish and perfect the text in a calm and supportive way. Thanks also go to John Haslam and his team at Cambridge University Press for their expeditious handling of the publication process and to the Cambridge readers for their helpful comments. Any errors that remain in the book are, of course, my own.

I am pleased also to have the opportunity to thank the three bodies who funded the research presented in this book: the German Research Foundation's Cluster of Excellence on 'The Formation of Normative Orders'; the German Academic Exchange Service; and the Peace Research Institute Frankfurt. I gratefully acknowledge permission by Oxford University Press to reproduce sections of 'Same Same or Different? Norm Diffusion Between Resistance, Compliance, and Localization in Post-conflict States' (*International Studies Perspective* 17(1): 98–115).

Last, but not least, I would like to thank my family and friends. They played a crucial part as the book took shape – sometimes with hands-on help, sometimes just by virtue of their enduring interest. Thank you, then, to Ellen Ehmke, Dorothea Gädeke, Lisa Groß, Angela Marciniak, Heather Renwick, Julia Strutz and, of course, my parents. Thanks also to my partner, Jannik Pfister, without whose help I can say, without exaggeration, this book would not have been written. The final coda belongs to baby Lukas, whose exemplary sleeping habits in the first few months of life enabled me to complete the bulk of revisions to the manuscript.

# 1 | Introduction: Between Global Norms and Local Translation

After the end of the Cold War, there was a strong belief throughout the Western world that intervention in countries ravaged by civil war could bring about stable democracies with functioning rule-of-law systems.[1] As a result, a whole industry grew up dedicated to promoting global rule-of-law and democratic norms in post-conflict states. These norms encompassed, amongst other things, prison standards, rules governing elections and political party donations, media guidelines and mechanisms of oversight for the military. However, in the 2000s, given the infrequency with which stable democracies were emerging – despite years of peacebuilding and democracy promotion – the high expectations in regard to post-conflict countries began to wane.[2] In addition, the idea of putting external pressure on people to adopt a specific model of liberal democracy was increasingly perceived as normatively problematic.[3]

In line with the more limited expectations, policy recommendations referred more and more to 'local ownership' (Diamond 2008b: 316; Youngs 2012: 115) and 'context sensitivity' (Hill 2010; Leininger 2010) as key factors in promoting democracy and the rule of law. In Afghanistan, Western donors set up a 'Tribal Liaison Office', the declared purpose of which was 'institutionalized engagement with customary structures, local communities and civil society groups'.[4] The United Nations explored the benefits of customary law as a means of improving legal systems in developing countries[5] and involved itself in attempts to find context-sensitive ways of promoting the rule of law in

---

[1] See e.g. United Nations Security Council (1992).
[2] See e.g. Bermeo (2009), Call/Cook (2003: 234), Ottaway (2003), Paris/Sisk (2009).
[3] For discussion of this, see Duffield (2007), Hobson/Kurki (2012), Robinson (1996).
[4] See TLO, 'Goals and Objectives', www.tloafghanistan.org/page30.html, accessed 1 March 2016.
[5] Wojkowska (2006).

areas where Islamic law pertains.[6] A well-known expert on US promotion of democracy denounced the marked 'externality' of such promotion and the low level of local ownership by recipient populations
(Carothers 2009b). 'Ownership' also became the new catch-all term in
the debate about development cooperation, whose purpose – according
to the 2005 Paris Declaration – must be to ensure that foreign aid was
distributed in line with strategies set by the recipients of that aid.[7]

The new policy paradigm dictates that norms should take on a local
face but at the same time 'reflect transcendent values that cannot be
modified' (Shaw/Waldorf 2010a: 5). A 2004 report on rule-of-law
promotion by former UN Secretary-General Kofi Annan typifies this
approach:

> Success will depend on a number of critical factors, among them the need to
> ensure a common basis in international norms and standards and to mobilize
> the necessary resources for a sustainable investment in justice. We must learn
> as well to eschew one-size-fits-all formulas and the importation of foreign
> models, and, instead, base our support on national assessments, national
> participation and national needs and aspirations.[8]

In the current global political context, promoters of democracy and the
rule of law assume they can simultaneously diffuse global norms and
give them a local face and local legitimacy. But this shift to a new
sensitivity of the 'local' brings with it a host of problems. To what
extent are global norms localized? And who decides whether global
standards or local particularities prevail? The ways in which external
rule-of-law promoters such as UN agencies, development agencies and
international non-governmental organizations (NGOs) deal with this
dilemma remain unresearched. The core question posed by this book is
therefore: how does external rule-of-law promotion affect norm
translation[9] in post-conflict states and how does interaction over global
norms and their local faces take place?

Although conflict relating to norms and their domestic reception has
become a vibrant area of research, current investigation neglects this

---

[6] The UN's Department of Peacekeeping Operations, for example, was one of the
co-organizers of an Expert Conference on 'Islamic Law, the Rule of Law, and
International Peace Operations' held in Cairo from 27 to 29 June 2011.
[7] OECD (2005/2008).    [8] United Nations Security Council (2004).
[9] In what follows here, I use the term 'norm translation' to mean the interpretation
of a norm in a new context. The term 'localization' is used to denote results of
such translation where these do not equate either to rejection or full adoption.

central question. Two particular approaches have been a major influence in the analysis of norm-diffusion processes and their dynamics: norm-socialization research and localization research; the former focuses on questions of compliance and asymmetric interaction, while the latter focuses on how local actors adapt global norms. Neither approach takes adequate account of interaction between norm promoters and domestic actors, however. In addition, they have opposing normative leanings, whereas norm-socialization research perceives anything less than full norm adoption as a 'watering down' of international standards, the localization approach often depicts localization as the desirable normative outcome on the basis that it ensures the legitimacy and stability of appropriated norms.

This book challenges some of the central assumptions of both the norm-socialization and norm-localization approaches in norm-diffusion research. It demonstrates that norm translation is the product of interactive 'feedback loops' between external norm promotion and domestic translation and that these loops are, in turn, affected by norm precision. Specifically, it analyses the interaction of rule-of-law promotion and domestic translation in the case of three rule-of-law norm sets[10] in Guatemala – a paradigmatic post-conflict state. The norm sets in question are children's rights, the right of access to public information and the scripts of international rule-of-law commissions, all of which were chosen for their different levels of precision. Based on this analysis, it also gives a more balanced account of the normative implications of global norms with a local face.

## 1.1 Shortcomings of the State of the Art

There are two major approaches to norm diffusion. Although the socialization approach has done much to help identify the effects of transnational norm promotion on domestic norm adoption, it has so far provided few insights into the interaction of norm promoters and their targets in relation to norm translation. The approach itself emerged in the context of the Cold War's end and was intended as a means of analysing how and why certain international norms were

---

[10] I will generally refer not to *one* norm but to 'norm sets', given that these – women's rights, for example, or standards for a democratic police force – usually comprise a collection of norms, or what Finnemore and Sikkink (1998) would refer to as institution.

being adopted by an increasing number of states. A first generation of scholars developed influential models to describe the ways in which states socialized into international communities. These models – including the 'norm life-cycle' (Finnemore/Sikkink 1998), 'boomerangs' (Keck/Sikkink 1998) and the 'norm-diffusion spiral' (Risse et al. 1999) – continue to shape this field of research. A second generation of researchers enlarged the focus to include the socialization of states into democracy and the rule of law in the context of the European Union (EU) (Kelley 2004; Magen/Morlino 2009a; Schimmelfennig et al. 2006). They also offered a refined account of the norm-diffusion strategies available to external actors (Magen/McFaul 2009; Risse/Ropp 2013) and of the possible domestic constraints to diffusion (Checkel 1999; Cortell/Davis 2000). The perceived endpoint of norm diffusion was not just change at the collective institutional level but 'internalization' or 'habitualization' (Checkel 2001: 556; Finnemore/Sikkink 1998: 905) – in other words, a process in which the individuals in a state adapt their behaviour to a norm because they accept it as the right or normal thing to do. The focus of this approach on seemingly stable, uncontested norms with unambiguous delimitation and clear content was later criticized (for example, Acharya 2004; Wiener/Puetter 2009: 4). In addition, this line of thought remains vague on concepts such as partial compliance, decoupling and adaptation,[11] and diffusion outcomes other than full norm adoption are explained in terms of the domestic factors – such as normative context, veto players and deficient capacity – through which external norm promotion is filtered.[12]

The norm-socialization approach has an 'outside-in' perspective. External norm promotion is generally seen as an independent variable influencing a dependent norm-diffusion outcome, with domestic factors hindering this process. The direction of causality is ostensibly clear. Interaction between domestic context and external actors does occur, but only to the extent that promoters may adapt their strategies to the specific domestic situation in the target country. For example, strategies may be adjusted to accommodate the presence of strong veto players (Morlino/Magen 2009a); norms may be framed in a way that resonates more directly with local culture; and specific problems of

---

[11] See e.g. Jetschke/Rüland (2009), Noutcheva (2009).

[12] For example, Börzel/Risse (2013), Checkel (1999), Cortell/Davis (2000), Flockhart (2005a).

capacity may be addressed (Börzel/Risse 2013; Keck/Sikkink 1998; Risse/Sikkink 1999). This asymmetric depiction of interaction severely limits the explanatory power of norm-socialization models.

An alternative approach focuses on norm localization and contestation. Instead of portraying norms and their interpretations as stable, it points to the dynamics surrounding them (Sandholtz/Stiles 2009; Wiener 2004, 2008) and explores the question of how norms are interpreted and modified in new contexts. Local actors are seen as engaging creatively in the combination and interpretation of norms in 'glocalized' normative orders (Acharya 2004, 2009; Zwingel 2012). Research into peacebuilding and the promotion of democracy has recently begun to focus on contestation and on hybrid outcomes of the everyday interaction involved in peacebuilding (Kurki 2010; Mac Ginty 2011; Richmond 2011). In IR research, however, localization is mostly seen as the product of domestic agency (see, for example, Acharya 2004; Liese 2009) and in this it too fails to take adequate account of the interactive nature of norm generation. In addition, the localization approach lacks a systematic model of translation and often replicates the linear perspective of norm socialization. A better analysis of translation and interaction is needed in order to establish why norms take on a particular 'local face' on the ground.

## 1.2 The Argument: Interactive Norm Translation

In response to the shortcomings just described, this book sets out to improve understanding of the political dynamics involved in the promotion and translation of rule-of-law norms. It offers a new, interactive perspective to norm translation – one that moves beyond the unidirectional perspective of norm socialization and the failure of norm localization to take account of interaction.

The book demonstrates that rule-of-law promotion affects domestic norm translation, but in unexpected ways. It traces the manner in which such promotion triggers domestic contestation, and thereby also 'feedback loops', which, in turn, bring about change in (1) the modes of interaction engaged in by external actors, and (2) the final form into which global norms are translated (see Figure 1.1). Although international promoters of the rule of law begin by trying to achieve full adoption of global standards using a conditionality-oriented mode of interaction, they subsequently respond to local interpretation and

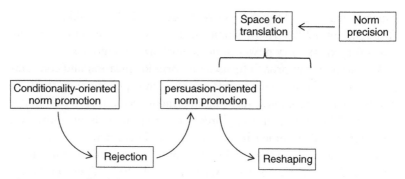

**Figure 1.1** Feedback loops in norm-diffusion processes.

contestation, changing to a more persuasion-oriented (and less transparent) mode of interaction and accepting a degree of leeway in regard
to local translation. This response is not a consciously thought-out
policy on the part of the external actors but an ad hoc reaction to
contestation. The actual amount of space afforded for translation,
however, depends on the degree of precision of the global norm set in
question: the more precise the norm, the less flexible the attitude of
both external and domestic actors and the less substantial the ultimate
localization.

In sum, domestic translation is a product of a process of interaction
between external and internal actors. Feedback loops lead to changes
that go beyond strategic bargaining with domestic elites over liberal
reforms (on this kind of model, see Barnett et al. 2014; Barnett/Zürcher
2009). External actors become enmeshed in domestic discourse, domestic frames and domestic contestation, and, in reaction to this, shift to
a more persuasion-oriented style of interaction and a joint re-discussion
of norms.

The book's findings also underline the desirability of an interactional
and deliberative approach to norms that stresses mutual processes of
construction as a condition for the legitimacy of global norms in local
contexts (Benhabib 2006; Brunnée/Toope 2010).

## 1.3 Design

In the absence of any systematic investigation of the patterns of interaction involved in external norm promotion and domestic translation,

this study, based on a theory-generating case-study design, aims to produce a model of these processes (Lijphart 1971: 692; Munck 2004: 119–20). Its inductively generated theoretical argument should therefore be regarded as requiring further empirical testing in order to be fully generalizable.

Case selection was based on the following considerations. First, investigation of translation processes requires a detailed analysis of the politics and political discourse involved in them. Accordingly, this study concentrates on in-depth analysis of interaction and norm translation in a single country and across several cases.[13] Second, the international donor community's approach of basing interaction in post-conflict states on peacebuilding and the promotion of democracy is a recent phenomenon, having evolved during the 1990s.[14] To accommodate this, the country selected for study is one in which civil war was brought to an end at the close of the Cold War and with strong support from external actors. More specifically, the country in question – Guatemala – was one of the first contexts in which wide-ranging peacebuilding activities were engaged in by the international donor community[15] (Paris 2004: ch. 7).

In addition, the particular norms on which the study focuses are rule-of-law norms. Norms are understood here as regulated modes of behaviour that are based on inter-subjective validity (Deitelhoff 2006: 39–44; Finnemore 1996: 22–23; Klotz 1995: 451). On this understanding, norms regulate interpersonal relationships by solving problems of collective action and also by constituting those relationships. They are 'prescribed patterns of behavior that give expectations as to what ought to be done' (Hurrell 2002: 143). As such, they serve internally as benchmarks for judging one's own behaviour and that of others.[16]

---

[13] This ensures that the context – e.g. the role of external actors, past and present, and the domestic political system – remain constant.

[14] See e.g. United Nations Security Council (1992).

[15] As I use it here, the term 'international community' is not intended to denote a normative concept. I employ it mainly to refer to the group of donors – whether states, international organizations or international NGOs – active in a country.

[16] From this constructivist perspective, norms endogenously influence the creation of identities and preferences by providing standards as to what is right or appropriate (for an overview, see also Deitelhoff 2006: 53–69; Kowert/Legro 1996). Norms here should be understood not as causes of action but simply as shaping the possibilities of action (Hurrell 2002: 144; Kratochwil 1989: 8). This point of view differs from that advanced in realist or liberal-institutionalist

Since the end of the Cold War, 'rule of law' has become a buzzword of development cooperation and an integral part of the 'good governance' agenda. Today, academics and practitioners describe rule-of-law promotion as an 'elixir for many ills' (Mani 2008: 29). It has gained such prominence amongst donors that 'virtually every government in developing and transition countries is involved in one or more internationally sponsored projects designed to strengthen their legal systems and institutions' (Faundez 2005: 567).

Although rule-of-law promotion has a long history in foreign policy, its meaning has changed over time. As early as the 1960s and 1970s, the US 'law and development movement' was viewing rule-of-law promotion as a strategy for fostering economic development in the Global South. In Latin America in particular, the United States was actively seeking to get law on investment and land ownership reformed. However, it was the 1980s that saw the greatest push for the rule of law, notably by the World Bank and the United States, who looked on it as part of the promotion of economic liberalism. In line with this 'governance paradigm', there was a belief that the only way in which underdeveloped states could achieve economic development was through an extensive reform of their institutions. Sections of the development-cooperation community, meanwhile, viewed rule-of-law promotion as the prime means of consolidating young democracies.

Not surprisingly, conflicts have arisen in academic and political circles as to the exact nature and purpose of the rule of law. Scholars often distinguish minimum and maximum concepts of it, the minimum version denoting a sound judiciary and stable institutions, the maximum version implying a more wide-ranging set of human rights and an understanding of law as having a content that is both substantive and moral.[17] In the minimalist version, it would be considered sufficient to reform market institutions and formalize property rights and investment laws; in the maximalist version, promotion of the rule of law would have to encompass questions of social justice and wealth

theories, which only refer to power, material factors and constellations of interests to explain the creation of norms in the international system. In these approaches, once norms are in place, they are understood either as exogenous constraints on action that feature in actors' cost–benefit calculations (Keohane 1984; Mearsheimer 1994/95) or as nothing more than patterns of standard behaviour (Axelrod 1985, 1986).

[17] On definitions of the rule of law, see O'Connor (2006: 518–20) and Stromseth et al. (2006: chap. 3).

distribution.[18] In the first concept, there is no integral link with democracy; in the second, democracy and justice are seen as key. The first 'runs the risk of turning toward revisionist authoritarianism' (Mani 2008: 28); the second risks, as it were, wanting too much. This study eschews the choice between minimalist 'procedural' and maximalist 'social justice' definitions of the rule of law, preferring for analytic purposes a concept that combines a minimalist definition with civil and political rights.

The debate about non-minimal perspectives on rule-of-law promotion led to a number of previously distinct issues being woven together. Discourse about human rights had formerly been seen as independent of concerns about security and development, but in the 1990s, a rights-based outlook brought these three areas together into a single discourse on the rule of law (Rajagopal 2008: 50–51). In the UN, the 1990s saw rule-of-law promotion become a key part of activity in post-conflict states, with state-building, peacebuilding and human rights all rolled into a single approach.[19] This triggered a new narrative about the 'indissociable' link between human rights and the rule of law.[20] All kinds of norms were combined here – from guidelines for judicial appointments, through standards for police reform and the demobilization of former combatants, to the promotion of women's rights, to name but a few. In this scheme of things, the rule of law forms part – indeed the key part – of an overall promotion of liberal democracy (Carothers 1998: 96–7; Magen/Morlino 2009b). It was this perspective that shaped peacebuilding in the 1990s and 2000s – and along with it the approach of external actors to Guatemala.

Over the years, Guatemala has been a major target of rule-of-law promotion by UN agencies, the World Bank, the Unites States and Europe. In 1996, its government signed Peace Accords with the guerrilla forces of the Guatemalan National Revolutionary Unity (Unidad

[18] Carothers (2003: 6), Rajagopal (2008: 55) and Upham (2002).

[19] Carothers (2003: 5), Mani (2008: 29–32), Sriram (2008), Trenkov-Wermuth (2010: 2–3).

[20] Rajagopal (2008: 54). However, Rajagopal, for one, argues that the rule of law has come to be used as a substitute for human rights discourse, explaining that: 'The human rights discourse is a discourse of social transformation and even emancipation, whereas the rule of law discourse does not have that ambition and may be seen as inherently conservative' (2008: 53).

Revolucionaria Nacional Guatemalteca – URNG).[21] These accords
ended a thirty-six-year civil war that had begun shortly after the
ousting, in 1954, of Guatemala's president, Jacobo Árbenz –
the second civilian to hold the post during a democratic interlude in
the country's history. The coup was led jointly by conservative forces
and the military, with strong support, including military backing,
from the United States (Handy 1994; Jonas 1991). The country continued to be governed by the military, or military-backed administrations, until the start of the 1980s, when it slowly began to open up to
democratic reform.[22] The Peace Accords were negotiated with the
support of the international community. From 1994 to 2004, a UN
verification mission, MINUGUA, was stationed in the country, initially to oversee compliance with human rights agreements and subsequently to monitor the implementation of the Peace Accords and
support the state in the democratization process (Franco/Kotler
1998; Stanley 2013).

There are a number of ways in which Guatemala is paradigmatic of
post-conflict spaces: its political system is more akin to a hybrid regime
(Karl 1995; Zinecker 2009) than a liberal democracy; organized crime
takes centre stage in the political discussion; domestic discourse remains
polarized; and the promotion of democracy by the international donor
community is often the subject of contestation. The ongoing frustration
of external actors in regard to norm adoption and compliance (Morales
López 2007) combined with the animated political discourse on internationally promoted reform projects make it an ideal source of systematic insight into post-conflict processes of translation and interaction in
general.

Magen and Morlino (2009b: 10) describe the following dimensions
of rule-of-law promotion:

(1)  protection of civil freedoms and political rights
(2)  independent judiciary and modern justice system

---

[21]  A process of democratization had begun in Guatemala as far back as 1983 and
this had led, in 1986, to a (limited) opening up to democracy. It was not until
1996, with the signing of the Peace Accords, that military oversight of the
fledgling democracy was cut back more thoroughly. Because of this gap between
the limited democratization of the 1980s and the final peace agreement of 1996,
external actors did not home in on the classic post-conflict field of electoral
procedure (Azpuru et al. 2004: XVI; de Zeeuw 2005).
[22]  See e.g. Azpuru (1999: 103), Jonas (2000), Ropp and Sikkink (1999).

(3) institutional and administrative capacity to formulate, implement and enforce the law
(4) effective measures against corruption, illegality and abuse of power by state agencies
(5) security forces that are respectful of citizens' rights and are under civilian control.

For the present study, the main norms associated with these dimensions were identified. Out of those that had been the subject of promotion following the signature of the Peace Accords, three sets were then selected according to precision. Precision was assessed against the specificity of the international standards involved and the degree of their formality (international treaty, soft law, best practice).[23] Thus *high precision* implies the existence of specific legal norms at an international level; *medium precision* implies there are 'soft' norms in place – i.e. that substantial international guidelines have been issued by international entities but these do not take the form of legal norms; and *low precision* implies the existence of 'global scripts'; in other words, particular models and best practices that guide the international community's approach.[24]

Some scholars argue that the more precise the norm, the greater its chance of being adopted and complied with (Finnemore/Sikkink 1998: 906–7; Legro 1997: 34); others contend that a lesser degree of precision improves compliance (Krook/True 2012; Van Kersbergen/Verbeek 2007). If an interactive process over norm translation can be observed in both cases – that of high precision and its opposite – this strengthens the argument for the existence of feedback loops.

The three norm sets selected are the high-precision *UN Convention on the Rights of the Child* (CRC); the *right of access to public information,* based on soft standards that developed around the human right to freedom of expression; and imprecise scripts relating to *UN rule-of-law commissions in post-conflict spaces.*

The high-precision UN Convention on the Rights of the Child, an international treaty setting out detailed standards, was opened for

---

[23] My use of the term 'precision' differs slightly from that of Abbott et al. (2000), who see it purely as meaning 'specificity' (and as being one of a trio of elements – alongside delegation and obligation – that make up their model of legalization).
[24] The notion of scripts – in other words, of institutional models – is more commonly found in 'world polity' approaches such as that proposed by Meyer et al. (1997: 149).

signature in 1989 and ratified by Guatemala in 1990. It contains a list of civil, political, social and cultural rights ascribed to children. Most importantly, it moves away from a depiction of children as persons in need of protection to one of children as holders of rights.[25] It includes some important rule-of-law features, in that it aims to enhance protection of children's civil freedoms and political rights and provides for the creation of relevant institutional and administrative capacities, including a juvenile-justice system and security forces that are respectful of children's rights. The key norm promoters in this case were the United Nations Children's Fund (UNICEF) and transnational and domestic NGOs such as Save the Children.

In 1996, a new children's code, drafted with the help of UNICEF, was passed by the Guatemalan Congress. This replaced an earlier law that did not match up to the provisions of the CRC. The code actually went beyond the rights-based approach of the CRC but never came into force, because a conflict over children's rights erupted on the domestic political scene, the most outspoken protagonists in the dispute being the religious authorities and the private sector. A good many years later, the debate was renewed in an inclusive form that brought together former promoters and opponents and this led, in 2003, to the passing of a new 'Comprehensive Protection Law'. The result was a Guatemalan translation of the CRC that put greater emphasis on family values. The CRC was thus reshaped, but the degree of reshaping was minor.

Global standards on access to public information developed in the 1990s and took on a more specific form during the 2000s. They evolved out of the right to freedom of expression, which includes a right to 'seek, receive and impart information' (Universal Declaration of Human Rights, art. 19). This right became the basis of a collection of guidelines, in both regional and international human rights systems, as to the best methods of ensuring access to public information. Several regional human rights systems actually issued model laws (Ackermann 2003; Blanton 2002; Michener 2011). The standards in question are of medium precision, being based on 'soft law' and guidelines of medium specificity. Up to 2016, the number of countries that had adopted laws falling under the rubric of 'freedom of information', 'right to know' or 'access to

---

[25] For an overview, see Holzscheiter (2010).

information' was just over 100 – of which eighty had adopted them after 1990.[26]

The standards on information were promoted not only as safeguards to civil freedoms but also as an effective tool in the fight against corruption. In Guatemala, following the failure of several drafts to make it through Congress despite international support, 2008 saw the adoption of a law on access to public information. The key actors in this case were the United States (via the United States Agency for International Development – USAID) and the Special Rapporteur on Freedom of Expression from the Organization of American States (OAS). These protagonists tried to diffuse distinct framings of the norm – as a tool to achieve transitional justice and as a weapon against corruption. Local partners, either human rights or transparency NGOs, used these frames in a keen contest with each other – and against the military, the private sector and parts of the Guatemalan government. However, both coalitions proved ready to accept a degree of leeway in respect of deviation from the global standards. In the end, a more inclusive dialogue took shape and this resulted in a modification of the global standards and a reshaping of the norm set for the Guatemalan context. This reshaping was more extensive than in the case of children's rights.

Rule-of-law commission scripts are the least precise norm set considered in this study. They include standards for the structure of international commissions in post-conflict states and guidelines specifying precisely which rule-of-law norms such commissions are meant to uphold. During the 1990s, a model for human rights commissions (mostly truth commissions) took shape in which the commissions' main task was the gathering of information on past human rights violations and the publication of reports setting out recommendations for the international community and the domestic governments in question. Examples of this model include the commissions in Sierra Leone and Timor-Leste. In the course of the 2000s, standards for international commissions and tribunals working variously on investigation and prosecution began to take shape within the UN. They covered areas such as civil freedoms and political rights, as well as the creation of modern justice systems, functioning administrations and

---

[26] Global Right to Information Rating, www.rti-rating.org/country-data, accessed 16 February 2016.

security forces respectful of citizen rights. These commissions operated in a 'hybrid' fashion in the sense that their work was carried out inside the legal system of the post-conflict state (and often with mixed international and domestic staff). Examples of such hybrid bodies are the Special Panel for Serious Crimes in Timor-Leste, the Special Court for Sierra Leone, the Bosnian War Crimes Chamber, the Extraordinary Chambers in the Court of Cambodia and the United Nations International Independent Investigation Commission (UNIIIC) in Lebanon.[27] The mandate of these commissions remained that of investigating human rights violations.

In the case of Guatemala, after years of intensive debate and with strong support from the UN, the United Sates and the EU, 2007 saw the ratification by the Guatemalan Congress of the agreement to establish a UN-sponsored International Commission against Impunity in Guatemala (Comisión Internacional contra la Impunidad en Guatemala – CICIG), based on an initiative by the Guatemalan human rights community.[28] An initial UN blueprint for the commission had been declared unconstitutional by the Guatemalan court in 2004, following contestation from domestic elites. The ultimate design was the product of a series of substantial changes to the international scripts for such commissions worked out in a dialogue-oriented process involving both international and domestic actors. In a departure from the initial script, the commission was modified into an assistive body designed to strengthen the state but not invested with autonomous prosecutorial powers. Its focus was widened beyond human rights issues to include the investigation of organized crime. In addition, it was much more deeply embedded in the domestic legal system than other hybrid commissions of this kind – which retained greater autonomy – and it was reshaped to have a strong capacity-building function.[29] The commission was the first of its kind, and its design emerged from a substantial reshaping of the scripts for bodies of this type.

---

[27]  Hudson/Taylor (2010: 6), Werle/Jeßberger (2014: 27–9, 121–8). Also UN General Assembly (2008: 92–3).

[28]  For NGO reports of the process, see Granovsky-Larsen (2007), SEDEM (2004), WOLA (2008). See also 'Agreement between the United Nations and the State of Guatemala on the establishment of an International Commission against Impunity in Guatemala' (CICIG) (CICIG Agreement 2006).

[29]  See Hudson and Taylor (2010), International Crisis Group (2011b), Schünemann (2010a).

In sum: by the time they found their way into Guatemalan law and practice, all three rule-of-law norm sets – children's rights, access to information and the scripts of rule-of-law commissions – had been reshaped, albeit to differing degrees. This evolution had involved external actors engaging in a shift of interaction mode and lending their support to domestic translation. They exhibited similar reactions to domestic contestation, even though the relevant coalitions of actors varied considerably. However, the degree of precision – meaning the specificity and formality of the norms in question – conditioned the space available for norm translation: it determined the rigidity of the text on the basis of which changes could be discussed and influenced perceptions of the level of normativity involved, with higher-precision norm sets being viewed as having greater normative authority.

This study is a theory-generating one and therefore stops short of providing a generalizable model. It does, however, suggest that in considering norm translation in post-conflict states, we should be looking beyond bargaining processes and considering circular patterns of interaction in which, on the one hand, domestic actors reinterpret norms in processes of contestation and, on the other, external actors get enmeshed in political controversies and react to them. While it is true that external actors retain considerable power over modes of translation, this study points to their engaging in something more than the mere application of a policy of 'context sensitivity' in their promotion of the rule of law: it suggests they actually participate in shaping the local faces of global norms – though only in ad hoc fashion and coupled with an informalization of activities, as will be shown in the following chapters. By shifting the analytical focus away from socialization and localization approaches to interaction and translation, the research presented here provides a more politicized and conflict-oriented account of these processes.

Although its intensity may vary from case to case, norm-related interaction between different contexts takes place all the time. Study of such interaction therefore need not confine itself to the sphere of post-conflict or aid-dependent states. 'Global' entities such as international organizations, courts and expert bodies all interpret norms to differing degrees and promote these interpretations around the world – often in concert (or conflict) with particular governments, foundations, international NGOs and others. Domestic actors, meanwhile, contest, reinterpret and reshape these norms and, in their turn, trigger reactions.

A case in point is the US attempt to reinterpret bans on torture; another is the German parliamentary debate on the ratification of the UN Convention against Corruption. Study of interactive patterns such as these suggests the incipient shift of focus in norm research away from diffusion and towards norm circularity (see Chapter 7).

Despite their ubiquity, the way in which such circular patterns of interaction take shape, and the type of content they involve, are highly case-dependent. Moreover, post-conflict states often exhibit specific structural conditions (high levels of military influence, for example) and a marked dependency on external support. These are the factors that shape the specific types of feedback loop described in this study.

## 1.4 Making Translation More Democratic?

What are the normative implications of these kinds of interactive translations – in other words, of global norms with a local face? Should there be public outrage at the fact that international rule-of-law promoters allow, indeed sometimes encourage, deviations from international standards beyond the notion of context sensitivity? Or should such reshapings be viewed as positive outcomes, in that they strengthen the domestic legitimacy, stability and 'authenticity' of norms translated to local contexts? Both positions are highly problematic in terms of democratic theory. In the first, damage will be done to the democratic self-determination of the particular state if international standards are forced through using sanctions and conditionality: while post-conflict countries may not score well on indicators of liberal democracy, the majority do at least aspire to democratic status. In the second, the socio-economic inequalities, discrimination and marginalization that shape most processes of localization in post-conflict states are ignored.

This book proposes a balanced strategy aimed at a democratic 'appropriation' of norms – in other words a process of democratically making norms 'one's own'. Amongst the scholars writing in this field, Seyla Benhabib (2006), adopting a deliberative perspective in democratic theory, points to the importance of so-called democratic iterations – in other words, the ongoing processes of appropriation by which democratic states subject universal values to constant reinterpretation. From an agonist viewpoint, James Tully (2002) similarly highlights continuing fundamental contestation of global norms as a key aspect of democracy.

Appropriation and contestation of global standards are therefore recognized as fundamental democratic rights, but in post-conflict states, the mechanisms for both deliberation and contestation are seriously flawed (and there is no doubt they could do with refinement in most Western liberal democracies as well). Postcolonial scholars, for their part, point to the dependencies inherent in the relationship between norm promoters and norm recipients and to the power constellations that trigger the emergence of specific global norms (Kapoor 2008; Mutua 2001; Spivak 2008; Tully 2008b). The quality of contestation and deliberation is therefore in need of enhancement from both points of view – domestic appropriation and the interaction between external and domestic actors.

A balance has to be found in which appropriation of global norms in domestic political processes becomes more democratic and interaction between democracy promoters and norm recipients becomes less patronizing; a balance between all-out adoption of international standards and a democratic translation of these. Where there is doubt, it may be more important for a more inclusive political discourse to emerge than for all international standards to be fully adopted. Appropriation is a vital element of democratic practice and the 'global norms versus local faces' dilemma engenders a constant but productive tension in the interaction between rule-of-law promoters and recipients.

## 1.5 Data Collection and Analysis

Many of the types of information used in the study of OECD countries are simply not available in the case of post-conflict states. The coverage of daily press reporting on political events is often poor, and digital access to daily newspapers is very limited, rendering keyword searches impossible. Guatemala is no exception. In addition, much conflict or contestation that has occurred will often not have done so openly – in the course of congressional debates, for example – but behind closed doors. The research for this study is therefore based on a triangulation of relevant data drawn from: elite interviews; general newspaper articles and 'opinion pieces'; 'grey' literature; and academic studies.

Any attempt to explain how international rule-of-law promotion affects norm translation in the three Guatemalan cases selected must involve looking at both elements – the promotion and the translation – in greater detail. Activities relating to rule-of-law promotion can be distinguished according to the modes of interaction used by external actors when engaging in them. The term 'modes of interaction' is here preferred over the more common one of 'strategy' to flag up the fact that the choice of activities is not purely strategic. Actors can make a choice from the incentives/sanctions and praising/shaming pair, both elements of which are more conditionality-oriented, or they can opt for teaching and arguing, which are more persuasion-oriented (see Chapter 2). Whereas the imposition of conditions and the use of praise and shame involve utilitarian calculations and considerations of what appears appropriate, the aim of teaching and arguing is to persuade, which leads to both sets of actors, international and domestic, being willing to engage in dialogue. Whereas teaching implies a unidirectional transfer of expertise, arguing implies a mutual process in which the aim is to convince others of a norm's validity.

In tracing the influence exerted by particular rule-of-law strategies in the Guatemalan examples, the key considerations are which particular mode of interaction promoters used in the three cases under review, and whether these modes changed over time. Analysis here is based on elite interviews, newspaper coverage and various reports and other publications issued by the government, NGOs and international organizations. Of course, it is unlikely that any one mode of interaction will be found in a pure or isolated form. In addition, different actors have different resources and instruments available to them. Having said all this, it is possible to determine which external actors used which modes in relation to which group of actors in a specific case, and which modes of interaction were predominant during particular phases.

In this study, 'translation' is taken to mean the process of interpreting a norm in a new context (Zwingel 2012). Although other terms such as 'norm contestation' (Wiener 2004) and 'norm localization' (Acharya 2004) point in a similar direction, I suggest using 'translation' because it is broader in scope and has wider currency in other areas of research – such as cultural studies and anthropology – which also concern themselves with the impact of contextual change on norms and cultural practices (see Chapter 2).

Chapter 2 of the present study proposes a system of categorization for (temporally stabilized) outcomes of norm translation. This makes possible the identification of subtypes. The system is structured around *three dimensions of norm translation*: translation into discourse, translation into law and translation into implementation (Zimmermann 2016).

(1) Every norm introduced into a new political context will be embedded into the political discourse – i.e. the discourse of political organizations – and into the media discourse. Here, norms are consciously or unconsciously linked to different frames.[30] These contain not only interpretations of events and of possible collective action but also patterns of interpretation that link norms to existing worldviews. Individual groups of external actors will try to influence domestic discussions and a number of different local frames will develop in what are often polarized framing contests (cf. Bob 2012; Payne 2001). The stance of a frame towards a global norm can be one of *rejection* – questioning its validity; one of *constructive criticism* – questioning its application and interpretation; or one of *support*. In the present study, analysis of domestic frames is based on a corpus of newspaper op-eds and editorials complemented by elite interviews. (2) Different frames are linked to different suggestions as to how a norm should be translated into law. During translation into law, the relevant legal text can be *rejected* or the international standards can be *adopted* in their entirety. However, the text can also be *reshaped* – i.e. parts of the international norm set can be left out, new elements can be added or existing elements can be modified. (3) Frames also influence translation into implementation, and this too can lead either to *rejection*, to *full adoption* or to *reshaping*. If the proposed system of categorization is applied, and the outcomes arrived at in these three dimensions are combined, it is possible to assess the results of norm translation in terms of more than just complete rejection or complete adoption.

The major source of information used in the investigation of international norm promotion and domestic translation was a series of sixty-three expert interviews during which first-hand knowledge of political processes and domestic discourses had been garnered. The interviewee cohort comprised experts in the general field of rule-of-law promotion and the role of external actors in Guatemala and experts in the specific areas covered by the three case studies. More

---

[30] Frames are a familiar feature of constructivist norm research (see e.g. Autesserre 2009; Keck/Sikkink 1998; Price 1998), having been inspired by social-movement research (Benford/Snow 2000; Snow et al. 1986). However, the effects which conflicting norm-related domestic frames have on their further translation have so far received little attention in norm-diffusion research. In general terms, frames are 'schemata of interpretation' (Goffman 1986: 21) which '[render] events or occurrences meaningful' (Snow et al. 1986: 464).

specifically, those interviewed included headquarters and field staff of international organizations and development agencies, embassy personnel, members of international NGOs working in the country, members of domestic NGOs and think tanks, members of other domestic civil-society groups and members of the Guatemalan government.[31] The use of semi-standardized interview-schedules ensured comparability of responses across individuals and cases. For the protection of interviewees, interviews are identified only by reference to the actor group involved (as in 'head of domestic NGO' – see Annex 1).[32]

Reconstruction of the discursive frames is based principally on qualitative content analysis of the media discourse. Analysis of the domestic frames that emerge when the norm sets are embedded into discourse is based on a compilation of newspaper op-eds and editorials. Over 400 op-eds and editorials dealing with the three selected norm sets were analysed using a single coding scheme. The articles were drawn from three major Guatemalan daily morning broadsheets (*Prensa Libre*, *El Periódico* and *Siglo Veintiuno*). Editorials and op-eds were collected cluster-fashion around major discussion points (such as the proposal, passing, or entry into force of a law), as these moments of contention were representative of the more general political discourse.[33]

Translation into law was evaluated by comparing major laws in draft and final form with existing international standards and assessing the extent to which the former differed from the latter as a result of

---

[31] Because they actually had limited expertise in the processes under review in the study, and because access to them was restricted, party members and members of Congress were not interviewed. Congressional debates were mostly reconstructed from interviews and newspaper coverage.

[32] Not all interviewees asked to remain anonymous, but in order to ensure anonymity for those who did request it, all interviews are treated in the same way. Anonymized transcripts and information on interview partners are available from the author. For an overview of interviews, see Annex 1.

[33] For an overview of discussion points, see Annex 3. Op-eds and editorials were analysed in relation to their stance to the norm set in question (rejection, constructive criticism, support) and in relation to their depiction of the norm set, the arguments and the groups of actors involved. The depictions were coded inductively. The main frames of the political debate were reconstructed along the dominant lines of interpretation. However, political discourse is not always so open and politicized that it gets taken up by the media. In these less overt cases, the study drew on expert interviews and 'non-opinion' newspaper coverage to reconstruct the discourse within political bodies and the frames they were using.

omission, addition or modification. Processes of discussion and negotiation surrounding the draft laws were investigated through interviews and analysis of documents and reports issued by domestic and transnational NGOs, the government and international organizations. Reports and public statements by domestic and international NGOs, development agencies and international organizations were also used as sources of data on the implementation of the norm sets. This data was then analysed using process tracing and a structured comparison.

## 1.6 Outline of the Book

Following the general introduction provided here, the Chapter 2 offers a review of existing research on norm diffusion and proposes a model of interaction of norm promotion and norm translation. The two major competing approaches to norms in IR research – socialization and localization – are compared and contrasted. The norm-socialization approach, it is argued, focuses on uncontested norms, full norm adoption and asymmetric interaction, with the result that anything less than full adoption is seen as indicative of inappropriate norm-promotion strategies and/or domestic constraints. The chapter then explains how this stance is called into question by the localization approach and by critical research on peacebuilding and the promotion of democracy. Here, it is claimed, norms are presented as contested and dynamic, and interest in the outcomes of diffusion extends beyond rejection or full norm diffusion. It is also suggested, however, that the localization approach focuses exclusively on domestic political processes and thus also neglects interaction. Both perspectives are also argued to have a normative bias: the first because it proposes a 'technical' version of global governance in which domestic conflict over norms precludes full diffusion; the second because it is often over-enthusiastic in its support for localization, which it sees as a means of securing local (democratic) legitimacy and stability for norms.

A system of categorizing norm translation, based on the three dimensions described above, is then proposed, along with a new explanatory model of the interaction between external rule-of-law promotion and local norm translation. The analytical framework is explained and a more detailed account is given of the book's main argument – namely, that international norm promotion triggers local contestation and thereby also feedback loops. This dynamic, it is argued, causes the external actors to shift from conditionality-oriented to more dialogue-oriented modes of interaction and from more transparent to less transparent types of interchange, at the same time opening up to the possibility of deviation from global standards. However, the extent of leeway accepted depends on the degree of precision of the norm set in question. This interactive feedback loop, it is argued, shapes the final outcome of domestic norm translation.

As a prelude to detailed analysis of the case studies, Chapter 3 traces the international donor community's involvement in Guatemala. It outlines the post-conflict setting, the history of the interaction between domestic and external actors in Guatemala and the immense rule-of-law and security challenges faced by Guatemala as a drug-trafficking corridor to the United States.

Chapters 4 to 6 present the three case studies – on children's rights, access to information and the scripts of rule-of-law commissions. Each chapter offers a short introduction to the norm set involved and analyses the interaction between the relevant processes of norm promotion and norm translation in Guatemala. Chapter 4 deals with the translation of the 1989 UN Convention on the Rights of the Child – the most precise of the three norm sets studied. Chapter 5 describes the translation of norms relevant to access to public information. This norm set was systematized in UN and regional human rights regimes in the 1990s and 2000s and is of medium precision. The translation of a low-precision script for commissions promoting the rule of law in post-conflict states provides the focus for Chapter 6.

Chapter 7 summarizes the book's findings on rule-of-law interactions and the implications of those findings beyond post-conflict Guatemala. It argues that a new type of norm research is called for – one which takes interaction seriously and addresses the norm-translation process. Chapter 8 considers the normative implications of the research findings: should the aim of external norm promoters be the fullest possible diffusion of norms, or should localized versions be their new goal? The book points to the problematic nature of both these positions and the need to balance them in a strategy for democracy promotion that aims at a more democratic process of appropriation.

# 2 | *To Socialize or to Localize?*

There are two major approaches to norm diffusion in IR norm research. The first focuses on norm socialization. Socialization is defined as 'a process of inducting actors into the norms and rules of a given community' (Checkel 2005: 804). In IR research, this means an international community of states. The basic idea of socialization is that 'norm takers'[1] have an interest in 'belonging to the club' (Flockhart 2005b: 14) and adapt their behaviour to the rules of that club either for strategic reasons or because they perceive these rules as desirable.[2] The second approach focuses on the contestedness and dynamic nature of norms as they undergo reinterpretation and reshaping for translation to a new context (Acharya 2004; Wiener 2008). Research in related fields such as peace-building and the promotion of democracy is also increasingly showing an interest in contestation.

Each of these perspectives proposes its own model of both what happens to norms during their diffusion and how the outcomes of these processes are to be explained. In addition, they have opposing (implicit) normative stances in regard to norm translation: whereas socialization research portrays domestic conflict over norms, and anything less than full adoption of them, as a watering down of global standards, localization research is often over-enthusiastic in its support for localization as a means of securing legitimacy and stability for the norms being diffused.

In an attempt to find a more promising path between these two alternatives, I propose a more thorough going analysis of the interaction

---

[1] The terms 'norm senders' and 'norm takers' or 'norm recipients' are used throughout this work wherever reference is made to approaches that operate with these terms. The use of such terms is not meant to imply that certain states or groups of actors are always 'norm senders' or 'norm takers', or that the terms fully captures norm-translation processes.

[2] See also Alderson – who, however, defines socialization as an outcome rather than a process (2001: 417).

between external norm-promotion activities and norm translation. I argue that rule-of-law promotion triggers domestic contestation, and thereby also 'feedback loops', which, in turn, bring about change in (1) the modes of interaction engaged in by external actors, and (2) the final form into which global norms are translated. The size of the space which emerges for domestic translation is, however, limited by the degree of precision of the norms in question – meaning their specificity and formality. This process goes beyond mere bargaining over liberal reform (on the bargaining model, see Barnett/Zürcher 2009).

This chapter will contrast the two dominant approaches to norm diffusion by describing (1) their models for the outcomes of norm diffusion; (2) their explanations of these outcomes and the role they ascribe to interaction; and (3) their own normative leanings. An account will then be given of the main argument and analytical framework of the present study.

## 2.1 Norm Socialization: Asymmetric Interaction

IR norm-socialization research has done much to help identify the role of international organizations and transnational NGO networks in the global diffusion of norms. A first generation of scholars developed models to describe processes of socialization, particularly the socialization of human rights norms. Their models – the 'norm life-cycle' (Finnemore/Sikkink 1998), the 'boomerang' (Keck/Sikkink 1998) and the 'norm-diffusion spiral' (Risse et al. 1999) – are still highly influential in the field today. A second generation turned its attention to the socialization of states into democracy and the rule of law, notably in the context of EU expansion (Kelley 2004; Magen/Morlino 2009a; Schimmelfennig et al. 2006). It also offered a refined account of both the strategies – coercion; conditionality; praising and shaming; teaching; and arguing – that are available to external actors when promoting norms (Magen/McFaul 2009; Risse/Ropp 2013) and the domestic variables that influence diffusion (Checkel 1999; Cortell/Davis 2000).

These developments resulted from a shift to a more constructivist outlook in IR research. From the 1980s, the purely rationalist explanations of behaviour that had come to dominate IR research were increasingly called into question, and the kind of constructivist thinking that had taken hold in philosophy and sociology was translated to IR (see, for example, Kratochwil 1989; Kratochwil/Ruggie 1986; Onuf 1989; Wendt 1987).

As a result of this overall shift, the study of norms – from human rights conventions through environmental standards to trade law – became a major theme in IR research. Early studies focused on the evolution of norms and often stressed the role which transnational advocacy networks (TANs) – meaning transnational networks of international and domestic NGOs, international organizations, foundations and other bodies promoting specific causes – played as norm entrepreneurs. They pointed to the way in which the activities of such networks influenced international agenda-setting and to their capacity to change the behaviour of target actors.[3] They explained how NGOs, for example, which are generally held to be weak from the point of view of resources, used the pressure generated through 'blaming and shaming' to increase the potential material and social costs which non-compliance would occasion to the targets of their campaigns. Invoking an IR version of the Habermasian concept of communicative action, scholars suggested it might also be the case that norms emerged in international negotiations as the product of arguing processes that played out on 'small islands of persuasion' (Deitelhoff 2009).[4]

This focus on the emergence of norms was very soon followed by more refined studies on their diffusion and socialization. The norm-socialization model of norm diffusion is one of linear steps towards an endpoint at which the norm in question is internalized or habitualized. The main reasons cited for a particular outcome to diffusion are the norm-promotion strategies used and the domestic constraints to diffusion.

## A Linear Model of Norm Diffusion

In the socialization approach, the outcome of diffusion is assessed according to the degree of norm adoption – in other words, the extent of institutional and ideational change – that takes place in the country in question. To put it another way, research focuses on the replacement of prior norms, institutions and practices that results from norm

---

[3] Busby (2007), Joachim (2003), Keck and Sikkink (1998), Nadelmann (1990), Price (1998).
[4] Neta Crawford (2002), Deitelhoff and Müller (2005), Deitelhoff (2006), Hawkins (2004) and Risse (2000).

promotion.[5] Scholars present outcomes either in a dichotomous fashion (see, for example, Finnemore/Sikkink 1998) or in terms of a linear
scale ranging from rejection to adoption. The first step on this scale is
*rhetorical adoption*, when governments adhere publicly to a norm set;
the next step is *legal adoption* into domestic law; this is followed by
*implementation* in government policies and practices; the final step –
the one that is regarded as ensuring full adoption – is individual
*internalization* of the norm set.[6] The field between rejection and full
adoption is presented as a qualitative continuum.

In this model, internalization takes different forms. For the first
generation of scholars, influenced as they were by sociological institutionalism, it was a kind of habitualization, a 'taking for grantedness'.
A norm is followed because it becomes the normal thing to do
(Finnemore/Sikkink 1998: 905). In the same vein, Koh (1996) refers
to internalization as a process of creating norm 'stickiness' through
iteration and practice.[7] This habitualization, so the authors argue, is
crucial for further compliance with a norm. It is needed, along with
implementation, '[in order to] "depersonalize" norm compliance and
to insure [norm] implementation irrespective of individual beliefs'
(Risse/Sikkink 1999: 17). For other scholars (Checkel 2001: 556;
2005: 804), internalization is the end of a learning process: the individual acquires the normative conviction that following a certain norm is
the right thing to do. Where political elites internalize a norm, it is
argued, general dissemination follows, in a kind of a trickle-down
effect, to the rest of society.

Awkward questions arise at this point. Whereas legal adoption and
implementation of a norm relate to the collective level of the state,
internalization has to do with individual conviction and habit. But
whose convictions and habits need to be changed?[8] And how can
a change in conviction be demonstrated and measured? Given these
difficulties, some scholars restrict their investigation to socialization
at the collective level – i.e. legal adoption and implementation (see e.g.

---

[5]  Acharya (2004); Wiener and Puetter (2009: 4).
[6]  Variations on this model are found in Risse (1999), Schimmelfennig et al. (2006),
     Magen and Morlino (2009a).
[7]  Koh (1997: 642) also distinguishes a number of dimensions of internalization,
     namely legal, social and political.
[8]  On the distinction between the collective and individual levels of socialization,
     see also Zürn and Checkel (2005: 1053).

Schimmelfennig et al. 2006: 4).[9] Others talk of internalization being a long-term process, and one that is not necessarily sequential with the other steps (Alderson 2001: 419; Morlino/Magen 2009a: 41). But even long-term trickle-down effects find themselves subject to question (Peshkopia/Imami 2008).

The focus on internalization presents other problems besides that of knowing who needs to do the internalizing. To some degree this model of adoption depoliticizes norm diffusion because it identifies the absence of political conflict as the endpoint of the diffusion. As Alderson puts it: 'There is an unfortunate tendency among scholars writing on state socialization to resort to psychological imagery to describe (and explain) an intrinsically political process' (Alderson 2001: 418). Instead of acknowledging political conflict and political discussion as central elements of norm-translation processes, this model suggests that the rapid depoliticization of a norm set is a clear indication of internalization, and therefore of full norm adoption.[10]

Re-politicization and contestation of diffused norms at a later stage do not figure in the linear model; nor does the idea of norm decay or the waning of norms once adopted.[11] Jetschke and Liese (2013: 33) point to this kind of problem with the 'norm spiral' model and human rights: 'once the promotion of human rights had become official state policy, the model did not expect political conflicts over human rights to occur'. This approach disregards the fact that norms are part of a 'constant process of negotiating and renegotiating' (Zwingel 2012: 12) in both the international and the domestic context. The model of norm diffusion which it proposes implies that contestation in relation to norms always hinders their full adoption.

Outcomes located somewhere between rejection and full adoption have only recently secured greater attention. Today, researchers will talk of 'partial compliance' (see, for example, Noutcheva 2009) or of 'incomplete internalization' (Goodman/Jinks 2008). Research on Europeanization in particular highlights the heterogeneity that characterizes the adaptation of European policies and norms to the domestic context (Björkdahl et al. 2015; Cowles et al. 2001; Knill/Lenschow

---

[9] Also Cortell and Davis (2000).
[10] On the problem of agency in this kind of model, see also Epstein (2012).
[11] For recent analyses of norm decay and backlashes against internalized norms, see e.g. Panke and Petersohn (2012), Rosert and Schirmbeck (2007) and Sikkink (2013).

2005). Over recent years, norm-diffusion researchers have also increasingly referred to 'decoupling' in relation to outcomes that go beyond rejection or full adoption and to disparities between adopted policy and actual practice.[12] The term was originally coined by scholars of sociological institutionalism, who argued that global scripts for administration, education and medicine (or human rights) do not always have functional equivalents in the states that adopt them (Meyer et al. 1997: 149). Developing states in particular, it is argued, are likely to display decoupling or loose coupling.[13] Although certain norms and ideas are embraced rhetorically by the government, and may be written into law, they are decoupled from any further implementation or actual practice. This, it is claimed, may either be a temporary phenomenon, ultimately giving way to full adoption (see, for example, Swiss 2009),[14] or it may prove a long-term outcome (Drori et al. 2003: 156; Meyer et al. 1997: 155), with international pressure for reform merely leading to renewed decoupling and a series of defunct global models populating the local context.

Clearly, then, new categories have emerged that seek to accommodate diffusion outcomes falling between rejection and full adoption. However, there has as yet been no attempt to systematize or further explore these within the existing models of socialization. Thus, sociological institutionalism, from which the concept of 'decoupling' is drawn, shows an interest in the diffusion of global scripts but only at the macro level, asking why states are so much alike globally and concentrating their attention on the occurrence of mimicry and emulation. From their perspective, local reshapings of norm sets are no more than slight deviations from global scripts. As a result, although they recognize that many norms become domestically decoupled, they make little effort to categorize individual instances of this or to engage in any detailed exploration of the ways in which such decoupling comes about.

In summary: there is no doubt that socialization research has shifted its position to try to account for what happens when norms are transposed to new contexts. Today's scholars are keen to improve their understanding of the gap between 'commitment and compliance' in

---

[12] Boswell (2008), Goodman/Jinks (2013), Hafner-Burton/Tsutsui (2005), Jetschke/Rüland (2009), Schmitz/Sikkink (2013: 836).

[13] Meyer and Rowan (1977: 357), Meyer et al. (1997: 154–55), Drori et al. (2003), Swiss (2009).

[14] Also Goodman and Jinks (2008).

norm diffusion (Risse et al. 2013). They have called for a more detailed study of norm diffusion, beyond the question of compliance or non-compliance (Morlino/Magen 2009a: 39) and are showing an interest in the processes of 'conflict, resistance and politics' surrounding norm diffusion (Börzel/Risse 2009: 5).[15] Despite all this, socialization research's linear perspective on norm adoption remains problematic. When viewed through the norm-socialization lens, the outcomes of norm diffusion can only ever be described as deficient, never as different. This is already implied in terms such as 'partial compliance', 'incomplete internalization' and 'decoupling'. Socialization research starts out from 'the notion that there is a stable and agreed meaning to a rule, and we need merely to observe whether it is obeyed' (Howse/Teitel 2010: 127).[16] A concomitant of this linear perspective – as I will go on to show here – is an asymmetric portrayal of interaction.

## Explaining Outcomes of Domestic Diffusion

Where diffusion is incomplete, the classic explanation offered by socialization research is that specific domestic constraints existed which the norm-promotion strategies employed by external actors were unable to overcome. What follows here is an overview of these domestic 'filters', international norm-promotion strategies and the role ascribed to interaction in socialization accounts. Although socialization research began to take a closer look at the ways in which such filters interacted with norm-promotion activities, they did so in asymmetric fashion.

### Domestic Constraints to Diffusion

The way in which domestic context conditions norm diffusion has become a major area of research. Political systems and local opportunity-structures are viewed as a primary filter. In line with rationalist-institutionalist argumentation, the conditions favouring local norm adoption are said to include a degree of societal openness; an absence of blocking factors such as strong elites or veto players; favourable decision-making structures and state–society relations; and

---

[15] Also Jetschke and Liese (2013).
[16] The remark is made about compliance studies but applies equally well to socialization research.

control of the policy-making process by state actors (Risse 2002: 266–7; Schimmelfennig 2002: 14–15). If these factors are not present, it is argued, either transnational networks will lack access points to the political system or the cost of adopting a new norm will prove too high for the government.

Recent research also points increasingly to problems of capacity to explain, not actual resistance, but decoupling. State elites, it is argued, feel compelled, or are pressurized, to adopt certain institutional models and ideas but do not have the capacity to implement them (Börzel/Risse 2013; Drori et al. 2003). Rationalists point to more strategic motives: they suggest it may also be the case that states have no interest in enforcement and merely seek international legitimacy (Levitsky/ Murillo 2009: 120–2). Norms, it is claimed, are frequently adopted by policy-makers even though they know that decoupling will take place (Levitsky/Murillo 2009: 127) and this expectation, according to some researchers, may even be shared by external actors and local supporters of the norm set (Deere 2009: 16).

Most of the literature in this field complements talk of filters with a cultural argument.[17] What is termed a 'cultural match' or 'normative fit' is defined as 'a situation where the prescriptions embodied in an international norm are convergent with domestic norms, as reflected in discourse, the legal system (constitutions, judicial codes, laws) and bureaucratic agencies (organizational ethos and administrative procedures)' (Checkel 1999: 97). In its most extreme version, the cultural approach envisages only two possibilities: local culture either provides resonance for a norm or it does not. Without resonance, it is argued, the probability of local norm adoption declines (Elbasani 2004: 29).

For many critics, the notion of a cultural match is not very helpful, analytically speaking, since it implies that new norms are only accepted if they already match existing ones.[18] In addition, resonance is rarely convincingly assessed ex ante. Rather, absence of resonance is used ex post facto as an argument to explain unsuccessful norm promotion (Deitelhoff 2006: 74). The explanatory power of cultural filters thus remains ill-defined and 'ideational (in)compatibility is still underspecified in the

[17] Brysk (2008), Checkel (1999), Cortell and Davis (1996, 2000), Flockhart (2005a), Legro (1997), Risse-Kappen (1994: 188), Schimmelfennig (2002: 14–15).
[18] Schmitz (2004: 411–12).

literature' (Risse 2002: 267). Overall, the filter approach paints a rather static picture of local structures and local culture.[19]

### Overcoming Domestic Constraints

In response to these difficulties, socialization research often points to framing activities in dealing with domestic filters of this kind. External actors, it is argued, may try to frame the norms that are being promoted in a way that increases their resonance with domestic normative structures (Keck/Sikkink 1998; Risse et al. 1999). In Keck and Sikkink's seminal work, framing is depicted as the central strategy in the activity of transnational advocacy networks. Such networks are described as linking norms and issues to particular interpretations and explanations in order to make them resonate with a wider public both internationally and in the target state. To ensure the success of a campaign, say the authors, an issue needs to be perceived as a problem and there must be easy solutions available to tackle that problem (Keck/Sikkink 1998: 2–3, 8).

Keck and Sikkink note that such framing activities are not uncontroversial. Within the advocacy networks (TANs) themselves, they point out, there are cultural and political differences between members from differing backgrounds and these need to be negotiated. They suggest that new frames may also stir up contention in a wider public. Constructing shared meanings around a frame is thus recognized to be a far from easy process (Keck/Sikkink 1998: 3, 8, 17). Moreover, the success of a specific frame is seen to be dependent on the political, social and cultural context at a particular point in time (Keck/Sikkink 1998: 73). This is quite a dynamic understanding of norm diffusion, since it stresses the contestation and the discursive processes inside the TANs – and to some extent in the wider context as well. In addition, the notion of framing presented here differs from the purely strategic version offered in many other IR studies.[20]

However, there is one further step missing in this account. Socialization research understands framing activities mostly as 'acts of reinterpretation or representation rather than reconstruction' (Acharya 2009: 13). Yet the reframing of a norm can also imply its

---

[19] Acharya (2004: 243), Cortell and Davis (2005), Risse and Ropp (1999: 271–75).

[20] See e.g. Barnett (1999), Payne (2001). See also Sect. 2.3.

reshaping: TANs do not 'sell' the same norm in different wrappings; they change the norm in a process of framing. Keck and Sikkink recognize that local actors in TANs are not mere 'enactors' but 'people who seek to amplify the generative power of norms, broaden the scope of practices those norms engender, and sometimes even renegotiate or transform the norms themselves' (Keck/Sikkink 1998: 35). But they do not go on to explore how framing activities can reshape norms as part of norm-diffusion processes. Framing is discussed only as a strategy for improving the chances of successful norm diffusion.

In addition to framing of this kind, actors such as international organizations, states (and their development agencies) and transnational NGOs may use different strategies to promote a norm in a specific domestic context.[21] In this connection, scholars – using slightly differing terminologies and typologies – distinguish between, on the one hand, indirect diffusion via emulation and, on the other, activities such as conditionality; praising and shaming; teaching/capacity-building; and arguing (see also Chapter 1).[22]

The way in which these strategies are categorized is often based on different logics of action. In the *logic of consequentiality*, norm promoters use sanctions and incentives to achieve norm adoption by norm takers. Norm takers, for their part, accept a norm on the basis of a rational cost–benefit calculation. If, for example, the material gain derived from aid money, or the cost of sanctions, is greater than the cost of overcoming internal opposition, a government will adopt a norm. In the *logic of appropriateness*, meanwhile, the behaviour of actors in recipient countries is based on imitation and learning. External actors promote cognitive scripts and categories, which local actors then adopt because the scripts, or the actors promoting them, are considered morally sound, legitimate or appropriate.[23] This categorization leads to confusion, as authors differ as to how they match up the logics of

[21] Each of these groups of actors obviously has different strategies available to it.

[22] Many scholars also include coercion. Coercion in the sense of the (violent) enforcement of a norm – e.g. by military intervention – is not considered in this book. For slightly different terms for, and conceptions of, the mechanisms used for diffusion, see e.g. Checkel (2005), who identifies strategic calculation, role play and normative suasion; and Magen and McFaul (2009: 12–15), who identify control, material incentives, normative suasion and capacity-building. In the democracy-promotion research field, see Whitehead (1996) and Schmitter (1996). Goodman and Jinks (2013) add more indirect acculturation processes.

[23] Kelley (2004), Checkel (2005), Magen and Morlino (2009a).

action with the different strategies.[24] Conditionality, praising and shaming and teaching can (to differing degrees) all influence utilitarian calculations, since they all produce costs and benefits of a material, political or social kind. And any strategy can involve indicating to a norm target that it is not following appropriate standards of behaviour.

There is also theoretical confusion when it comes to distinguishing between praising and shaming, teaching and arguing. In older studies, praising and shaming were often equated with arguing (Risse/Sikkink 1999: 13), even though the latter implies deliberation and justification (cf. Deitelhoff 2006: 75–7), and these have little to do with the kind of 'arm-twisting' (Risse/Sikkink 1999: 14) actually described. Similarly, teaching situations involving international organizations (as teachers) and state actors (as learners) have, along with framing activities by transnational non-governmental groups, been depicted as examples of arguing (Zürn/Checkel 2005: 1056). Yet teaching involves asymmetries of power untypical of arguing. In a teaching process: '[T]he relationship between socializer and socializee is an unequal one where the socializer either has, or believes itself to have, a greater knowledge or understanding of the norm set than those that are being socialized, and that it has the power to judge whether the required norm changes have been undertaken satisfactorily' (Flockhart 2005b: 15–16). This accords with its representation as a unidirectional process (Checkel 2005: 813) in which the only side to change its preferences is the norm-taking side. This view, in turn, differs from IR interpretations of Habermasian 'communicative action',[25] in which, in an ideal version of arguing, actors enter into a discourse on an equal footing (Deitelhoff 2006; Risse 2004). On this view, the possibility of learning – and thus also of changing one's ideas and preferences – exists on both sides. Adoption of a norm is then seen as being linked to conviction of its validity. Such conviction is depicted as resulting either from the well-foundedness of the norm in question[26] or from the validity of the decision-making procedures that produced it (Risse 2004: 293).

The question of which strategies are successful in producing norm adoption is a much-researched one. The main approach here has been

---

[24] As an example of this, see Magen and McFaul (2009) versus Busby (2007).
[25] For the original, see Habermas (1981).
[26] What this consists in depends on the discourse and cannot be predicted externally; see Deitelhoff (2006: 95–96).

either to compare the effectiveness of conditionality with that of other strategies or to attempt to identify pure teaching relationships – particularly in the context of the enlargement of the EU.[27] In general, studies on the socialization of the European neighbour states into the European Union conclude that strong conditionality is the only means to successful norm adoption. Schimmelfennig and company, for example, argue that only 'credible EU and NATO membership conditionality' combined with progressive party-constellations in the norm-taker state have led to norm adoption (Schimmelfennig et al. 2006: 9–19).[28] Similarly, Vachudová (2005) and Kelley (2004) contend that only membership conditionality and material incentives have had any significant influence on potential member states.[29] Elsewhere, however, Schimmelfennig, with Sedelmeier (2005: 219–20), points out that the use of teaching and persuasion can lead to a less contested adoption of norms.

Remaining with the European example, where there are no attractive membership-options and no other strong incentives or sanctions – and this is often the case outside the immediate European neighbourhood – socialization becomes more complicated. Bauer and company (2007) argue that persuasion and inter-state competition can lead to a certain amount of medium-term norm adoption in non-candidate countries. Magen and Morlino (2009a) compare EU strategies in candidate and non-candidate countries in Europe and conclude that membership conditionality can indeed lead to the adoption of norms into law but that in situations where an issue is not very politicized and few veto players exist, other types of conditionality can also exert influence. These authors also underline the fact that, historically, conditionality has had little influence on the internalization of norms and that where the EU has exerted strong pressure to bring about reform, fake compliance has resulted (Morlino/Magen 2009b: 237, 42–3). This research thus questions the central role of conditionality in norm diffusion for anything beyond adoption into law. However, studies in this area remain scarce for countries beyond the European near abroad. Recent norm-diffusion research has tried to fill this gap by looking at

---

[27]  See e.g. Checkel (2005) or Gheciu (2005).
[28]  For a similar argument, see Linden (2002) and Schimmelfennig and Sedelmeier (2004).
[29]  For a discussion of successful and unsuccessful strategies of influence by the EU, see also Grabbe (2006), Haughton (2007).

the diffusion of European models – such as European regionalism – around the world (Bicchi 2006; Börzel/Risse 2012; Grugel 2007).

Given that the norm-promotion strategies they describe are themselves interactive in nature, interaction proves to be a key feature in all these depictions: teaching requires long-term interaction; conditionality signals to targets which behaviour is expected and targets then respond in this or that way. Interaction may also lead to changes in the strategies of external actors: provided adaptation does not put any major interests at risk, norm promoters may adapt strategically to the specific domestic context in order to increase their chances of achieving full norm adoption. A case in point is the triggering of different strategy choices by differing types of regime – conditionality-oriented for authoritarian regimes, persuasion-oriented for democratizing regimes (Hüllen/Stahn 2009). In addition, different strategies may also work better in different sequences in the norm-diffusion process (Risse/Sikkink 1999: 11) or be of greater influence on certain types of players. Veto players, for example, may be more responsive to conditionality than to other strategies (Morlino/Magen 2009a: 42–5). Essentially, then, interaction here means a process in which norm promoters adapt their strategies in order to ensure more successful diffusion.

**Factors beyond External Strategies and Domestic Constraints**
Other factors have been cited as affecting the chances of successful norm adoption and compliance, but research into these has, again, remained within the asymmetric model of socialization. The factors in question include, most importantly, the characteristics of the norm promoters, the diffused norm and the interaction process (intensity of contact, for example, or consistency). It is argued that diffusion is most likely to succeed if the 'socializer' is perceived as having substantial authority, if the norm is regarded as important and legitimate and if the 'norm takers' see themselves as learners being taught by external norm promoters.[30] Finnemore and Sikkink's list also includes interest in international legitimacy of the target state; a high degree of precision and specificity of the norm set; and, content-wise, reference to issues of bodily integrity and equal opportunity and

---

[30] Finnemore and Sikkink (1998: 905–09), Zürn and Checkel (2005: 1055) Schimmelfennig (2003: 412–15).

links to existing norms (see, for example, Finnemore/Sikkink 1998: 905–09).[31]

Of these conditions, the one to have attracted the most empirical and theoretical attention is norm precision, but it has done so not from the point of view of the shaping of spaces for translation (as described in this study) but in terms of its upping the chances of compliance. Franck, for example, considers that transparency and the existence of clarificatory procedures will lend a norm greater legitimacy (1990: 52–83).[32] For Schimmelfennig and Schwellnus, meanwhile, precision reduces the chances of deviation (2007).

One general observation that can be made in relation to this research on scope conditions is that more attention needs to be paid to attendant micro processes and that there is too great a focus on unidirectional causal arrows from socializer to socializee (Zürn/Checkel 2005: 1071).[33] In general, the targets of diffusion do not 'talk back'. All the conditions mentioned are clearly of importance. However, their effect on the ground, the reaction they elicit from targets, the way in which, for example, precision creates legitimacy for actors or deters them from deviation – these issues remain empirically unexplored. One of the objectives of the present study is to throw light on the mechanisms at work here, notably the link between norm precision and domestic translation.

What emerges from socialization's account of the measures to deal with domestic constraints is therefore an asymmetric picture in which external actors adapt their strategy choices to the domestic context in order to achieve full norm adoption. If norm promotion fails, or is only partially successful, the explanation offered is that external input was just not forceful enough to prevail over domestic constraints such as the cost of reforms, the normative structures or a dearth of capacity, and that certain characteristics of norms and norm senders were absent.

---

[31]  The last two items in this list actually tie in with framing strategies: international and local actors regularly seek to frame issues in terms of bodily integrity or equal opportunity and the success of 'grafting' (establishing links to existing norm sets) is, likewise, a question of active framing.

[32]  Permutations here include specificity (Legro 1997: 34); specificity and clarity (Finnemore/Sikkink 1998: 906–07); determinacy (Franck 1990: 52–83); precision (Abbott et al. 2000: 401).

[33]  In their examination of human rights practice in Latin America, Lutz and Sikkink (2000) do consider the role of legalization as construed by Abbott et al., but they do so from the point of view of the channels and mechanisms by which change of human rights practices is brought about.

## Norms Watered Down?

In the socialization approach, the outcomes of norm diffusion are described either in dichotomous terms or as points on a linear scale ranging from rejection to full adoption. Although socialization research has made some moves towards exploring resistance and contestation in greater depth, empirical analysis here is still thin on the ground – as are investigations of the implicit normativity of models of socialization.

In recent years, an important explication of the normative stances adopted in norm research has been conducted by scholars from the constructivist field.[34] So far, however, these debates have related mainly to the moral dilemma opposing military intervention and self-determination (Finnemore 2008) or to the problem of how to assess moral progress in general (Price 2008b; Sikkink 2008).

The more subtle normative dilemmas associated with human rights and the promotion of democracy have not yet been analysed in this context.[35] However, one identifiable feature of norm socialization's analytical models is their implicit bias. The endpoint of norm diffusion remains full adoption – meaning not only the legal adoption and implementation of a norm set, but also its internalization. This preoccupation with internalization inevitably casts local contestation in a negative light: local actors have only successfully adopted a norm if they no longer reflect on it or discuss it. This model leaves little room for more complex processes of interpretation and translation and assigns a passive, reactive role to targets of socialization (Acharya 2004: 242; Epstein 2012).[36] Difference can only be described as deviation from a 'correct' interpretation of standards – which in most cases means existing international rules and conventions. Cases in which not

---

[34] See the contributions to the edited volume by Price (2008a).

[35] See e.g. Engelkamp et al. (2012, 2013) and Deitelhoff and Zimmermann (2013a).

[36] For some scholars, this normative bias means that the whole norm-research enterprise is fundamentally flawed. They point out that such research ignores the part played by colonial and postcolonial power constellations in the generation of liberal norms and that it presents norm diffusion as a more power-free process than is actually the case. Some also argue that research into diffusion appears to assume the latter always travels in a north–south direction and that, again, this field of study does not engage with postcolonial agency. For more on this, see Epstein (2014).

all the standards in question are followed are equated with a 'watering-down' of the norm.[37]

This is not to say that normative judgements of this kind are wrong in every case and for all international standards that may be studied. However, norm socialization's analytical perspective on the diffusion of human rights regimes and democratic norms results in there being only one possible normative judgement, while more balanced normative assessment is frequently absent. This means that in much of socialization research, conditionality, rather than being problematized, is perceived as being an effective – and therefore 'good' – strategy for achieving diffusion. The contention of the present study is that these models are overly functional and geared more to norm senders than to norm addresses. That said, the second major research-perspective – that of norm localization – has its own, contrasting drawbacks, tending as it does to romanticize norm adaptation.

## 2.2 Norm Localization: Local Agency Only

Norm-socialization research is often contrasted with more recent approaches that focus on norm contestation and localization. Research into peacebuilding and the promotion of democracy have recently also taken a 'critical' turn and begun to explore contestation and hybrid peacebuilding outcomes.[38] These approaches do manage to overcome some of the difficulties attached to norm-socialization research; however, as will be shown here, the analytical tools they use to assess diffusion are still only at the development stage, and the bulk of IR norm research in this area neglects the interaction element, explaining localization purely in terms of domestic factors. Since the focus of the relevant branches of research differ, their respective methods of categorizing norm diffusion, and their explanations of this diffusion, will be explained in separate subsections. The first of these will deal with research on international norm contestation and norm localization, while the second addresses research on peacebuilding and the promotion of democracy.

---

[37] See e.g. the wording in Noutcheva (2009: 1077) or Liese (2009).
[38] Since both these branches deal with the reinterpretation of norms in new contexts, they are brought together here under the heading of norm localization.

## Contestation and Localization

Research on norm contestation and norm change focuses on the dynamics of norms at the international level. Localization, by contrast, studies the reinterpretation of norms in regional, domestic and local contexts. Authors in these two areas criticize the structural bias of existing IR norm-diffusion theories, in which, they argue, the application and implementation of norms is represented as unambiguous (Van Kersbergen/Verbeek 2007: 221). They contend that contestation around norms emerges not only from overlap with other norms but also from different interpretations of those norms (Krook/True 2012: 2). They then spotlight the contention over the meanings of norms and the process of their reconstruction.[39] Although such interpretive processes and changes in perceived meaning already featured in constructivist research of the 1990s (see Keck/Sikkink 1998; Koh 1998: 649–51), the focus in those accounts was on norm entrepreneurs rather than on contestation more generally.

In research on contestation, emphasis is placed on changes in the interpretation of norms at international level and an account is given of the factors influencing such changes. Badescu and Weis (2010), for example, show how contestation in regard to the (mis)application of 'responsibility to protect' helped create a more robust consensus on the scope and boundaries of that norm. Van Kersbergen and Verbeek (2007) investigate changes that came about in the interpretation of the European subsidiarity norm as a result of the empowerment of new actors. From a slightly different perspective, some researchers focus on stigmatization rather than socialization and reflect on the contested nature of stigma attribution in the international system (Adler-Nissen 2014; Zarakol 2014) and how this may actually create norm change (Chwieroth 2015).

The most advanced model of norm change proposed by scholars in this area is that put forward by Sandholtz and Stiles (2009).[40] They argue that disputes about a norm's application are a recurrent phenomenon: 'The inevitable gap between general rules and specific actions ceaselessly casts up disputes, which in turn generate arguments, which then reshape both rules and conduct' (2009: 3). They go on to develop

---

[39] See e.g. Reus-Smit (2001), Van Kersbergen and Verbeek (2007), Wiener (2004; 2007: 58; 2008).
[40] See also Sandholtz (2008); on norm change also Müller and Wunderlich (2013).

a model conceptualizing the different steps leading to norm change at the international level and argue that such change is more likely to happen if the variant interpretations have the support of major powers, if they are consistent with existing meta-norms and if they have the authority of precedent (2009: 18). Amidst all this investigation, however, one question none of these scholars has so far addressed is: what brings about a deepening or weakening of a norm and how should such norm change be categorized?

This step is also missing in the work of Antje Wiener (2004, 2008, 2014), who has been instrumental in the shift of focus towards contestation in norm research. For Wiener, contestation 'involves the range of social practices, which discursively express disapproval of norms' (Wiener 2014: 1). It means conflict over the meanings[41] of norms, and these meanings, in the words of Weldes (1998: 218), are '[i]ntersubjective structures ... that provide the categories through which we represent and understand the world'. According to Wiener, negotiating processes relating to norms and their meanings present a particular challenge at the international level, where individuals bring their 'normative baggage' (2008: 57) to the task of interpretation: 'It is through this transfer between contexts that the meaning of norms becomes contested, as differently socialized actors such as politicians, civil servants, parliamentarians or lawyers trained in different legal traditions seek to interpret them' (2008: 33). Even if international negotiators manage to agree on one particular interpretation of a norm within the negotiating setting, says Wiener, contestation and reinterpretation will occur in every new context.

Despite this recognition of contestation, the actual concept remains vague. What is actually contested – a norm's validity or its application – and how this influences the outcome of contestation, remains an open question.[42] In addition, the individual 'normative baggage' (Wiener 2008: 57; 2014: 41–42) that is said to trigger contestation is mostly a consequence of domestic socio-cultural context and thus offers an only slightly more dynamic equivalent to domestic 'culture' as cited in socialization research.[43] One key insight that this approach does offer, however, is that norms, far from being stable and unambiguous, give

---

[41] Termed 'meanings-in-use' by Weldes (1998: 218).

[42] See also Deitelhoff and Zimmermann (2013b).

[43] This focus results from what Wiener calls an 'inter-national' perspective on global politics (Wiener 2014). She firmly rejects the idea that something like

rise to differing interpretations depending on the actor group and context involved.

The multi-directional transfer of cultural concepts, ideas and norms in global contexts has long been a subject of study in sociology, history and postcolonial studies. In these fields of research, the term 'appropriation' is used to describe the creative modification that takes place in groups confronted with new norms or ideas. Eisenstadt (2000) coined the term 'multiple modernities' in this connection. In the postcolonial context, it is also linked to the notion of creating agency and space for resistance.[44] Worldviews, ideas, norms and practices are thus seen as the product of prior processes of construction, redefinition and appropriation. A degree of cultural hybridity or 'glocalization' (Robertson 1995) is considered to shape all local spaces.

The terms used to describe the results of this interaction are manifold: 'hybridization' (Peterson 2012), 'creolization' (Hannerz 1996; Stewart 2006), 'vernacularization' (Levitt/Merry 2009), 'syncretism' (Galvan/Sil 2007) and 'bricolage' (in cultural studies). Each of the implied concepts has its critics. There is condemnation of the 'pure' Westernness on which such notions are based and of the assumption of 'unhybridized' Western and non-Western institutional and cultural priors that underlie them (Randeria 2007: 100–2). Scholars cast doubt on the whole idea of norm takers and norm makers and of independent cultural, political and economic spheres. As an alternative, they propose concepts such as 'entangled history' (Conrad/Randeria 2002; Randeria 2005) or 'histoire croisée' (Werner/Zimmermann 2006). These are intended to supersede an academic tradition in which European experience gives rise to supposedly universal concepts, which are then used as yardsticks to document the 'deviation' of non-European societies (Randeria 2005: 169–70). In fact, say the scholars, European modernity can only be understood as the product of Europe's (colonizing) relations with the rest of the world. This points up a need for more in-depth study of multi-directional processes of interaction and flows of ideas and power.

From this point of view, local culture does not constitute 'authentic tradition' or 'national essence'. In her study on the diffusion of

a shared life-world or a shared value system can exist at the international level (see also Vetterlein/Wiener 2013).

[44] Bhabha (1985; 1994).

human rights norms, Merry states: 'Culture in this sense does not serve
as a barrier ... but as a context that defines relationships and meanings
and constructs the possibilities of action' (Merry 2006: 9). Such a view
also militates against the practice of presenting domestic contexts as
'tradition-bound' and international spaces as 'culture-free' (Zwingel
2012: 120).

Inspired by historical research on South-East Asia, Amitav Acharya
has translated this perspective to the International Relations domain.
He highlights how local actors actively link international norms to
local normative orders by a process of grafting and framing (2004:
254). During this process, he argues, norms undergo modification in
both meaning and scope. A successful localization, he says, '[does not]
extinguish local beliefs and practices' but 'may instead universalize and
amplify the latter' (2009: 5). As opposed to what happens in the
socialization model, which depicts external actors linking up with
domestic partners to promote specific norms, the emphasis here is on
independent local actors adapting international norms to their needs in
order to enhance their domestic legitimacy (2004: 247–8).

Acharya mentions four factors that increase the likelihood of successful localization: the capacity of the external norm to strengthen
legitimacy and authority for local actors; the existence of strong local
orders; the presence of powerful local actors to safeguard existing
orders; and a strong sense of identity underlying the local order (2004:
248–50). Mac Ginty, meanwhile, identifies a number of factors that
contribute to hybridity in peacebuilding (2010). Aspects such as the
compliance power of peacebuilders,; the incentives linked to norm
adoption; the ability or power of local actors to resist, ignore or
adapt norm sets; and the existence of the option to propose alternatives
can all, he says, result in different 'degrees' of hybridity.

This implicitly echoes the explanation of partial norm adoption cited
in the socialization approach: while external actors seek to achieve full
norm adoption, local actors – if powerful enough to resist full adoption –
may achieve localization. Such accounts neglect the element of interaction and the possible role of external actors in the localization of global
norms. The same applies in the case of research into norm dynamics and
contestation, which bases its explanation of domestic contestation and
resultant reinterpretation on local factors such as the particular constellation of actors or the particular regime (Joachim/Schneiker 2012; Liese
2009: 45). While this may be adequate for the case studies in question,

for post-conflict states like Guatemala, greater attention needs to be paid to the interactive nature of the norm-translation process.

Scholars point out that actors at a variety of levels become active in the translation process: translators, they say, may be found at global or local level, at the centre or at the periphery (Levitt/Merry 2009: 448–9). Transnational actors, it is argued, are just as likely as domestic actors to be 'downloaders' of international norms or to try to create alternative norms or adapt global norms to local contexts (Boesenecker/Vinjamuri 2011: 1163). Indeed, in some areas, it is argued, transnational networks of non-state actors are the main drivers of translation processes (Brake/Katzenstein 2013). There is also a long-standing debate – particularly amongst scholars of anthropology and International Relations – about the translation, appropriation and vernacularization of norms by groups in different societal contexts (Levitt/Merry 2009; Merry 2006; Orr 2012).

Research here also focuses on the contested nature of such translation – after all, the kinds of norm translations the previously mentioned groups come up with may be a long way off enjoying consensus amongst the supposed beneficiaries (Cheng 2011). The outcomes of translation, too, are often contradictory and contested (Großklaus 2015).[45] Notwithstanding these insights, the role of external actors and transnational networks in the domestic translation process, and their reaction to contestation, still await systematic exploration.

Precise categorization of the outcomes of such localization is also lacking. Acharya's proposed scheme (2004) remains broad: he is concerned with the adaptation of norms by regional actors in regional organizations. As he describes them, these regional actors seek discursively to connect existing regional norms and practices to external norm sets (grafting); or they may prune external norm sets, removing any parts that do not seem compatible with the particular local normative order. Drawing on his case studies of regional organizations, he argues that changes to the diffused norm may take place at the level of the scope and tasks of an institutional set or at the level of linked instruments and procedures (Acharya 2004: 252). He does offer insights into possible differences between types of appropriations, but he does not systematize these.

---

[45] In addition, localization often functions as a mechanism for warding off international norm promotion (Capie 2008; Jetschke/Rüland 2009; Rüland/Bechle 2014: 237; Williams 2009).

IR research on localization also frequently echoes the socialization paradigm. The work of IR scholars exploring regional organizations and regional norm-diffusion is a case in point. Researchers here have taken up Acharya's concept of localization,[46] but their accounts differ little from those offered in the socialization approach: the 'local' again becomes a barrier through which certain parts of a norm enter and others are filtered out. Localization here is not a reinterpretation of meaning; instead, the talk is still of norms being 'weakly diffused' (Capie 2008: 640) or lacking internalization (Williams 2009: 416). In other words, although the terms have changed, IR translation-research retains a norm-diffusion bias. This may be due to the exclusively strategic view of localization in Acharya's work. In approaches such as his, localization is seen as a rational strategy employed by local actors to regain local legitimacy (Acharya 2004).

To sum up: the approaches described here explore the reinterpretation and contestation of norms. The localization viewpoint, in particular, offers the most fully developed instrument so far for analysing and explaining outcomes of norm diffusion that go beyond full adoption or rejection. However, this approach has not yet come up with a systematic model or method of categorization for dealing with such outcomes and, in addition, it remains unidirectional: it explains localization exclusively in terms of local factors, neglecting possible interaction with external actors in regard to norm translation.

## Contestation and Hybridity in the Wider Research Field

Contestation and hybridity have both found their way into research on peacebuilding and the promotion of democracy. Traditionally, most scholarly engagement with the promotion of democracy and the rule of law proceeded along the same lines as IR research into norm socialization: it focused on orientation, asking what areas were being targeted, what strategies were being used, and what models of democracy were being promoted.[47] Such research was thus supply-side oriented and, in addition, it tended to spotlight the activities of the EU and the United

---

[46]  Capie (2008), Jetschke and Murray (2012), Prantl and Nakano (2011), Williams (2009). Use of the concept in relation to domestic reactions to norms has been less frequent (Aharoni 2014; Großklaus 2015; Vaughn/Dunne 2015).

[47]  Robinson (1996). See also Hobson (2009: 393).

States (see Magen 2009: 16; Schraeder 2002).[48] Regarding 'impact', one major debate centred on sequencing – in other words, the timing of democracy promotion to enhance its effectiveness. This entails determining which promotion strategy should be applied when, whether rule-of-law reform and state-building should happen before or after further electoral democratization,[49] what the different phases of promotion are (Brown 2005), which specific actor groups are involved[50] and, most importantly – as in norm-socialization research – which strategies are the most effective overall.[51] Debates on rule-of-law promotion followed along much the same lines.[52]

Researchers soon realized, however, that the goal of democracy promotion – namely, achieving fully democratic states – was only very rarely realized.[53] They noted that, rather than changing into stable liberal democracies, many states had become 'stuck' between different political regimes.[54] Some scholars even talked in terms of a 'democratic recession' (Burnell/Youngs 2010; Diamond 2008a; 2008b: ch. 3), of a 'backlash' against external democracy promotion (Carothers, 2006; Gershman/Allen 2006) or, more recently, of policies of 'closing space' (Carothers/Brechenmacher 2014; Mendelson 2015).[55] This led to wider-ranging reflection, with scholars highlighting the negative long-term effects of democracy promotion and criticizing overly 'technical'

---

[48] On the varying strategies used by different actors to promote democracy, see Carothers (2009a), Gerrits (2007), Kopstein (2006), Magen et al. (2009), Youngs (2001, 2004, 2008), Wetzel et al. (2015), Wolff et al. (2014).

[49] See e.g. Fukuyama (2005) and Carothers (2007). Carothers argues that proposed models of sequencing do not coincide with political realities in target countries.

[50] See Magen/Morlino (2009b: 15).

[51] See Gordon Crawford (2002). Linking in with this is the question of whether strategies that stress ownership by recipient states are truly dialogue-oriented (Molenares/Renard 2003).

[52] See only Carother (2003), Magen/Morlino (2009a).

[53] More quantitatively oriented studies have explored the effects of foreign aid (Finkel et al. 2007; Henderson 2002; Knack 2004), and the overall impact of democracy assistance (Azpuru et al. 2008). Burnell (2007) argues that we do not know whether democracy promotion works or which strategies work best. Quantitative and qualitative studies seek to measure the impact of some very abstract foreign-aid variables in bringing about regime change or altering the level of democracy in a country; they make no attempt to explore the causal mechanisms between these variables (Leininger 2010: 64).

[54] O'Donnell (1996), Karl (1995), Collier (1997), Diamond (2002), McFaul (2002).

[55] Critically, Wolff and Poppe (2015).

approaches both to this and to the promotion of the rule of law (Goetschel/Hagmann 2009; Grugel 2005: 42; Harrison 2001; Leininger 2010).[56]

The situation in post-conflict states in particular made the promotion of democracy even more difficult and the prospects for lasting democratization, according to the scholars, were dim (Call/Cook 2003: 240; Zuercher et al. 2009). Local conditions were not conducive to peacebuilding: local infrastructure had in many cases been destroyed; governmental and administrative capacity was non-existent; and local elites were not interested in reform. Resources for peacebuilding were limited and the timeframe for engagement was often tight. In addition, peacebuilding had grown quite complex, embracing anything from security sector reform to disarmament, demobilization and reintegration (Call/Cook 2003: 243; Debiel 2002; Ottaway 2003), and the degree of success peacebuilding missions could achieve was limited. Many countries relapsed into conflict and the security situation in some places (including Guatemala) often worsened, so that 'post-conflict spaces' were frequently more violent than their name suggested (Barnett 2006: 92; Paris 2004).

The new paradigm that has been suggested as a means of overcoming an overly 'technical' approach to the promotion of democracy, and of improving the latter's chances of success, is 'context sensitivity'. Its stated aim is to search out 'appropriate' versions of democratic institutions (Mandaville/Mandaville 2007: 10). Democracy promoters are urged to abandon the 'one-size-fits-all' strategy and start taking into account local conceptions, meanings and political processes. Such context sensitivity, it is claimed, will preclude the promotion of any Western-biased projects or any unrealistic models that disregard local forms of democracy.[57] Despite their common thrust, however, all the authors cited here would probably differ considerably as to how far context sensitivity can go and who should decide which models are context sensitive and which not. The following description of rule-of-law promotion illustrates the difficulties here:

---

[56] Actual promoters of democracy and the rule of law often view their activities as unproblematic *because* purely technical (critically also Carothers 1998: 99; Mani 1998: 1; Peterson 2010; Rajagopal 2008: 47; Upham 2002: 8).

[57] This is a popular claim in research on democracy and rule-of-law promotion (Carothers 1998: 104; Channell 2006: 130; de Zeeuw 2005: 482–3; Golub 2006: 125; Hobson 2009: 400; Jawad 2008; Leininger 2010; Mani 1998; 2008: 38; O'Neill 2008: 101; Pouligny 2003).

Donors attempt to work 'with' local governments to improve the delivery of justice, but such improvements are defined by the donor, usually reflecting Western expectations for how a legal system should operate and what interests it should protect. These interveners will tolerate local variation, but only as long as the central rule of law principles are not compromised.[58]

Hobson and Kurki also criticize the fact that context sensitivity remains '[at the level of] policy and implementation, with insufficient consideration given to the theoretical and conceptual frameworks that inform these practices'.[59] Thus, they argue, context sensitivity entails external actors deciding what form adapted versions of liberal democratic institutions should take. The concept of liberal democracy itself is not questioned. What is needed, therefore, is not simply that those involved be context sensitive but that democracy promotion undergo a conceptual rethink at the analytic and normative levels. Kurki goes even further here.[60] She argues that the conceptual contestability of democracy, beyond its liberal version, has been overlooked in the research on democracy promotion and that this research ignores theory-of-democracy debates in which a variety of concepts of democracy have been identified, each with its own, very different, set of justifications. In addition, she says, it ignores the ways in which concepts of democracy are interpreted in different contexts. The concept of democracy, as it figures in democracy promotion, must be pluralized and contextualized.[61] And contextualization implies considering models of democracy in context, and also listening and being open to different meanings.[62] Normatively, so both authors argue, this shift also entails a change to real dialogue rather than an exclusively teacher–student relationship between promoters and recipients of democracy.[63]

Scholarship in this area thus takes a broader view on norm promotion. However, it has so far given rise to very little empirical research into the precise nature of the kinds of local interpretations and conceptions of democracy promotion involved. Only very few studies explore cases in which promoters of democracy actually did have to rethink their template and adjust it to processes of democratization outside the

---

[58] Pimentel (2010: 34).   [59] Hobson/Kurki (2012: 2).
[60] Kurki (2011a, 2011b, 2013).   [61] Hobson/Kurki (2012: 7–10).
[62] Kurki (2010: 375–6).   [63] Hobson (2009: 400), Kurki (2010: 381).

liberal paradigm (but see Wolff 2011, 2012).[64] The upshot is that neither translation nor interpretation, nor their role in the external promotion of democracy, have so far been adequately captured in this branch of research.[65]

Research into democracy promotion may nowadays have widened its scope to cover possible contestation of the 'liberal' view of democracy, but an even more radical shift can be observed in research into peacebuilding. The more marked intrusiveness of many peacebuilding activities, the greater forcefulness of the interventions involved, and the fact that peacebuilding missions often take over government functions – all this has generated a particular interest in the problems and limits of such activities. As a result of the particular conditions prevailing in post-conflict states, researchers have developed a special interest in local agency and interaction as well as in the hybrid outcomes of peacebuilding. Some even talk of a 'local turn'.[66]

Overall, peacebuilding research has seen a shift of normative emphasis towards 'ownership'. Where there is deliberation, representation and constitutionalism, argues Barnett (2006), the outcome of peacebuilding need not be a fully fledged liberal polity; it can be a republican one – which establishes framing-institutions that are then 'filled in' domestically. Other scholars go even further in their rethinking of liberal peace, arguing in favour of peacebuilding that only fosters mutual recognition and bottom-up ownership (Donais 2009; Schaefer 2010).

Research into 'post-liberal' peacebuilding is one area in particular where there has been a shift to the analytical and normative study of peacebuilding outcomes both under the rubric of 'hybridity' (Mac Ginty 2010; Richmond/Franks 2009; Richmond/Mitchell 2012a)[67] and in relation to 'frictions' in the encounter between international interveners and local actors, discourses, and practices (Björkdahl/ Höglund 2013; Millar et al. 2013). This branch of research argues

---

[64] See also Poppe and Wolff (2013). For an account of democracy promoters dealing with a dilemma of choice between institution-building and local empowerment, see Lemay-Hébert (2012).

[65] But see a current research-network dedicated to studying 'democracy promotion as interaction': http://external-democracy-promotion.eu/, accessed 24 February 2016.

[66] Mac Ginty/Richmond (2013), Hughes et al. (2015).

[67] For a valuable overview of the advantages and drawbacks of this kind of research focus, see Peterson (2012).

that the promotion of democracy and the rule of law seldom results in working institutions and that post-conflict spaces are shaped by hybridity (Richmond/Franks 2009: 211). As understood by these scholars, 'hybridity' refers not to local reaction to norm diffusion (as in IR norm research) but to emerging interfaces between international and domestic actors (Peterson 2012), which can be 'composite forms of practice, norms and thinking that emerge from the interaction of different groups, worldviews and activity' (Mac Ginty/Sanghera 2012: 3).[68] The objects of study here are, on the one hand, the many ways in which local actors interact in peacebuilding interventions by hybridizing, coopting and resisting (Björkdahl/Höglund 2013: 297; Richmond/ Mitchell 2012b: 9–10), and, on the other, the many ways in which peacebuilders try to adapt to the new paradigm of context sensitivity (Hellmüller 2014; Mac Ginty 2008; Mac Ginty/Richmond 2015; Shaw/Waldorf 2010b; Sriram 2012).

This analytical approach forms the basis for some strong normative claims. Hybridity, it is argued, should be accepted as a normal outcome of peacebuilding rather than being regarded as deficient (Richmond 2011). It is also employed as a problem-solving device for achieving more context-sensitive peacebuilding (see e.g. Millar 2013; Schia/ Karlsrud 2013). Hybridity and resistance even becomes a central emancipatory concept: 'Peacebuilding as resistance appears, at least from the local level, to offer the main avenue through which to shape the emerging political environment' (Richmond 2010: 685).[69] Calls are made for peacebuilding activities to undergo radical change. Where traditional practices 'that may be at odds with Western expectation and interests' lead to 'plural-indigenous' systems that are legitimate in the eyes of the local population, internationals are called upon to show 'acceptance, not tolerance' of such hybridity (Roberts 2008: 80) – though more recently a shift towards more postcolonial perspectives amongst scholars in this area has led to greater caution in regard to claims of 'authenticity' and 'localness' (Lidén 2011; Richmond/Mitchell 2012b: 10–11).[70]

To sum up: whereas research into the promotion of democracy seeks to explore domestic contestation and the reinterpretation of democracy,

---

[68] See also the edited volume by Richmond and Mitchell (2012a) or Mac Ginty (2011).

[69] See also Laffey and Nadarajah (2012).

[70] See also the critiques by Chandler (2010), Nadarajah and Rampton (2015) and Sabaratnam (2013).

research into peacebuilding has undergone a more radical shift and is looking at everyday interaction in post-conflict spaces and at the ways in which actors use resistance and hybridity in the context of intervention and state-building. In addition, research here is characterized by strong explicit normative claims. Despite the changes described, the focus in these areas of research continues to be located at the micro and meso level. The aim is to give a picture of hybridity and of the complexity of global–local encounters (Millar et al. 2013: 140); no consideration is given to patterns of translation or interaction. Why a particular kind of norm translation or a particular kind of interaction takes place is not properly explored.

## *Romanticizing Localization?*

As indicated, socialization research is strongly focused on the notion of *full* norm adoption, while localization research homes in on the contestation and localization of norms. Underlying this latter stance is the belief, on the one hand, that norm legitimacy can only be produced through deliberative and contestatory processes, and, on the other, that because of its better fit with local normative structures, the outcome of translation – namely, localized norms – will be more stable and secure a higher level of compliance.

To those researching norm dynamics and contestation, and studying changes at the international level, conflicts over the meaning of norms can be a 'good thing'. They are considered to be an inevitable feature of the application of norms (Sandholtz/Stiles 2009) and can, it is claimed, lead to greater consensus in regard to interpretation and application (Badescu/Weiss 2010). Provided it is channelled through the appropriate arenas, contestation, it is argued, is necessary to produce norm legitimacy.[71]

Research also claims that localization can invest diffused norms and institutions with greater stability because, thus localized, they fit in better with the local context. Norms, as it were, have to be 'remade in the vernacular' in order to take on meaning (Merry 2006: 1). Similarly, peacebuilding researchers hope for the emergence of 'a new, post-liberal, politics, which is more locally "authentic", resonant and agential' (Richmond 2009: 326, 28) and leads to 'a more sustainable form

---

[71]  Wiener (2004, 2008) and Zwingel (2012: 126).

of peace in local terms' (Richmond 2011: 144). Rather than being 'artificial' – meaning created by external actors – this hybridity must be 'locally legitimate' (Mac Ginty/Richmond 2015: 1).

Scholars recognize that translation processes are inevitably shaped by power and interest: 'the politics of contestation over culture and historical memory – who is able to define authentic local tradition in terms that are socially acceptable and emotionally compelling – can set the terms for adaptation, rejection, or acceptance of new institutional forms' (Galvan/Sil 2007: 17). When it comes to influencing translation, it is argued, elites enjoy special advantages in terms of various forms of economic, cultural and social capital available to them (Galvan/Sil 2007: 11). This means that 'local' agency does not necessarily lead to fairer and more accountable politics (Lidén 2011: 65; Mac Ginty 2008: 149–50; Peterson 2010). As Richmond argues, contestation can 'enable, emancipate, include, exclude, self-determine, marginalize, silence or govern' (Richmond 2011: 29). Despite these reservations on the part of this branch of research, localization is at least recognized as having the potential to produce outcomes of a more legitimate, more stable and locally more appropriate kind. However, whether or at what point it actually does so when the target locality is a post-conflict space shaped by strong socio-economic inequalities, exclusion and marginalization remains moot. In addition, underlying these accounts is an assumption that contesting actors will hardly ever question the validity of norm-promotion activities and will instead readily engage in dialogue that is deemed to help produce more legitimate, 'appropriated' norms (see the critical discussion in Wolff/Zimmermann 2016).

## 2.3 Beyond Existing Norm-Diffusion Research

Interaction between norm-promotion activities and domestic translation do not form part of either of these approaches to norm diffusion: socialization research focuses on the methods norm senders use to achieve full norm adoption and on domestic constraints to such methods; IR localization research depicts local translation processes as independent of, or resistant to, outside influence. In what follows, patterns of interaction between rule-of-law promotion and domestic translation will be examined, along with one of their scope conditions – precision – and evidence will be offered of how external actors become involved in conflictual domestic translation as a result of feedback loops.

As has been indicated, the question of how norm translation is best analysed remains an open one. That norm translation takes place is now well established; by contrast, the ways in which translation processes differ, and how best to categorize their various outcomes, remains poorly explored. Socialization research offers an exclusively linear model of norm adoption, and localization research is overly broad in its categorization of norm reinterpretation and change. In the following sections, I set out a systematic model for analysing, and differentiating between, norm-translation outcomes.

A further contrast between the socialization and localization approaches is that they find themselves on opposing sides of a normative dilemma. Norm-socialization research holds that the promotion of specific standards relating to democracy and the rule of law ensures that the minimum requirements for just and democratic governance are met. The use of conditionality to achieve norm adoption is seldom questioned at a normative level. Norm-localization researchers, meanwhile, believe that norm translation offers a way of ensuring the local legitimacy and stability of norms. Drawing on the empirical insights afforded by the Guatemalan case studies, Chapter 8 will reflect in greater depth on this conundrum.

The aim of this study is to analyse norm translation as a dynamic component and product of interaction and, on the basis of this analysis, to accommodate norm contestation and norm reinterpretation within a theoretical and empirical framework. The model proposed goes beyond a purely rationalist account such as that offered by Barnett and Zürcher (2009), who use a strategic-choice approach to model the interaction between peacebuilders and domestic elites in post-conflict states (see also Barnett et al. 2014). These scholars argue that the outcome of such interaction is in most cases a negotiated compromise (Barnett/Zürcher 2009: 34). Although elites are attracted by the prospect of obtaining outside resources, reform is a costly proposition for them and a potential threat to their interests and power base. Peacebuilders therefore compromise on the extent of proposed liberal reforms in order to retain local support and safeguard stability. The result, say these scholars (Barnett/Zürcher 2009: 24, 35), is a symbolic adoption, or what sociological neo-institutionalism would describe as a decoupling (see above). Similarly, Groß and Grimm (2014) explore the 'interplay' of promoters and recipients of democracy and also find it leading ultimately to compromised reform. The process they depict is one of the rational use of a variety of instruments both by democracy promoters pressing for reforms and by domestic elites seeking to adapt, slow down or jettison these in line with their own interests.

In the rationalist approach, neither domestic political processes nor discourses around norm promotion dynamically influence the negotiations between domestic elites and external actors. By contrast, in the cases that will be presented here, interaction over translation involves more than a mere bargain with elites; it is a reaction to framing and contestation within broader domestic translation processes and, in addition, is influenced by the degree of precision of the norm sets in question (see Chapter 7). A purely rationalist model is not able to explain the shifts that occur from more conditionality-oriented interaction modes to more persuasion-oriented ones, in which there is (limited) space for arguing. Why particular standards are translated, how the translation occurs and how far it goes can only be understood by focusing on the interaction between norm promotion and norm translation.

The model of interaction proposed in this study also reaches beyond latest constructivist research into loops and cycles of norm change; such research does not include domestic norm translation in the cycles it identifies. Park and Vetterlein, for example, focus solely on cycles of contestation in international organizations (2010). Wiener, meanwhile, though proposing a model for contestatory cycles, has so far not taken this beyond the theoretical stage (2014). Börzel and Risse's (2000) model of feedback loops in Europeanization processes, for its part, remains structuralist and top-down in character.

Although norm change between more global and more local contexts has been specifically highlighted in research into the dynamics of Responsibility to Protect (R2P) – being variously termed 'feedback loops' (Job/Shesterinina 2014; Prantl/Nakano 2011) or 'norm circulation' (Acharya 2013) – these studies have so far ignored interaction over domestic translation. They focus first on localization and then, separately, on the effect these have on international norm dynamics. The present study, by contrast, devotes its attention to the interactive process in between, asking how this drives translation.

Interaction, as described in this study, is a 'back and forth' process driven interdependently by domestic norm translation and rule-of-law promotion. In order to capture this interaction more fully, a type of 'bracketing'[72] will be used involving analytically condensed steps. This entails devising a better system of categorization for norm translation and for the modes of interaction linked to norm promotion.

## Norm Translation

As indicated earlier, research along both norm-socialization and norm-localization lines fails to provide much in the way of a model for analysing translation processes or distinguishing the types of outcomes that result from these.

How can norm-translation processes best be analysed? As with any analysis, the first step must be to try to identify constituent elements or dimensions. A pointer here is provided by Elgström in a case study on the European Union (2000). Here, the process of negotiation around new norms is identified as having two distinct steps: negotiation of the text and negotiation of the implementation, with the latter involving a slightly different constellation of actors. Both steps entail conflict and resistance, hence 'we cannot expect the convinced advocate's version of the norm to come through this process unaffected' (Elgström 2000: 461). But there is one step missing from Elgström's account: to understand the negotiations in question, we need first to analyse the way in which a norm set is interpreted in a new context. This step – translation into discourse – shapes the further translation of a norm into law and into implementation. Overall then, translation from the 'global' to the 'local' takes place in three dimensions: translation into discourse, translation into law and translation into implementation (see Table 2.1). The dimensions are, of course, not temporally distinct. They should, however, be distinguished analytically. Again, translation is never 'complete' and we can therefore only study temporally stabilized outcomes on the three dimensions.

### Translation into Discourse

When global norms enter domestic political discourse, they are linked, consciously or unconsciously, into frames (see Chapter 1). Frames can be defined, in general terms, as 'schemata of interpretation' (Goffman

---

[72] The notion of bracketing was introduced by Giddens (1979: 49–95) as a means of exploring the interdependence of structure and agency. I use it here to distinguish the steps involved in interaction.

**Table 2.1** *Categorization of norm-translation outcomes*

| Dimension | Resistance | Localization | Full adoption |
|---|---|---|---|
| Translation into discourse | Resistance | Constructive criticism | Support |
| Translation into law | Rejection | Reshaping (omission, addition, modification) | Full adoption |
| Translation into implementation | Rejection | Reshaping (omission, addition, modification) | Full adoption |

1986: 21) which '[render] events or occurrences meaningful' (Snow et al. 1986: 464). They provide a means of analysing world views and particular constructions of social reality and are thus key elements in helping us to understand the political debates about translation into law and into implementation that take place in domestic contexts. Of course, domestic contexts are not independent of other, regional or global, contexts and some actor groups will try to link up debates occurring in different settings. In addition, frames will seldom be completely coherent and unchanging over time (see above).

Some scholars in IR see frames merely as a strategic device used by agents 'to situate events and to interpret problems, to fashion a shared understanding of the world, to galvanize sentiments as a way to mobilize and guide social action and to suggest possible resolutions to current plights' (Barnett 1999: 15).[73] On this view, frames are tools for collective action (Benford/Snow 2000: 614) resulting from strategic negotiation and interaction. But frames can develop from a combination of discursive and strategic processes both inside and outside the frame-bearing group (Benford/Snow 2000: 623–27). Hence, they do not develop merely from rational considerations (Donati 2001: 151–52). They are based on processes of reconstruction in which events are given meaning. Although culture plays a part here, it does so not in the sense of dictating a specific frame (the 'cultural match') but as a kind of 'toolbox' or

---

[73] This strategic understanding tallies with the 'core framing tasks' that feature prominently in most of the literature on social movements (Benford/Snow 2000: 615–22; Gerhards/Rucht 1992; Snow et al. 1986). Barnett (1999) is particularly strong in his emphasis on strategic framing as a causal mechanism, but many other IR scholars also point to the strategic use of frames – by agents such as norm entrepreneurs – as a means of promoting policy change or policy implementation (Barnett/Finnemore 2004; Keck/Sikkink 1998; Price 1998).

'reservoir' to be drawn upon during the frame-construction process (Swidler 1986).[74]

Frames encompass more than an interpretation of events and a construal of possible collective action (see Autesserre 2009: 252). In relation to norms, they comprise:

- an interpretation of what the norm set is about
- a reservoir of arguments for and against the norm set
- depictions of actors supporting or rejecting the norm set.

Different groups of international and domestic actors, often with differing interpretations of particular norm sets, will naturally try to influence domestic discussions in their preferred direction. This process of embedding into divergent frames emerges, for example, in the case of political and civil rights, a broad norm set that is open to very different types of framing at the local level: Domestic human rights groups may frame such norms as key elements of a democratization and good-governance agenda; adherents of a law-and-order coalition may object to this interpretation and discursively link it to leftist radicalism and an intention to afford protection to criminals; and indigenous groups may see the norms as tools in the struggle for emancipation and the fight against a neo-liberal state (Zimmermann 2016). These are only a handful of the possibilities: society is made up of myriads of subgroups, each of which may operate with slightly different framings.

Contrary to what is implied in the literature on transnational advocacy (see, for example, Keck/Sikkink 1998), TANs are not the only actors to project frames; in fact, various parties generate them, often as part of polarized framing contests (Bob 2012; Payne 2001: 44). Domestic debate and contestation thus always involve a plurality of frames: 'The process is essentially dialogic in that the actions of one speaker or voice are oriented to the ... performances of other voices – reacting, projecting, transforming, anticipating discourse of other speakers or voices' (Mehan et al. 1990: 135). The distance between these frames and those at a global level will vary.

Based not on their content but on their relation to a 'given' global norm set, I distinguish three types of frames:

---

[74] For this kind of view of frames in IR, accommodating both the strategic element and the meaningful interpretation of events, see Brysk (1995), Klotz and Lynch (2007: 51–57), Autesserre (2009), Charnysh et al. (2015).

- *frames of open resistance*, which question the validity of the norm set
- *frames of constructive criticism*, which openly propose modification of the norm set but do not question its validity
- *frames of support*, which completely support the global norm set.

Some argue that states are now so closely integrated within an overall global system that national borders are of little consequence and the international and domestic are inextricably enmeshed (see, for example, Leininger 2010). By contrast, the present study highlights the impact which differences of context, power asymmetries, the existence of differentiated networks and the potential for agency of different groups have on translation. It shows that domestic political processes are key factors in shaping translation into law, guiding policy formulation and defining the course of implementation. Although domestic discursive spaces are not independent of regional and global spaces, they nonetheless have unique characteristics and present different constellations from those operating at these other levels, thus creating a specific space for interaction.

### Translation into Law

The aim of global promoters and local supporters of a norm set is to get that norm set translated into law and invested with binding force in the domestic setting. IR norm-socialization scholars call this 'adoption', but this concept, as they define it, fails to capture the plurality of ways in which translation into law can take place.

As will be shown in the present study, the first of the three dimensions mentioned above – translation into discourse – strongly influences translation into law: the frames that emerge in political discourse determine which options are discussed during translation into law. This account of norm translation challenges the norm-diffusion paradigm, in which frames have no implications as regards the contents of the norm set that are diffused. A frame merely provides an 'intact' norm set with a better 'wrapper' (see above). By contrast, the present study contends that different frames entail different propositions as regards translation into law and translation into implementation. Political discourse can, of course, be dominated by one particular frame and in this case translation into law will be based on the latter. More often, however, there will be a clash of frames in the domestic setting and political actors will have to open a dialogue or negotiate a compromise.

External actors, meanwhile, will naturally try to influence the choice of translation.

Based on the degree to which they tally with the global norm set in question, I distinguish three types of translation into law:

(1) *complete rejection* of the norm set
(2) *reshaping* of the norm set through modification, addition or omission
(3) *full adoption*, meaning adoption of the international norm set as it stands.

Turning again to the example of civil and political rights, translation into law might be shaped by the following frames: human rights groups might well press for full adoption of the rights in question; proponents of a law-and-order approach might try to block adoption of those parts of the norm set that provided for greater safeguards on due process; and supporters of indigenous rights and emancipation might fight for the inclusion of indigenous rights and autonomy.

In analysing such processes, the present study compares the main drafts and adopted versions of the laws in question with the relevant international standards. It also reconstructs the political process, show-ing which groups supported which proposed versions of the legislation and what degree of negotiation took place between the different groups. Where a draft law tallies in every respect with the norm set in question, this is classified as full adoption; if it omits particular provi-sions, makes additions or institutes significant modifications, this is classed as reshaping – and particular attention is paid to the nature and degree of that reshaping.

### Translation into Implementation

When a norm has been translated into law, a period of at least tempor-ary stability follows. This is not so true of translation into implementa-tion. As the norm sets begin to inform official policy and activities and institutional development,[75] new groups of actors – frequently from the bureaucracy – are brought into the political process (Elgström 2000; Van Kersbergen/Verbeek 2007). Again, these groups may

---

[75] As described by Raustiala and Slaughter (2002: 539). I differ from these authors, however, in distinguishing legislation from implementation and introducing the element of 'translation into policy'.

support new or modified frames, and renewed contestation may break out over the 'correct' way to implement the norm set. In post-conflict states, the implementation dimension is much more strongly influenced than the legal one by financial constraints and lack of capacity.

Based on the extent to which the norm set in question is implemented, I distinguish three types of translation into implementation:

(1) *complete rejection* of the norm set, with no effort to put it into practice
(2) *reshaping* of the norm set through modification, addition or omission during implementation, which may involve the government or responsible agencies only partially implementing the norm set or linking previously unrelated policy-areas to implementation
(3) *full adoption*, which involves intensive activity by the government or responsible agencies with a view to implementing all parts of the norm set.

I go on to assess whether reshapings made during implementation relate to the same areas as those made during translation into law or whether new ground is covered.

Using these categorizations – translation into discourse, translation into law and translation into implementation – it is possible to distinguish (temporally stabilized) subtypes of norm translation. The proposed system is also useful when it comes to assessing the strength of modifications made to norms in specific categories and analysing translations on the different dimensions over different time-periods.

## Norm-Promotion Activities

How do norm promoters actually go about influencing translation processes?

One conclusion that can be drawn from the present study is that a straightforward external–internal division of the actor groups and activities involved would be too simplistic: external actors in Guatemala are seen to be active in local political discourse, in local political processes, including the drafting of legislation, and in critical 'closed doors' consultations with government leaders; conversely, local actors are seen to operate within, or be employed by, international organizations.

In addition, the case studies show interaction occurring at different levels, with different partners and audiences. Internationally, it may take place at the diplomatic level or, more publicly, via statements and reports issued by external actors – in Guatemala these were, amongst others, international NGOs, UN Rapporteurs, the European Parliament and the OAS. Locally, international organizations have offices in the countries concerned and resident ambassadors regularly invite government members and other politicians to informal talks and meetings. Again, development agencies engage in capacity building and information sharing, and international NGOs support specific development projects and campaigns run by local NGOs. Although the activities by these different actors at different levels are not synchronized, the present study indicates that there are phases where particular activities dominate.

How might these activities be analysed more accurately? This book proposes a classification of interaction modes according to the following types (based on the discussions above): incentives and sanctions; praising and shaming; teaching; arguing. Norm promoters can opt for one of the more conditionality-oriented alternatives – incentives/sanctions or praising/shaming – or for one of the more persuasion-oriented approaches of teaching and arguing. The conditionality-oriented options are driven mainly by utilitarian calculations and by considerations of what appears appropriate; the persuasion-oriented options are aimed ultimately at bringing both parties, international and domestic, into dialogue – with a unidirectional transfer of expertise in teaching and a two-way exchange in arguing (Risse 2004: 293).

Attempts by norm promoters to influence the course of events take place in all three of the dimensions outlined previously: translation into discourse, translation into law and translation into implementation.

The activities engaged in by the promoters are not necessarily different in kind; they are simply targeted at different dimensions of the translation process. International organizations may, for example, finance public campaigns in support of a norm set; they may recruit experts to assist in drafting legislation; or they may build the capacities of the government employees who work on implementation after the law has been passed. All three sets of activities would be categorized as teaching. In addition, it is unlikely that any of the three activities will occur in a pure, isolated form; some kind of combination is always observable. In the Guatemalan case, for example, the United States organized teaching activities with the government whilst threatening sanctions if Congress did not approve particular legislation. Activities

Table 2.2 *Operationalization of interaction modes*

| Mode | Conditionality | | | Persuasion |
|---|---|---|---|---|
| *Form* | Incentives/ sanctions | Praising/ shaming | Teaching | Arguing in dialogue |
| *Indicators* | *Sanctions*: threat to cut aid or suspend preferential political arrangements  *Incentives*: offers of aid, credit, preferential political arrangements | Positive/ negative comments regarding political figures or programmes | Workshops, training sessions, conferences aimed at capacity-building, transfer of expertise, awareness-raising | Exchange of arguments within dialogue-based fora and on basis of mutual recognition |

may also differ depending on the external actor involved: in Guatemala, a major international NGO chose to organize a retrospective shaming campaign against the government when a particular piece of legislation failed to be adopted; the European Union, by contrast, preferred to act prospectively, with a promise of aid should the legislation go through. Clearly this also has to do with differences in the resources and instruments available to each actor. With all these variables in mind, the present study will seek to establish which activities are used locally by which external actors in relation to which actor groups and in which phase or dimension. It will also ask whether dominant modes of interaction in these activities change as a result of interplay between norm promotion and domestic translation.

## 2.4 Acknowledging the Interactive Element

The present study contends that analysis of the interaction between external norm-promotion activities and domestic norm translation points to the formation of 'feedback loops' in reaction to the activities of rule-of-law promoters. It contrasts this process with the unidirectional sequence depicted in most existing IR norm-socialization research: the reactions of external actors to local contexts are not simply technical adjustments to strategy; they are substantive responses to contestation and political conflict in the societies in question. The study will also show that the outcomes of these 'loops' are shaped by the degree of precision of the norm being promoted. The cases under review demonstrated that, in general, the less precise the norm, the greater the space for translation. Even very precise norms, however, underwent some modification and reshaping, the extent of this being limited by the perception of them as having greater normativity and the fact that the stricter 'text' allowed less variation in standards.

The translation of three norm sets of differing precision in post-conflict Guatemala formed the basis for the present study. Analysis of this pointed up a pattern of interaction between external actors' norm-promotion endeavours and the domestic translation process. Initial norm-promotion activities based on conditionality elicited domestic contestation and a rejection not only of the content of the norm sets in question but also of the strategies used to promote them. External actors reacted by shifting to a more persuasion-oriented style of promotion and adopting a less transparent mode of operation. Dialogues were set up with presumed veto players and this created scope for translation, resulting, in every case, in some kind of reshaping of the norm set in question. The scope for reshaping was, however, conditioned by the precision of the norm set involved: in the case of the high-precision norm set on children's rights, it was narrow; when it came to global scripts for rule-of-law commissions, it was considerable (see Figure 1.1).

To set the scene for the detailed analysis that will follow, Chapter 3 outlines the evolution of rule-of-law promotion in Guatemala and the international community's involvement in the country. It outlines the post-conflict setting, the history of the interaction between domestic and external actors and the immense rule-of-law and security challenges faced by the country.

# 3 | Guatemala and the International Community

Promotion of the rule of law was the approach adopted by the international donor community towards Guatemala after the signing of the 1996 peace agreement. The ultimate aim was a radical overhaul of Guatemala's political and social structure, with a view to securing peace and promoting democracy. In what follows here, light is thrown on the role which the international donor community has played in Guatemala – taking the latter as a paradigm of a post-conflict country.

Lasting more than thirty years, Guatemala's civil war was one of the longest and bloodiest in twentieth-century Latin America, and the war's root causes – colonial land-seizures and massive socio-economic inequality – continue to shape the country today. Opinions as to the impact of the peacebuilding process in Guatemala since the 1990s are mixed. On the one hand, peace was assured with only modest UN intervention (to oversee elections, demobilization and the human rights situation). There was no relapse into conflict, the human rights situation improved and, so far, all newly elected governments have pledged to further the peace process. On the other hand, when it comes to tackling the root causes of conflict, the picture is rather dim (Paris 2004: 113–14; Stanley/Holiday 2002: 441). Guatemala exhibits a number of traits typical of post-conflict spaces: its political system is more akin to a hybrid polity than a liberal democracy (Karl 1995); organized crime, drug trafficking and social violence have transnational reverberations and are viewed as signs of potential 'state failure'; and domestic 'ownership' of the peace agenda is weak and the activities of the international donor community are often subject to contest.

This chapter describes the background-factors that shape interaction regarding the translation of specific rule-of-law norms in Guatemala. It traces the history of Guatemalan conflict and of external actors' involvement in the country (3.1). It looks in particular at the attempts at peacebuilding that followed the signing of the peace agreement in 1996 and at the current post-conflict setting, including not only the challenges which Guatemala faces in regard to security and the rule of law (3.2) but also the difficult conditions these create for the international donor community as it seeks to promote the latter (3.3). Armed with this information, the reader will, it is hoped, have a better appreciation of the immense challenges and often problematic socio-political power constellations with which post-conflict countries more generally are confronted.

## 3.1 External Actors in War-Torn Guatemala

### *Guatemala's Civil War*

Guatemala's current political situation is shaped by its historical experience of colonialism and authoritarian structures. The country gained independence from Spain in 1821. During the nineteenth century, agricultural exports became its main source of income and, even today, products such as coffee and bananas rank alongside textiles and processed food as key exports.[1] At the start of the twentieth century, Guatemala came under the dictatorship of Jorge Ubico (president from 1931 to 1944), who opened up the country to greater foreign investment – a well-known beneficiary of this policy being the United Fruit Company.[2] A brief interlude of democratic government under Presidents Juan José Arévalo and Jacobo Árbenz (the 'Ten Years of Spring' from 1944 to 1954) ended in a US-backed military coup launched in response to President Árbenz's attempts to bring about moderate land reforms (Handy 1994). Until the democratic opening-up of the 1980s, Guatemala was governed by a series of presidents, both military and civilian. These were dependent on backing from the military – which became the most important institution in the country, dominating not only the state but the country's social and economic life. Underpinning this authoritarian system of rule was an ideologically based entente with Guatemala's oligarchic agro-export elites (Briscoe/ Pellecer 2010: 7–9). As Kurtenbach puts it (2008: 10):

[A] repressive regime was established which rested on the traditional features of Guatemala's society: [an] agro-export economy based on the exploitation of [a] cheap indigenous labour force; political exclusion of the majority of the

---

[1]   Taft-Morales (2013: 8).

[2]   For a history of the company's operations in Guatemala, see Dosal (1993).

indigenous and ladino population; and violent repression of any forms of opposition.[3]

Revolt against this political regime began early on. During the 1960s, young leftist military officers fled the army, formed insurgency groups and began a guerrilla war in the east of the country. Although these groups were crushed, the 1970s saw the build-up of a new wave of insurgency that brought leftist guerrilla groups and indigenous rural movements into closer contact with one another. Chief amongst the grievances aired by these groups were socio-economic inequality and, linked to this, inequitable land distribution and discrimination against indigenous populations in rural areas.[4] During this second phase of insurgency, the various guerrilla groups operated mostly out of the country's western highlands, inhabited predominantly by indigenous peoples.[5]

Although the Guatemalan military had been proactive in fighting this new wave of insurgency from the time it began in the 1970s, at the start of the 1980s, under General Ríos Montt – installed as de facto head of state in a coup in 1982 and holder of the presidency until 1983 – the war attained new dimensions. The military targeted the rural Mayan population as presumed guerrilla collaborators and cruel 'scorched earth' campaigns saw whole villages slaughtered. Overall, the civil war in Guatemala cost 200,000 lives, making it the bloodiest Latin American civil war in the twentieth century (Brands 2011: 12). Eighty-three per cent of those victims who were identified were Mayan. In addition, experts estimate that between half a million and one and a half million Guatemalans were victims of forced displacement between

---

[3]  On state-building and Guatemala's social evolution, see Williams (1994) and MacCreery (1994). On the construction of ladino and Mayan identities in relation to a resource-extractive development model, see Kurtenbach (2008).

[4]  For excellent overviews of the civil war in Guatemala, see e.g. Jonas (1991) and Handy (1984, 1994).

[5]  In the east of the country, the population is majority 'ladino', i.e. Hispanicized. It has no links with the former colonial elites but does not see itself as indigenous either. Although more than 50% of the Guatemalan population do identify themselves as indigenous, this group is rather fragmented, consisting of Mayans (e.g. the K'iche', Mam and Q'echi'), members of the Xinca people and a group of people of African descent called the Garifuna. Mayans, a very diverse group who speak around 26 different languages (including Quiche, Cakchiquel, Mam, Tzutujil, Achi and Pokoman), dominate the population in the western highlands. For a rights-based account of Guatemala's indigenous peoples, see Minority Rights Group International (2015).

1981 and 1983. A truth commission set up in later years found that the overwhelming majority of human rights violations that took place at this time were perpetrated by Guatemalan military and paramilitary groups.[6] In its report, published in 1999, the commission stated that in the four heavily affected areas which it had analysed, 'agents of the State of Guatemala ... committed acts of genocide against groups of Mayan people'.[7] These massive military campaigns left the guerrilla forces virtually destroyed.

Following a further coup in 1983, a number of internal and external factors led to a slow democratic opening-up of the country. These factors included economic mismanagement and changes in attitudes amongst the oligarchic elites, the middle class and certain sections of the military. Further impetus was provided by the wave of democratizations and the operations of increasingly well-organized human rights networks in Latin America as a whole (Azpuru 1999: 10; Pearce 2005: 16). In 1985, the military handed power to a civilian government set up in accordance with a democratic constitution. Even under this constitution, however, leftist parties were banned from political life and democratic presidents continued to be subject to major military constraints, making this a fragile hybrid of authoritarianism and democracy (Karl 1995).

## International Involvement

Until the 1990s, Guatemala remained isolated internationally. Leaving the United States aside, the role which other countries played in Guatemalan politics was minimal and transnational contacts were essentially limited to economic exchange. Compared with the transnational networks that existed in the Southern Cone at that time, Guatemala's civil-society links continued to be relatively weak (Baldwin 2009: 85).[8]

The prime external actor in Guatemala was, without a doubt, the United States. It took a hand in the overthrow of President Árbenz in

---

[6] It is estimated that 93% of documented human rights violations were perpetrated by Guatemalan military and paramilitary groups and only 3% by the guerrilla. See Commission for Historical Clarification (1999: paras. 15, 21, 66).

[7] Commission for Historical Clarification (1999: para. 122).

[8] During the 1970s and 1980s, however, a European solidarity movement, concerned mainly with development and the rural situation, took active steps to try to inform the European public about the political situation in Guatemala.

1954[9] and its strongly anti-communist foreign policy and powerful economic interests served to stabilize the power of the military and the oligarchic elites in Guatemala.[10]

Until the 1990s, apart from one brief interlude, the approach of the US administration to the Guatemalan military remained one of cooperation. From the 1960s, the United States provided financial backing for the military and helped train it in counter-insurgency techniques, seeing it as a bulwark against a presumed communist threat across the continent. With the presidency of Jimmy Carter (in office 1977–81), who made US aid conditional on improvements in human rights,[11] this relationship underwent a brief period of change. However, during Ronald Reagan's tenure (1981–9), internal conflict in Central America – notably in Nicaragua and El Salvador – once again took centre stage in US foreign policy. Although expressing approval at the democratic opening-up of Guatemala, the Reagan administration resumed the strong cooperative relations previously maintained with the Guatemalan military.[12] Once the Cold War was over and various civil wars in the area had come to an end, the prominence of Central America in US foreign policy diminished and the countries in question were left with the task of redefining their roles as states which, other than in relation to drug trafficking, now held little interest for their dominant neighbour (Falcoff 1991).

The role played by Europe in Guatemala developed as a counterpoint to US foreign policy but remained more limited in scope. It was only in the 1980s that European countries began to devote greater attention to the conflicts in Central America, chiefly as a result of European dissent from US Cold War politics. European countries saw the various conflicts in Central America as deriving from poverty and repression rather than as a potential opening for communism. Amongst Scandinavian populations in particular there was a deeply felt sympathy for the Central American revolutionary struggles (Falcoff 1991: 368). Against this

[9] On US involvement in this coup, see Marks (1990).
[10] For a discussion of the role played by the United States in the civil war in Guatemala, see Jonas (1991: 28–38).
[11] Resulting in the US Congress making a series of cuts to Guatemalan security-assistance between 1977 and 1983. See Jonas (1996: 147–8).
[12] Stanley and Holiday (2002: 426); Jonas (1996). However, in the wake of the democratic opening-up of the country, the US Congress did approve a new ban on direct military assistance – still partially in force today. For details of this, see Taft-Morales (2004, 2013).

background, Central America became one of the first areas of the world to be the target of a joint European foreign-policy approach. The San José Dialogue mechanism – which facilitates dialogue between Central American presidents and the European Community, not only on matters of trade but also in regard to the maintenance of peace in the area – was initiated in 1984 and continues to form the basis of EU–Central American relations (Rey Marcos 2000: 173).[13] Nowadays, the EU regards the Central American experience of the 1980s as having played a key role in shaping its own approach of 'socializing' countries into democratization and the opening-up of socio-economic life (Youngs 2002: 155).

As a result of this growing international attention, the Guatemalan conflict began increasingly to be perceived as part of a regional problem. Guatemala was not the only country overtaken by civil war in the 1980s: El Salvador and Nicaragua were equally shaped by these kinds of conflicts. However, whilst the Salvadorean struggle mirrored the Guatemalan one in that it involved violence between a military-led government and a guerrilla movement (the Farabundo Martí National Liberation Front – FMLN), in Nicaragua the Sandinista National Liberation Front (FSLN) had actually managed, at the end of the 1970s, to oust the country's dictator, Anastasio Somoza. Subsequently, however, the Sandinista government found itself under attack from rightist counter-revolutionary groups in the so-called Contra War. These events triggered a Central American peace-initiative, which took formal shape in the second half of the 1980s.[14] In the Esquipulas II Accords of 1987, the presidents of El Salvador, Guatemala, Nicaragua, Costa Rica and Honduras undertook to further the peace process in their respective countries within a framework of democratization and international verification. As well as normalizing relations between the other Latin American states and Sandinista-ruled Nicaragua, these accords laid the foundations for peace agreements in Nicaragua itself (1989) and in El Salvador (1992). Guatemala followed suit, though with some delay (1996).

[13]  The Dialogue's full members are Guatemala, Honduras, El Salvador, Nicaragua, Costa Rica and Panama.

[14]  The Contadora group, comprising several Latin American countries (Colombia, Mexico, Panama and Venezuela), lent regional support to the Central American peace process from the start of the 1980s. However, because of the group's quasi-recognition of Sandinistan Nicaragua and its critical stance towards US foreign policy, US backing was not forthcoming and the process therefore failed to advance as expected.

This 'created a particular landscape for international involvement in the region based on particular norms' (Short 2007: 71). The norms in question related to the institution of electoral democracy, the free operation of civil society and the creation of relevant political institutions. All three peace agreements were drafted with the help of the UN or other international mediators, and all the countries involved hosted UN observer or verification missions to monitor their implementation (Paris 2004: 113).[15] As later sections will show, the Guatemalan Peace Accords institutionalized the role of the international donor community in Guatemala without securing broad domestic 'ownership' of the peacebuilding process.

## Rule-of-Law Promotion as a Post-Peace Focus

Relations between the international donor community and Guatemala during the 1990s were shaped first by the negotiation of the Guatemalan Peace Accords and later by their implementation. The main approach adopted during both phases was that of building peace through democracy and the rule of law.[16] However, once the Accords were signed, the international donor community's agenda seldom tallied with domestic political constellations.

### Negotiation of a Peace Agreement

The democratic opening-up of Guatemala lent added importance to transnational contacts. As well as creating spaces in which the evolving Mayan movement and NGO sector could articulate their views, it opened the country up to tourism as a major source of income (Kumar/Lodge 2002: 9–10). Democratization also made it easier for donor states to establish official relations with the country and to

---

[15] The official title of the Nicaraguan mission was the 'United Nations Observer Group in Central America'.

[16] Although the country's overall donor dependency remains low, the political influence of the donor community has been considerable. Foreign aid makes up only 1% or so of Guatemalan GNI (Gross National Income) but 10% of government expenditure: World Bank (2007: Sect. 6.11). In the current donor structure, the United States is the most important donor, followed by the EU, Japan and the non-EU European states. See the OECD ranking at www.com pareyourcountry.org/chart.php?cr=347&lg=en&project=aid-statistics&page=21, accessed 26 January 2016.

allocate aid and loans to the Guatemalan government (Rey Marcos 2000: 174; Youngs 2002: 117–18).

However, it was only in 1996, after another ten years of internal and external pressure, that the Guatemalan peace negotiations were brought to a successful conclusion. Not until the start of the 1990s had the Christian-democratic government of Marco Cerezo shown itself willing to initiate serious talks with the URNG – the umbrella organization for the various, now weakened, guerrilla groups (for a list of Guatemalan presidents who have held office since democratization, see Annex 2). The decision to do so was motivated primarily by the desire of the Guatemalan government to improve its international standing: domestic impetus for such negotiations was minimal, as the political elites were convinced they had won the war (Azpuru 1999: 107).[17] It was only when the UN took on a more proactive role in the negotiations that the process moved forward. This shift came in response to an attempted 'self-coup'[18] by the next president, Jorge Serrano. When Serrano was forced to leave office, Ramiro León, a former human rights ombudsman, served as interim president. León had very little domestic political support but enjoyed positive international standing. In addition, increasing diplomatic pressure was exerted, notably by the United States and the European countries, in order to keep negotiations on the Peace Accords going and steer them in the desired direction.[19] Ex post conditionality[20] was offered, with promises of generous aid should the Accords be signed (Morales López 2007: 87). With UN mediation, the process gained momentum and in 1996 the URNG and the newly

[17]  On the negotiations, see Stanley and Holiday (2002: 428–29).

[18]  The term 'self-coup' denotes a coup in which the head of government of the country in question assumes extra-judicial powers, dissolves the legislature and, in some cases, suspends the supreme or constitutional court. One of the effects of the self-coup in Guatemala was to make clear to the Guatemalan military the limits of the international donor community's tolerance. The United States, the EU and the governments of Europe as a whole condemned the action and threatened a 'suspension of trade privileges, economic aid, and access to international credit' (Jonas 1996: 158). This strategy was successful and Serrano handed over power to an interim president.

[19]  Stanley/Holiday (2002: 432); Schultze-Kraft (2012: 147). The negotiation process was supported in particular by the UN and a 'Group of Friends' consisting of Columbia, Mexico, Norway, Spain, the United States and Venezuela. The Latin American members of this group, however, were quickly excluded from any major roles of influence during the implementation of the peace agreement (Whitfield 2007: 95–96).

[20]  Material incentives accorded only after a particular provision has been fulfilled.

Table 3.1 *Peace accords between the URNG and the Guatemalan government*[1]

| | |
|---|---|
| 1994 | Comprehensive Agreement on Human Rights |
| 1994 | Agreement on Resettlement of the Population Groups Uprooted by the Armed Conflict |
| 1994 | Agreement on the Establishment of the Commission to Clarify Past Human Rights Violations and Acts of Violence that have Caused the Guatemalan Population to Suffer |
| 1995 | Agreement on Identity and Rights of Indigenous Peoples |
| 1996 | Agreement on Social and Economic Aspects and Agrarian Situation |
| 1996 | Agreement on the Strengthening of Civilian Power and on the Role of the Armed Forces in a Democratic Society |

[1] Table based on: United States Institute of Peace, 'Peace Agreements: Guatemala', www.usip.org/publications/peace-agreements-guatemala, accessed 26 April 2014.

elected government of Álvaro Arzú (president from 1996 to 2000) signed a final Peace Accord which brought together six separate agreements concluded between 1994 and 1996.

The Guatemalan Peace Accords not only put an end to violent conflict and provided for the demobilization of former combatants and their reintegration into society, they also laid down a comprehensive set of provisions relating to human rights, democracy, indigenous rights and social and economic policy. They represented not only an attempt to establish peace but a bid to tackle the root causes of conflict (see Table 3.1).[21] They are therefore regarded as one of the first examples of substantial peace-*building* activities by external actors.

In contrast to the interplay of factors in El Salvador, where peace negotiations had been brought about by a stalemate-situation, the internal pressure for peace negotiations in Guatemala was very weak. The process was driven mainly by the specific interests of the two groups involved in the negotiations. The guerrilla groupings were very conscious of the fact that these negotiations represented their last chance to transform themselves into legally recognized actors in

[21] In this respect, the Guatemalan Peace Accords differed from the other peace accords concluded in Central America. The Salvadorean agreement, for example, dealt only with issues of demilitarization and democratization – albeit in a more specific and detailed way (Azpuru 2006b: 103).

the political system. The government, meanwhile, was keen to open up internationally and secure the financial input (aid and investments) which it had been promised.[22] The international attention and resources that the peace process brought with it made it possible to circumvent the country's classic veto players,[23] and the Accords 'promised the government a framework to rally support for modernization, while retaining the option of blaming unpopular measures on international pressure and the demands of economic globalization' (Stanley/ Holiday 2002: 430). The success of this strategy of circumvention, however, was short-lived.

### Implementation of the Peace Agreement
In the years that followed, it became obvious to the international community that there was no domestic consensus in favour of the peace agreement – and indeed no domestic ownership of it at all: the influential business sector and the traditional political parties viewed it in a negative light; the professional NGO constituency that had grown up around the peace negotiations remained small and urban-based; the indigenous movement focused more on issues such as security, decentralization and self-determination and not so much on state reform; and the broader population, whose overall perception of the state was a negative one, generally had low expectations in regard to the ideas the Peace Accords proposed for bolstering the latter – with the result that active involvement by the public was minimal.[24]

Given this situation, MINUGUA – the United Nations Verification Mission in Guatemala – found itself with very little room for manoeuvre. Initially sent to Guatemala in 1994, when an early human rights agreement was concluded, the Mission stayed beyond the signing of the final Accords in order to monitor their overall implementation, and finally left in 2004.[25] Despite the constraints, the mission to

---

[22] On this constellation of interests, see Pásara (2001: 14) and Franco and Kotler (1998: 41).

[23] Kumar and Lodge (2002: 11). Still, without at least some support from classic veto players such as certain sections of the military, no peace agreement would have been possible (Stanley/Holiday 2002: 430–31).

[24] Schultze-Kraft (2012: 149), Kumar and Lodge (2002: 16), Pásara (2001: 5–7).

[25] On the history of MINUGUA in the country, see Stanley (2013).
The peacekeeping and demobilization part of the mission was mandated by the Security Council in 1997 and comprised 188 military personnel. The rest of the mission (more than 250 personnel in all), which was dedicated to verification,

Guatemala was a highly ambitious one. Instead of being geared to assist with relief and rehabilitation, as had been the case for former UN missions, it worked proactively on institution-building, notably in the area of civil and political rights and the rule of law. As the UN saw it, the judiciary, the police, the military, the prison system and all the institutions of the justice system needed to be reformed in order to secure human rights (Kumar/de Zeeuw 2006: 3; O'Neill 2008: 94). The funding and capacity needed to help create new institutions and carry out the planned reforms was provided by the donor community.[26] Despite the efforts of the majority of donors to coordinate their actions within a consultative group,[27] all this activity culminated in the familiar phenomenon of 'overrun', identified by Thomas Carothers (1999: 165) as early as 1999:

Rule-of-law aid programs are multiplying: the U.S. government, the Inter-American Development Bank, the World Bank, the Swedish government, and the Dutch government are all sponsoring rule-of-law aid activities in the country. The various donors have commissioned more than thirty separate diagnostic studies of Guatemala's legal and judicial system in recent years.

Further down the line, this agenda of state reform was judged by many scholars to have been an over-ambitious project that was doomed to failure because it went beyond the vision of the domestic actors themselves (see, for example, Kumar/de Zeeuw 2006: 4; Pásara 2001: 31). The problem of general 'ownership' soon became apparent with the election of a right-wing government headed by the Guatemalan Republican Front (Frente Republicano Guatemalteco – FRG) and with the failure of a referendum on constitutional reform initiated as part of the peace agreement in 1999. In signing the peace agreement, President Álvaro Arzú had had the backing of the oligarchic land-owning elite, but the success of the FRG at the polls pointed to a new diversification in the country's elites and to the advent to power of groups that had not supported the peace agreement. This diversification had an impact on

was mandated by the General Assembly. This was said to have resulted in its having less leverage, but it may also explain why it was accepted by Guatemalan actors normally very reluctant to countenance foreign intervention.

[26] In the wake of the devastation caused by Hurricane Mitch in 1998, funds were subsequently diverted from direct institution-building to disaster relief (Youngs 2002: 124).

[27] This wave of reform was taking shape even before the signing of the Peace Accords: Carothers (1998: 103).

subsequent elections. At the same time, the political representatives of the former guerrilla groupings ceased to have any real influence in Guatemalan politics after 1999 (Holiday 2000).

Since the 1980s, the land-owning elites had found themselves in competition with new elites springing up in finance and industry. In addition, organized crime and drug trafficking offered new revenue flows that posed a threat to oligarchic dominance. The presidency of FRG-representative Alfonso Portillo (2000–4) relied for its support on the popularity of the party's leader and former de facto head of state Ríos Montt and on funds provided by a section of the emerging elites.[28] With its populist, conservative stance, the party also attracted a large number of indigenous votes. For the international donor community, however, the electoral success of the FRG was a sign of a deterioration in the peacebuilding process and of the increasing infiltration of criminal and clandestine groups into government (Pearce 2005: 20).

A referendum in 1999 was related to the parts of the peace agreement that proposed constitutional changes – changes affecting a range of areas from military responsibilities to the strengthening of indigenous rights. The failure to get these proposals confirmed precluded any profound change in Guatemalan political structures. Getting the reforms through the preliminary stages in Congress had in itself proved a major obstacle: changes of content were required and the whole process was seriously delayed, only moving forward when pressure was applied by international donors. After all this – and despite a large-scale internationally financed publicity campaign and extensive 'voter education' – the turn-out for the referendum was only 18 per cent. None of the four parts of the referendum secured a majority.[29]

Many of the referendum's supporters blamed its failure on both the anti-reform campaign conducted by the right and on the absence of a clear public stance by the political parties (despite their official support for the referendum). In an attempt to persuade the middle and upper classes to vote against the proposals, the right's campaign invoked the threat of left-wing dominance, a rise in indigenous power and international intervention. A hostile debate about indigenous rights flared up amongst the white middle classes, stoking fears of a 'balkanization' of Guatemala. An increase in 'lynchings' in rural areas seemed, in this

---

[28] Briscoe and Pellecer (2010: 8–22); Schünemann (2010a: 19).
[29] Stanley and Holiday (2002: 437).

context, to militate against the idea of voting for any kind of indigenous rights (Sieder 2002: 198–201).

In addition, a substantial proportion of the indigenous population – who would have been the main beneficiaries had the referendum's proposals been adopted and implemented – either failed to vote or voted 'no'. This can be explained in part by a lack of information and by the inaccessibility of polling stations, but, as Carey argues (2004), it also had to do with a lack of 'ownership' on the part of indigenous groups. Many amongst these regarded the peace process and the formal human rights agenda as an outside project that did not necessarily help their cause. The state – and with it elections – were viewed with suspicion.

Other long-term peacebuilding tasks that were financed, and sometimes directly managed, internationally also showed very mixed results – partly because the tactic of 'circumventing' the veto players in the peace process backfired. According to observers, the scope and complexity of the agreements were not made clear to the public (Azpuru 1999: 120). The numerous tasks deriving from the peace agreements were dealt with in a host of different committees, and although elements of civil society were involved, the process remained diffuse, failing to connect with local representative structures or be submitted to broader public debate.[30]

An outline will now be given of the main areas addressed in the efforts to implement the provisions of the peace agreement.

The international donor community concentrated its efforts on reform of the security sector and judiciary (Pearce 2005: 17; Schultze-Kraft 2012: 148). That it was able to do so was due in part to the fact that the tasks of resettlement and demobilization proved quick to complete. The resettlement of internal refugees and refugees who had fled to Mexico[31] (mostly indigenous people fleeing from the Guatemalan military) was funded mainly by EU money. In fact, most refugees had returned by the start of the 1990s, making resettlement a manageable task. As for demobilization, this went relatively smoothly in the case of the weakened guerrilla forces but was more complicated when it came to the right-wing paramilitary groups – the so-called Civil Self-defence

---

[30] Stanley and Holiday (2002: 424); Pásara (2001: 15).
[31] Approximately 250,000 fled over Guatemala's northern border to Chiapas, in Mexico (Kurtenbach 2008: 14).

Patrols or PACs (Patrullas de Autodefensa Civil). During the early 2000s, the mobilization potential of the Patrols was regularly used by the FRG as part of a strategy of political intimidation.

Reform of the police was one of the international donor community's major undertakings in Guatemala and is now judged to have been a failure. The former police forces were dissolved and a new 'Civilian Police Force', modelled on the Spanish Guardia Civil, was created under the supervision of the Spanish – with little attempt to reflect the requirements set out in the Peace Accords. In addition, in order to fill the ranks – and tackle a crime wave then sweeping across the country (see below) – former police officers were re-hired. Corruption, low wages and poor resourcing and capacity continued to afflict the police and from early on the military were called on to provide 'temporary' back-up for them.[32]

In regard to the military itself, drug-trafficking activities, the security situation and its own continuing economic power have ensured that it has retained its influence on 'national security' right up to the present day. Military numbers and budgets were reduced – both following the peace agreements and later, under the presidency of Óscar Berger – but '[d]espite these losses of power and privileges [the military] still retains formidable quotas of power' (Spence 2004: 52). This situation was not helped by the failed attempt to introduce a constitutional reform imposing further limits on the military's internal role. As for the Guatemalan intelligence agency – the notorious Estado Mayor Presidencial or Presidential Guard – this was dissolved only at the end of President Portillo's term of office (2004) and only under strong international pressure.[33]

The institution of a transitional-justice process was another of the international community's major aspirations – but found little favour with the various Guatemalan governments. An internationally financed truth commission[34] (the Commission for Historical Clarification – CEH) was set up to document the ill deeds perpetrated by both the

---

[32] On the reform of the police, see e.g. Azpuru (2006b: 113), Kincaid (2000), International Crisis Group (2010: 8–9), Sieder (2002: 39–41), Spence (2004: 62–64), Taft-Morales (2013: 6).

[33] For an overview of military reform, see Pearce (2005: 21–22); Schultze-Kraft (2012: 148).

[34] The brief of a truth commission is to investigate, and report on, wrongdoings committed by governments and other parties to a conflict.

guerrilla forces and the Guatemalan military during the civil war but was prevented, by the stipulations of the peace agreement, from naming offenders. Its report, published in 1999, shocked the international donor community, as did a 1998 report by the Catholic Church, published under the title *Guatemala: Nunca Más* ('Guatemala: Never Again') (Sieder 2001: 175–76). The government showed little interest in following up the Commission's recommendations – the payment of reparations, for example; the provision of financial assistance for exhumations; or the implementation of reforms in the military and judiciary (Stanley/Holiday 2002: 456). What was more, an amnesty introduced in 1996 exempted perpetrators of political crimes from prosecution. The amnesty did not, however, cover genocide, torture or forced disappearance, with the result that, with the backing of the Inter-American Court of Human Rights and the Inter-American Commission on Human Rights, some prosecutions at least have now finally been brought against former members of the military. Even former dictator Ríos Montt was convicted of genocide by a Guatemalan court – the first-ever genocide conviction by a domestic court anywhere in the world. However, the conviction was later ruled to be invalid by the Guatemalan Constitutional Court, on the grounds of procedural irregularity.[35] A reparations programme established in 2005 has enjoyed mixed success,[36] and at local-community level the exhumation of mass graves that has been carried out has often been the work of civil-society groups operating with international support (Biekart 2009: 154–57).[37] The question of whether the Guatemalan conflict had genocidal dimensions is one that still sparks major domestic debate as well as controversy with external actors – and vigorous denial by Guatemala's elites.[38]

Efforts at reform in the socio-economic area, over and above classic development aid, have been of lesser scope. A major bone of contention that persists between Guatemala and the international donor community is the dual problem of the country's tax ratio[39] and the government's

---

[35] For a detailed account of this case, see International Crisis Group (2013). On further developments in the re-trial, see www.ijmonitor.org/category/guatemala-trials/, accessed 16 January 2016.

[36] United States Institute of Peace (2011).

[37] In 1999 President Bill Clinton offered a historic apology to the Guatemalan people for activities engaged in by the United States in their country (Camilleri 2005: 25). On transitional justice, see Sieder (2001: 177–78), Isaacs (2010).

[38] Taft-Morales (2013: 2).    [39] Tax revenue as a percentage of GDP.

social spending. Even international financial institutions agree that in order to achieve any kind of functioning state apparatus, a rise in the tax ratio is unavoidable.[40] Despite the repeated formation of coalitions to secure such a rise, the Guatemalan private sector has always managed to block major reform in this area. But it is not only the Guatemalan oligarchy and private sector who oppose such a move: owing to the '[t]raditionally conservative attitudes and distrust of state intervention [shared] by most Guatemalan sectors' (Kumar/Lodge 2002: 5), support for it is also lacking amongst the indigenous population and the middle class. At the same time, external actors have strongly supported liberal trading policies in Guatemala – as reflected in the ratification of a free trade agreement between the Dominican Republic, Central America and the United States (DR-CAFTA) and the 2011 Association Agreement with the EU. These pacts have made the possibility of any change to the current – highly unequal – distribution of land even more remote (Shamsie 2007: 263).

## 3.2  Guatemala Today: Engulfed by Violence?

The slow and often uncoordinated process of reform in the security and justice sectors is seen as one of the major causes of the 'crisis of national and citizen security driven by (transnational) organized crime' (Schultze-Kraft 2012: 137). What gives rise to this perception of crisis? Indicators of the country's 'post-conflict plight' are to be found in its political institutions and socio-economic structure. Socio-economically, inequalities between the rural population and the urban middle and upper classes have not diminished.[41] Land-distribution rates in Guatemala are worse than in any other Central American country (Spence 2004: 82),[42] and this situation is one of the main reasons for the mass

---

[40]  A rise to 12% by 2002 was suggested in the Peace Accords and by the international community (Paris 2004: 128–32). By 2012 the figure stood at 10.9%, which was still significantly lower even than that recorded in neighbouring Central American countries. See the World Bank ranking for 2012 at http://data.worldbank.org/indicator/GC.TAX.TOTL.GD.ZS, accessed 26 January 2016.

[41]  Over 50% of the overall population fall below the national poverty-line and amongst the rural population the figure rises to over 70%: UNDP (2009: 8–11).

[42]  The configuration of land ownership in Guatemala is the result of colonial land seizure and the fact that the agricultural industry is concentrated in the hands of oligarchic elites: 2% of the population owns 70% of the land (2004). Guatemala

emigration of Guatemalans to the United States and the high dependency of the rural population on remittances from those who make this move.[43]

In terms of political institutions, the system in Guatemala may be described as being in an ongoing state of 'hybridity' (Zinecker 2009). Although there are democratic institutions in place and democratic elections are held, operation of the rule of law is poor and there is a prevalence of capture and rent-seeking economies. Guatemala's state institutions have been indirectly dominated by the interests of oligarchic elites since authoritarian times, but these interests are now being openly challenged by emergent elites of a different kind. Despite these challenges, there has been no shift away from the 'captive state'. In fact, these developments have exacerbated the phenomenon, bolstering a system in which competing elites fight for influence over state institutions and in which the principle of representative government is trumped by allegiance to elite money (which in the case of most political parties includes profits from drug-trafficking). The party system, meanwhile, is shaped by voter volatility and by *transfugismo* – the practice frequently indulged in by congressional representatives of changing sides after an election.[44]

Guatemalan civil society is a poor counter to this institutional set-up. The term has essentially come to denote a small number of professional, urban-based NGOs[45] that have assumed central roles as agenda setters and opponents of government, drafting legislative proposals and engaging in lobbying activities. As there is no domestic system for financing such groups, mostly all their activities are funded externally. Given the need to compete for these funds, NGO work is characterized by fragmentation and antagonism (Azpuru 2006b: 118–19). In contrast to the indigenous movement in South America – in Ecuador, for example, or Bolivia – the Guatemalan equivalent has not had much success in securing indigenous rights or political influence.[46] Currently, its major campaigns centre on the prevention of resource extraction,

---

also has the second-highest Gini coefficient in Latin America (55.1): UNDP (2009: 9–10).

[43] UNICEF (2011).    [44] Sánchez (2008); Briscoe/Pellecer (2010: 7).

[45] Examples include the Fundación Myrna Mack, the Centro para la Acción Legal en Derechos Humanos (CALDH) and Acción Ciudadana.

[46] An exception is its success in the field of 'cultural and language revitalization' (Jackson/Warren 2005: 562). For an overview of the Guatemalan indigenous movement, see Warren (1998) and Fischer (2004).

which is both socially and ecologically extremely damaging to many indigenous communities. These campaigns are subject to constant restrictive action by government (Fulmer et al. 2008; González et al. 2014).

For the majority of the Guatemalan public, the agenda of the Peace Accords was quickly displaced by what were, from their perspective, much more pressing problems. During the 2000s, Central America became the principal conduit for the trafficking of cocaine from South America to the United States.[47] In addition, the Mexican 'war on drugs' drove Mexican drug-cartels into Guatemala's northern territories (International Crisis Group 2010). As a result of this, there has been a steep rise in the incidence of criminal violence. But other types of violence are also on the increase. In this connection, Kurtenbach (2008: 38) distinguishes between political violence (in the run-up to elections, for example), social violence (where groups engage in what they call 'social cleansing'), violence for personal enrichment and, lastly, situational violence. With over 6,000 murders a year, Guatemala's annual homicide rate of 39.9 per 100,000 inhabitants is one of the highest in Latin America.[48] This makes Guatemala in peace-time more violent than it was at most times during its civil war.[49]

Given the criminal networks and everyday violence in Guatemala, foreign-policy observers and think tanks – notably those from the United States – have, over recent years, begun to warn of a new type of 'irregular warfare' and state failure (see, for example, Brands 2011: V; International Crisis Group 2011a). Despite this, the nature and operational structure of the various drug-trafficking networks are neglected as areas of research.[50] By way of example, the extent to which organized crime and drug-trafficking are linked to youth gangs (the so-called *maras*[51]) and to the old networks of military and secret-service personnel (Peacock/Beltrán 2003) remains largely unexplored.

---

[47]  US interdiction programmes in the Caribbean had forced traffickers to opt for routes via Mexico.

[48]  See the ranking by the United Nations Office on Drugs and Crime at www .unodc.org/documents/gsh/data/GSH2013_Homicide_count_and_rate.xlsx, accessed 24 February 2016.

[49]  For a discussion of 'low intensity peace,' see Kurtenbach (2008).

[50]  Though some work has been done on the differences in the structure and politics of the various gangs; see International Crisis Group (2011a); Brands (2011: 15–17).

[51]  Brands (2011: 23–24).

The International Crisis Group (2010: 9) argues that the so-called 'parallel powers' – in other words, the former military generals and members of the intelligence agencies – who also tried hard to influence post-conflict politics no longer loom large in organized crime. By contrast, contacts between drug-traffickers and the *maras* are apparently intensifying.[52] And criminal networks also appear to pursue political interests – or are used by political actors for their own ends. As a result, justice personnel and human rights activists are the target of constant threat, harassment and assault.[53]

This combination of socio-economic marginalization, institutional hybridity and violence has been dubbed *impunidad* ('impunity') by the general public. The term encapsulates the public's overall perception that criminals go unpunished and that state institutions cannot be trusted as potential sources of security and stability (Azpuru 2006a: 18–20; Fischer 2004: 97). In the quest for a remedy, the urban and middle classes have turned to private security[54] – and the rural populations to indigenous dispute resolution and vigilante justice.[55]

## 3.3 A Difficult Relationship: Domestic Contestation of Rule-of-Law Promotion

The long years of military dominance and civil war and the persistence of the 'root causes' of the conflict continue to shape the social, economic and political system of Guatemala. Guatemalan society is highly conservative and marked by profound socio-economic inequalities. The rural indigenous population remains marginalized and a process of empowerment such as that initiated in the Andean countries has yet to occur. The political system is dominated by conflict between different sections of the Guatemalan economic elite.

The key political issue in Guatemala is that of security. 'Impunity' generally denotes a failure to convict a perpetrator, but in Guatemala it has acquired the wider sense of a situation of insecurity encompassing crime, the corruption of state institutions and a non-functioning justice system. For years, the international donor community's main concern in Guatemala has been to ensure implementation of the Peace

---

[52] International Crisis Group (2011a).   [53] Amnesty International (2011).
[54] On the development of private security, see Argueta (2013).
[55] Snodgrass Godoy (2002); Sieder (2011). On the struggle for control over local justice systems, see Handy (2004).

Accords. But these Accords have never been seen as a Guatemalan project, and public support for them – and for the activities of the UN Verification Mission (MINUGUA) – has been minimal. Most of the proposed reform projects have been subject to what has often been vigorous contestation – not only from the political elites, but also from the wider public. As will be demonstrated in the following chapters, it is this context that has shaped the discussion, adoption and implementation of the three sets of norms examined in this study – norms relating to children's rights, access to information and scripts for rule-of-law commissions.

# 4 | *Translating Children's Rights*

The Convention on the Rights of the Child,[1] adopted by the UN General Assembly in 1989, is the most widely ratified human rights convention in the world today. Its rapid diffusion came as something of a surprise, given that it promulgated an entirely new view of childhood: it was the first piece of international legislation to adopt a human rights–based approach in this area, superseding international declarations in which children were described only in terms of their need for protection and not as holders of rights. Guatemala was one of the first states to sign the CRC, but following the adoption of the Peace Accords, a major conflict erupted around the translation of children's rights and this became one of the most heavily contested issues of the early post-conflict period. Against this background, the role played by UNICEF, the major promoter of children's rights across the world, came under particular scrutiny.

This chapter explores the way in which the norm set relating to children's rights was translated in Guatemalan domestic politics and how this process interacted with external rule-of-law promotion. It focuses on those aspects of the CRC that relate to the civil and political rights of children and the treatment of children in conflict with the law. The first section takes a detailed look at the high-precision norm set of children's rights and the way this has developed; the second outlines the three steps of interaction, as envisaged in the 'feedback model'. In the first of these steps (1990–6), UNICEF promoted full legal adoption of the CRC in Guatemala and an initial code of rights for children was enacted. In the second step, however, major contestation erupted and the code never came into force. UNICEF then revised its interaction strategy and, in a third step (2003), the Guatemalan Congress passed a new law effecting a modest reshaping of the CRC standards in line with a 'family-based' approach to children. The new mode of interaction persisted, but

---

[1] United Nations (1989).

the way in which the issue of children was framed domestically shifted towards one of impunity, and this was a key factor in shaping translation into implementation.

## 4.1 The Convention on the Rights of the Child: The Shift to a Rights-Based Approach

The CRC lays down a series of civil, political, economic, social and cultural rights for children. Its adoption in 1989 marked a crucial shift away from welfare and protection and towards human rights.[2] Instead of portraying children merely as needful of protection, it conceived of them as evolving rights-holders. It introduced the guiding principle of the 'best interests of the child' and established a list of freedoms for children, counterbalanced by provisions setting out the rights and duties of parents and guardians (see Table 4.1). Compliance by CRC members is monitored by a Committee on the Rights of the Child. Since 1989, three additional 'Optional Protocols' have been passed relating to: the involvement of children in armed conflict (2000); the sale of children, child prostitution and child pornography (2000); and the institution of an individual complaints procedure (2011).[3]

The CRC was the product of ten years of painstaking negotiations set in train by Poland's proposal – issued in 1979, the UN Year of the Child – for a legally binding covenant on children's rights. The Convention was finally adopted by the UN General Assembly in November 1989. It has been ratified by more states than has any other human rights treaty – the United States being the only United Nations member which has so far failed to take this step. That said, the number of opt-outs and modifications has also been very high.[4]

Various international declarations and standards relating to children had been in existence before 1989, but these had largely been shaped by the image of the child as an innocent and helpless being.[5] This 'protection' discourse was a product of nineteenth-century European industrialization and the resultant improvements in the material conditions of large sections of the population, which meant that child labour was no longer indispensable to family survival. The earliest international norms in this

---

[2] See also Holzscheiter (2010: 2).    [3] United Nations (1948–2006).
[4] For details, see Krappmann (2006: 146–7).
[5] Examples here are the 1924 League of Nations' Geneva Declaration on the Rights of the Child and the 1959 UN Declaration on the Rights of the Child.

**Table 4.1** *Main rule-of-law areas covered by the Convention on the Rights of the Child*

| | |
|---|---|
| Guiding principles | Best interests of the child (art. 3) |
| | No discrimination on grounds of race, colour, sex, language, religion, political or other opinion, national, ethnic or social origin, property, disability, birth or other status (art. 2) |
| Civil and political rights | Right to be registered, right to identity (arts. 7, 8) |
| | Right to freedom of expression (art. 13) |
| | Right to freedom of thought, conscience and religion (art. 14) |
| | Right to association and peaceful assembly (art. 15) |
| | All these rights are *delimited* by: rights and duties of parents, provisions such as freedom of religion and public order, and the evolving capacities of the child |
| Inter-country adoption | Should be a last resort and is managed by state authorities |
| | Requires informed consent of parents and must not involve any improper financial gain (art. 21) |
| Social rights | Right of access to health-care (e.g. preventive health-care, family planning education and services) (art. 24) |
| | Right to social security, an adequate standard of living and education (primary education should be compulsory and free) (arts. 26–8) |
| Indigenous people | Right to practise own culture and religion and use own language (art. 30) |
| Children and work | Minimum (unspecified) working age, ban on economic exploitation (art. 32) |
| | State to protect against abduction, trafficking, exploitation (arts. 34–36) |
| Children in conflict with the law | Ban on torture, capital punishment and life imprisonment of children (art. 37) |
| | Access to appropriate juvenile justice system (art. 40): alternatives to judicial proceedings, alternatives to institutional care |

area thus focused on the regulation or prohibition of child labour. Global regulation of childhood continued to expand in the twentieth century and as early as the 1920s, child-welfare organizations such as Save the Children began to be set up. Gradually, a transnational social movement took shape which promoted the notion of children as rights-holders in the making – notably in cases where abuse was involved (Holzscheiter 2010:

103–10). The notion of children as individuals with rights, as formalized in the CRC, eventually superseded the previous exclusively 'protective' approach.[6]

Although stress was often laid on the inclusivity of the CRC process, and much was made of the involvement of Southern countries and NGO groups in this regard, the shift to a children's rights approach in fact triggered major contestation as the negotiations proceeded (Holzscheiter 2010: 16–17, 99–100). Contentious topics included: inter-country adoption; freedom of speech and religion; the rights of the unborn; traditional practices and their potential harm to children; and the absence of any mention of children's duties towards their parents.[7] Several of these issues, having initially been neglected, re-emerged in regional norm-setting processes – in Africa, for example, where a regional convention on children's rights questioned the idea of treating a person as a child until the age of 18 and placed greater emphasis on the protection of the child and the duties of children towards their parents (Holzscheiter 2010: 241–47).

The inter-American human rights system – in other words, those conventions and institutions of the OAS specifically aimed at safeguarding human rights – for the most part adopted the CRC–based interpretation of children's rights. Although the 1969 American Convention on Human Rights had made reference to the special situation of children, this mention was confined to a single article and was couched in terms that reflected the previous, protection-based, approach.[8] During the 2000s, the interpretation of this article was considerably widened and in 2002 the Inter-American Court of

---

[6] On the standardization of a *global* childhood in the twentieth century, see Holzscheiter (2010: ch. 5), Linde (2014) and Moody (2014).

[7] For an overview, see Johnson (1992), Krappmann (2006: 153), Oestreich (1998: 186). More radical critics also try to deconstruct the universality of concepts of childhood. Thus, Nieuwenhuys (1998) points out that the notion of 'innocent childhood' implies that conceptions of childhood in other parts of the world are deficient. Others point out that the rights-based approach focuses the attention of international organizations on policy formation and policy reform, with no thought of trying to change the socio-economic situation of children in the 'Global South' (Pupavac 2011). Pupavac (2001) also argues that the Western concept of 'innocent childhood' devalues adults in the South because they cannot offer their children a Western-style experience of childhood.

[8] 'Every minor child has the right to the measures of protection required by his condition as a minor on the part of his family, society, and the state': OAS (1969: art. 19).

Human Rights published an 'Advisory Opinion' on children's rights which embraced the central CRC principle of 'best interests'.[9] Since then, children's rights have been a key theme of reporting by the Inter-American Commission on Human Rights (IACHR), operating through its Rapporteur on Children.[10]

The situation of street children and other children living in poverty has elicited particular attention in the Latin American context (Oestreich 2007: 54). Following the adoption of the new, human rights-based approach, this area has seen a shift away from the notion of 'irregular situation' and towards that of 'comprehensive protection' – in other words, from 'managing' children living outside the family (which was often equated with a life of crime) to promoting rights-based protection and prevention. Since the 1990s, in line with these changes at the global level and in the Americas, almost all the countries in the American hemisphere have reformed their legal codes on children (CEJIL 2006: 1).

The children's rights norm set is the most precise of the norm sets considered in this study. As set out in the CRC, children's rights are legal norms; expectations in their regard are laid down in the CRC itself and in its Optional Protocols; and practical measures for their implementation are set out by the Committee on the Rights of the Child, a body of eighteen independent experts.[11] The Committee publishes 'General Comments' containing guidelines as to how states are to interpret particular provisions of the CRC.[12] It considers reports by the signatory states – texts which are in many cases based on preliminary investigations by NGOs in the respective countries and by local UNICEF offices. Based on these reports, the Committee drafts and publishes 'Concluding Observations', in which it highlights particular problems and specific areas in which it expects better compliance.[13]

---

[9] On the court's incorporation of children's rights, see also Young (2015).

[10] On this development, see CEJIL/Save the Children Sweden (2005 14–16, 22–30) and CEJIL (2006: 1).

[11] United Nations Office of the High Commissioner for Human Rights (2013).

[12] So far, the Committee has published twenty such Comments: United Nations Office of the High Commissioner for Human Rights (2017).

[13] Whether or not the Committee offers any leeway on the interpretation of the CRC is a vexed question: Harris-Short (2001), for example, argues that the Committee generally views 'culture' as a problem to be expunged; Krappmann (2006: 158–59) meanwhile – himself once a member of the Committee – regards dialogue within the Committee as highly inclusive and culture-sensitive.

Although not involved in the early negotiations on the CRC,[14] UNICEF has since assumed a central role in the diffusion of children's rights.[15] Despite having begun to reorient its mandate from protection to rights in the early phase,[16] it was not until 1998 that it officially adopted the human rights–based approach across all its activities.[17] Dedicated supporters, however – particularly in its Latin American field offices – had been implementing this approach throughout the 1990s (Oestreich 2007: 48–49) and had supported local adaptation of the CRC across the hemisphere.[18] Legislative reform was seen by both UNICEF and the Committee on the Rights of the Child as the first and most important step towards compliance with the CRC (Krappmann 2006: 153; Oestreich 2007: 40).

The strategy adopted by UNICEF to promote the CRC was a decentralized one aimed at canvassing support for the CRC norm set in a locally sensitive way. However, UNICEF itself came to wield considerable interpretive power:

> The vertical integration of UNICEF activities – from the interpretation of rights, to the creation of programs, the drafting of reports to the committee in Geneva, and even the consideration of those reports – suggests an opportunity for a single agency to have a very large say in what is and is not acceptable behavior. (Oestreich 1998: 195)

In sum, the CRC is a high-precision norm set and the interpretations of the Committee on the Rights of the Child have made it even more so. UNICEF played a key part in the diffusion of the CRC and this gave it a pivotal role in determining what degree of deviation was acceptable in domestic translation. How this affected the interactive translation and feedback loop in the Guatemalan case will now be explored in greater detail.

---

[14] UNICEF's involvement during the latter years of the negotiations was the result of a strategic decision on its part and of lobbying by international children's NGOs (Oestreich 1998: 185; 2007: 26, 30–3).

[15] Although not part of official CRC monitoring, UNICEF can be called as an expert witness by the Committee on the Rights of the Child and can (and does) take part in all Committee meetings. The Committee frequently commissions reports from UNICEF, and host countries also request its help in drafting reports of their own (Oestreich 1998: 186, 190–1).

[16] This shift was an extremely complex one and in all likelihood has never been fully implemented internally: Oestreich (2007: 44–5).

[17] Holzscheiter (2010: 244). On the turn to a human rights–oriented approach, see also Jolly (2014: ch. 6).

[18] Lewin (2000); Grugel/Peruzotti (2010).

## 4.2 Interactive Translation of the CRC in Guatemala: In Search of a Family-Based Approach

### Step 1: Promoting Full Adoption: UNICEF as an Over-Achiever in the Guatemalan Context

When Guatemala ratified the CRC in 1990, it was only the sixth country to do so since the finalization of the Convention in 1989.[19] Guatemala's first democratically elected government, under President Vinicio Cerezo (see Annex 2), was keen to show the international community that it meant business with democratization and that the country was eager for reform (see interviews [hereinafter 'ints.'] 54 2011, 56 2011; list of interviews, see Annex 1).[20] At the time, no thought was given to the implications of this ratification. As one of those interviewed for this study comments: '[T]he convention was ratified ... without weighing up the significance or implications. It was more of a political tactic' (int. 56 2011).

Once the CRC had been ratified, UNICEF encouraged the creation of children's rights NGOs in Guatemala and many came into being at around this time.[21] It also worked with the Commission in Favour of the Convention on the Rights of the Child (Comisión Pro-Convención sobre los Derechos del Niño, known as 'PRODEN'), a section of the Guatemalan Human Rights Ombudsman's Office, with a view to developing a network of domestic partners and getting a replacement drafted for the Guatemalan Minors Code, in existence since 1979.[22] It promoted a joint CRC–based drafting process in which it worked together with the new NGOs and members of the Guatemalan government – notably the office of the First Lady, which had also supported the ratification of the CRC. The UN Verification Mission (MINUGUA) was also involved (Franco/Kotler 1998: 58).

---

[19] OAS (2001: para. 12).
[20] Unless otherwise indicated, all translations are by the author.
[21] These included the Coordinadora institucional de promoción por los derechos de la niñez, Save the Children Guatemala and Casa Alianza.
[22] See La Rue et al. (1998: 4, 35). This code was not based on children's rights but instead took an 'irregular situation' line. Street children, for example, were regarded not as needing treatment in rehabilitative institutions but as juvenile delinquents. See e.g. United Nations Committee on the Rights of the Child (2001: paras. 10–11); Kolbay (2005: 4–5); int. 50 (2011).

The whole process relied on technical, financial and political support from UNICEF (see ints. 54 2011; 56 2011; 59 2011), and UNICEF facilitated exchanges with 'international consultants and experts' (La Rue et al. 1998: 4). These were mostly Latin American lawyers working for, or closely with, UNICEF's Latin America office – well known at the time as a strong supporter of the CRC (Lewin 2000). The Brazilian code of the time, which was based on a decentralized system of municipal and departmental responsibilities, was considered particularly suitable as a model for Guatemala, which was itself undergoing decentralization at that time.

Interaction in the forum mainly took a 'teaching' line, with UNICEF experts advising the small drafting-group as to how the CRC might best be translated. There was, however, consensus within the group on the need for a rights-based approach (ints. 59 2011; 61 2011).

The draft code that emerged was translated into law without any major set backs. Although there was conflict between the political parties as to the overall direction and financial implications of the code,[23] there was no public debate on children's rights during this period[24] – not even when the first draft came before Congress. Despite some dissension in the chamber, in September 1996 the Guatemalan Congress unanimously approved the new 'Children and Youth Code' (Código de la niñez y la juventud, hereinafter 'CNJ'[25]).[26] It was assumed that the funds needed to implement the Code would be provided by international donors.[27]

The final version of the CNJ is an example of 'over-achievement' in translation into law: UNICEF and the combined domestic actors had managed to produce a law that not only incorporated all the CRC standards but went beyond this, adding to its provisions. Whereas in

---

[23]  Int. 54 (2011). The majority party in government, the National Advancement Party (Partido de Avanzada Nacional – PAN), for example, was reluctant to support the draft law because it was officially sponsored by the congressional Commission on Women, Minors and the Family (Comisión de la Mujer, el Menor y la Familia), whose president, Nineth Montenegro, was a member of the leftist New Guatemala Democratic Front (Frente Democrático Nueva Guatemala – FDNG). In addition, there was concern about the budgetary implications of implementation.

[24]  In the period immediately before and after the passing of the law on children's rights, not one editorial or op-ed on the topic appeared in Guatemala's main newspaper – *Prensa Libre*.

[25]  Congreso de la República de Guatemala (1996).    [26]  Larra (1996).

[27]  'Q38 millones costar' (1996).

the CRC children's rights were balanced by provisos regarding children's capacities and the duties of parents, the CNJ included no such mentions. Instead, it expanded the list of freedoms, enhanced the rights relating to protection from discrimination and abuse and guaranteed priority to children in the formulation of policy and in access to social services. The only area in which it did not incorporate all the standards was adoption, which it made the subject of separate legislation (see Table 4.2). The precision of the CRC played a key role during the first phase: the drafting-group adhered closely to the Convention's standards, adding to them where they thought civil and political rights, and protection from abuse, needed even greater emphasis.

The CRC itself does not indicate what institutional arrangements are to be made for implementation. The Guatemalan CNJ followed the Brazilian model, opting for a decentralized system with national, departmental and municipal commissions for children and young people. The Human Rights Ombudsman was also expected to establish a post of ombudsman for children (Defensoría de Derechos de Niñez y Juventud) to monitor violations of children's rights. Municipal protection councils (Juntas Municipales de Protección a la Niñez y Juventud) would provide a local mechanism for reporting such violations.[28] The CNJ thus amplified the CRC provisions with the addition of an elaborate decentralized system of child protection focusing on the violation of rights.

This 'over-achievement' later came to be regretted, when strong currents of opposition to the CNJ began to emerge:

The result was perhaps the most advanced Code on Children and Youth in Latin America. But from today's point of view, that process took place 'behind closed doors' with little or no participation of other sectors and without mechanisms to consult with civil society. (La Rue et al. 1998: 26)

The rationale for the CNJ's focus on bolstering freedoms and protection from abuse only becomes apparent when one looks at the way in which children's rights were framed by support groups in Guatemala. These groups viewed children primarily as being in need of protection against authoritarian parents and an authoritarian

---

[28] Congreso de la República de Guatemala (1996: arts. 96, 112).

**Table 4.2** *Children and Youth Code additions to the Convention on the Rights of the Child*

|  | CRC | CNJ |
|---|---|---|
| Children as rights-holders | Rights-holders with need for comprehensive protection (art. 3) | Precedence accorded in all policy-making areas and in access to social services (arts. 4, 6) |
| Discrimination | No discrimination 'irrespective of the child's or his or her parent's or legal guardian's race, colour, sex, language, religion, political or other opinion, national, ethnic or social origin, property, disability, birth or other status' (art. 2) | Sexual orientation added to list of outlawed grounds for discrimination (art. 10) |
| Freedoms | Right to freedom of thought, conscience and religion, right to freedom of expression, right to freedom of association, but parents and guardians provide direction consistent with the evolving capacities of the child (art. 14). Rights are delimited by rights of others, national security and public order (arts. 13, 15) | No restraint on any freedom (art. 13) Freedom of movement (and other freedoms) added to list (art. 13) |
| Rights violations | State protects against rights violations | Stipulation of child's right and duty to report violations (arts.17, 61) |
| Adoption | Last resort, managed by state authorities Informed consent of parents, no financial gain (art. 21) | Provision for further regulation in separate legislation |

society. Since public dissension only emerged after the Code had passed into law, the following account of its framing is based on an analysis of press discourse as conducted in op-eds and editorials between 1996 and 2004.[29]

As part of the major supportive framing, many of the op-eds backing the Code criticized the Guatemalan social and political system and – sometimes explicitly, sometimes implicitly – identified Guatemalan family relations as the root cause of the long history of authoritarian government and civil war in Guatemala. The argument thus transcended the sphere of children's rights. There was a more generalized questioning of power relations, and translation of the CRC became a battle to secure a more thoroughgoing renewal of the political system in the wake of the Peace Accords. The CRC was seen by its supporters as a means of changing society and creating a new, democratic citizen – an attitude summed up in the following quote: 'The truth is that the forms of power in the Guatemalan family (which is a mirror of the state) ... have produced generation upon generation of unhappy individuals conditioned to the situation.'[30] The CRC thus became a symbol of the kinds of changes that could be brought about in the country's power structures: 'This is why the Children and Youth Code inspires such fear. Repealing it would mean we were kept in a state of Third-Worldism, where it is much easier for someone to wield obscene degrees of power.'[31]

As supporters of the law saw it, Guatemalan families, with their tendency to revert to machismo and their insistence on strict obedience, were the cause of the stagnation of democracy in the country and of the violence in society. One op-ed argued that 'the top-down, closed-minded, inconsiderate family is the main reason why our society is as it is'.[32] Another observed that: 'From the time we are little, we learn to keep our thoughts and feelings to ourselves for fear of being punished by parents and teachers. As adults, we maintain this silence for fear of suffering political and economic repression.'[33] As seen from within this frame, this authoritarian culture had to be changed if Guatemala was to move beyond state repression and violence and see the emergence of a free citizenry:

---

[29] On the methodology of the analysis, see Chapter 1.
[30] Mario Alberto Carrera (1998).    [31] Mario Alberto Carrera (1998).
[32] Mendoza (1998).    [33] Margareta Carrera (2000).

To judge from what those who oppose the Code's entry into force have been writing and saying, it would seem they are hoping for a return to the old 'usted papá, usted mamá' rant and the bullying, accusatory finger-wagging of the person who turned the country into a gigantic secret cemetery.[34]

International aspects did come up in this narrative but were not of central importance – though the example of other countries was sometimes invoked to support the case for children's rights:

Does it not strike you as rather odd that so many other countries, governments and law-making bodies of every ideological persuasion and political leaning are prepared to accept legislation in favour of children and young people and don't think of it as some kind of monster that will wreak havoc on the family, or as some kind of bogeyman of Marxist, socialist or satanic provenance?[35]

One of the products of Guatemala's authoritarian family structures, claimed the Code's supporters, was the outrageous situation of Guatemalan children, notably in regard to physical and sexual abuse. The problem of child labour and exploitation was also mentioned, but poverty in general did not figure to any great extent in the supportive frame. Criticism of the Code's opponents was couched in terms of throwbacks to a feudal era and examples of the Guatemalan elites' consummate capacity for domination. Public opposition, meanwhile, was interpreted as a sign of the Guatemalan population's ignorance: 'We are a people reluctant to change. We have limited vision. We are ill-informed and blinkered.'[36] Supporters of the Code viewed themselves as an avant-garde group ushering in the conditions needed to establish democracy in Guatemala.

To sum up: the first step in translation involved the UNICEF field office fostering the creation of a domestic coalition that would promote reform of Guatemalan legislation in line with the CRC. As a result of the experience of conflict in Guatemala, this coalition saw children's rights as a means of breaking with the authoritarian past and shaping a democratic citizenry of the future. In line with this, the Code did not just incorporate the entirety of the standards set out in the CRC; it redoubled the latter's stress on a rights-based approach.

---

[34] Albizures (1998). This is a reference to the diatribes of Ríos Montt and the catchphrase he famously used when lecturing parents on their duties.
[35] Albizures (1998).    [36] Escobar Sarti (1998).

## Step 2: Contestation and Rejection

Despite securing the approval of Congress and passing into law, the Code never actually came into force in its original form. Once it had been officially adopted, a broad-based public campaign of opposition to it was launched – backed mainly by the religious and business sectors.[37] The two aspects particularly targeted for criticism were the Code's progressive stance on children's freedoms, life choices and sexual orientation, and the decentralized human rights infrastructure called for by the Code. In addition, lawyers feared that if international adoptions from Guatemala were made to comply with the provisions of the CRC, much lucrative business would be lost to them. Private schools and hospitals, meanwhile, were afraid they would be obliged to offer services free of charge (int. 56 2011).

The parties to the argument did not sit entirely squarely along existing political divides. Although there was a fixed core of supporters and opponents, some sections of the business sector supported the Code, and some sections of the progressive pro-democratization camp spoke out against it (La Rue et al. 1998: 20). The Catholic Church in particular found itself internally riven.[38]

The children's rights NGOs were taken completely aback by this critical outburst. With support and funding from UNICEF and Save the Children, they launched a public lobbying and information campaign – but to no avail (int. 56 2011). In spring 1997, the Guatemalan Congress approved an initial suspension of the entry into force of the CNJ, citing implementation problems as grounds for this.[39] The public debate then rapidly turned into a general deliberation as to the validity of the CRC as a whole.

Whereas within the support frame children's rights were presented as an indispensable tool in ensuring a break with society's authoritarian past and the creation of a democratic Guatemala, those working within the dominant frame of resistance regarded the Guatemalan family as

---

[37] Catholics are in the majority in Guatemala, but Pentecostalists make up the second largest religious grouping. On the expansion of Protestantism in Guatemala during the twentieth century, see Garrard-Burnett (1998).

[38] Representatives of the Church's human rights office, for example, took part in the drafting of the CNJ, but higher-ranking Catholic officials spoke out against the Code: Arellano (1998a); González Merlo (1998).

[39] The governing party (PAN) was itself divided in its opinion on the Code (La Rue et al. 1998: 7).

the one good aspect of Guatemalan life that needed to be safeguarded against external influence. Children's rights were thus embedded in a central conflict about the impact of historical violence in Guatemala and about what steps should be taken to bring peace and democracy to the country.

Within the rejectionist frame, the validity of the CRC was called into question, fear of statism and state intervention prevailed and the Guatemalan CNJ was portrayed as a device for destroying Guatemalan families. According to representatives of this frame, not only were child-related issues already sufficiently regulated; the new code was not suited, either culturally or politically, to the Guatemalan context: 'Guatemala is not a completely Western country and our successes and failures therefore cannot be measured purely according to the parameters of Western democracy.'[40] It was clear that '[t]he reformed Children and Youth Code was conceived by minds ignorant of our customs and distinctive traits and should therefore be definitively revoked'.[41] Little indication was given of which issues were considered particularly problematic, but there was general agreement that the rights-based approach at least was not appropriate in dealing with Guatemalan children.

Many also criticized the political process surrounding the CNJ, claiming that it had not been inclusive and that it had resulted in a poorly thought-out law. International aspects lay at the heart of the criticisms from this quarter: op-ed writers claimed that Guatemala had been pressurized into adopting the Code by various international organizations. UNICEF in particular was criticized for its attempts to influence public opinion. This bond, op-ed writers argued, must be broken:

Having undergone this very sad and demeaning experience, we should seize this critical political opportunity to affirm our independence. We should exercise our right to be free and creative. We should summon up the courage and ingenuity we need to sever these invisible golden ties, with their underlying presumption that we can continue to be controlled remotely through spurious agreements that undermine our sovereignty.[42]

Pursuing the cultural line, many also questioned the Western paradigm of family life and child-rearing, arguing instead for a hypothetical 'Guatemalan' model of the family. Life in Canada, the United States

---

[40]  Gutiérrez (1998).     [41]  Barrios Peña (2000).     [42]  Barrios Peña (2000).

and Europe, it was claimed, was marked by family disintegration, drug addiction and violence. In Guatemala, by contrast, 'the family is the thing that works best … it is a strong institution that ensures survival … richer in values and convictions than the European or North American family – and much more so than the Scandinavian'.[43]

It was not just intervention by external actors in the country's affairs but also state intervention in family life that was rejected. 'Statist ambitions'[44] were criticized and concerns were expressed about the advent of an 'all-powerful state'.[45] Op-ed writers warned of the demise of parental and teacher authority and the end of fathers' rights over their children. The Code would make children into rebels and bring not freedom but 'licence'.[46] The ultimate fear was thus that the family – 'the only sanctuary left to us'[47] – would be destroyed. The family represented what was good in Guatemalan society and it had to be protected from Western influence, which would surely bring about disintegration, anarchy and disorder. In this frame, the intervention of Western states, and of the Guatemalan state, in Guatemalan private life was indicative of dependency. What was more, the Code had been drafted without any allowance being made for the unique features of Guatemalan life. The fact that these 'Western influences' derived from an international convention was hardly ever mentioned.

Only a small minority of commentators offered 'constructive criticism' – in other words, did not openly question the validity of children's rights but still issued their remarks from within a family frame. These critics supported children's rights and the protection of children in general, but argued that the current law needed to be modified, notably by putting 'the family' at its heart. However, op-ed writers were less specific as to the parts of the CNJ that did not tally with the unique aspects of Guatemalan life, or about what could be done to rectify this – though one commentator did refer specifically to the EU's and NGOs' emphasis on reproductive health and sex education as inappropriate to the Guatemalan setting.[48] One writer cited the Honduran code as an example of good practice, claiming that 'it doesn't just mention the family – it takes it seriously into account'.[49] Others were critical of the institutional arrangements for the Code;[50] and yet others were simply concerned that the process of reform

---

[43] García Molina (1998).　[44] García (1998).　[45] Jacobs (1998).
[46] Lineares Beltranena (2000).　[47] Barrios Peña (2000).　[48] Camacho (2002).
[49] Camacho (1998).
[50] See e.g. Ríos de Rodríguez (1998); Orantes Troccoli (1998).

should be more inclusive and reflective: 'The ultimate outcome should be legislation that is well executed, fair and consonant with the socio-cultural realities of Guatemalan life.'[51]

Although taking a more broadly family-oriented view, this constructive frame ultimately sought the reform and 'customization' of the CNJ rather than its abolition. However, there was little support for this approach amongst political actors at that time and so the conflict around the Code dragged on. Civil-society groups opposed to the CNJ organized marches, demonstrations and petitions against it.[52] In 1998, the congressional committee with oversight of these matters agreed to take part in a round-table discussion to debate proposed modifications with both supporters and critics of the Code. Chief amongst the topics up for debate were the various freedoms accorded to children by the Code, and the duty it imposed to report abuse and breaches of rights. State involvement in sex education was condemned and the private sector sought the removal of those articles of the Code which they believed granted a right to receive private health services free of charge. Another aspect that came in for strong criticism was the institutional set up at the municipal level.[53] The governing PAN party cut these renegotiations short, bowed to public pressure and postponed the decision on entry into force, initially until September of that year and later until 2000.[54] Following the 1999 elections, the presidency and congressional majority passed to the right-wing FRG, which had been part of the coalition that opposed the Code. The new president of Congress (and former de facto head of state), Ríos Montt, proposed that the Code be suspended indefinitely.[55]

---

[51] 'En torno a las reformas' (1998).

[52] These groups included: the Liga pro Patria (Pro-Fatherland League), the Asociación para el Poder Local (Association for Local Power), Madres Angustiadas (Anxious Mothers), the Alianza Evangélica (Evangelical Alliance), and a 'Círculo de Empresarios de la Educación' (Association of Educational Entrepreneurs). See Arellano (1998b), Maldonado/Larra (1998).

[53] Dubón (1998), Larra (1998), Martínez (1998).

[54] Entry into force was postponed three times between 1997 and 2000: from September 1997 to March 1998, from March 1998 to September 1998, and from September 1998 to March 2000. See Larra et al. (2000), Larra (2000b). By that stage, half a dozen or so revised or newly drafted versions had been put forward by various coalitions of actors: Ríos de Rodríguez (2000), Sandoval (2000c).

[55] Suggesting as an alternative the creation of a 'family institute' under the direction of the Churches: Larra (2000a).

External actors openly sought to save the Code, employing a rather conditionality-oriented mode of interaction to achieve this. When public opposition first emerged after the Code's adoption in 1996, UNICEF's initial strategy was to wage a campaign in which it used shame and public pressure as levers (ints. 4 2009; 56 2011). It also joined with the Guatemalan Consultative Committee of International Organizations for Child Protection (Comité Consultivo de Organismos Internacionales para la Protección Integral de la Niñez Guatemalteca – CCOIPINGUA) in supporting a campaign organized by the Social Movement for Children (Movimiento Social para los Niños), a body coordinating pro-code NGO action (La Rue et al. 1998: 24). Later, when definitive suspension was on the table, it organized emergency meetings with President Portillo and Ríos Montt – to no avail.[56] The Code also featured on the agenda of the Consultative Group – the donor forum charged with monitoring implementation of the Peace Accords – and whenever donors met to evaluate Guatemala's progress in this respect, the failure to bring the Code into force was publicly criticized.[57] This meant, essentially, that compliance with the CRC was one of the conditions the Guatemalan government had to fulfil if it wanted to retain the international funding associated with the Peace Accords. The Committee on the Rights of the Child, meanwhile, repeatedly expressed deep concern at the continuing absence of legislation that would bring Guatemala into line with the CRC.[58] Despite the efforts by all these parties, the ruling FRG exploited its majority in Congress to get the law suspended indefinitely.[59]

## Step 3: Revised Modes of Interaction and Collaborative Reshaping

After the definitive suspension of the Code, there was a move away from this kind of conditionality-oriented mode of interaction. In addition, profiles were lowered in response to the criticism, and UNICEF in

[56] Luisa Rodríguez (2000), 'Ríos Montt se reunió' (2000).

[57] Chay (2003b); Guoz (2003).

[58] United Nations Committee on the Rights of the Child (2001: paras. 11–12).

[59] Sandoval (2000a). Neither did a 1999 decision by the Inter-American Court of Human Rights on the assassination of five Guatemalan street children by Guatemalan police officers in 1990 change this negative stance. On this case, see www.corteidh.or.cr/docs/casos/articulos/seriec_63_ing.pdf (accessed 24 February 2016).

particular adopted a less public role in regard to children's rights (ints. 56 2011; 4 2009). One element of the rejectionist frame had been a negative depiction of the activities of UNICEF and its partners: UNICEF was portrayed as a politicized actor that orchestrated public campaigns and tried to influence the Guatemalan political discourse.[60] Critics also accused it and other international organizations of having leftist tendencies and supporting the guerrilla movement: 'The Human Rights Ombudsman [and] other international bodies, no longer able to push the socialist line openly, are trying to reduce us to slavery by destroying the family.'[61] Civil-society organizations that supported the Code were depicted as having mercenary motives. NGOs, said the critics, were only after the aid money; the only thing that motivated them was 'the promise of thousands of dollars that will help them survive another few years without money worries'.[62] Viewed from within a resistance frame, the NGOs thus appeared as 'obedient spokesmen'[63] of UNICEF, as conscript propagandists with no opinions of their own. The 'arrogance' of the children's rights coalition had also provoked criticism:

some Mayan organizations have expressed their unease with the type of attitude that is found among some directors of NGOs for children, who intend to teach them the relevance of the topic and the legal aspects without opening a bilateral dialogue of mutual understanding. (La Rue et al. 1998: 28)

UNICEF itself was accused of treating this local coalition simply as a local implementer of projects rather than as a group of social actors with opinions and agendas of their own (La Rue et al. 1998). Critics also claimed it viewed reform of the Code as a technical enterprise that did not require further local discussion (int. 61 2011).

In the wake of this intense criticism, UNICEF and its partner NGOs in Guatemala switched to a strategy that sought to ensure greater inclusion of opponents in the campaign to get the Code redrafted (int. 57 2011). The principal roles were now left to the NGOs, and UNICEF took more of a back seat in the public debate (int. 56 2011). However, the evolving dialogue mechanism was still organized and managed by UNICEF: it met on UNICEF premises and UNICEF provided technical, financial and expert input (ints. 51 2011; 54 2011).

---

[60] See e.g. Palmieri (1998); Preti (1998).    [61] Bauer Rodríguez (1998).
[62] Canteo (2000).    [63] Barrios Peña (2000).

UNICEF instituted a *mesa de diálogo* (lit. a 'table for dialogue') bringing together all the groups who were willing to consider a re-drafting of the Code. Participants to the *mesa* included: the offices of the Human Rights Ombudsman (Procuraduría de los Derechos Humanos) and the attorney general (Procuraduría General de la Nación); a number of judges from the Supreme Court; and various representatives of the religious sector[64] – including members of the Evangelical Alliance, which had previously been one of the Code's fiercest opponents.[65] In 2002, following several years of discussion, the forum secured consensus on a new draft of the Code. The dialogue had elicited compromise from the adherents of both the rights-based and the family-based frames. Only lawyers specializing in adoption retained their position of open rejection. Other formerly hostile groups – notably the religious sector and the governing FRG party – shifted to a position of constructive criticism.

According to its members, the dialogue process was based on a more persuasion-oriented mode of interaction. However, opinions differ as to whether the interaction took the form more of 'teaching' or of 'arguing' (on these categories, see Section 2.1). In retrospect, it would appear that the pro-Code NGO coalition failed to present the critics' opinions as valid points of view. As far as they were concerned, the dialogue was a teaching process, in which particular sectors were expected to learn what the Code was really about:

in 2003 the religious sector was already involved [and] was saying 'We definitely want a children's code. We didn't know [what this entailed]. We thought it was something different. Now we understand the situation, we've got to know the laws, we've discussed things with civil-society partners.' It was, shall we say, a very healthy educational experience ... for all those involved (int. 54 2011).

Another interviewee remarks: 'I believe we managed to convince [the Code's] legitimate opponents – the churches, the professional bodies, the politicians – that the law on [child] protection was simply the

---

[64] The Catholic and Anglican Churches, the Alliance of Evangelical Churches and the Jewish Community (int. 57 2011).

[65] Int. 56 (2011). However, the Evangelicals were still divided in their opinion of this process. Though the dialogue was supported by the president of the Alliance of Evangelical Churches – Cesar Vasquez – certain Alliance members found the change of vision unacceptable and condemned the collaboration with UNICEF: Sandoval (2000c).

embodiment of an international convention' (int. 56 2011). By contrast, interviewees from the religious sector see the process as a real dialogue, in which both groups had to take steps towards a joint position (ints. 57 2011; 61 2011).

In the year consensus was reached, a window of opportunity opened up in regard to getting the renegotiated code through Congress. The children's rights NGOs mounted a legal challenge against the indefinite suspension of the CNJ and, as a result, its non-enactment was declared unconstitutional by the Constitutional Court.[66] Following this, in 2003, the new 'consensus' version of the code was introduced into Congress under the designation 'Comprehensive Child and Adolescent Protection Code' (Ley de Protección Integral de la Niñez y Adolescencia – Ley PINA).[67] The change of name was a strategic move to uncouple the new legislation from previous contestation (int. 59 2011). It also reflected a shift from the open children's rights approach to a family frame and a more 'protection-oriented' perspective.

The proposed new code was still essentially rights-based but was couched in more 'family-oriented' terms and was stripped of the additions made by the CNJ (see Table 4.3). Such changes as there were to the original CRC standards were minor: sexual orientation and political opinion were omitted from the list of possible grounds for discrimination and freedom rights were not specifically named but only referred to as existing in international conventions which Guatemala had ratified.

The institutional arrangements as set out in the proposed new code were slightly reworked and the institutional structure at national level was laid down in greater detail. The departmental commissions were scrapped, but the rest of the decentralized set up contained in the CNJ of 1996, and centred mainly on rights violations, was retained.[68] In the final negotiations in Congress, however, in a bid to ensure the support of the FRG and its partners, the entire decentralized infrastructure – in

---

[66] Citing art. 180 of the constitution, the Court argued that the power to suspend a piece of legislation indefinitely did not lie with Congress. See López (2002); also Sandova (2002).

[67] Congreso de la República de Guatemala (2002). The initiative was sponsored by: Alianza Evangélica de Guatemala; Conferencia Episcopal de Guatemala; Conferencia Latinoamericana de Iglesias (CLAI); Movimiento Social por los Derechos de la Niñez y la Juventud de Guatemala; Procuraduría de los Derechos Humanos.

[68] Congreso de la República de Guatemala (2002).

**Table 4.3** *The transition from the Convention on the Rights of the Child to the Ley PINA*

| | CRC | CNJ | PINA |
|---|---|---|---|
| Children as rights-holders | Rights-holders with need for comprehensive protection (art. 3) | Precedence accorded in all policy-making areas and in access to social services (arts. 4, 6) | Emphasis on 'family integration' (art. 1), 'family interest' (art. 5) and rights and duties of parents (art. 3). Central aim of state policy is to 'strengthen the institution of the family' (art. 81) No precedence in policy-making or social services |
| Discrimination | No discrimination 'irrespective of the child's or his or her parent's or legal guardian's race, colour, sex, language, religion, political or other opinion, national, ethnic or social origin, property, disability, birth or other status' (art. 2) | Sexual orientation added to list of outlawed grounds for discrimination (art. 10) | Sexual orientation and political opinion omitted from list of outlawed grounds for discrimination (art. 10) |
| Freedoms | Right to freedom of thought, conscience and religion, right to freedom of expression, right to freedom of association, but parents and guardians provide direction consistent with the evolving capacities of the child (art. 14). Rights are delimited by rights of others, national security and public order (arts. 13, 15) | No restraint on any freedom (art. 13) Freedom of movement (and other freedoms) added to list (art. 13) | All freedoms in CRC are valid but subject to limits imposed by child's own capacities and parents' right to 'guide, educate and discipline the child' (art. 13) |

Table 4.3 (*cont.*)

| | CRC | CNJ | PINA |
|---|---|---|---|
| Rights violations | State protects against rights violations | Stipulation of child's right and duty to report violations (arts. 17, 61) | In case of abuse, a child may only 'seek help' (art. 17) or 'seek protection' (art. 61 n). |
| Adoption | Last resort, managed by state authorities Informed consent of parents, no financial gain (art. 21) | Provision for further regulation in separate legislation | Managed by state authorities. Provision for further regulation in separate legislation based on existing international norms (arts. 22, 23) |

which children's rights NGOs were to have played a major role – was dropped. The provision establishing a children's ombudsman was also excised – and along with it the institutional structure's strong rights-based orientation. In addition, as a result of an accommodation between the governing FRG party and the conservative Unionist Party, the sentence explicitly conferring the status of rights-holders on children was cut from the final version. The rest of the Code, however, remained rights-based. Thus modified, the Code was adopted by Congress.[69]

Retrospective evaluation of these changes varied depending on the actor group involved. Members of the rights-oriented coalition were generally critical of the congressional decision to jettison the institutional structure (which was not part of the CRC) but were still confident that the new code complied with international standards – despite being less precise in formulation than the earlier versions (ints. 51 2011; 56 2011; 59 2011). As one representative of this group comments: 'Changing the name, making the structure different, was really just a strategy. It did improve things in some respects, and it brought the opposition onside' (int. 56 2011). By contrast, an interviewee from the religious sector views the transition from CNJ to PINA as marking a profound change – one that accommodated the country's distinctive economic, cultural and religious traits (int. 61 2011).

When the revised code finally passed into law, in 2003, it did so without large-scale public debate: the issue of children's rights had already disappeared from the public agenda and the law's once vociferous opponents had either been brought into the fold or (as in the case of adoption lawyers) discredited as having purely mercenary motives. There were, says one interviewee, no demonstrations or celebrations, no discussions or objections: 'And then of course in 2003 what was missing [was] that there wasn't that political interest in the topic – the implementation of the law happened without anyone noticing' (int. 54 2011).

The relevance of the debate in determining the country's overall direction had diminished. Nonetheless, the final process of adoption in Congress saw a number of European embassies rallying to lend behind-the-scenes support (ints. 56 2011; 61 2011).[70]

---

[69] See Benavente (2003,); Chay (2003a); Valladares (2003).
[70] US input was not to be expected here, as the country has so far not ratified the CRC.

### The Scope for Reinterpretation: How Precision Came in

Throughout this whole renegotiation process, it was mainly UNICEF that acted as 'interpreter' in construing the space between precision and deviation in the Guatemalan case. It had been criticized – particularly in the first phase – for adopting a 'technical' approach to children's rights and for not including any Guatemalan voices beyond those in the government and in its own NGO coalition. It then adopted the dialogue mechanism as a strategy to open the process of translation up to the concerns of those who opposed the CNJ. In the case of the Ley PINA, however, the renegotiation debate was not a 'tabula rasa' enterprise to identify a local understanding of children's rights: the discussion had to begin from the CNJ and changes could only be introduced as part of this. The changes made were therefore minor and the text remained essentially the same. The only major alterations were those made by Congress, and they related to institutional structure, which was not regulated in the CRC. On the whole, however, the Convention's legal status meant that its standards were perceived as having high normativity and this was underlined by the pro-Code coalition, which spent considerable time persuading the Code's opponents of the need to include these standards.

At somewhat of a distance from the contestation and debate associated with the domestic framing, the international Committee on the Rights of the Child declined to enter into a discussion about Guatemalan 'family values'. It made no comment, good or bad, on the changes made in the transition from the CNJ to the Ley PINA. Although severely critical of Guatemala's slow 'progress' in regard to the CRC, the Committee repeatedly acknowledged the country's special situation and limited capacities.[71] It did, however, express its disapproval of the Guatemalan government's attempts to defend deviations from the CRC by reference to indigenous practices (for example, in calling for a lower marriage age).[72] In sum, UNICEF facilitated a degree of local reshaping, but the Ley PINA continued to be classified as 'non-deviating' at the international level.

[71] United Nations Committee on the Rights of the Child (2010a: para. 10).

[72] The Committee's preferred lower age limit for marriage is 18 (Rodríguez Fernández 2001: 9; Tostensen et al. 2011: 017) but it would be happy even to secure an increase to bring the current marriage age for girls (14) into line with that for boys (16). Guatemala, however, argued that this would go against indigenous practice. See United Nations Committee on the Rights of the Child (2008: para. 45); United Nations Committee on the Rights of the Child (2010a: para 38). Guatemala brought marriage age in line with the Committee's interpretation in 2015.

The ultimate form in which the CRC was translated into law displays a modest degree of reshaping (for categorization, see Section 2.3). This came about as a result of a compromise in the two-frame discourse into which the issue had been translated and which presented children's rights in terms either of protecting children from their families (support) or of protecting the family itself (shift from rejection to constructive criticism). The family element was given greater emphasis than in the CRC, and the rights to freedoms were subject to stricter parental oversight. The 'add-ons' made in the first version of the legislation (CNJ) were jettisoned.

## Implementation Brings Further Shifts of Frame

The key shift which the international bodies had made in their mode of interaction at the discourse and drafting stages persisted during the subsequent phase – that of implementation. Domestically, however, there was a further shift, in which both the rejection and the support frames were subsumed within a single 'impunity' frame. This had a considerable impact on translation into implementation, with reshaping becoming more substantial. At the same time, the shift helped minimize reshaping at the legal level.

### Reframing Child-Related Issues

Once children's rights had been translated into law, they disappeared from view and there was no public discussion about how they should be implemented. However, certain topics that had already figured in the debate during the translation, and which called for additional regulation, began to loom large in public discourse – one notable example being international adoption. The major clash of frames that had pitted protection of the child against protection of the family had also died down: child-related policies were now widely understood as part of a broader meta-frame of impunity. This led to a securitization of child and youth policies. The idea of showing leniency towards members of youth gangs, or of reintegrating them into society, was viewed extremely critically and government representatives defended this law-and-order approach even at the international level.[73] 'Social cleansing'

---

[73] This led to disagreement between the government representatives and the Committee on the Rights of the Child. Whereas the Committee emphasized the

and the extra-judicial killing of members of youth gangs found strong support amongst the Guatemalan population.[74] The rights of young people in conflict with the law therefore met with little favour from adherents of an impunity frame. As one op-ed argued: 'What a flabby, floppy piece of political decision-making it is that worries about the "human rights" of the butcher and neglects the right to life of the butchered. . . . The "poor you" policy for halting the spread of juvenile thievery is an ineffective and costly one.'[75]

By contrast, child-related issues that fell within the ambit of this 'security frame' – the suppression of child-trafficking, for example, or the prevention of kidnapping – did meet with strong support. This frame shift was openly exploited by the groups who had previously made up the children's rights coalition. These included UNICEF, which sought, in its public campaigns, to link the topic of children and young people to the powerful Guatemalan discourse about impunity and criminal violence,[76] decoupling it from overt rights-based language and attempting, with some success, to make it resonate with the public (int. 54 2011). A good example is the 2010 'Te toca' ('It's your turn!') campaign, which wove the issues of malnutrition and abuse into the core Guatemalan security-based discourse about impunity. In essence, UNICEF's new position was that a rights-based approach would only gain support in Guatemala if the core security situation was tackled.[77] UNICEF itself kept a low profile – some of its public campaigns were conducted without featuring its logo, in order to maximize support (int. 54 2011). The children's rights coalition thus to some extent reified the securitized framing of childhood.

A good example of the broader impunity-based framing is the debate that took shape around the further regulation of international adoption. Internationally, UNICEF itself, and the UN Committee on the Rights of the Child, take a quite explicit stance against inter-country adoption, accepting it only as a last resort, as stipulated in the CRC.[78] Meanwhile, adoption agencies and prospective adopters from Western

---

need for better care of adolescents, and an avoidance of criminalization, the Guatemalan delegation insisted a tough stance must be taken against youth gangs. See United Nations Committee on the Rights of the Child (2010c: para. 35, Ms De Valle); United Nations Committee on the Rights of the Child (2010b: para. 11, Ms Ortitz).

[74] See e.g. Sonia Pérez (2006).    [75] Zapeta (2005a).
[76] 'Una campaña para despertar' (2011).    [77] UNICEF (2010c: para. 18).
[78] See UNICEF (2007).

countries – notably the United States – work transnationally to counter this stance.[79] In Guatemala, prior to the reforms, international adoption was managed by notaries and state oversight was minimal. There was evidence of various kinds of abuse of the system – financial inducements to give up children for adoption, for example, interference with DNA testing, or child-stealing. Ninety-eight per cent of all adoptions were inter-country and Guatemala ranked third in the list of major exporters of children to the United States (McCreery Bunkers et al. 2009).

During the 2000s, UNICEF and the children's rights NGOs reframed international adoption as a security issue under the rubric of child trafficking. The chief strategy used in this connection was to present inter-country adoption as a trafficking activity organized and run by nebulous mafias whose origins, it was suggested, lay in the country's unsettled past. A key element in this reframing was its repeated reference to the validity and legitimacy of the CRC and other international norms.[80] It may therefore be said that, in general, there was a more open use of international norms, and notably of the CRC, to justify policy in Guatemala.

Supporters of a resistance frame on adoption were less successful. The majority of these were adoption lawyers, who had a considerable financial interest in maintaining an inter-country system of adoption and had not joined in the dialogue mechanism on children's rights at the earlier stage. They kept up the narrative that had dominated earlier resistance – namely that the new arrangements constituted illegal state interference and excessive state bureaucratization.[81] They set this firmly within an overall political impunity-based frame, a feature of which was criticism of state interference in family decisions and the claim that such interference would result in rising numbers of street children, increased youth criminality and a growth in the number of abortions.[82]

---

[79] At first, the position of the United States – the country to which there was the greatest number of adoptions – was unclear. US adoption agencies in particular sought to influence US policy in this area and triggered a heated discussion on the work of UNICEF in the United States. At the same time, having signed up to the Inter-country Adoption Convention in 2007, the United States publicly supported legislation in this area (int. 51 2011).

[80] See e.g. Roesch (2004). [81] See e.g. Escaler (2005), Jacobs (2007).

[82] See e.g. Alonso (2004), Escaler (2005).

**Bolstering the Legal Structure**

Surprisingly, the impunity framing led to the already modest legal reshaping of the CRC being further narrowed. A number of anti-rights proposals that would have reinforced the reshaping were introduced into Congress at regular intervals throughout the 2000s but were rejected. These included legislation lowering the age of criminal responsibility, imposing stronger penalties for juvenile delinquency and banning rights-based youth policies.[83] At the same time, most of the UNICEF–backed proposals that took the legal focus back to security-related issues detailed in the CRC and its protocols made it successfully through Congress. This was the case with the legislation on international adoption, which brought Guatemala into line with both the CRC and the 1993 Convention on the Protection of Children and Co-operation in Respect of Inter-country Adoption.[84] Another success story here was the rapid adoption of a draft law on child protection – modelled on the American 'Amber Alert' system – which gave the police the power to institute an immediate search for any missing children suspected of being victims of abduction.[85] Also passed with strong backing from UNICEF was the Law against Sexual Violence, Exploitation and Trafficking in Persons (2009), which brought Guatemala into line with the relevant CRC protocol. Domestically, these impunity-related initiatives in the legal field were spearheaded by the Guatemalan NGO Fundación Sobrevivientes (Survivors' Foundation), but once again it was UNICEF that facilitated the legal debate and provided the necessary funding and expert input.[86] International diplomats lobbied Congress to get the legislation passed.[87] The Committee on the Rights of the Child also engaged in a degree of shaming – for example, by publicly calling for the cessation of international adoptions from Guatemala and by condemning Guatemalan practice in this area.[88]

---

[83] UNICEF (2010a: 9).
[84] In preparing the ground for this legislation, UNICEF specifically returned to the Ley PINA dialogue mechanism and its former members.
[85] UNICEF (2010b).
[86] Ints. 51 (2011), 54 (2011). Also: Siu (2014); UNICEF (2010a: 15).
[87] Ramírez/Marroquín (2007), int. 54 (2011).
[88] Luisa Rodríguez (2004), Palma (2004).

**Institutions and Policies**

Whilst the impunity framing helped to reduce reshaping at the legislative stage, it did the opposite during translation into implementation. To obviate any further circumvention by Congress, the Ley PINA was brought into force the day after its adoption in July 2003. However, this also meant that Guatemala's institutions were totally unprepared as far as implementation was concerned.[89] International experts thus feared that the Ley PINA was 'nothing more than a symbolic gesture rather than an *effective instrument of protection of children's rights*' (Kolbay 2005: 13, author's emphasis) and that 'children remain a low priority of the state' (Tostensen et al. 2011: 109). The institutional system, they claimed, was too weak and centralized to be effective. 'Furthermore, there is a tendency to treat children in a highly patronizing and bureaucratic manner, instead of basing strategies on a rights perspective and offering opportunities for children to be heard' (Tostensen et al. 2011: 110).

In general, institutional structures remained scarcely functional. Although the percentage of the budget allocated to children had grown from 1.3 to 2.8 between 2004 and 2007, it was still far too low, claimed the international experts, to maintain any properly functioning system for implementing child-related policies (Tostensen et al. 2011: 107). In fact, Congress never allocated sufficient funds for the institutional implementation of the Ley PINA – nor, it appears, did it ever intend to (int. 51 2011). The principal body in charge of formulating and implementing child-related policy in line with the Ley PINA – the National Commission on Children and Adolescents (Comisión Nacional de Niñez y Adolescencia) – was not established until four years later, in 2007, along with a new Secretariat for Social Welfare (founded in 2006) to implement its policies.[90] All this happened before the UN Committee on the Rights of the Child was due to publish its latest report.[91] UNICEF, together with various development agencies and international NGOs, sought to encourage CRC implementation with technical and financial assistance. A key initiative in this connection was the development of child-related policies at municipal level, and the creation of municipally based child-related councils.[92]

---

[89] Apart from some minor changes in 2004 (Congreso de la República de Guatemala (2004)), no further reshaping of the actual law took place after 2003.
[90] Gobierno de Guatemala (2007).    [91] Kolbay (2005); int. 51 (2011).
[92] UNICEF (2010c: para. 16).

Shaped by the meta-frame of impunity, the implementation phase saw a further securitization of youth policy.[93] The main victims of the wave of 'social cleansing' (carried out by private security-firms) and arbitrary police arrests that followed were street children.[94] Adolescents were particularly affected, falling victim to the increased criminalization of young people and being subject to arbitrary arrest and harsh treatment for suspected gang membership. Rather than a last resort, detention was a favoured option amongst the judiciary in the juvenile justice system (Kolbay 2005: 9) and the prisons were over-whelmed by the sheer numbers of adolescent detainees (int. 51 2011).

Overall, international bodies maintained their essentially persuasion-oriented mode of interaction but publicly canvassed issues that tallied with the impunity-based meta-frame then dominant in the country. On the one hand, this led to increased protection of children against crime (particularly at the legal level); at the same time, however, when it came to translation into implementation, it gave rise to substantial reshaping (omission) in regard to the rights of children who found themselves in conflict with the law.

## 4.3 Reshaping Children's Rights

As analysis in this chapter has shown, the interactive process by which the Convention on the Rights of the Child was translated for the Guatemalan context ran along a feedback loop, eventually leading to a minor reshaping of the rights in question. During the initial phase after ratification (1990–6), UNICEF worked with others to assemble a domestic coalition in support of children's rights (Step 1). This very small group of dedicated children's rights advocates drafted a new children's rights code that did not merely comply with all the CRC standards but actually expanded the Convention's rights-based vision. The drafting process was shaped by UNICEF's strategy – one it commonly employed in Latin America[95] – of taking a small group and teaching it (and thereby the government) what it thought constituted a children's code. As well as progressive provisions on life choices,

[93] United Nations Committee on the Rights of the Child (2010b: para. 11, Ms Ortitz).
[94] Kolbay (2005: 9–10), OAS (2003b).
[95] See e.g. Grugel and Peruzzotti (2010) on Argentina and Maclure and Sotelo (2004) on Nicaragua.

political opinions and sexual orientation, the draft included a duty to report abuse and a requirement to accord absolute primacy to children in all Guatemalan policy-making. Alongside these measures there were provisions for an elaborate decentralized institutional structure aimed chiefly at tackling human rights violations. The reason for this legislative 'over-achievement' lies in the support coalition's understanding of children's rights in the Guatemalan context. Members of the coalition saw these rights on the one hand as a tool with which to democratize and refashion the country after years of conflict and, on the other, as a means of protecting children from authoritarian parents and an authoritarian society. At this stage, the topic of children's rights had not yet become politicized and in 1996 the resultant draft law made its way through Congress without substantial debate.

Only after it had been approved by Congress did the Code trigger large-scale contestation from the religious and business sectors – in a second phase that lasted roughly from 1996 until 2003 (Step 2). The contestation related not only to the content of the law but also to the political role played by UNICEF. The law became the focus of a polarized conflict over the legacy of Guatemala's past and the values to be pursued in future. In the view of the law's opponents, the 'Guatemalan family' was superior to Western equivalents and must be rescued from erosion and anti-authoritarianism. UNICEF and the donor community responded with an open, conditionality-oriented mode of interaction involving praising, shaming and provisions about aid money. This was unsuccessful and the law's entry into force was postponed indefinitely.

In a third phase, UNICEF altered its mode of interaction to one based more on persuasion (and less formal in nature), bringing previously hostile groups – notably the religious sector – into a dialogue mechanism (Step 3). The product of the years of renegotiation that followed was a compromise between those who supported a children's rights frame and those who favoured a family frame. Renamed the 'Comprehensive Protection Code', the refashioned law was approved and brought into force in 2003. The text was marked by its use of a strong, family-based vocabulary and the various freedoms were subject to a greater degree of parental oversight – leaving the CRC standards only modestly refashioned in legal terms. The support coalition's additions to the CRC were done away with and the provisions establishing a decentralized institutional structure designed to safeguard against human rights violations were completely excised by Congress. Although UNICEF worked through persuasion-oriented dialogue with most former opponents, a degree of shaming by the donor community helped keep up the pressure for adoption of the re-drafted law by Congress. Precision made itself felt in two ways in this renegotiation: firstly, because the debate took the CRC and the former law – the CNJ – as its starting point, the room for manoeuvre was more limited; secondly, the support coalition expended a great deal of effort in 'bringing round' those who formerly opposed the CRC, presenting the inclusion of the CRC rules in the domestic legislation as indispensable. Although the second drafting process was more inclusive than the first, overall management was still in the hands of UNICEF, which had accepted the need to move from an 'over-achieving' code to one with a stronger family-oriented rhetoric and more limited freedoms. In the perception of the support coalition at least, the scope for reshaping was kept within bounds by UNICEF, and the ultimate result was not viewed by the international community as deviating from the CRC.

A frame shift in child-related policy during the 2000s led to a paradoxical situation in which reshaping of the CRC, having diminished at the legislative stage, increased during translation into implementation. Child-related policy in Guatemala became part of a new 'impunity' frame and, as a consequence, was securitized. The idea of protecting children against crime won strong support; that of protecting children in conflict with the law hardly any. Within this frame, legislative initiatives protecting children against crime prospered, closing the gap that separated domestic arrangements from CRC standards and optional protocols. Thus, international adoption, presented as a major child-trafficking issue, led to the enactment of corresponding regulation. Congressional support was also forthcoming for legislation on missing children and trafficking. These various laws produced some positive results when implemented. At the same time, however, the new frame led to increased criminalization of children and adolescents – most notably members of youth gangs. A working institutional framework capable of formulating policy never emerged and no country-wide diffusion of the rights-based approach took place. Apart from a degree of praising and shaming on the part of the wider donor community, the persuasion-based mode of interaction continued to be used during implementation, with UNICEF focusing on teaching strategies (capacity-building and awareness-raising) to encourage further implementation. In response to the securitization of

Table 4.4 *Stages in the translation of children's rights in Guatemala*

| Translation | Resistance | Localization | Full adoption |
|---|---|---|---|
| Into discourse | Call for protection of Guatemalan families | Adaptation of CRC to family values<br>Eventual shift to impunity frame | Emphasis on protection of children against families |
| Into law | | Re-centring on family | |
| Into implementation | | Greater emphasis on impunity-related areas in implementation (protection against crime) | |

Guatemalan politics, and the lack of support for a rights-based approach, UNICEF adapted its day-to-day policies: it sought to garner support by reframing the issues in terms of security rather than in terms of children's rights, often combining this tactic with less overt forms of interaction.

One notable feature of the Guatemalan dissension over children's rights is the virtual invisibility of the transnational organizational dimension on the resisting side, despite the fact that critics such as the Guatemalan Evangelical Alliance (initially the chief opponent of the process) and the lobby on inter-country adoption had access to an extensive transnational network and to powerful external partners, notably in the United States. This was in marked contrast to the breadth of contacts in the children's rights coalition. Also surprising was the speed with which domestic frames shifted and the difference in the way they shaped translation into law as opposed to translation into implementation. Although reshaping became more pronounced during translation into implementation – partly because of capacity problems and a specific constellation of interests – this stage of translation was not entirely decoupled from the norm translation that occurred at the two other stages: translation into discourse and translation into law.

In sum: the Guatemalan case traces a progression from contestation to a more inclusive form of translation on the part of international and domestic actors, the result being a modest reshaping of international norms. Translation into law led to minor reshaping and the omission of certain standards; translation into implementation produced more significant omissions, occasioned by a shift in the framing of child-related policy (see Table 4.4). By contrast, the translation as it occurred in the Guatemalan context had little influence on the interpretation and promotion of children's rights at the international level. The particular translation into discourse that characterized this case elicited very little discussion outside the UNICEF field office. Indeed, in the international context, the reshaping was presented as being 'in line with' CRC standards.

# 5 | Translating a Right to Access Information

The idea that access to official documents is a universal right and should be part of every democratic system is a relatively new one, globally speaking. It was not until the 1990s that a campaign launched by international NGOs triggered a wave of access-to-information (ATI) legislation around the world. By the beginning of 2016, just over 100 countries had adopted relevant laws – under the various guises of 'freedom of information', 'right to know', and 'access to information' – and around eighty of these had done so only after 1990.[1] ATI, a medium-precision norm set, was systematized in UN and regional human rights regimes shortly after its emergence. In Guatemala, it was incorporated into the reform agenda adopted after the conclusion of the Peace Accords in 1996. Particularly active in supporting this norm set in Guatemala were the United States and the OAS Special Rapporteur for Freedom of Expression, working alongside domestic partners. There were, however, two distinct framings of the norm set – as an aid to transitional justice and as a means of fighting corruption. When resistance made itself felt, a more inclusive process of dialogue took place, in which both coalitions showed themselves willing to accept modifications to the global standards – as reflected in the reshaped version of these embodied in the legislation of 2008. The deviation here was more extensive than in the case of children's rights.

The first section of this chapter traces the development of the global 'access to information' norm set. The interactive process by which this norm set was promoted and translated in the Guatemalan context is then examined. This process began after the signing of the Peace Accords, when the OAS Special Rapporteur in particular – and later USAID – promoted discussion of ATI legislation (Step 1). The draft law that resulted, completed in 2004, was rejected by Congress due to opposition

---

[1] See Global Right to Information Rating, www.rti-rating.org/country-data, accessed 16 February 2016.

from the military and certain sections of the government (Step 2). In 2008, following a shift of frames and the opening of a dialogue with former opponents, a reshaped version of the ATI legislation made its way successfully through Congress (Step 3). The influence of international bodies was much more indirect here than in the case either of children's rights or (as we shall see later) of the scripts for a rule-of-law commission. This mode of interaction persisted during the phase of translation into implementation. At the same time, reshaping became more pronounced, leading not to a complete decoupling of law and practice, but to a decoupling of the realities of ATI from the many presumed advantages – such as greater citizen participation and transparency – which its introduction had been expected to result in.

## 5.1 The Development of a Global Right to Information

Before the 1990s, only a handful of states worldwide had legislation regulating access to public information. Sweden, which has an ATI law dating from 1766, is most commonly cited as the first country to have legislated in this area. Another well-known example is that of the United States – although its Freedom of Information Act, brought into force in 1967, did not become operative until the 1970s, in the aftermath of the Watergate scandal. Most Scandinavian countries had also adopted ATI legislation prior to the 1990s. By 2002, the number of states with such legislation had risen to twenty-six; by 2016 the figure stood at just over 100.[2]

The spread of ATI legislation was occasioned by a change in the interpretation of Article 19 of the 1948 Universal Declaration on Human Rights, which recognizes the right 'to seek, receive and impart information'.[3] Before the 1990s, this article had been interpreted as referring to 'press freedom, propaganda and censorship in an *international framework*' (Darch/Underwood 2010: 77, original emphasis) – in other words, as a right to disseminate and receive (press-related)

---

[2]  Blanton (2002: 50), Michener (2011), Relly (2008: 24), Global Right to Information Rating, www.rti-rating.org/country-data, accessed 16 February 2016.

[3]  'Everyone has the right to freedom of opinion and expression; this right includes freedom to hold opinions without interference and to seek, receive and impart information and ideas through any media and regardless of frontiers' (Universal Declaration of Human Rights, art. 19). The same form of words – 'freedom to seek, receive and impart information' – is used in the 1996 International Covenant on Political and Civil Rights (also art. 19).

information across state borders. During the 1990s, a network of NGOs concerned with transparency and freedom of expression (the 'Article 19' group, for example, and Transparency International) sought proactively to broaden the interpretation of this article to include the right of access to official sources of information (Blanton 2002). This interpretation challenged 'the long-dominant norm of the sovereign right of states to maintain secrecy about all security matters' (Florini 1996: 381).

This shift in interpretation was rapidly reflected in the human rights systems at UN and regional level.[4] The NGO 'Article 19' was particularly active in promoting the transformation of the original right, initially elaborating a set of standards (Article 19 1999) and later drafting a complete model law (Article 19 2001). These documents widely influenced later norm-setting: the 1999 standards were endorsed by the UN Special Rapporteur and, together with the 2001 model, were extensively referenced elsewhere (Berliner 2016: 126–27).[5] As early as the end of the 1990s, a number of human rights bodies were backing the right of access to information both at the global level (see Table 5.1) and within the inter-American system (see Table 5.2). And in 2006, the Inter-American Court on Human Rights became the first body of its kind to embrace the right of access to public information.[6]

The standards most commonly adopted in relation to ATI are based on those specified by the 'Article 19' group. They include maximum disclosure; obligation to publish; promotion of open government; institution of a 'harm versus public interest' test for exceptions to ATI; limits on the cost of access; precedence of ATI laws over other regulations; institution of an independent review body and stipulation of penalties for public officials who obstruct or interfere with ATI (see Table 5.3).[7]

---

[4] Most notably in the Inter-American, European, African and Commonwealth systems – which, however, all showed slight variations in their approach to the right and their interpretation of its scope (Bishop 2009; Mendel 2009).
[5] The Article 19 group also became proactive in analysing draft ATI laws around the world.
[6] In its decision in *Reyes v. Chile*, a Chilean NGO had made a request to the government for information about a major logging contract in the south of the country. When this was ignored, the NGO had appealed to the Chilean Supreme Court, which had ruled the appeal inadmissible. For the Inter-American Court's ruling, see www.corteidh.or.cr/docs/casos/articulos/seriec_151_ing.pdf, accessed 1 March 2016.
[7] The last two standards were added in the 2001 model law. Article 19 (2001).

**Table 5.1** *Global support for access to information*

| | |
|---|---|
| 1998 | In line with directives of the UN Commission on Human Rights,[8] UN Special Rapporteur on Freedom of Opinion and Expression expresses view that 'the right to seek, receive and impart information imposes a positive obligation on States to ensure access to information'.[9] |
| 1999 | UN Special Rapporteur, OSCE Representative and OAS Special Rapporteur for Freedom of Expression jointly express their support for a right of access to public information[10] |
| 2011 | Human Rights Committee[11] publicly endorses right of access to public information and *habeas data*[12] |

**Table 5.2** *Inter-American support for access to information*

| | |
|---|---|
| 1994 to date | Inter-American Press Association supports right to ATI, as enshrined in Chapultepec Declaration, currently endorsed by numerous heads of states on the continent[13] |
| 1999 to date | OAS Special Rapporteur for Freedom of Expression, supported by IACHR, actively develops and monitors right of ATI in the region[14] |
| 2003 | OAS General Assembly recognizes right of ATI[15] |

Other standards proposed by Article 19 did not prove as popular and are not reflected in the provisions of the various human rights systems. These include the principle that all meetings of public bodies should be open and the guarantee of protection for whistleblowers who 'release

---

[8] Established in 1946 by the UN Economic and Social Council (ECOSOC), the Commission was replaced by the UN Human Rights Council in 2006.

[9] Report of the Special Rapporteur. United Nations (1998).

[10] International Mechanism for Promoting Freedom of Expression (1999).

[11] The body monitoring implementation of the International Covenant on Civil and Political Rights.

[12] Human Rights Committee (2011: para 18–19).

[13] Hemisphere Conference on Free Speech (1994).

[14] Office of the Special Rapporteur for Freedom of Expression (1999: ch. III). See also Special Rapporteur for Freedom of Expression (2003: para. 32–40); Inter-American Commission on Human Rights (2000).

[15] OAS (2003a).

**Table 5.3** *Most commonly adopted standards in regard to access to information*

| | |
|---|---|
| Maximum disclosure | All government information is public. Only very limited exceptions to this principle are permissible. |
| Obligation to publish | Key information must be proactively published by government |
| Promotion of open government | Open government to be fostered via government-initiated educational campaigns and capacity-building |
| Harm v. public interest test | Any proposed exceptions to open access must undergo a 'harm v. public interest' test |
| Limits on cost | The cost of access to information must not be excessive |
| Precedence | Disclosure takes precedence over other regulations/laws |
| Independent review body | An independent review body rules on appeals and monitors implementation |
| Penalties | Public officials to be penalized for obstruction or interference |

information on wrongdoing'.[16] In relation to the American region, a model law on ATI was published by the OAS in 2010 and approved by the OAS General Assembly in June of that year.[17] This law extends the right of access to information to cover data held by private organizations that administer public funds.

Apart from the emergence of this body of 'soft law' on ATI, there has been a trend more recently for international and regional treaties on transparency and the prevention of corruption to include general provisions on access to information. These treaties do not specify standards; they simply call for the adoption of ATI legislation. The 2005 UN Convention against Corruption, for example, contains clauses on the

[16] The ranking of ATI laws produced by the Global Right to Information Rating is also based on the standards mentioned here but is organized differently, under the rubrics of: right to access, scope, requesting procedures, exceptions and refusals, appeals, sanctions and protections, promotional measures. See http://new.rti-rating.org/wp-content/uploads/Indicators.pdf.

[17] OAS Plenary Session (2010). Further model laws were developed by the African Union and the Commonwealth: African Commission on Human and Peoples' Rights (2013); Commonwealth (2003).

regulation and facilitation of public access to information.[18] Again, the 1999 Inter-American Convention against Corruption makes no explicit reference to access to public information, but since 2005 part of the brief of its follow-up mechanism is to check that ATI legislation is in place in the countries under scrutiny.[19]

In terms of the indicators of norm precision used in this study – the formality of international agreements and the degree of specificity of the standards involved – the ATI norm set may be said to be of medium precision. Over the last twenty years, the stipulations of international and regional human rights treaties in respect of freedom of expression have been reinterpreted to include a universal right of access to public information. However, this right is not laid down in any detail, either in these treaties or in those relating to corruption. In 2006 the Inter-American Court of Human Rights became the first of the international courts to embrace the right of access to public information, but again did not specify standards.[20] In the area of 'soft law', meanwhile, a dynamic process of formulation of standards and model laws has been under way since the late 1990s.

## Patterns of Diffusion

Nowadays, access to information is widely regarded as a core element of democratic governance (Blanton 2002: 56), but the pattern of its diffusion around the world has varied from region to region. In Eastern Europe, the adoption of ATI legislation in the 1990s came as a reaction to the secrecy of former authoritarian regimes and was linked to 'lustration' – the process by which the newly democratizing countries purged themselves of former officials of the Communist establishment.[21] Compared with these countries, certain members of the OECD were latecomers to the

---

[18]  See arts 10 and 13b, United Nations (2004).    [19]  See OAS (2011).
[20]  For an overview of ATI rulings by international courts, see Right2Info, 'RTI case law', www.right2info.org/cases, accessed 28 February 2016.
[21]  The Soros Foundation was a particularly proactive supporter of ATI legislation in the region (Banisar 2006: 19; Blanton 2002: 53). Some also see the wave of new legislation as a reaction to the Chernobyl cover-up and the emergence of a European right of access to environmental information, resulting ultimately in the signing of the Aarhus Convention on Access to Information, Public Participation in Decision-making and Access to Justice in Environmental Matters, drawn up under the auspices of the United Nations Economic Commission for Europe (Relly 2008: 25–26).

process: in Japan, there was no ATI legislation in force until 2002; in Britain entry into force did not come until 2005, and in Germany legislation was adopted in 2005 but not brought into force until the following year. Motives here also differed, the trigger in many countries – Canada, Ireland and Japan – being a series of corruption-related scandals throughout the 1990s (Blanton 2002: 50–53; Florini 1999: 29–30). In Africa, South Africa's adoption of a highly progressive law in 2000 made it a global model in this area.[22] In Latin America, a number of countries had ATI clauses in their constitutions but had never enacted them. During the 1990s, driven by a wave of World Bank policies to combat corruption and by evolving OAS standards on ATI (see below), more and more countries introduced relevant legislation. With the adoption of its progressive federal legislation in 2002, Mexico became another global model and is considered to have some of the strongest ATI regulations in the world. By contrast, diffusion in the Middle East and Asia has been slow and so far only a handful of countries have drafted any ATI legislation – Jordan being one example, with its law of 2007.[23] Over recent years, however, some have expressed the fear that a counter-wave is already under way: the privatization of government functions is limiting citizens' access to information and the 'war against terror' is fostering a new culture of secrecy and a ruthless attitude to whistleblowers in many countries (see, for example, Ackerman/Sandoval-Ballestreros 2006: 124, 27–29; and Callamard 2008: 8).

The various coalitions that helped promote the right of access to information around the world, and lobbied for corresponding legislation, did so for varying reasons. Activist Agnes Callamard from the 'Article 19' NGO thus talks of 'not just one movement, but many *movements*', which, she says, may give priority either to transparency, good governance or openness more generally (2008: 7, emphasis by author). The group of international NGOs that had played a pivotal role in creating the ATI norm set was the driving force behind the diffusion of ATI as a human right inextricably bound up with democratization and accountability. These groups included: Transparency International, the International Federation of Journalists, Article 19, the Open Society Institute

[22] Though the law never actually functioned as intended (Mendel 2006: 10).
[23] For an overview of regional developments, see Relly (2008: 29) and Banisar (2006: 19). For accounts that attempt to explain diffusion patterns chiefly as a function of domestic institutional structures, see Berliner (2014) and Michener (2015a, 2015b).

and – from 2002 – the Freedom of Information Advocates Network. For state agencies such as USAID and the British Council as well as for international organizations such as the World Bank, by contrast, ATI fell within the transparency and anti-corruption remit they were pursuing as part of their worldwide campaign for market reform.[24]

These two approaches – rights versus transparency – reflect the two chief framings of ATI worldwide. In the first, ATI is a citizen right that promotes participation in society, is essential to democratic governance and is a precondition for the fulfilment of a wide range of other human rights (Banisar 2006: 7–8; Bishop 2009: 43–98). In the second, ATI has to do with transparency and accountability and is closely related to market regulation and economic growth. This second perspective also dominates much of the academic literature (see, for example, Ackermann 2003: 87; Florini 1999, 2007; Grigorescu 2003: 7–8).

A number of less well-developed perspectives also exist. One such – linked to the debate about transitional justice – focuses on the right to uncover the truth about past crimes, including human rights violations. It emerged during the 1980s and 1990s, when relatives of the disappeared in Latin America demanded to be told their loved ones' fate. Another perspective links ATI with the right to a healthy environment and to access to information on environmental policy; and yet another defines it as the right to know what personal data is held in public and private databases – a right commonly termed *habeas data*.[25]

All these perspectives can, to some degree, be found in the Guatemalan debate, but it was the framings based on truth about the past, *habeas data* and transparency that dominated the early discussion – as we shall now see.

## 5.2 Interactive ATI Translation in Guatemala: Securing Justice or Fighting Corruption?

*Step 1: Promoting Access to Information as an Aid to Transitional Justice*

Guatemala has traditionally been a country with a strong culture of state secrecy. Although such secrecy was a widespread norm of state

---

[24] Ackerman/Sandoval-Ballesteros (2006: 121–3), Banisar (2002: 2) and Darch/Underwood (2010: 52).
[25] Banisar (2006: 7–8), Bishop (2009: 101–28).

governance right across the world during much of the twentieth century, in Guatemala it was reinforced by a legacy of authoritarianism and civil conflict. The military traditionally tended towards secrecy on the basis of national security; state agencies in general were characterized by corruption and a lack of transparency; and certain sections of the economic sector strove to maintain secrecy in matters of banking and taxation.[26]

It was at the end of the 1990s, as part of the discussion surrounding the Peace Accords, that the debate about ATI took shape in Guatemala – although provisions on access to information had been present in the constitution since its re-drafting in 1985. Born of the experience of civil war and military dictatorship, the new Guatemalan constitution lays stress on the safeguarding of political rights. It accords free access to all official information, with two exceptions – information relating to military or diplomatic matters affecting national security and information given in confidence. It also recognizes the right of individuals to know what information is held about them in state archives (*habeas data*).[27] These rights were never translated into practice.[28]

In the 'Agreement on the Strengthening of Civilian Power and on the Role of the Armed Forces in a Democratic Society' (one of the thematic components of the Peace Accords – see Section 3.1), the government was required to encourage the Guatemalan Congress to adopt 'a law regulating access to military or diplomatic information relating to national security, as provided for in article 30 of the Constitution, and containing provisions on classification and declassification procedures and levels'.[29]

This understanding of ATI tallied with that of both the domestic and the international human rights communities at that time, who saw ATI as an aid to transitional justice and as a means of curtailing the power of the military in Guatemala. The discussion centred on ways of bringing perpetrators to justice and finding out what information the government was illegally holding on its citizens (int. 60 2011; Darch/ Underwood 2010: 186). The practical limitations under which ATI

---

[26] Gramajo Valdés (2009: 2–3, 62–70).  [27] Arts. 30 and 31.
[28] Jonas (1995: 28) and Gramajo Valdés (2003: 12).
[29] See art. 52b of the Agreement on the Strengthening of Civilian Power and on the Role of Armed Forces in a Democratic Society, available at United States Institute of Peace (1996).

laboured in Guatemala became even more apparent when the CEH – the Guatemalan truth commission – failed to gain access to government files and was forced to rely entirely on US documents to reconstruct events that had occurred during the civil war (int. 55 2011). In line with these preoccupations, MINUGUA, the UN verification mission to Guatemala, highlighted the issue of the classification and declassification of government archives – but not that of access to information in general (Gramajo Valdés 2003: 81–82).

It was only after 1999, when the then OAS Rapporteur for Freedom of Expression, Santiago Cantón, began to take a greater interest in ATI, that thoughts turned to the regulation of access to information in general (see Section 5.1). In April 2000, during a visit to Guatemala, Cantón proposed joint drafting of relevant legislation with the Guatemalan government.[30] The proposal was followed up, at the end of May, with a conference entitled 'The Right to Access to Information in Guatemala', which brought together members of the Guatemalan government, representatives of domestic human rights NGOs and members of international NGOs with expertise in the declassification of state archives and in ATI more generally.[31]

In the years that followed, monitoring of the right to ATI became a formal part of the OAS Rapporteur's annual report. Legislation in different areas of the world was compared and trends in ATI adjudication in national and international courts were discussed, thus helping to advance the ATI debate.[32] In addition, in a 2003 country report on Guatemala, the government was specifically reminded of its commitment to legislate on ATI.[33] In this first phase of translation, therefore, the Special Rapporteur played a central role, working with groups specializing in the declassification of military archives to bring ATI and *habeas data* to public attention as human rights issues. Via the Rapporteur's annual reports, public shaming was used to highlight deficiencies in this area, and pressure was exerted on the Guatemalan government to

---

[30] Special Rapporteur for Freedom of Expression (2000: paras. 21, 32).

[31] One such expert was Kate Doyle from the US NGO 'The National Security Archive', who had been working on the 'Guatemala Project' since the 1990s, searching through formerly classified US government files on the Guatemalan civil war (see National Security Archive n.d.). A member of the 'Article 19' NGO also attended the conference: Ruiz (2000).

[32] See Annual Reports of the Special Rapporteur for Freedom of Expression (2000, 2001, 2002; 2004: ch. IV).

[33] See OAS (2003b: paras. 402, 10, 59).

proceed to legislation. This was in contrast to the less proactive approach on ATI legislation adopted by MINUGUA[34] and to the line taken by the key bodies operating in this area in Latin America – the Carter Center and the Open Society Institute, for example – whose work on ATI in Guatemala was restricted to basic information exchange.

ATI legislation did, however, make it onto the agenda of the Consultative Group – the major donor forum monitoring the implementation of the Peace Accords.[35] The reason it did so was twofold: firstly, the donor community was displeased at the failure to grant the Guatemalan truth commission proper access to government files; and secondly, it was concerned that the development aid then flowing into Guatemala should be put to effective and transparent use.[36] Given that the major flows of aid to the country were managed by the Consultative Group, the legislative reforms which it proposed carried with them overtones of conditionality (see Step 2).

During this first wave of norm promotion, then, external actors canvassed ATI chiefly as an aid in gaining better oversight of the military and ensuring transitional justice. Strategies in regard to the Guatemalan government were geared to conditionality, and the main domestic partners were human rights organizations.

## Step 2: Rejecting Access to Information as an Aid to Transitional Justice

In 2000, as a result of these norm-promotion activities, the Portillo administration began the process of drafting appropriate legislation.[37] It agreed to joint discussions with Guatemalan human rights groups – who were perceived as the main civil-society groups affected.[38]

---

[34] It merely mentioned the Special Rapporteur's recommendations and the drafting process in its annual reports and did not do any work of its own in this area. See UN General Assembly (2000: para. 48); UN General Assembly (2001).

[35] Guoz (2003d); 'El mensaje del Grupo' (2003).

[36] Gramajo Valdés (2003: 80–81; 2009: 84).

[37] Draft legislation for the translation of ATI into law had first been presented to Congress as early as the end of the 1990s, by supporters of the human rights and transitional-justice agenda. These proposals (e.g. Iniciativa 2339, put forward by the congressional representative Nineth Montenegro), which focused on *habeas data* and the classification of archive information, did not prompt any further debate (Blanco/Zapata 2007: 466).

[38] Most importantly CALDH, Fundación Myrna Mack, Grupo de Apoyo Mutuo (GAM) and SEDEM. For a list of all invited groups beyond the human rights

The discussions were led by the then Guatemalan secretary of strategic analysis (Secretario de Analysis Estratégico), Edgar Gutiérrez, a former human rights activist. The aim was to draft legislation that would cover not only the opening-up of official transactions but also *habeas data* and the classification and declassification of official archives (Gramajo Valdés 2003: 28).

Although the negotiations did produce a draft law, they also flagged up the main battle lines between the two sides.[39] In the view of the human rights groups – the main source of domestic support for the process – ATI legislation had to do mainly with the right to be told the truth about the civil war and about what information the secret services had gathered on political activists during the conflict. It was also about cutting back the power of the military. This perspective translated into a preoccupation with access to archives and access to personal information (*habeas data*). As one human rights activist explained, having good ATI legislation 'would also serve to shed light on some unknowns of the past'.[40] This emphasis was also reflected in the media discourse, where the legislation was often referred to as a 'habeas data law'.[41] One of the members of the Guatemalan government at that time, Francisco Jiminez, remarked that the human rights groups were '[more interested] in recalling the past than in subjecting public administration to scrutiny'.[42] On the government side, there was no notion of ATI as a human right; the prime concern was the maintenance of secrecy in matters relating to national security, particularly in the military sphere.[43] The positions taken in the FRG-ruled Congress were similar:

organizations, see Gramajo Valdés (2003: 27–8). Organizations linked to the press and other media seemed particularly uninterested in the issue and did not cover the drafting process in any detail. Political parties were also absent from the discussions.

[39] In the initial stages, political discussion on ATI was confined to a very small group and was given very little coverage by the media. To get a fuller picture, the media discourse therefore has to be supplemented with information from other sources (such as interviews).

[40] Frank la Rue, as reported in Arellano (2000).

[41] See e.g. 'Privacidad: Luces y sombras' (2003). Argentinian and Chilean 'habeas data laws', which were not ATI laws in the strict sense, were also proposed as models for the Guatemalan legislation.

[42] As quoted in Gramajo Valdés (2003: 81).

[43] During the visit of the OAS Special Rapporteur to Guatemala in 2000, the Minister of Communication, Palacio Luis Rabbé, openly opposed this type of legislation, but generally speaking members of the government were careful not to reject it publicly: González Moraga/Arellano (2000).

any access to state information concerning the civil war was out of the question (int. 49 2011) and issues relating to the transparency of public services as a whole were considered secondary.[44]

There was an added difficulty in that international standards in this area were only just beginning to take shape, and domestic drafters were therefore not sure what draft legislation of this kind should contain. As one of those involved in the process commented: 'All this was very vague, and we didn't really understand either. We followed the Mexican model, for example, but we didn't understand it. We knew we had to lay down rules about transparency or about paperwork – we knew all that. But we didn't know how' (int. 60 2011).

At the end of 2001, a first draft of the legislation was sent to Congress by the Guatemalan government. Overall, the draft showed very little evidence of having been influenced by international principles and it contained no mention of any institutional mechanism through which requests for information might be made. It did, however, make a degree of provision for access to classified and confidential information and to public and private archives (see Table 5.5).[45]

The influence of the external actors on the drafting process was not as direct here as it was in the case of the other two areas under consideration in this study (children's rights and rule-of-law commissions – see Chapters 4 and 6). The only point on which the Guatemalan donor community insisted was that legislation should be adopted (Step 1); it made no stipulations as to content. However, a number of international experts did comment publicly on the draft. These included the OAS Special Rapporteur and representatives of the US NGO 'Center for National Security Studies', who provided extensive critical advice on basic definitions and the drafting process.[46] The NGO 'Article 19' also commented on the draft,[47] listing the many areas in which it diverged from ATI standards, pointing to the problematic nature of its 'harm versus public interest' test and criticizing its over-generous exemptions. Comment on the law thus came mainly from organizations involved in the human rights scene, a number of whom were engaged explicitly in work on national security exemptions and oversight of the military.

---

[44] Gramajo Valdés (2003: 29–34; 2009: 92–5).
[45] Congreso de la República de Guatemala (2001).
[46] Gramajo Valdés (2003: 30).    [47] Article 19 (2000, 2003).

These critical voices had little influence on discussions in the Guatemalan Congress, where the legislation was viewed as low priority. Although the government formally supported the law, it was clear that, in Congress, the governing FRG party would not give its backing to any legislation involving elements of transitional justice.[48] The FRG's strategy was to delay the draft law's progress through Congress.[49]

It was only at this point that the United States joined the ranks of those publicly promoting ATI legislation. The US embassy in Guatemala lent its support to public events relating to legislation.[50] From 2003, USAID joined with the Danish development agency Prodeca in financing the activities of a coalition of transparency NGOs – headed by Acción Ciudadana – which was campaigning in favour of legislation and had begun monitoring the state of ATI in Guatemala (int. 49 2011). The agenda of this coalition differed from that of the human rights NGOs. Its aim was not to secure access to military archives but to 'promote accountability of their administrative acts among public servants' (Pape-Yalibat 2003: 1) – in other words, to ensure transparency. USAID also financed the preparation of domestic reports as part of the monitoring process operated by the Inter-American Convention against Corruption.[51] Some observers argue that the US interest in ATI legislation in this part of the world was linked to the regional negotiations that were then under way on the DR-CAFTA free trade agreement – which contained a chapter on transparency and timely access to information (see Grimes 2011: 8).[52]

The focus here differed markedly from that which had dominated the drafting process, where human rights groups and representatives of the government had pitted transitional justice against national security. At the same time, this transparency discourse to some extent tallied with the (very limited) presentation of ATI in the media. Access to

---

[48] In addition, a number of congressional representatives introduced their own draft laws into Congress (initiatives 2624, 2641) – though these were not debated.

[49] The relevant congressional committee did report positively on the proposal in October 2002 (Del Cid 2002) and the draft did manage to progress through several congressional debates, 'Piden cambios en Ley' (2002); 'Hábeas Data' (2002).

[50] Alberto E. Ramírez (2002).

[51] See USAID contract: Casals and Associates. (2004: para. III.A.i).

[52] See ch. 18 of DR-CAFTA, Office of the United States Trade Representative (n.d.).

information was seen as part of an overall agenda of transparency and good governance. Democratization also featured heavily, with ATI being viewed as a means of breaking with the repressive past. In the media discourse in particular, the press was regarded as the chief enactor of ATI, exercising its right of access to information under the rubric of press freedom.[53] According to the media discourse, ATI legislation would bring about accountability and transparency in the daily work of public servants.[54] People would have greater control over officialdom and would be able to find out what their taxes were spent on. ATI would also lead to improved political processes and the provision of 'reliable public information that will help the public servant, the entrepreneur, the investor, the analyst, the consultant and the student to understand current realities, design projects for the future, propose changes and make good decisions'.[55] Access to information would help to fight corruption and modernize the Guatemalan administration.[56] But ATI was also seen as part of a democratization-agenda: 'As a people, we like to boast about our new-found democracy, but it seems the concept has not advanced very far with us and we are content simply to vote freely every four years and call ourselves democratic on the strength of it.'[57] Greater access and transparency were thus needed to create a democracy that went beyond the ballot box. Editorial and op-ed writers also underlined the fact that access to information was a symbol of victory over the authoritarianism of the past, the 'old tradition of concealment'[58] and the 'legacy of internal armed conflict'.[59]

The new transparency-based campaign had little impact on the congressional delaying tactics. However, in 2003, with a meeting of the Consultative Group – the major donor forum – about to take place, there was renewed pressure for the draft law to be adopted.[60] In spite of this, when the closing discussions on the draft took place, the majority FRG party first watered down its provisions and ultimately sent it back to the relevant committee – a move tantamount to final rejection.[61] Opposition to the legislation was rarely expressed openly in the media

[53] See e.g. Fuentes Destarac (2004), 'Nuevo golpe a la Libertad' (2000).
[54] See e.g. 'Diputados urgidos' (2003), 'Ejército, obligado' (2003).
[55] Bonilla (2002).   [56] See e.g. 'Ante la Farsa' (2004).   [57] Bonilla, (2002).
[58] Vásquez Araya (2004).   [59] 'Debe romperse cultura' (2004).
[60] Del Cid, (2003b), Chay (2003b).
[61] Del Cid (2003a). 'Agenda de leyes' (2004).

or in Congress; it was coordinated from behind closed doors.[62]
By *introducing* legislation into Congress, the government had fulfilled
its obligations under the Peace Accords; it was less concerned with
actually *enacting* it.[63]

To sum up: access to information was translated into three key frames
in the Guatemalan political discourse, but the one maintained by key
political actors was that of resistance and, despite the conditionality-
oriented activities of external actors, these actors ultimately rejected
draft legislation. The first of the three frames, one of support, focused
on transitional justice. Human rights groups saw ATI as a means of
gaining access to information held by the military, of curtailing the latter's
power and of uncovering past crimes. In the second frame, also a support
frame, ATI was portrayed – particularly by transparency NGOs, but also
(very occasionally) by the media – as a weapon against corruption and an
aid to transparency. The transparency frame was also linked to democratization and the modernization of state structures. The third frame –
a resistance frame – saw the government and the dominant party in
Congress, the FRG, opposing ATI (mostly behind closed doors) on the
grounds of national security and its own rejection of transitional-justice
measures. Even the conditionality-oriented strategy adopted by the norm
promoters vis-à-vis government and Congress failed to secure the adoption of the legislation against such powerful opposition. External actors
had used shaming strategies, and, to some degree, a teaching approach, to
get the government to address the issue of ATI. The Consultative Group
had also used conditionality – in the form of threatened cuts in aid – to
persuade the government to get to work on draft legislation. The drafting
process that was eventually initiated as a result of these pressures was
conducted in concert with the Guatemalan human rights community and
this led to the draft law focusing on oversight of the military and access to
classified information– a framing of ATI that was ultimately rejected by
Congress.

---

[62] In contrast to the situation in the two other areas explored in this study, there is
almost no expression of resistance in the media in this area. Overall, the press is
very much in favour of ATI – not one op-ed argues against its general
desirability. Op-eds thus report but never support the dissenting views of
politicians and members of the government.

[63] A number of laws passed at that time – such as the 2002 Municipal Code and the
General Law on Decentralization of the same year – did include some ATI
standards for specific areas.

## Step 3: Framing Contests and the Shift to Dialogue

The election of Óscar Berger to the Guatemalan presidency in 2004 raised new hopes amongst supporters of ATI legislation. Berger, a candidate of the oligarchic elite, had included adoption of this legislation in the list of promises made during his election campaign.[64] At the same time, the new Guatemalan government was concerned about its international image in regard to corruption and one strategy it adopted to rectify this was to work to ensure a positive assessment from the Inter-American Convention against Corruption, whose criteria (from 2005) included ATI legislation (see Section 6.1).[65] In line with this, President Berger set up a vice presidential Transparency Commission to coordinate the government's policies in this area. The new government's approach to ATI was thus directly shaped by an anticorruption and pro-transparency frame.[66]

The two support frames in use amongst Guatemalan non-governmental organizations underwent only marginal shifting. The transitional-justice frame was still dominant amongst the human rights groups, but some of these groups began to display a more general concern in regard to criminal violence and impunity, notably in relation to the military and the police (see int. 52 2011). Transparency-oriented NGOs, by contrast, sought to exclude the contentious topic of exemption on national security grounds and to narrow down translation into law to the single issue of institutionalized access to official information as a means to transparency and accountability. Meanwhile, *habeas data* – now viewed not as an aid to discovering what kind of information the state was holding on an individual's past but rather as a means of preventing the misuse and sale of personal data – was incorporated into the transparency framework (see subsequent transparency-inspired drafts, Table 5.4). The transparency frame also continued to dominate the press discourse, but a shift in perception is observable here – from ATI as a press right to ATI as a citizen right and cornerstone of participatory democracy: 'We urge

---

[64] Portillo (2003), Palencia (2004).
[65] Mechanism for Follow-up on the Implementation of the Inter-American Convention against Corruption (2005: ch. 4.2); Mechanism for Follow-up on the Implementation of the Inter-American Convention against Corruption (2008).
[66] Thus, in talking to civil-society groups, the vice president invited only the transparency NGOs and not the human rights groups working on ATI (Gramajo Valdés 2009: 106–9).

Table 5.4 *Progression of ATI legislation in Guatemala*

| | 2002 | 2005 | 2005 | 2008 | 2008 |
|---|---|---|---|---|---|
| | First draft | Initiative 3165 | Decree 645–2005 | Initiative 3768 | Decree 57–2008 (final law) |
| Drafted by: | Government, human rights coalition | Human rights and transparency NGOs | Government | Transparency coalition | Government, human rights groups, transparency groups |
| Focus | Transitional justice v. national security | Transitional justice, oversight of military | Limited transparency | Transparency | Transparency and oversight of military |
| Summary of content | No explicit human rights focus<br>Focus on rules for access to public and private archives, *habeas data* and national security<br>No institutional mechanism for information requests | No explicit human rights focus<br>No institutional mechanism for information-requests | No human rights focus, ATI presented as part of anti-corruption conventions<br>No reference to access to archives or *habeas data*<br>Limited institutional mechanism for information requests | ATI as human right<br>No reference to access to archives<br>Elaborate institutional mechanism for information requests<br>Inclusion of *habeas data* to prevent commercialization of data | ATI as human right<br>Access to archives and *habeas data*<br>Elaborate institutional mechanism for information requests |

people to put this success to good use in overcoming the attitude of resignation in regard to understanding the workings of the state: only those who are well-informed can play an active part in shaping the country's choices.'[67]

Once again, there was no open expression of resistance in the media. Urban politicians were particularly anxious not to be singled out as 'untransparent' by the press (int. 49 2011). Álvaro Arzú, former president of Guatemala and subsequently mayor of Guatemala City, was one of the few politicians to reject the ATI legislation openly.[68] The military, too, continued to view transparency of classified information with considerable suspicion (int. 62 2011). But the transparency framing, now encompassing not only declassification and access to archives but also the day-to-day operations of the state, elicited resistance from new quarters as well. Members of the government feared that publication of details about their salaries would lead to extortion and that governmental departments would be swamped with ATI requests. Many of them were also afraid that the advent of ATI would unleash a wave of corruption scandals (int. 62 2011).

This constellation of opinions resulted in a major framing contest between the human rights community and those NGOs who promoted ATI as an issue of transparency and good governance. The split is evident in the different stances adopted by two major NGOs then seeking to rekindle public debate in this area: Acción Ciudadana, which pursued a heavily transparency-oriented agenda, and DOSES[69] – and its offshoot Centro Civitas – which promoted coverage of human rights and other social issues in the media.[70]

Because the constellation of international norm promoters had changed, it was the transparency coalition that gained the upper hand. The OAS Special Rapporteur for Freedom of Expression was no longer as involved in the Guatemalan political process as had been the case when Santiago Cantón held the post (1996–2002),[71] and with the

---

[67] 'Informarse es derecho' (2005).
[68] Ana Lucía Blas (2008b), 'Arzú monta falso show' (2008).
[69] Associación de Desarollo, Organización, Servicios y Estudios Socioculturales.
[70] Gramajo Valdés (2005: 2; 2009: 89). The NGO coalition 'Citizen Observatory', set up by Acción Ciudadana, became active again, began a new lobbying campaign, and produced reports on ATI in Guatemala – see Garmendia (2004a, b).
[71] There were no more visits to the country and no specific exchanges regarding the new drafts. The only public statement made by the OAS Rapporteur in regard to

closure of the MINUGUA office in 2004, the Consultative Group had also discontinued its annual meetings for several years. The role of major supporter of ATI legislation in Guatemala was thus taken over by USAID, working within a transparency frame. USAID continued to fund local supporters of Guatemalan ATI legislation, notably Acción Ciudadana, and was the major donor in this field (ints. 49 2011; 62 2011) – a situation that irked the human rights NGOs, who now felt sidelined (int. 60 2011).

An initial re-drafting of the ATI legislation was set in motion by the human rights NGOs,[72] this time with the participation of Acción Ciudadana, but without active government support.[73] Transitional justice featured even more heavily than before (see Table 5.5)[74] and without official support this version also died in Congress.[75] Existing international standards were used much more extensively than before as a basis for discussion and drafting, with the result that a number of new aspects of the international debate made it into the document. These included the right of access to information held by private organizations in receipt of public funds and the principle that where information is exempted from ATI provisions its existence must be made public.[76]

ATI came in response to the publication of the 2005 government decree. See Sonia Pérez (2005).

[72] Centro Civitas, Fundación Myrna Mack, SEDEM, FOSS, amongst others.

[73] Although welcomed by the government, the process took place without the involvement of government representatives – in contrast to what had happened in the first phase. Media groups were officially invited to join the process but declined (Gramajo Valdés 2005: 3) – which also helps to explain why media coverage was so poor.

[74] The civil-society groups doing the drafting refrained from including any penalties for public servants. In addition, despite a great deal of discussion about the possible inclusion of provisions for an independent review body, as called for by the international standards, these were excluded from the draft: most groups were critical of this kind of set-up, as exemplified in the Mexican model, and were afraid to further inflate bureaucracy (Gramajo Valdés 2009: 95). See the summary of initiative 3165 in Table 5.5.

[75] Some important social sectors did open themselves up to discussion about possible ATI legislation: both the military and the CACIF – Guatemala's main business-association, interested in particular in the management of state funds and the commercialization of public databases – invited representatives of the NGO groups to present the draft legislation to them. They did not, however, make any public pronouncements on the matter (Gramajo Valdés 2009: 100–1).

[76] On the drafting, see Gramajo Valdés (2009: 91–5)

Table 5.5 *Incorporation of international standards into Guatemalan legislation*\*

| | 2002 First draft | 2005 Initiative 3165 | 2005 Decree 645–2005 | 2008 Initiative 3768 | 2008 Decree 57–2008 (final) |
|---|---|---|---|---|---|
| Maximum disclosure | ✗ (Extensive interpretation, no disclosure) | ✓ | ✗ | ✓ | ✓ |
| Obligation to publish | ✓ (Limited) | ✓ | ✓ (Limited) | ✓ (Extensive list incl. both private and public entities) | ✓ (Extensive list incl. both private and public entities) |
| Promotion of open government | ✗ | ✗ | ✗ | ✗ | ✓ |
| Harm v. public interest test | ✓ (Limited) | ✓ (Limited, with extensive exemption) | ✗ | ✗ | ✓ (With limited exemption of confidential information) |
| Limits on cost | ✗ | ✗ | ✓ | ✓ | ✓ |
| Precedence | ✗ | ✗ | ✗ | ✗ | ✗ |
| Independent review-body | ✗ | ✗ | ✗ | ✗ (But government commission to review exemptions and reservations) | ✗ (Monitoring by Ombudsman's office, review by courts) |
| Sanctions | ✗ | ✗ | ✓ (Limited) | ✓ (Administrative and penal) | ✓ (Administrative and penal) |

\* ✓ indicates standard is included, ✗ not included

In 2005, independently of these re-drafting activities by civil-society groups, the Berger government decided that, rather than enacting legislation on ATI, it would issue a decree on the matter. This was binding only on the executive branch and was centred entirely on transparency.[77] It was intended as a token, to the international donor community, of Guatemala's good faith in regard to implementing the Inter-American Convention against Corruption. Formulation of transparency standards as human rights was virtually absent, and regulations regarding information relating to national security were entirely excluded (see summary of decree in Table 5.4).[78] Nonetheless, many senior members of the Guatemalan government remained sceptical in regard to the decree and were worried about the operating costs.[79]

The support coalitions, meanwhile, kept up the pressure for a dedicated domestic law and in 2008, with the advent of a new president – Álvaro Colom – a window of opportunity opened up.[80] The subsequent debates show that members of the ATI support coalitions were ready to allow considerable space for changes to international standards. However, differences had now emerged between the two support groups as to the areas in which such space should be granted in order to secure the adoption of ATI legislation. The supporters of the transparency frame – Acción Ciudadana, backed by USAID – drafted their own new version of the law (initiative 3768 of 2008, see Table 5.4). Though transparency-centred, this allowed considerable leeway on national security, which was still a major concern for sections of the government, the military and Congress. Aspects of ATI that related to transitional justice and the removal of constraints on information relevant to national security were excluded and it was argued that this agenda had prevented previous drafts from getting through Congress.[81] By contrast, the main human rights groups canvassed an only slightly reworked version of the 2005 draft (initiative 3165 of 2005 in Table 5.4). Focusing on classified information, this neglected many of the features considered important by the transparency coalition, such as sanctions for officials and an institutional

---

[77] Ángel (2005).     [78] Presidencia de la República Guatemala (2005).
[79] Gramajo Valdés (2009: 99, 105).
[80] In March 2008, Colom signed the Chapultepec Declaration, which includes a right of access to public information. He also promised better access to military archives. See 'Presidente Colom suscribirá la declaración' (2008); 'PDH manejará archivo militar' (2008).
[81] This elicited a strong response from human rights NGOs in Guatemala. See Alvarado (2008), 'Piden ley que no restrinja' (2008).

mechanism for requesting information – in other words, issues relating to everyday transparency and efficiency in the public services.[82]

This public split prompted the institution of a more inclusive dialogue mechanism, extending even to the government sceptics. The mechanism comprised members of the government, the Human Rights Ombudsman, representatives of the press, Acción Ciudadana from the transparency coalition and Centro Civitas from the human rights coalition, who also chaired the mechanism. The goal of the process was a new, jointly elaborated draft law to which all groups could give their assent (int. 55 2011).

The tussle between the two support coalitions was not restricted to the content of the legislation: there was also much vying over the management of the dialogue mechanism. Although Centro Civitas, with its human rights focus, officially headed the dialogue process, Acción Ciudadana, the chief promoter of transparency, availed itself of USAID funds to hire an international expert – Ernesto Villanueva – to completely re-draft the legislation. Villanueva, a Mexican specialist on ATI, had been involved in the drafting of Mexico's federal legislation on ATI and was a member of a regional network of NGOs working on ATI from a transparency perspective.[83] Despite these affiliations, however, Villanueva took into account all the formal requests submitted by the members of the dialogue mechanism and combined the differing priorities – on the one hand transparency and on the other concerns regarding national security exemptions – into one document. The result was a piece of legislation that incorporated many more existing international standards on ATI than any of the previous drafts had (Gramajo Valdés 2009: 112).

During the dialogue process – as in the case of children's rights – the support coalition sought to conceal the degree of external input. The major role played by the external drafter was either passed over or downplayed in the domestic debate. Thus in its public pronouncements Acción Ciudadana talked only of a combination of previous, domestically produced drafts, not of an entirely new version (ints. 49 2011; 55 2011; 59 2011). USAID too sought to maintain a low profile in the campaigns promoting legislation (int. 62 2011). Discursively

---

[82] This version went before Congress as initiative 3755.

[83] Acción Ciudadana was also a member of this network – the Alianza Regional por la Libertad de Expresión e Información. The network is funded by the Canadian International Development Agency, the Open Society Institute, the Trust for the Americas and the National Endowment for Democracy.

speaking, pride of place was given to the dialogue mechanism and stress was laid on domestic 'ownership'.

This indicates that the support groups in this area were open to granting considerably more space for the domestic adaptation of international standards than their counterparts in children's rights – bearing out the thesis that translation space grows in inverse proportion to norm precision. As a result of the dialogue mechanism, however, the respective spaces accorded by supporters of the transparency frame and supporters of the transitional-justice frame to some extent cancelled each other out. Nevertheless, the human rights group resented the way in which Acción Ciudadana and USAID had commandeered the process by hiring an external drafter and thereby curtailing the influence of the dialogue forum on the drafting process. Although they were content with the legislative outcome, they were not content with the actual dialogue process (ints. 55 2011; 60 2011). As one interviewee observes, the dialogue was something of a fig leaf for the transparency coalition, satisfying the requirement for consultation (int. 62 2011):

But you have to remember . . . there's the real version and there's the politically correct version. The politically correct version is that there were meetings, that groups of people discussed the legislation . . . suggested changes . . . The reality is that . . . although the discussions held by this group were taken into account, the changes that were ultimately made were minimal because everyone knew certain principles had to be observed. But yes, this group did lend legitimacy [to the process].

Despite all this, the final draft did include a number of departures from the international standards. A major discussion point between the groups was the creation of an independent review body. Acción Ciudadana in particular promoted a permutation of this: the Human Rights Ombudsman, it suggested, should assume responsibility for monitoring ATI but should not have the power to review decisions on access. Some participants undoubtedly supported this curtailment of powers because they feared that without it the proposed arrangement would not get past Congress. However, there were also some who criticized the review body (modelled on the Mexican Federal Institute for Access to Information and Data Protection – IFAI) as unsuited to the Guatemalan context (ints. 47 2011; 49 2011; 62 2011). The principle of precedence was also omitted.

Acción Ciudadana – again with USAID funding[84] – lobbied intensively in favour of the final draft. For the first half of 2008, Congress dragged its heels over enactment,[85] but fortune then smiled on the supporters of ATI: a major scandal erupted in Congress over the embezzlement of 82 million quetzals (over 10 million US dollars) from the Congressional budget. This opened up a window of opportunity for ATI legislation and triggered a press campaign in its favour (int. 49 2011).

Despite this development, the final negotiations in Congress were a nail-biting affair. Various parties attempted to water down the text but were prevented from doing so[86] and the final version of the draft law was unanimously approved in September 2008.[87] This contained a number of additional changes, notably in relation to confidential information: such information, in contrast to the classified kind, was exempted from the rule requiring publication after a fixed time period. This provision was essentially adopted to accommodate private economic interests – and, so analysts feared, potentially corrupt practices (see final law/Decreto 57–2008 in Table 5.5).[88]

Essentially, then, only the final drafting process in 2008 adhered systematically to international standards (ints. 60 2011; 62 2011). During the 2000s, actors' awareness of the detail of international ATI standards increased, as did the number of references to these in the domestic discourse, and this was reflected in the increasing precision of the domestic legislation itself. Whereas in the earlier drafts, the omission of specific international standards was not always the result of a conscious decision, this was not the case in the final drafting process.

---

[84] It also hired former foreign minister Edgar Gutiérrez as a consultant and lobbyist. It was Gutiérrez who had initiated the first discussions on ATI between the NGOs and the government in 2000.

[85] Initially, the relevant committee failed to reach a decision and requested further technical reports: Barrera (2008). In addition, a number of parties in Congress were unwilling to support the law openly: Ana Lucía Blas (2008b).

[86] Osorio (2008), Morroquín (2008). The Partido Unionista – the party of Álvaro Arzú, former president of Guatemala and later mayor of the Guatemalan capital – openly argued against the legislation: León Blas (2008).

[87] Ana Lucía Blas (2008a).

[88] See Villagrán (2015). The final version also laid down sanctions for official misconduct that were even more stringent than those stipulated in the draft. Some of the bodies covered by the provisions were changed. A last-minute definition of national security was also added. See Congreso de la República de Guatemala (2008).

This difference was due mainly to the emergence of a more organized expert network in Latin America and the attempts of this network to standardize ATI legislation across the region. The upshot is a law which, compared with similar legislation elsewhere in the world, adheres quite closely to international standards. Its overall score in the Global Right to Information Rating exceeds that of (amongst others) Germany and the United States.[89]

International groups welcomed the adoption of the Guatemalan legislation. The main modification that had resulted from the drafting process – namely, the decision not to include provision for a review body – was not criticized, particularly as this institutional option had also been rejected by the majority of other countries in Latin America.[90] By contrast, the failure to regulate confidential information drew strong criticism, given that it constituted an active piece of watering down by Congress for the clear purpose of protecting economic interests (ints. 47 2011; 60 2011).

Overall, the influence of external actors was more indirect than in the other two areas under investigation in this study. In addition, the shift in the mode of interaction was mainly due not to a conscious decision by the actor groups, as in the other cases, but to a reconfiguration of international norm promoters that left USAID as the main advocate of ATI, working to a transparency-based agenda and using a capacity-building approach. However, the decision which USAID took, during the dialogue process, to intervene through behind-the-scenes funding and capacity-building, and by coordinating groups with similar outlooks, *was* a conscious one. USAID and its domestic partners were willing to grant leeway on the difficult question of ATI standards on national security. By contrast, those domestic actors who had been involved in a transnational network promoting ATI within a transitional-justice framework were left to fend for themselves. They nonetheless stuck to their focus on oversight of the military and access to archives and continued to give less priority to standards on day-to-day administration. In addition, although

---

[89] See Global Right to Information Rating, www.rti-rating.org/country-data.
[90] Two of the models for the drafting process in Guatemala were Ecuador and Chile (ints. 47 2011; 49 2011). Generally speaking, however, ATI developments in other countries played little or no role in the Guatemalan process: examples from outside the Americas had no influence at all; those from Latin America, with the exception of the above countries and Mexico, were little known; and those from Guatemala's neighbours in Central America had no effect at all on the process (ints. 47 2011; 60 2011).

the United States exerted a degree of diplomatic pressure to advance the overall transparency agenda, ATI was in fact just one of a number of items on this agenda. The debate never assumed the same importance for the United States as did, say, the discussions on scripts for a rule-of-law commission (see Chapter 6). That said, the US ambassador in particular supported the ATI legislation during the final stages of discussion in 2008, putting pressure on Congress and publicly praising and shaming as appropriate (ints. 49 2011; 52 2011; 62 2011).[91] The support that many other international bodies offered for ATI legislation often came at the urging of the transparency coalition (int. 49 2011). Transparency International,[92] the OAS Rapporteur, the United Nations Development Programme (UNDP) and the Inter-American Press Association[93] publicly praised the new law. In addition, the well-known Guatemalan human rights lawyer Frank La Rue had just been appointed to the post of UN Special Rapporteur on the Promotion and Protection of the Right to Freedom of Opinion and Expression and actively supported the draft legislation via op-eds and public statements.[94]

**Translation into Implementation: Expectation and Reality**
In contrast to developments in the area of children's rights, translation into implementation in ATI was not shaped by a renewed shifting of discursive frames – although a number of new actor groups did become involved in the implementation process. International promotion of ATI in this phase tended even more than before towards capacity-building and an interactive teaching mode. Economic interests and the lack of institutional capacity meant that translation into implementation resulted in an even more pronounced reshaping of ATI standards. The outcome was not so much a decoupling of law and practice; rather it became clear that the many expectations associated with ATI in both the international and the domestic discourse were essentially unrealizable.

Translation into implementation was shaped by a change in actor groups. It was the government who had to implement the law; and the municipalities, as the key bodies mandated in this area, were also

---

[91] European ambassadors showed support but were not as emphatic (int. 62 2011). See Ana Lucía Blas (2008a).
[92] 'Transparencia Internacional urge a aprobar' (2008).
[93] See e.g. 'No hay mejora en la situación' (2008).
[94] See e.g. 'Sectores aplauden paso' (2008).

expected to put it into action – without having been involved in the prior discussions. The office of the Human Rights Ombudsman, having assumed responsibility for monitoring application of the ATI law, also acquired greater prominence in the debate.

Although ATI improved after the law's entry into force in April 2009, its quality varied from level to level. Most state institutions introduced mechanisms for requesting information; the majority managed, as a minimum, to carry out the proactive publication required by the law; and the proportion of requests deemed to have been dealt with satisfactorily by the various ministries and other mandated entities increased. At the same time, the way in which government institutions handled ATI varied widely: some offered virtually full access, others none at all.[95] At municipal and departmental level, the quality of ATI was generally very poor: the institutional mechanisms put in place seldom worked and most information was, in any case, centralized in Guatemala City and had to be accessed from there, making the process difficult for the rural population. Where a request was denied, at whatever level, an appeal could only be lodged in the capital and was a costly undertaking.[96] In addition, ATI implementation in Guatemala relied heavily on online channels of publication, but as of 2014 only around 23 per cent of the population had access to the Internet.[97] In the case of other bodies, serious capacity problems meant that monitoring was non-existent and any kind of reporting to the Ombudsman's office was impossible. These bodies included: regional and local development councils; NGOs and trusteeships (*fideicomisos*); and organizations (such as the extractive industry) that were bound by the ATI legislation because they handled public funds or licences.[98] Although the Ombudsman's office was officially charged with monitoring and promoting implementation of the ATI legislation (but not reviewing decisions), Congress had never allocated it the funds for these tasks, thus limiting its capacity to fulfil its functions.[99] Relevant NGOs such as Acción Ciudadana and Grupo de Apoyo Mutuo offered help with legal proceedings in cases where requests for information had been turned down by state institutions.

[95]  See Acción Ciudadana (2010), Cerigua (2014).
[96]  See int. 52 (2011), GAM (2011).
[97]  See World Bank ranking at: http://data.worldbank.org/indicator/IT.NET.USER
.P2, accessed 16 Feb. 2016.
[98]  Alejandra Álvarez (2009); Bonillo (2010b).
[99]  'Falta de voluntad política' (2009), ints. 47 (2011), 49 (2011).

As time went on, it also became clear that the ATI legislation owed its passage through Congress to the previously mentioned window of opportunity. Subsequent proposed ATI-related legislation – on the organization of archives in Guatemala, for example, or on the handling of personal data by private actors – was not adopted (ints. 49 2011; 50 2011; 62 2011). Similarly, government initiatives to curb bank secrecy – a major subject of discussion since 2010 – have so far come to nothing.[100] Instead, the deteriorating security situation has actually prompted new initiatives aimed at limiting access to information, notably classified material concerning police and military matters.[101]

ATI attracted a degree of public attention in the wake of a number of scandals that prompted congressional representatives, the Human Rights Ombudsman and the NGO Acción Ciudadana to avail themselves publicly of the ATI legislation in order to request information.[102] During this period of debate, the media discourse remained located within a supportive, transparency-based frame. Expectations that ATI would be used as a tool in the fight against corruption figured prominently,[103] whereas other notions of ATI – as a means to democratization and participation, for example – had vanished. In the discourse of the human rights NGOs, meanwhile, a new theme counterpointed the urban 'good governance' approach that characterized the transparency frame: ATI was no longer supposed simply to generate well-informed citizens who are better able to participate in democratic activities; it was now seen as a tool for empowering and emancipating the marginalized and getting them to understand that they are in charge – 'Yo soy el patrón' ('I'm the boss') – and that they are the driving force behind democracy (int. 52 2011): 'And there's a shift to thinking that it isn't necessarily to do with public spending – people begin to think access to information is a human right – so there's a change as well' (int. 55 2011). With the emergence of ATI's new role as an emancipatory tool, the focus on past crimes faded and the new preoccupations were reflected in a shift of NGO teaching activities and

[100] See e.g. 'Elaboran proyecto' (2010).
[101] See Noticias de Guatemala (2012). On a recent government initiative, see Carlos Álvarez (2015).
[102] Areas involved here included (amongst many others) the social programme 'Mi Familia Progresa' and various issues in the education, health and energy sectors. See e.g. Alianza Regional por la Libertad de Expresión e Información (2010: 50–53), Cardona (2010a, b).
[103] See e.g. Ajanel (2009); Montenegro, (2009).

capacity-building towards the municipalities and their marginalized rural populations.

It was the government that took the biggest steps in regard to ATI implementation. The process was organized by a core group of ministries – who also established links with Mexico's independent ATI review body, the IFAI. Government members undertook a number of exchanges and capacity-building trips to Mexico at which various aspects of implementation were discussed.[104]

On the down side, the keenness with which ATI implementation was pursued varied from one institution to another[105] and a number of government bodies continued openly to express their opposition to the legislation on the grounds that it endangered individual officials, notably by exposing them to the threat of extortion.[106] Several implementing institutions tried to interpret the law to their own advantage[107] and in the case of journalists, access actually became more difficult once the law was in place, as they were now frequently obliged to follow the formal route when requesting information.[108] State officials, meanwhile, quickly learned to keep their books clean (int. 62 2011).

The most proactive forms of resistance to ATI implementation were to be found in Guatemala's autonomous municipalities and in their representative body – the National Association of Guatemalan Municipalities (Asociación Nacional de Municipalidades – ANAM).[109] The challenges which the new legislation would bring for the municipalities had been given no consideration at all during the drafting process; and the municipalities themselves had not been involved in the political discussions (int. 48 2011). They suffered from a dearth of funds, were ignorant of their obligations and traditionally favoured a non-transparent style of governance (ints. 47 2011; 49 2011; 52 2011; 60 2011).

This asymmetry remained largely unredressed by the capacity-building, awareness-raising and teaching activities of the external

---

[104]  The government's Transparency Commission also sought to keep the discussion on an independent administrative authority alive by holding a series of workshops and drawing up a proposal for reform of the ATI legislation (ints. 50, 55 2011). These efforts, however, found no support (int. 47 2011). On the Mexican links, see 'Funcionarios aprenden' (2009), 'Delegación va de nuevo' (2009).

[105]  Espada (2009).

[106]  See ints. 47 (2011) and 55 (2011) and e.g. 'Surge primera queja' (2009).

[107]  Ajanel (2009), Arévalo (2009).     [108]  Véliz (2009).

[109]  Bonillo (2009); Cardona (2009).

bodies – notably USAID, GIZ (the German government development agency) and the Open Society Institute (which financed campaigns by Acción Ciudadana and Centro Civitas to promote awareness of ATI legislation amongst Guatemalans) (int. 60 2011). All the manuals on ATI legislation – both for ordinary citizens and for officials – were developed either by Acción Ciudadana, USAID or GIZ.[110] USAID and GIZ in particular concentrated on promoting ATI as part of an accountability and transparency agenda and provided citizens with practical information on how to deal with state institutions. GIZ also aimed at capacity-building in the municipalities,[111] and USAID, besides supporting both the central government and the municipalities (ints. 16 2010; 47 2011; 49 2011; 60 2011; 62 2011), also funded monitoring by NGOs.[112] Funds were also made available by the Open Society Institute to develop guidelines for the classification and declassification of archives (ints. 55 2011; 60 2011). The UNDP and the International Republican Institute, meanwhile, funded more general workshops to analyse the progress of implementation.[113]

Indirect pressure from the US administration ensured the cooperation of the Guatemalan Ministry of Defence in complying with requests for information: the United States had made the lifting of a ban on the supply of most kinds of military aid to Guatemala conditional on Guatemalan support for human rights and the fight against impunity.[114] In addition, the US Congress attached a number of conditions to the funding provided under the terms of the Central American Regional Security Initiative (a counterpart to the US's Mérida Initiative on Central America). These included improved investigation and prosecution of human rights offences committed by members of the police and military.[115] All this gave the Ministry good reason to want to portray itself as open to requests for information.[116]

---

[110] Ints. 48 (2011), 49 (2011). See Anam/Promudel (2010); Acción Ciudadana/Promudel/USAID (n.d.).

[111] But in only three out of twenty-two departments (int. 48 2011).

[112] Int. 62 (2011), Blas (2009), USAID Guatemala (2012), US State Department/USAID (2009).

[113] See int. 62 (2011); Méndez Villaseñor (2010).   [114] Associated Press (2012).

[115] Meyer/Ribando Seelke (2012: 22–24).

[116] One NGO – the Grupo de Apoyo Mutuo (GAM) – exploited this situation by copying every information request it sent to the Ministry of Defence to the US embassy, ensuring a high rate of response (int. 52 2011).

Thus a whole series of 'teaching' activities took place during the implementation phase. Most of these centred on transparency, but some gentle indirectly applied diplomatic pressure by the United States also helped maintain the Guatemalan government's efforts in the field of national security exemption.

Over and above these problems of capacity, and the active resistance of the municipalities and certain mandated bodies, the major obstacle to a properly functioning ATI norm set was the lack of demand for it from anyone beyond a tiny educated elite – a problem encountered in many other countries attempting to introduce ATI legislation (Callamard 2008: 9–10). Some municipalities even had difficulty maintaining the information-units which they were obliged by law to set up but which often received no more than five or six requests for information per year.[117] A study carried out across six municipalities in 2010 showed that 90 per cent of the population were unaware of the existence of ATI legislation:[118] 'It's always the same organizations ... always groups working to a centralized agenda that ask for information ... nobody else' (int. 50 2011).[119] The press too was reluctant to make use of official requests as a means of obtaining information, feeling that this process hindered rather than facilitated direct access to government.[120] Government fears about a flood of requests thus failed to materialize:

there was an expectation which then turned out to be unfounded ... we thought ... the offices would be [flooded] with people asking for information. Even the people from the Ministry of Defence ... thought they would need to open up a whole stadium because of all the people who would turn up. (int. 50)

For many, ATI had a rather symbolic quality: it was not so much about the actual use of institutions, more about the fact that they existed at all (int. 55 2011). The many different expectations associated with ATI, and the effects it was hoped would follow from it – namely, the advent

---

[117] Int. 48 (2011). See also Cereser (2009).     [118] Casasola (2010).
[119] For an overview of trends in information requests, see Vera Martinez et al. (2015: 94).
[120] Int. 60 (2011). This did prompt some efforts to reshape the norm set: an initiative launched by the transparency-based support group with the aim of strengthening the powers of the Ombudsman and guaranteeing preferential treatment of the media came to nothing. See Hernández (2009); Bonillo (2010a).

of greater emancipation and citizen participation as weapons in the fight against corruption and the struggle to secure transitional justice – remained entirely unfulfilled.

In this area, then, in contrast to the course of events in children's rights, the implementation phase in ATI brought no major new additions or omissions – though existing reshaping was reinforced. Capacity-related constraints and a strong economic interest in the maintenance of secrecy meant that implementation was only partially successful. The mode of interaction did not change and the initial framing, pitting oversight of the military against transparency, persisted, with international bodies attempting to work on both aspects but focusing more on transparency-related teaching activities.

As it stands, developments in this case seem, on the face of it, to support a neo-institutionalist interpretation: international standards were in large part adopted but practices were decoupled. In fact, the picture is a more complex one. The legislation was the subject of active political contention within the Guatemalan political system. In addition, following its adoption, it became one of the key tools used by NGOs based in the capital and by the Ombudsman's office in its clashes with the government over transparency and the collection of personal data. The lack of public demand for ATI legislation dispelled many of the fears which members of the government and officials in the municipalities harboured in regard to bringing it into effect, and most observers soon realized that the passage and implementation of the law would fulfil few of the expectations associated with it.

## 5.3  Reshaping Access to Information

ATI did not emerge as a global norm set until the 1990s, and yet only ten years later it was being described all over the world as a key characteristic of democratic governance. Since then, standards for the translation of ATI into domestic law have gradually been honed – a process that has taken place in the 'soft law' area of human rights regimes, resulting in a norm set of medium precision.

When one looks at the parallel political process of international standardization and domestic conflict over legislation, it is clear that standardization and further formalization of the global standards exerted considerable influence on domestic translation in Guatemala – albeit with something of a time lag. Guatemalan support-group actors looked to existing international standards for 'guidance' in drafting domestic legislation. In the early phase, the issue of access to information came to the fore in relation to the Peace Accords and as a result of active promotion by the OAS Special Rapporteur for Freedom of Expression (Step 1). An initial version of the ATI legislation was drafted but – in a second phase – was rejected by Congress (Step 2). Negotiations at this time were centred on a small group of domestic actors from the government and various human rights groups. In the minds of these groups, ATI formed part of the general settlement laid down in the Peace Accords; it was linked to the right to learn the truth about past events and was located within a transitional-justice frame. On this view, the central issues which ATI legislation had to address were the opening-up of the military's archives, disclosure of the types of information which the state was holding on private individuals and improved oversight of the Guatemalan national security apparatus. Amongst members of the Guatemalan government and Congress, by contrast, the dominant frame was one of resistance – including vis-à-vis the issue of transitional justice. The focus on transitional justice contrasted with the approach that dominated in the press and in the increasingly widespread activities of transparency-oriented NGOs, notably Acción Ciudadana. Here, ATI formed part of a transparency frame and was seen as an anti-corruption tool that would improve administrative efficiency.

That the government entered into negotiations with the human rights groups at all was mainly due to the shaming tactics and threat of sanctions employed by the OAS Special Rapporteur and the Consultative Group – the major donor forum in Guatemala. Despite this positive turn, once it had introduced draft legislation into Congress, the government considered its obligations in this matter discharged and the draft went on to be rejected by a majority of congressional representatives – thus completing the first two steps of a feedback loop. During this phase, there was little discussion about international standards amongst domestic actors – and external actors too were only partly aware of the latest provisions in this area.

The third phase saw a major framing contest emerge in Guatemala. With strong support from the United States (specifically USAID), the chief transparency NGO – Acción Ciudadana – pushed a transparency agenda. In-country ATI promotion by the OAS Rapporteur and the Consultative Group ceased, but domestic human rights groups continued to push for a concept of ATI centred on transitional justice and improved oversight of the military, with little energy being expended on everyday transparency. The draft legislation proposed by the supporters of the transparency frame, in contrast, contained provisions for practical institutional mechanisms through which requests for information might be made. At the same time, it allowed considerable leeway on national security exemptions and the declassification of official files.

Clearly, then, for 'soft' medium-precision standards such as this, the support coalitions were prepared to allow space for local adaptation. In the end, however, the particular constellation, involving two distinct support groups, meant that the changes made to the international standards were relatively minor (Step 3). The conflict between these groups, which saw each fighting for its particular version of ATI, led to the institution of a dialogue mechanism in which the two sides could work with members of the government and other groups to develop more inclusive draft legislation. Although the influence of external actors was more indirect here, USAID (via Acción Ciudadana) effectively determined the direction of the process by hiring a Mexican expert to produce a new draft of the ATI legislation. The resultant text did, however, take both of the opposing positions into account, proving acceptable to both sides and adhering to existing international standards to a much greater degree than any of the previous drafts. As the two support groups continued to champion their respective priorities but had to accommodate each other's priorities, the overall degree of reshaping was more modest than anticipated. That said, wherever government and civil-society groups could agree, modifications were introduced: in lieu of a fully fledged review body, for example, the draft proposed assigning simple monitoring functions to the Human Rights Ombudsman; and the principle of the precedence of ATI over other regulatory arrangements was omitted. In addition, during the closing discussions in Congress, a decision was taken to exempt 'confidential information' from the rule requiring publication after a set period. This latter exemption drew criticism at the international level, but the omission of arrangements for an independent review body passed without major comment, given that this kind of modification had been made in other Latin American states as well.

With the cessation of the OAS Rapporteur's high-profile involvement and the disappearance of the conditionality imposed by the Consultative Group, it was not so much a conscious shift in interaction

**Table 5.6** *Stages in the translation of access to information in Guatemala*

| Translation | Resistance | Localization | Full adoption |
|---|---|---|---|
| Into discourse | Against transitional justice and transparency | | ATI for transitional justice v. ATI for transparency |
| Into law | | Modification of oversight mechanisms, omission of precedence and confidential information | |
| Into implementation | | Limited implementation (but no major shift in reshaping), poor take-up | |

mode as a reconfiguration of norm promoters that dictated the course of the third phase. USAID's support in getting the legislation through took the form mainly of teaching and a limited amount of shaming. It opted for a more persuasion-oriented mode of interaction and sought to keep its major role in proceedings hidden from public view. The transparency coalition too avoided publicizing the extent of its own activities and the role played by the outside expert recruited to draft the legislation: it knew how poorly this kind of 'external influence' was viewed. The idea of a domestic dialogue process was supported and the concerns of the other groups were more inclusively reflected in the new ATI draft, but the transparency coalition did not relinquish its overall management of the drafting process.

In contrast to the course of events in the case of children's rights, translation into implementation brought with it no major reshaping or shift of frame. The persuasion-oriented approach of the main norm promoters also persisted. At the same time, translation into implementation made existing economic interests and problems of capacity even more apparent. Government institutions fared relatively well in complying with the requirements imposed on it by ATI; other entities – notably private organizations entrusted with public funds and licences – were less successful. Resistance, both active and passive, was encountered in the autonomous municipalities, which had not been included in the political negotiations relating to the legislation. They claimed that issues of security and capacity made it impossible for them to fulfil their obligations in regard to ATI. The institutions in charge of national security, meanwhile, felt somewhat less fearful of the ATI legislation once they realized how few requests were being made. The main users of the legislation were NGOs from the support coalition, businesses and academics. This led to a decisive decoupling of ATI from the expectations that had initially been associated with it – the defeat of corruption, greater citizen participation, the emancipation of the marginalized and the institution of measures for transitional justice.

To sum up: the interactive translation process in the case of ATI was dominated on the one hand by two support frames – centred respectively on transitional justice and transparency – and on the other by a resistance frame. As a result of negotiation and dialogue between these three groups in regard to translation into law, a number of modifications were made to the international standards. These were more substantial than had been the case with children's rights. Implementation brought no major changes to these modifications but was hampered by economic interests and problems of capacity (see Table 5.6).

# 6 | *Translating Scripts for Rule-of-Law Commissions*

The Commission against Impunity in Guatemala (Comisión Internacional Contra la Impunidad en Guatemala – CICIG) is an international commission that works within the Guatemalan legal system. It investigates high-profile cases involving illegal networks inside state structures. It also has a legislative-reform mandate and organizes capacity-building with the Public Prosecutor's Office and the country's police forces. The creation of the commission aroused some of the most intense opposition seen since the signing of the Peace Accords in 1996 and a major political conflict developed with regard to the scripts relating to it. When designing the first version, human rights groups in Guatemala drew inspiration from the scripts used for rule-of-law and truth commissions in the region and proposed a format aimed at protecting human rights activists against abuse by clandestine 'security organizations'. However, by the 2000s, the global script for bodies charged with post-conflict rule of law had already undergone a change: preference had shifted away from the 'external commission' of the 1990s to the 'hybrid commission', working inside the domestic legal system and with an extended remit covering various combinations of investigation and prosecution. The focus in this chapter is not on a precise, internationally decreed norm set but on an evolving global script for rule-of-law promotion and on the way in which that script is translated in the domestic context. The standards generated by the script – in regard to the form that the UN and other international rule-of-law commissions should take in post-conflict countries and what problems they should address – were promoted and disseminated in an interaction process led by the UN, with support from the United States, the EU and the Guatemalan human rights community.[1]

The section that follows here will describe the emergence and evolution of the script for international rule-of-law commissions at a global level.

---

[1] The mode of translation into law in this case differs slightly from that in the two other areas investigated in this study, in that it involves the conclusion of an international agreement between the Guatemalan government and the UN.

154

An account will then be given of the three-step interactive process of translation of the script in Guatemala. In the period of 2000 to 2004, a first version of the commission was designed and debated (Step 1). This drew its original inspiration from regional scripts for external investigative commissions but was later heavily influenced by the UN-backed 'hybrid' scripts that emerged in the 2000s. In August 2004, this design was declared unconstitutional by the Guatemalan Constitutional Court (Step 2). A more dialogue-oriented process then took place, which involved reshaping and reframing the commission scripts to conform both to the interests of Guatemala's elites and to wider security concerns amongst the population (Step 3). The translation into implementation did not bring with it any further shift in the mode of interaction, but it did occasion additional domestic reshaping, as CICIG increasingly replaced Guatemalan institutions both in general discourse and in practice.

## 6.1 Emerging Scripts for Rule-of-Law Commissions

The standards embodied in scripts for rule-of-law commissions are the least precise norm set considered in this study. They detail best practice in regard to the appointment and practical operation of international commissions in post-conflict states and stipulate which rule-of-law norms such commissions should uphold.

During the 1990s, the international 'tool box' for post-conflict countries contained a number of different instruments such as international tribunals (like those in Yugoslavia and Rwanda), technical-assistance programmes and fact-finding missions (Hudson/Taylor 2010: 6; Roht-Arriaza 2008–2009). International tribunals prosecuted those responsible for violations of international humanitarian law – i.e. such prosecutions took place outside the domestic legal system. Technical-assistance programmes concentrated on promoting the rule of law through capacity-building and the transfer of expertise – delivered via training sessions and workshops and the provision of funds for equipment. Fact-finding missions, meanwhile, followed the classic route of gathering information on possible violations of international humanitarian and human rights law and reporting them to the international community.

In addition, the tool box also contained international investigative commissions. Being part of work on peacebuilding and transitional justice, the 1990s' versions of scripts for international 'commissions' were concerned primarily with the investigation of human rights violations either committed during civil war or directly linked to it.[2] The resultant commissions worked outside domestic legal systems, operating essentially as gatherers of information (mainly the testimony of victims – and perpetrators) and analysing any government documents that were available. They generally concluded their work by publishing a report that also included recommendations for the government in question.

In the course of the 2000s, these different tools came under increasingly heavy criticism. Tribunals and external investigative commissions were held to have had little impact in terms of strengthening the rule of law in the countries concerned, and the simple provision of technical assistance had clearly also failed to have any effect. International experts took the opportunity to reconsider the ways in which rule-of-law problems were tackled within the fragile justice systems characteristic of post-conflict states (see, for example, Castresana 2004: 106). Scripts for international commissions and tribunals empowered variously to investigate, or investigate and prosecute, human rights crimes began to take shape within the UN:[3] experiences were gained with hybrid judicial bodies such as the Special Panel for Serious Crimes in Timor-Leste (2000), the Regulation 64 Panels in Kosovo (2000), the Special Court for Sierra Leone (2002), the Extraordinary Chambers in the Court of Cambodia (2003) and the Bosnian War Crimes Chamber (2005). These bodies imposed sanctions for violations of international humanitarian and human rights law and they were 'hybrid' in the sense that their work was carried out inside the legal system of the post-conflict state (and often with mixed international and domestic staff) (Dickinson 2003: 295).

A number of investigative commissions were also created. In 2005, the UN granted 'Chapter VII authority'[4] to its Independent Investigative Commission (UNIIC) to look into the assassination of President Hariri of Lebanon. Operating within the framework of Lebanese law, a mixed team of internationals and locals investigated the case and referred it on for prosecution.[5] In Timor-Leste, a Serious Crimes Investigation Team

---

[2]  Examples here are the internationally backed truth commissions set up in Sierra Leone, Timor-Leste, El Salvador and Guatemala.

[3]  See UN General Assembly (2008: 92–3). For a systematic discussion, see Werle/ Jeßberger (2014: 27–9, 121–8) and Williams (2012).

[4]  Authority under Chapter 7 of the UN Charter, which invests the Security Council with the right to 'determine the existence of any threat to the peace, breach of the peace, or act of aggression'.

[5]  The case was prosecuted by the Special Tribunal for Lebanon, a hybrid body set up in 2007 to deal with the Hariri murder.

Table 6.1 *The evolution of UN rule-of-law commissions*

| Style of commission | External investigative – 1990s | Hybrid – 2000s |
|---|---|---|
| Matter | Violation of international human rights law during/in connection with civil war | Violation of international human rights law during/after civil war |
| Mandate | Information-gathering Policy recommendation | Investigation/investigation and prosecution Capacity-building (training and assisting domestic judicial personnel) |
| Institutional setting | Operates outside domestic legal system | Operates inside domestic legal system but autonomously |

began work in 2008, assisting the prosecutor-general with investigations and training domestic counterparts. Cases were then prosecuted by the Timorese courts (Hudson/Taylor 2010: 7).

This, then, was how new scripts for hybrid post-conflict mechanisms were evolving in the UN during the 2000s: the bodies concerned would work inside the domestic legal system and would have powers either of straightforward investigation or of investigation and prosecution. Human rights crimes committed during and after civil war continued to be a prime focus. The precision of the scripts in question remained low. Expectations were only loosely formulated and no law, hard or soft, was generated. Instead, the standards had the status of 'best practice'. The main standards, and their evolution from the 1990s to the 2000s, are summarized in Table 6.1.

## 6.2 Interactive Translation of the Scripts: Human Rights or the Fight against Crime?

### Step 1: CICIACS: *International Defence for Human Rights Activists*

The idea of setting up an international rule-of-law commission in Guatemala arose from a transnational campaign conducted by Guatemalan human rights groups. A number of key actors in the human rights community had become concerned about the ever more frequent threats and acts of violence against human rights activists in Guatemala.[6] They assumed these were the work of 'parallel powers' or illegal security forces known by the Spanish acronym 'CIACS' (standing for Cuerpos Ilegales y Aparatos Clandestinos de Seguridad – Illegal Groups and Clandestine Security Structures). The name was used to designate networks of former high-ranking military and intelligence personnel 'left over' from the era of military dictatorship and authoritarianism in Guatemala and suspected not only of being involved in crime but also of having powerful political interests and of using threats and violence to intimidate human rights activists (Peacock/Beltrán 2003). The human rights community, looking round for suitable weapons with which to defend itself, found inspiration in the international commissions set up in the region in the 1990s. From 2001, the heads of a number of urban human rights organizations in Guatemala met regularly to discuss possible strategies for responding to the threats (Ganovsky-Larsen 2007: 25).[7] Their view of how CIACS should be dealt with[8] was influenced by the international community's experience both in Guatemala itself and in Central America as a whole, and by the analyses and opinions of their transnational NGO partners, the UN rapporteurs visiting the country and MINUGUA.[9]

Two models in particular were given in-depth consideration. UN staff who had worked in other Central American missions suggested studying the experiences of the so-called Joint Group established in El Salvador in the early 1990s. This group, comprising a mixture of international and local personnel, had investigated, and reported on, the death squads which had persisted after the civil war in El Salvador

---

[6] The numbers of these declined steadily after the signing of the Peace Accords in 1996 but began to rise again during the Portillo presidency (2000–4). See e.g. Ganovsky-Larsen (2007: 15) and Samaoya (2004).

[7] The heads in question were: Helen Mack (Fundación Myrna Mack), Nery Rodenas (ODHAG), Mario Polanco (GAM), Frank La Rue (then at CALDH), and Claudia Virginia Samayoa (Fundación Rigoberta Menchú). These individuals were well known in the international community and functioned as the main conduit between the international and national levels. They had influential contacts in the UN and in US and European foreign-policy circles (SEDEM 2004: 7).

[8] These ideas are collected in a publication by the NGO Sedem (SEDEM 2004).

[9] See e.g. Naciones Unidas, Comisión de Derechos Humanos (2000); SEDEM (2004: 16); Ganovsky-Larsen (2007: 26); MINUGUA (2001: paras. 51, 81).

and had gone on to engage in human rights violations and political assassinations.[10] The experiences of the Guatemalan truth commission (the CEH) also served as a major template in devising a mechanism for investigating the assaults on human rights activists (Hudson/Taylor 2010: 5; SEDEM 2004: 9). When overtures to the government produced no support or action, the Dutch NGO Plataforma Holandesa funded a more formal analysis of the 'Joint Group' model by the US NGO WOLA (Washington Office on Latin America, int. 63 2011; SEDEM 2004: 17). It was WOLA's findings which then determined the shape of discussions amongst human rights organizations in Guatemala.

The Joint Group's mandate had included the production of a report and the compilation of a list of recommendations for the Salvadorean government;[11] the Guatemalan truth commission had a similar set-up (but focused on events during rather than after civil war). In the view of the Guatemalan civil-society actors, neither body had produced entirely satisfactory results: though successful on the reporting front, they had had little impact in terms of policy reform and legal action in the Guatemalan courts.[12] Building on their analysis of these bodies, Guatemalan human rights groups developed a design for an international commission entitled 'Commission for the Investigation of Illegal Groups and Clandestine Security Structures' (Comisión de Investigación de Cuerpos Ilegales y Aparatos Clandestinos de Seguridad – CICIACS, see SEDEM 2004: 18). At the same time, it formed the Coalición para la CICIACS (Coalition in Support of CICIACS).[13] The proposal for the commission was channelled into the public domain via the Guatemalan Human Rights Ombudsman in January 2003.[14]

In contrast to the direction of flow in the two other cases presented in this study, promotion of this human rights tool thus came *from below*: when the human rights groups sought to communicate their concerns

---

[10] Int. 52 (2011). The Group was established in 1993 and presented its findings in 1994. See United Nations Security Council (1994).

[11] United Nations Security Council (1994). The Group was made up of international experts, the majority of them Spanish police officers (SEDEM 2004: 17–18).

[12] See int. 44 (2010), SEDEM (2004: 9). Despite this, the Joint Group is considered to have helped reduce levels of political violence in El Salvador: (WOLA 2008: 5–6). See also Guoz (2003a).

[13] For an overview of all NGO members, see SEDEM (2004: 4).

[14] SEDEM (2004: 21–3), Ganovsky-Larsen (2007: 27).

to their international partners and contacts outside their transnational NGO network, they had to adopt active strategies of persuasion because CIACS were not widely perceived as a threat at that time (WOLA 2008: 5).

Surprisingly, this initiative also elicited rhetorical support from the government (SEDEM 2004: 5). It was only behind closed doors, as negotiations between the government and the human rights groups proceeded, that fundamental divisions made themselves apparent. The human rights groups and their transnational NGO partners were seeking an international mechanism that would enable them to address the violence against human rights activists – a kind of 'bodyguard commission'.[15] The government, meanwhile, sought to widen the mandate in order to cover organized crime, private security and even drug trafficking.[16] In the end, the focus on 'defending human rights defenders' was retained. A final agreement between the Human Rights Ombudsman and the government was signed on 13 March 2003 and submitted to the UN – as the prospective international senior partner (along with the OAS) in the proposed commission.[17]

What the Guatemalan NGOs envisaged was an ad hoc commission made up of international investigators and modelled on the human rights commissions instituted in Central America in the 1990s (Table 6.2). It would work outside the domestic legal system and focus on information-gathering. It was to resemble the Salvadorean Joint Group in that it would not target past crimes but rather current crimes perpetrated by illegal networks 'left over' from the civil war:

> The CICIAS will investigate illegal groups and clandestine security-structures operating in Guatemala, in particular those that are responsible for the assaults and threats suffered by defenders of human rights, judicial personnel, witnesses, journalists, members of trades unions, and [representatives of] other social sectors. Likewise, it will investigate illegal or clandestine activities engaged in by public and private security-organizations.[18]

Besides making policy recommendations, the commission was to collect information and make this available to the Guatemalan Public Prosecutor's Office.[19]

---

[15] See (int. 53 2011), Guoz (2003b, c, e).  [16] Guoz (2003c).
[17] SEDEM (2004: 60–4).  [18] SEDEM (2004: 61).
[19] The original proposal for the creation of this commission is reproduced in SEDEM (2004: 53–9).

Table 6.2 *CICIACS 1.0: A 1990s-style commission*

|  | External investigative commissions – 1990s | *CICIACS 1.0* |
|---|---|---|
| Matter | Violation of international human rights law during/in connection with civil war | CIACS and their human rights violations<br>'Left over' structures from the civil war |
| Mandate | Information-gathering<br>Policy recommendation | Information-gathering<br>Public reporting and policy recommendation<br>Provision of information to Public Prosecutor's Office with a view to prosecution of perpetrators and potential purging of government institutions |
| Institutional setting | Operates outside domestic legal system | Operates outside domestic legal system<br>25 members<br>6-month mandate<br>3 commissioners |

Although influenced by outside expertise and strongly inspired by regional scripts for previous human rights commissions, the drafting of this first design – CICIACS 1.0 – was mostly an internal process.

Analysts wondered why President Portillo chose to promote this project, given the scant support for it within his own party – the right-wing FRG – which had little inclination to back a project emanating from the human rights community (and indeed later ensured its defeat in Congress). However, the corruption scandals surrounding the Portillo government and the worsening human rights situation in the country were damaging the government's international standing. Portillo's support for CICIACS was therefore part of a strategy to improve the government's international image (Ganovsky-Larsen 2007: 31). After all, this was a project supported by the United States, Canada, Holland, MINUGUA and a number of NGOs.[20] But

[20] SEDEM (2004: 20, 25). Also, Méndez Villaseñor (2003c).

although pressure from the United States and Canada was of particular importance in fostering these initial negotiations between the government and the human rights groups, the undertaking as whole ranked low on foreign-policy agendas outside the confines of the diplomatic community in Guatemala.[21] In addition, during this first phase some countries, particularly in Europe, viewed the project as cleaving to a US agenda and were less forthcoming with their support. Only after the CICIACS agreement had been signed did the EU officially endorse it.[22] At UN headquarters too, interest was minimal – outside of the relevant department – since the project did not derive from an official UN mandate.

The UN Department of Political Affairs did show some interest in the CICIACS proposal and in July 2003 sent a team of experts to Guatemala to assess its feasibility (SEDEM 2004: 27). From the very start, however, the Department envisaged a body going beyond that proposed by the Guatemalan human rights community – a commission 'with teeth', consistent with the emerging scripts for hybrid commissions and judicial bodies. In line with this vision, the Department put together a technical mission – comprising experts on drug trafficking, corruption and organized crime – to explore the scheme's potential in consultation with domestic experts (int. 63 2011). In September 2003, the mission delivered a moderately positive report (SEDEM 2004: 29–30).

When it came to the mandate and style of the commission, the mission envisaged something quite different from the CICIACS 1.0 proposal put forward by the human rights groups (Castresana 2004: 107). The exclusive focus on crimes against human rights activists was perceived as too narrow and the style was seen as too limited and not consonant with the new scripts on international rule-of-law commissions that were emerging at that time. In line with this perception, the technical mission proposed an international commission that would conduct investigations and prosecutions independently but from within the Guatemalan legal system. Legislative reform was added to the mandate: the commission would be empowered to draft legislation and pass this on to Congress and would thus have the opportunity to help modernize Guatemalan criminal law.[23]

---

[21] In 2004, Otto Reich, then US Assistant Secretary of State for Western Hemisphere Affairs, was unaware of the project. See Del Cid (2004).

[22] 'Canciller pidió a Europa' (2003).

[23] See Castresana (2004: 107) and Méndez Villaseñor (2003b).

This was a major shift away from the CICIACS proposal canvassed by the Guatemalan human rights community, and certain human rights sections of the CICIACS support coalition were strongly critical of the new blueprint. They doubted the constitutionality of both the commission's prosecutorial role and its legislative mandate: 'The UN notion that CICIACS should be an investigative and prosecutorial entity which, while subject to Guatemalan law, would operate independently of the country's judicial system is worrying', commented the Human Rights Ombudsman.[24] Some human rights groups were worried that they were losing ownership of the scheme (int. 63 2011): their prime concern – the defence of human rights defenders – was no longer the only focus. In addition, the commission as proposed by the UN had much greater independence than had been accorded it in the domestic draft. Despite the changes to the mandate and institutional arrangements, and under considerable diplomatic pressure – notably from the United States (int. 52 2011) – on 7 January 2004, with the end of its term of office approaching, the government appended its signature to the CICIACS agreement between itself and the United Nations (CICIACS Agreement 2004).

The resulting arrangement was a textbook example of a script for a hybrid commission. CICIACS was to work inside the Guatemalan legal system. Besides investigatory powers, its mandate included autonomous prosecution (art. 3), meaning that it could initiate prosecutions independently, play the role of private prosecutor (*querellante adhesivo*) and join prosecutions even where there were objections from domestic actors. The mandate still only covered CIACS, but the latter's links to organized crime now also fell within the commission's purview and investigation of these was linked to human rights violations or to the state's failure to protect such rights (art. 2; see also Table 6.3). Crimes against human rights groups were given less prominence than in CICIACS 1.0, but their investigation remained a central task (art. 2a).

CICIACS 2.0 was designed as a body working within the Guatemalan legal system but enjoying substantial autonomy and empowered to bring cases before the Guatemalan courts.[25] It was an entity designed in line with the ideas and conditions proposed by the UN, for whom the best practice at that time was the 'hybrid commission'.[26]

---

[24] Méndez Villaseñor (2003a). See also Castresana (2004: 107).
[25] CICIACS Agreement (2004).
[26] Castresana (2004: 109). See also Martín P. Rodríguez (2004).

Table 6.3 *CICIACS 2.0: A 2000s-style commission*[27]

|  | Hybrid commissions – 2000s | CICIACS 2.0 |
|---|---|---|
| Matter | Violation of international human rights law during/ after civil war | CIACS and their human rights violations |
|  |  | Legislative provisions |
| Mandate | Investigation/investigation and prosecution | Investigation and prosecution of CIACS |
|  | Capacity-building (training and assisting domestic judicial personnel) | Investigation of CIACS attacks on HR defenders and deleterious effect of CIACS on state capacity to protect human rights |
|  |  | Reform of legislation on organized crime |
| Institutional setting | Operates inside domestic legal system but autonomously | Operates inside domestic legal system but autonomously |
|  |  | Small commission |
|  |  | 2-year mandate, extendable |
|  |  | One commissioner |

## *Step 2: Rejection*

In the months that followed, the scheme to establish a rule-of-law commission became a major source of contention in the Guatemalan political system and was ultimately rejected. Three framings of the issue can be distinguished in the debate. In the first frame, one of support, CICIACS was presented – in line with the vision of the Guatemalan human rights groups – as a mechanism for defending human rights defenders against the actions of CIACS. In the second – a resistance frame especially popular with rightist groups and the private sector – the commission was rejected on the grounds that it was unconstitutional, usurped the authority of state institutions and breached sovereignty. On top of this came the refusal of the FRG, the party of government, to back the agreement negotiated by its own leaders. Adherents of the third, less dominant frame, which centred on constructive criticism,

---

[27]  CICIACS Agreement (2004).

called either for greater concentration on the strengthening of local institutions or for a widening of the mandate to include organized crime and not just abuses against human rights defenders.

In the rejectionist frame, the commission was portrayed as illegally interfering in the country's affairs, as arrogating state powers to itself and as failing to provide any opportunity for active participation by the Guatemalans themselves. Critics claimed to support the commission's overall objectives – such as the fight against organized crime and parallel powers – but strongly rejected the concept of an international commission as a means of achieving these. The main bone of contention was the question of the commission's legality: CICIACS was described as unconstitutional and as breaching Guatemalan sovereignty. The commission, it was argued, was a ploy: rather than seeking to fight parallel powers, it was intent on supplanting state institutions:

There is no doubt that a series of treacherous blows have been inflicted on the country's institutional integrity and dignity. That integrity is now weakened because CICIACS, behind all the fine talk about 'acting without prejudice to the functions which the Guatemalan legal system assigns to the office of Public Prosecutor', is actually putting in place a structure endowed with super-powers that will reduce the Public Prosecutor's office to a travesty of itself.[28]

The rhetoric of slighted dignity was linked to the notion of dependency on the international community and an inability to solve one's own problems: 'We Guatemalans are a decent, upstanding, hard-working and essentially peaceful people and we are quite capable of extricating ourselves from the situations we have got ourselves into without shackling ourselves with "help" from outside "experts".'[29]

Intermeshed in this overall framework were a number of other strands of contestation. The way in which the commission had been given credence, for example, provoked annoyance: 'We lily-livered Guatemalans really have no dignity at all if we can't stop and say "Hang on a minute: if they're going to sign some piece of nonsense, they should be asking us about it first."'[30] Critics expected the commission to weaken rather than strengthen Guatemala's institutions and to bend to the specific interests of its supporters.[31] They feared it would have too much power inside the domestic system and that its

[28] Rosales (2004).     [29] Minondo Ayau (2004b).
[30] Luis Enrique Pérez (2004).     [31] See e.g. Figueroa (2004), Zapeta (2005b).

international staff would not have enough knowledge of local circumstances to function effectively.[32]

In the support frame, the focus, as explained before, was on safeguarding human rights activists from abuse by 'parallel powers'. These powers were presented as a major threat and were described as having connections to organized crime and exploiting state institutions for their own benefit.[33] The main victims of these CIACS, it was argued, were human rights activists:

As time has gone on, human-rights violators have developed ever stronger roots and these roots have worked their way down into dark, sanction-free domains of organized crime, making the task of breaking them down extremely complex. The situation at the moment is alarming – they are refusing to halt their absurd intimidation of indigenous people in the countryside, of human-rights activists, journalists, judges, prosecutors and key witnesses in judicial proceedings.[34]

As with CICIACS 1.0, this version of the commission was promoted as a protection mechanism. Attempts were made to counter the allegations of unconstitutionality in the media discourse, and the arguments about loss of sovereignty were condemned as nationalist and out of step with a globalized world: 'The claim that the institution of this commission violates sovereignty is pure jingoism. What sovereignty? When did we have any real sovereignty in this country?'[35] The commission, it was argued, would strengthen state institutions, not weaken them, and would bolster democracy.[36] The issue of the autonomous 'international prosecutor' was barely mentioned.

Constructive criticism was much rarer during this phase. Where it did occur, the arguments mounted against the commission coincided with those advanced in the resistance frame – but then went on to propose alternatives. Instead of creating new commissions, it was argued, the international community should strengthen local institutions.[37] Others called for the commission to be adapted to the local system, or for its mandate to be extended – if a commission was necessary, it should be one that looked beyond the narrow circle of human rights activists.[38]

---

[32] See e.g. Rosales (2004), 'Triunfo del estado de derecho' (2004).
[33] See e.g. Minondo Ayau (2004a), Monzón (2003).     [34] Ochaeta (2003).
[35] Colop (2004).     [36] See e.g. Ángel Albizures (2004).
[37] See e.g. Luis Enrique Pérez (2004).     [38] See e.g. 'Ventajas y riesgos' (2003).

The resistance frame was most prominent amongst members of Congress from the governing FRG and its coalition partners – in other words, amongst representatives of the rising elite. However, the old oligarchic elite were also sceptical in regard to the proposed body (Schünemann 2010a: 20). The CICIACS agreement was therefore given the thumbs-down by a number of parties in Congress. A change of administration (with the ascension of Óscar Berger, a representative of oligarchic interests, to the presidency) brought no shift in this negative stance. An ad hoc committee referred the matter to the Constitutional Court, via the Guatemalan president, and in August 2004, the court ruled CICIACS unconstitutional on the grounds that it was not a human rights instrument and was therefore not covered by Article 46 of the Guatemalan constitution, which accorded such instruments precedence over domestic law. The Court also argued that functions relating to independent investigation and prosecution could only be performed by state institutions. It did, however, rule as admissible a legal entity that could both assist the Public Prosecutor's Office in bringing a case and act as a *querellante adhesivo* – in other words, join in an existing case as a private prosecutor.[39]

In the run-up to the final political decision on CICIACS 2.0, the UN, along with the European and US ambassadors,[40] engaged in shaming tactics to ensure acceptance of the proposal.[41] According to the NGOs supporting the project, European and US diplomatic personnel made considerable use of this tactic behind closed doors, combining it with conditionality. The need for this kind of pressure increased when the Berger administration began its term of office in early 2004 and showed itself reluctant to lend any further support to the CICIACS proposal (WOLA 2008: 7).

To sum up: an initial design for a rule-of-law commission drawn up by Guatemalan human rights groups envisaged its task as the investigation of crimes committed against defenders of human rights. The commission was to work outside the Guatemalan legal system and its brief was to gather information, write reports and make recommendations to state institutions. This was, in other words, a 1990s-style rule-of-law commission. CICIACS 1.0 was inspired by external

---

[39] See Corte de Constitucionalidad (2004).
[40] See e.g. Guoz/Herrera (2003); Pérez/Rodríguez (2004); Nájera/ Barrilas (2004).
[41] See Martín P. Rodríguez (2004).

actors but not directed by them: in developing the scheme, domestic actors, communicating closely with their transnational network, drew both on 'best practice' in their own region and on the standards for human rights commissions prevalent in the 1990s. This 1990s-style proposal was, however, viewed critically by the UN, which, having consulted with domestic parties, proceeded to develop a new version of the commission – CICIACS 2.0 – designed to tally with the 'hybrid' paradigm of the 2000s. The government support given to this version was the result of considerable diplomatic pressure applied behind closed doors. The dominant mode of interaction was thus a conditionality-oriented one.

This second model of the commission was to work inside the Guatemalan legal system but investigate and prosecute cases independently. It was also mandated to propose reforms to Guatemalan legislation. Departing as it did from the focus on human rights activists, this model proved unacceptable to certain sections of the Guatemalan human rights community. It also elicited strong opposition from the governing FRG and from a great many conservative sectors of Guatemalan society. This resulted in a negative reception in Congress, after which CICIACS 2.0 went on to be definitively quashed by the Constitutional Court. CICIACS 2.0 had thus been rejected by the Guatemalan political system: the international donor community had tried to promote a 'hybrid' style of commission that did not have the full support either of the whole domestic human rights community or of the elite factions within Guatemalan society.

## Step 3: From Autonomy to Assistance

Amongst CICIACS support groups at both domestic and international level, this whole process proved instructive. It was clear that any new version of the commission would need to command the support of both government and a wider domestic constituency, implying a more flexible design (WOLA 2008: 14). Dialogue on the next remodelling of CICIACS – between the UN and the new government and between opposing blocs in the Guatemalan political system – was therefore more broadly based.

Some in the transnational human rights network concluded that the failure of the previous schemes was due to poor exposure amongst the population at large, the absence of any kind of pro-commission coalition within society and the lack of support for the 'international prosecutor' model. Outreach, they said, had been poor – social movements had not been included and there had been no support from the wider public (Ganovsky-Larsen 2007: 33). Both the format and the mandate of the previous models had been tailored to the agenda of a small group of human rights activists (int. 30 2010) and a broadening of the mandate from human rights to impunity more generally was seen by certain sections of the human rights network (including the influential Fundación Myrna Mack) as a necessary step in making the idea of the commission resonate with a wider constituency in Guatemala. There were others, however, who favoured a shift back to the CICIACS 1.0 model, with its focus on defending human rights defenders and exposing the connections between present-day groups and the past crimes of the civil-war period (ints. 13 2010; 44 2010). There was also a fear that the CICIACS model would be watered down in further negotiations.[42]

Effort was also required to keep the international support coalition together. Many countries believed that the attacks on human rights defenders were a phenomenon specific to the Portillo government and that the Berger administration would not be troubled by these kinds of problems (WOLA 2008: 9). Opening up the framing of the commission was therefore also, to some degree, a strategy to enhance international support in cases where the 'defence of human rights defenders' frame resonated less strongly with external actors. Thus, a more open frame chimed more closely with US foreign-policy concerns such as the advance of transnational crime – including drug trafficking – in Central America, and in 2006 the US administration renewed its support for the CICIACS proposal and offered financial backing for measures specifically targeted at organized crime.[43] Opinions at the UN, meanwhile, were mixed: at UN headquarters, the uncoordinated creation of investigative commissions in different departments of the UN led to a degree of scepticism vis-à-vis such instruments (int. 63 2011). All in all, then, it is clear that reinterpretation of the commission's mandate and format was a process that took place at international as well as domestic level.

---

[42] Samayoa in WOLA (2008: 11), Frank la Rue in Luisa F. Rodríguez (2006). See also int. 30 (2010).
[43] See Castellanos (2006); Martín P. Rodríguez (2006b).

The Berger administration (2004-8), mainly in the person of Vice President Eduardo Stein, showed an interest in giving the CICIACS proposal further thought following its rejection by the Constitutional Court. This decision was not due only to incentives and pressure from the international diplomatic community (int. 52 2011; WOLA 2008); the traditional elites' analysis of the Guatemalan domestic situation had also begun to evolve. The old oligarchy had become increasingly worried about the power shifts that were going on within the elite system and was trying to contain the indirect influence being exerted by emerging elites – whether in business or in organized crime – who lay beyond the old guard's control (Briscoe/Pellecer 2010: 25; International Crisis Group 2011b: 9; Schünemann 2010a: 19–20). One incentive for the Berger administration to reconsider CICIACS was therefore the idea of having an external tool with which it could refashion state structures in line with its own preferences – particularly as GANA, the governing party, had no majority in Congress.[44] If the commission was to satisfy this objective, however, it had to undergo considerable reshaping.

The Berger government entered into informal talks with the UN about the possibility of redesigning the commission[45] and in 2006 a revived UN expert mission consulted intensively with: 'the executive branch, Congress, the justice system, the Constitutional Court, the Human Rights Ombudsman, the National Civilian Police, the Army, political parties, unions, private sector organizations, media, human rights groups representatives, [and] indigenous organizations' (WOLA 2015a: 24). At the same time, Vice President Eduardo Stein began a process of consultation and lobbying – directed both at the various parties in Congress and at the human rights community – in which the shape of the commission's mandate was once again discussed.[46] Agency in this process lay to a much greater extent with the government than had been the case previously:[47] the administration conducted the dialogue with the UN and coordinated a large-scale campaign to persuade members of elite groups in Congress of the value of such a commission. Its preferred focus for the commission was organized

---

[44] GANA – Gran Alianza Nacional (Grand National Alliance). See int. 40 (2010).
[45] 'Remoará la Ciciacs' (2005).
[46] See International Crisis Group (2011b: 5), Mynor Enrique Pérez (2005), 'Ciciacs, a discussion' (2005).
[47] Martín P. Rodríguez (2006a).

crime and it lobbied for an advisory role for the commission and for capacity-building functions.[48] Most members of Congress objected to the preoccupation with human rights defenders and therefore took the same line.[49] Certain sections of Congress also had to be assured that the new commission would not have a 'transitional justice' bent and would not touch upon the matter of past crimes.[50]

In the subsequent negotiations with the UN,[51] the leeway for discussion of a new version of the rule-of-law commission was considerable, given that both groups were looking for a formula that would work in the Guatemalan context. The new design retained a 'hybrid' style. It embedded the commission even more deeply within the Guatemalan legal system and dispensed with its autonomous elements: the commission was to assist Guatemalan institutions but not have an independent prosecuting role.

A complete shift of focus from human rights and illegal groups to organized crime alone did not take place. Within the UN, this would have implied a shift of responsibility from the Department of Political Affairs, overseen by the secretary-general, to the Office on Drugs and Crime – a change the government preferred to avoid.[52] The compromise was a mandate formulated in terms that facilitated the inclusion of corruption and organized crime but retained a degree of linkage to human rights matters:

The fundamental objectives of this Agreement are: (a) *To support, strengthen and assist institutions* of the State of Guatemala responsible *for investigating and prosecuting crimes allegedly committed in connection with the activities of illegal security forces and clandestine security organizations and any other criminal conduct related to these entities* operating in the country, as well as identifying their structures, activities, modes of operation and sources of financing and *promoting the dismantling of these organizations* and the prosecution of individuals involved in their activities.[53]

When the revised body was unveiled in 2006, it bore the new title of 'International Commission against Impunity in Guatemala' (CICIG), underlining the shift in its mandate. CIACS were now defined more

---

[48] Int. 13 (2010).   [49] Paredes/Rodríguez (2006).   [50] Int. 58 (2011).
[51] The parties involved were the vice president's office, the Presidential Commission for Human Rights (COPREDEH), the UN Department for Political Affairs and the UN Office for Legal Affairs. See WOLA (2015a: fn. 151).
[52] Ints. 58 (2011) and 63 (2011).
[53] CICIG Agreement (2006: art. 1a), emphasis mine.

generally as groups that engaged in illegal acts affecting the exercise of civil and political rights and that had some link to state structures (art. 1d). Any focus on specific crimes against human rights groups was dispensed with.

The new design laid stress on capacity-building and did away with the elements of autonomy contained in the previous scheme. A special unit at the Public Prosecutor's Office was charged with bringing matters investigated by the commission to court. The commission itself would only be allowed to participate in legal proceedings as a private prosecutor (*querellante adhesivo*) and would only be able to do so if the matter bore some relation to its mandate and if the presiding judge approved (art. 3.1b). The legislative-reform mandate was retained and clauses were included which allowed the commission to recommend policy reforms, propose purges of public officials and participate in disciplinary proceedings (art. 3.1).

At an organizational level, it was envisaged that, over its lifetime, the commission would take on a total of ten to fifteen high-profile cases, with human rights being only one of several areas addressed – along with corruption, drug trafficking and organized crime.[54] The commission was to be funded by voluntary contributions from UN members and would be staffed by a mixture of international and domestic experts operating under the guidance of a UN-appointed commissioner.[55]

The commission thus became 'a complement to the State of Guatemala rather than an independent tribunal' (Carvill 2009; see also WOLA 2008: 7–13). The strong focus on human rights violations was lost and the mandate was set much wider in regard to the kinds of 'crimes' committed by CIACS and the decision as to which cases should be investigated (see Table 6.4). Compared with CICIACS 2.0, CICIG had a quite distinctive character:

CICIG is more rooted within the local legal system than UN hybrid tribunals, but gives the international community a more systematic influence over local institutions than technical assistance programmes. CICIG is also unusual as it maintains the investigatory powers associated with a prosecutor, but it

[54] Int. 63 (2011).
[55] It did not become an official UN body, however, because the UN's legal department was worried about the budgetary implications (ints. 10 2010; 58 2011).

Table 6.4 *The CICIG: reshaping the standards of the 2000s*[56]

| | Hybrid commissions – 2000s | CICIACS 2.0 | CICIG |
|---|---|---|---|
| Matter | Violation of international human rights law during/ after civil war | CIACS and their human rights violations<br>Legislative provisions | CIACS and associated crimes |
| Mandate | Investigation/ investigation and prosecution<br>Capacity-building (training and assisting domestic judicial personnel) | Investigation and prosecution of CIACS<br>Investigation of CIACS attacks on HR defenders and deleterious effect of CIACS on state capacity to protect human rights<br>Reform of legislation on organized crime | Assist Guatemalan state in investigating and prosecuting CIACS and associated crime<br>Strengthen institutions<br>Assist in the reform of legislation on organized crime |
| Institutional setting | Operates inside domestic legal system but autonomously | Operates inside domestic legal system but autonomously<br>Small commission<br>2-year mandate, extendable<br>One commissioner | Operates inside domestic legal system but has no power to prosecute independently<br>Small commission<br>Works closely with special unit in office of Public Prosecutor<br>2-year mandate, extendable<br>One commissioner |

lacks independent prosecutorial powers and must act within the Guatemalan judicial system (Hudson/Taylor 2010: 3).

[56] CICIG Agreement (2006).

Despite the substantial reshaping, strong opposition to the commission persisted and the resistance frame through which this operated was similar to that used during the contestation regarding CICIACS. The shift from independent prosecution to assistive legal role got barely a mention and the commission continued to be presented as an international prosecuting body intervening in domestic affairs.[57] The predominant feeling was one of fear of being subject to outside interference and not having any voice or influence in the international community.[58] On top of this came the legal argument about the commission's unconstitutionality:

Surrendering sovereignty is tantamount to allowing individuals outside our electoral system to take decisions for us. Politicians from Norway or Japan should not be allowed to determine public policy in Guatemala, because they can impose burdens on us without suffering the consequences themselves.[59]

The democratic ownership of the process by which CICIG had been developed was called into question: 'If the executive is now to determine the actions of the legislature, and is to do so with New York's help, there is no point in having a Congress.'[60]

In the earlier phases, the international donor community had not figured as a key player in discussions, but this changed significantly during debates on CICIG. The United States was portrayed as the chief external actor, resorting to threats and sanctions to get CICIG established. It was criticized for its intervention in domestic political decisions (the sovereignty problem) and for its breach of fairness norms. A particular bone of contention was the power asymmetry between the two states as well as the complete disregard shown by the United States for Central American opinions – concerning US migration policy, for example, 'It would be good to hear one or other of the 158 honourable members of the Guatemalan Congress putting the US government on notice that the country will not be participating in any regional security agenda until [the United States] has passed the law on migration.'[61] The United States was also depicted as one of the principal causes of various security-related problems in Guatemala: in the case of drug

---

[57] See e.g. Figueroa (2006); Minondo Ayau (2007b).
[58] See e.g. Ríos de Rodríguez (2006); Preti (2007a).
[59] Ríos de Rodríguez (2006).   [60] Zapeta (2007b).
[61] The op-ed from which this quote is taken does not in fact openly oppose CICIG: Mérida (2007).

trafficking, for example, critics pointed out that 'if there were no demand (US), there would be no supply (drug traffickers)'.[62]

Within the resistance frame, there was considerable preoccupation with historical experiences of peacebuilding in Guatemala and elsewhere. MINUGUA in particular was condemned as a failed enterprise that had brought no positive change to the country. Its staff were portrayed as indolent leftists with a penchant for the good life and it was accused of acting as a parallel executive, controlling the operations of the Guatemalan government – just as the future rule-of-law commission would do.[63] Peacebuilding activities and interventions in other countries – those of the UN in Haiti, for example, or of the United States in Iraq – were also cited as warnings of the failure that could be expected from a strategy of external state-building and democratization.[64]

Any kind of constructive-criticism frame at work in this phase was much less coherent in form. The main arguments against the commission centred on its purported lack of independence and the lack of local knowledge from which staff on an international commission would suffer. The chances of bringing any real change to Guatemalan institutions were considered minimal. Writers in this frame were also concerned about scope, and, as in the first phase, called for a mandate that went beyond support for human rights groups only.[65] In addition, they said, the commission should be adapted to the Guatemalan system and its problems. One new aspect was the emphasis on accountability: if a commission was inevitable, remarked a number of op-eds, then it must have better mechanisms for ensuring accountability.[66]

In the support frame, the central framing of the mandate shifted significantly to accommodate the new aim of broadening the support base for the commission. Whereas opponents generally focused on the ways in which CICIG would weaken state institutions, supporters presented it as helping to underpin these and foster trust in them.[67] The situation was so desperate, claimed supporters, that arguments about 'sovereignty' and 'dignity' must be set aside and international help must be sought.[68] Guatemala's long experience of international development aid was invoked and CICIG was framed as a technical instrument on a par with other types of technical development aid:

---

[62] Minondo Ayau (2007a).    [63] See e.g. Preti (2007b); Jacobs (2007).
[64] See e.g. González Merlo (2007).
[65] See e.g. Mayora Alvarado (2007); Preti (2006).    [66] See e.g. Zapeta (2007a).
[67] See e.g. Gálvez Borrell (2007), La Rue (2007).    [68] See e.g. Arévalo (2006).

Guatemala is already host to international technical assistance missions in the fields of health, agriculture, education and food security. Why should it not also have a technical-assistance body to support the justice system?[69]

The reshaping of the commission was praised as an example of successful adaptation to local conditions.[70] Rather than being presented as a means of combating CIACS and defending human rights defenders, CICIG was spoken of exclusively from within an organized-crime frame. Organized crime was no longer linked to the political agendas of parallel powers deriving from the civil war. It was now presented as transnational in scale; the forces that drove it (drug trafficking) lay outside Guatemala and were linked to terrorism.[71] The victims here were not human rights activists: impunity was the major threat and affected everyone's security:

The majority (politicians or otherwise) are no longer interested in activists. Their object is to build up criminal networks based on terror, disregard for life and the profligate use of resources to buy or intimidate officials at every level ... Nowadays, the cause of our concern is not an army engaged in murder and repression, or a brutal guerrilla force busy liquidating members of the business community. What really has our country stalemated – checkmated almost – is organized crime.[72]

Although they remained a major component in the official CICIG mandate, CIACS, as a left-over of the civil war and as a prime focus of the commission's activities, had virtually disappeared from the rhetoric.

This overall shift in framing is mirrored in the commission's change of name, which implied a move from a project designed to benefit human rights activists to one designed to benefit the public as a whole: 'To begin with, the name was thought of in terms of protection for human-rights defenders, judicial personnel and journalists. Now, the main idea is the guaranteed exercise of fundamental rights in all sectors.'[73] Although created to investigate a small number of high-profile cases, the commission was thus framed as combating a more generalized impunity, arising from organized crime, and as doing so for the population as a whole.

---

[69] La Rue (2007).
[70] See e.g. 'Calvario de CICIG' (2007); 'Cicig, un debate' (2007).
[71] See e.g. 'Plausible apoyo' (2006), Porras (2007).   [72] Valenzuela (2007).
[73] Frank la Rue in López (2006). See also Preti (2006).

Even after this explicit reframing and reshaping, the ratification process in Congress did not prove easy, dragging on for nine months. After a number of delays, the Foreign Relations Committee sent the agreement to the Constitutional Court to rule on its constitutionality – which, in this instance, it duly confirmed.[74] CICIG then became the major bone of contention in the subsequent presidential campaign. Both leading candidates – Otto Pérez Molina of the Patriotic Party (Partido Patriota, PP) and Álvaro Colom of National Unity of Hope (Unidad Nacional de la Esperanza, UNE) – endorsed the CICIG agreement, but it continued to be hotly debated in the relevant Congressional committee and was ultimately rejected there. Finally, after a scandal involving the murder of three Salvadorean congressmen and their driver by Guatemalan police had opened up a window of opportunity, a coalition of Congressional representatives scheduled a plenary vote on CICIG. Dramatic scenes ensued but a two-thirds majority[75] was secured and the agreement was approved.[76] Since adoption, the commission's initial mandate of two years has been extended four times by the UN and the Guatemalan Congress and is currently due to expire in 2017.

Because of the much broader dialogue that preceded it – encompassing external actors, Guatemalan human rights groups and domestic oligarchic elites – CICIG had much more of an air of compromise than earlier versions of the commission. Final adoption was not possible without a degree of conditionality, but this was aimed not at the government but at possible veto players in Congress.[77] A number of organizations and platforms issued public statements of support,[78] and members of the US Congress[79] praised the initiative and warned opponents of negative consequences if they voted against it. Although the open opposition elicited by this external activity led to greater caution

---

[74] Corte de Constitucionalidad. Expediente 791–2007.

[75] Required to override the decision of the Foreign Affairs Committee to reject the agreement.

[76] Pérez Molina and Colom both ignored a bomb threat to the Congress building and forced their parties into the chamber en bloc to vote for the CICIG agreement.

[77] Int. 16 (2010).

[78] The list here included the Inter-American Commission on Human Rights; a group of forty-four European, US and Canadian NGOs; and the European Parliament. See WOLA (2008: 13); European Parliament (2007).

[79] Senator Patrick Leahy and Congressmen Eliot Engel, both involved in work on Latin America (WOLA 2008: 12).

in the public discourse of outside supporters – notably members of the US government – President Bush himself endorsed CICIG during his visit to Guatemala in March 2007. As WOLA (2008: 13) observes: 'If backing had once been discreet, it was now open and emphatic.'

To sum up: the UN and certain sections of the domestic support coalition moved in the direction of renegotiation, recognizing that other sectors of society – notably critical elite groups – needed to be brought onside and involved. The mode of interaction here was therefore much more persuasion-oriented. The commission was reshaped in line with the main points of contention and its brief was changed to one of assistance to Guatemalan institutions in the tasks of investigation and prosecution. The purview was extended beyond human rights to problems of organized crime, drug trafficking and corruption – a shift mirrored in the change of name from 'Commission to Investigate Illegal Groups' to 'Commission against Impunity'. CICIG was thus the first UN-supported post-conflict rule-of-law commission explicitly to take on the issue of organized crime. In its reshaped form, the commission resonated more strongly with the Guatemalan elites' notion of sovereignty and with the public's major preoccupations – impunity, organized crime and the threat to security. A learning process thus took place in regard to leeway. Whereas during the negotiations on CICIACS 2.0 the UN and the domestic support coalition had ignored concerns about the institution of an independent international prosecutor, when it came to reshaping the latter document into CICIG, it showed itself more heedful of such anxieties. The discussions took CICIACS 2.0 as their starting point, but the UN allowed for deviation and took on board the need to consider the issue with wider sections of society and to adapt proceedings to the domestic discourse. Given that the standards here were of very low precision, there was considerable room for manoeuvre in regard to the exact institutional set-up to opt for within the parameters of the 'hybrid' script for rule-of-law commissions.

### CICIG in Action: Security for All?[80]
The perception and framing of CICIG as a commission that would ensure 'security for all' was at odds with what negotiators had

---

[80]  Implementation in the case of CICIG differs from that in the other two cases in that what is implemented is an international commission. Nonetheless, translation processes are observable here too.

envisaged. In fact, CICIG was originally designed to take on only a small number of high-profile cases and to do no more than demonstrate the possibility of professional-level investigation and prosecution within the Guatemalan system. This reframing of CICIG in general discourse – at odds with its actual translation into law – involved the commission in a major struggle to satisfy the resultant expectations during translation into implementation.

The first phase of implementation of CICIG saw considerable time being devoted to the establishment of institutional structures and the development of mechanisms of cooperation with state institutions (CICIG 2010: 5).[81] Gradually, however, the commission grew and as of 2013, CICIG had 162 staff – seventy-two people in substantive positions, twenty-eight in administration and sixty-two in security-related posts.[82] A little more than half were Guatemalan and most of the rest came from other countries in Latin America.[83] In addition, since 2007 the commission has had three commissioners. The first was Carlos Castresana, a Spanish prosecutor specializing in human rights, organized crime and corruption. He was replaced in 2010 by Francisco Dall'Anese, a former Costa Rican attorney general with a special interest in organized crime. The latest incumbent, appointed in 2013, is Iván Velásquez Gómez, a former investigating magistrate with the Colombian Supreme Court.

The commission had to play a difficult double role in its work: on the one hand, it conducted investigations and assisted the Public Prosecutor's office in bringing cases to court; on the other, it was expected to make recommendations in regard to legislative and institutional reform. In other words, it had to push politically for reform whilst collaborating closely with state institutions. Having no enforcement mechanism, the commission was obliged to rely on the goodwill of local actors in its work with Guatemalan institutions (Schünemann 2010a: 7, 17). However, this goodwill tended to fluctuate according to domestic political dynamics and the dissension between the elites.

---

[81] CICIG is not a UN mission and this made the process of recruitment more complicated. Despite its non-UN status, CICIG does, however, have the support of the UN General Assembly (2009).

[82] CICIG's funding is provided by: Canada, Denmark, Spain, Finland, Germany, Ireland, Italy, the Netherlands, Norway, Sweden, the United Kingdom, the United States and the European Union (CICIG 2013: 4).

[83] See CICIG (2015: 6).

The conflictive public debate around CICIG continued and the commission's activities prompted regular surges of rejection, often in relation to specific cases being investigated by CICIG. This embroiled the commission in political squabbles and reduced it to the status of just another domestic player – so much so that even some sections of the support coalition began to wonder if it was involving itself too deeply in political manoeuvrings (Schünemann 2010a: 24). The need constantly to strike a balance – effecting internal change without losing international support – made the job of the CICIG commissioner a particularly delicate one: Carlos Castresana left the post after precipitating a major crisis by claiming that a nominee for the post of public prosecutor had links with criminal networks;[84] Francisco Dall'Anese, for his part, quit following CICIG's public pronouncements on the trial of Ríos Montt for genocide (see Section 3.1) and the adverse reaction these had elicited from Guatemalan public figures.[85]

As regards interaction with the international donor community, no major shift is observable during implementation. Foreign ambassadors in the country gave official support to CICIG's reform agenda and practical work, and because almost all the countries of Europe and North America were involved with CICIG, it became a kind of 'donor harmonization' project (Hudson/Taylor 2010).[86] At the same time, diplomats had to act as a buffer between CICIG and the Guatemalan actors, lobbying behind closed doors for the reforms which the commissioner was demanding in public (int. 30 2010). Some UN agencies, meanwhile, fearing a complete securitization of the UN agenda in Guatemala, were reluctant to accept CICIG leadership in the beginning. All in all, external actors found themselves having to learn the rules of a new and complex game of interaction that was centred on CICIG and was liable to result in a powerful backlash from elite groups in cases where they felt threatened by CICIG activity. Most recently, the question of the renewal of CICIG's mandate has triggered a major domestic debate

---

[84] This was not the only reason for his resignation: a major campaign had been conducted against him in the Guatemalan press and there had been some unhappiness with his work amongst the international community (int. 58 2010).

[85] 'Francisco Dall'Anese renunciará' (2013).

[86] CICIG brought all the ambassadors together in a joint project (ints. 1 2009; 2 2009).

and international donors have openly applied pressure on the Guatemalan president to get him to support an extension.[87]

CICIG's formal mission is to solve high-impact cases and build capacity. Its work is currently held up as proof that such cases can be successfully investigated, but whilst the commission's effectiveness in investigative work may have been demonstrated, there is as yet no evidence that this work leads to conviction in the Guatemalan courts.

The type of investigative activities opted for also reflects the overall reshaping of the commission's mandate. The central hypothesis advanced from the very start of discussions on a rule-of-law commission – namely, that networks left over from the civil war had mutated into organized-crime groups which specifically targeted defenders of human rights – has never been proved, and this 'political' element has played a minor role in the commission's work. What has happened, rather, is that a whole range of issues – extra-judicial killings, smuggling, drug trafficking – have been investigated and this probing has revealed how state structures and organized-crime networks intermesh and cooperate (CICIG 2012: 3; 2013: 21). Key cases investigated by CICIG include that of extra-judicial killings at Pavon prison, in which high-ranking members of the Berger administration were implicated. CICIG investigation led to the capture of members of one of the major drug-trafficking clans in eastern Guatemala (headed by Haroldo Mendoza). The commission was also involved in the notorious Rosenberg affair, where its investigation prevented the Colom administration from descending into chaos.[88] Equally high profile was its break-up of an extortion ring operating out of a Guatemalan prison (the Byron Lima case).[89]

Corruption has also become an increasingly prominent focus of the commission's work, with the latest commissioner arguing that, instead of concentrating on CIACS, CICIG should turn its investigative attention to so-called Illicit Political-Economic Networks (Redes Político-Económicas Ilícitas) and their involvement in contraband, illegal campaign financing and judicial and administrative corruption. The direct discursive link from the commission's mandate back to the post-peace agenda and human rights has gradually dissolved and been replaced by a discursive

---

[87]　Reynolds (2015); Schlesinger (2015).

[88]　Rodrigo Rosenberg, a lawyer and member of the traditional elite, had organized his own death at the hands of hitmen and left a videoed message blaming his 'murder' on the then president, Álvaro Colom.

[89]　For details of these high-profile cases, see WOLA (2015).

preoccupation with corruption and concomitant financial flows and economic substructure.[90] One case in line with this shift was the accusation of former president Alfonso Portillo of committing embezzlement. Later cases concerned corruption in Congress and fraudulent activity in the Guatemalan Institute of Social Security. Of much greater impact was the commission's investigation of a tax-fraud scheme allegedly managed personally by President Otto Pérez Molina and his vice president.[91] Both were forced to resign and are now awaiting trial.[92] As of 2013, CICIG had investigated 150 cases and had been auxiliary prosecutor in fifty (WOLA 2015: 16). What had originally been planned as a small-scale commission with a short-term mandate had assumed rather more extensive proportions.

Although these cases have had a major impact on Guatemalan political discourse and political life, the number of successful convictions in the Guatemalan courts has remained very low, even where CICIG was involved as an auxiliary prosecutor. Practice shows that working within the domestic legal system imposes severe constraints and over the last few years CICIG has concentrated specifically on highlighting the dependency and resultant partiality of the Guatemalan judiciary.[93] Case selection has been another bone of contention: which clandestine networks will be investigated, and therefore which elite-groups will be put at risk, are matters of huge political import.[94] Modernizing Guatemalan legislation also fell within CICIG's mandate. Although it had no power to actually table new legislation, the commission, working through a technical unit specializing in law on organized crime, designed legislative-reform packages and rewrote draft

---

[90] See CICIG (2015: 13–14); International Crisis Group (2016: 6).
[91] On subsequent developments, see 'Bad apples everywhere' (2016).
[92] For details, see International Criminal Group (2016).
[93] CICIG (2012: 40; 2013: 35).
[94] Some observers claim that CICIG initially deliberately focused on corruption under the Portillo government – i.e. on the corrupt networks operated by the emerging entrepreneurial elites that made up the FRG – and neglected other clandestine security structures. They even claim this may have been done as a concession to the former Berger administration for having got CICIG through Congress (int. 2 2009). Some CICIG investigators themselves quit their jobs over the lack of action against the oligarchic elites, the mainstay of the Berger administration (Schünemann 2010a: 21–2). However, under the next commissioner, Francisco Dall'Anese, evidence of wrongdoing by these elite groups – specifically extra-judicial killings – was made public, leading to enormous friction with members of the former Berger administration.

legislation (int. 44 2010). Areas covered by the packages which CICIG has drawn up since its establishment include reform of the penal code; the institution of a witness-protection programme; wire-tapping; organized crime; human trafficking; and constitutional reform. A small number of these draft laws went on to be adopted, but the majority – including those dealing with constitutional reform and the organic laws relating to the judiciary and police that were crucial to CICIG's own functioning and to the overall fight against impunity – were blocked by Congress (CICIG 2013: 31–2). Again, although CICIG's many thematic reports – on illegal adoption, for example, on the financing of political campaigns, and on the judicial selection process – have increased public scrutiny of these matters (the campaigns regarding elections to the Supreme Court in 2009 and 2014 are a case in point) and have flagged up areas for political reform, fundamental changes are still awaited in all these domains.

One of CICIG's early tasks was to scrutinize the qualifications and past activities of government officials and police officers. Although these investigations led to the forced resignation of a significant number of prosecutors and the expulsion of 1,700 police officers, it is generally believed that the Guatemalan state institutions continue to be steeped in corruption and dominated by clandestine networks (Hudson/Taylor 2010: 17–18).

Interaction between CICIG and state institutions has varied in quality. On the one hand, there have been constant changes in top-level staff at the Ministry of the Interior and the National Police – often because of corruption or other criminal activity – and this has hampered the consolidation of working relations (CICIG 2010: 11). Work with the police has produced very little in the way of functioning working relationships or joint investigative enterprises (CICIG 2013: 4; International Crisis Group 2010: 21).[95] One the other hand, CICIG has established, and works closely with, a special investigative unit in the Public Prosecutor's Office. The unit's staff, handpicked and trained by CICIG, work in isolation from the rest of the Public Prosecutor's personnel (int. 44 2010, CICIG 2010: 11; Schünemann 2010a: 22). In addition, several specialized departments have been set up, with staff trained to carry out professional investigative work (CICIG 2013: 5).

---

[95] CICIG's international staff say they are unable to trust local staff completely (International Crisis Group 2010: 21).

The result has been a marked professionalization of prosecutorial work in units that cooperate with CICIG: techniques have shifted from individual to group investigation and increasing use has been made of scientific evidence, witness protection and plea bargaining. At the same time, however, the more generalized modernization of prosecutorial work has stalled as a result of – amongst other things – budgetary constraints (International Crisis Group 2016: 16).

In domestic discourse on CICIG, elite conflict came to loom less large, and in the support frame there was increased emphasis on the reframing of CICIG as a means of generating security for all.[96] Stress was laid in particular on the demonstrative effects of CICIG:

CICIG created a space for hope in Guatemala and showed that a whole host of what we thought were insurmountable obstacles in the fight against the mafia are actually not insurmountable at all. We now know that it is possible to see solid investigations through to a successful conclusion, assemble a convincing body of scientific evidence and organize successful police-operations that culminate in the arrest of suspects.[97]

Organized crime was increasingly mentioned in conjunction with state corruption.[98] Despite the fact that investigation of groups classed as CIACS was still officially part of the CICIG mandate, as the commission's work developed, the term gradually disappeared from the media discourse. Although increasingly framed as an assistive body, the commission was seen by some as a substitute for dysfunctional domestic institutions, or was expected to undertake a reorganization of Guatemalan institutions and powers. The perception of CICIG as a substitute even began to worry the commission itself. Guatemalan society, it said, needed to understand that the work of CICIG was intended to support the work of the Public Prosecutor's Office and not the other way round. Guatemalans would then feel able to look to the prosecutor or other responsible body for answers and cease to view CICIG as the source of solutions to all the country's problems with security, justice and impunity (CICIG 2010: 8). The successful investigation of the Rosenberg incident – which had brought the administration of former president Álvaro Colom to the brink of collapse – played a major role in fostering over-reliance on CICIG during its early years, the belief being that it was the only institution capable of making justice

---

[96] Analysis of the media discourse ends in 2010.   [97] Fernández (2010).
[98] See e.g. Ruano (2010), 'La CICIG debe continuar' (2009).

a reality (International Crisis Group 2010: 21). In 2015, following the disclosures associated with the La Linea corruption case, in which the president himself was implicated, CICIG was rated by the Guatemalans as being the most trusted of a variety of institutions (66 per cent said they had confidence in it – a score that put it ahead even of the Churches).[99] CICIG's shift of focus to corruption appears to have particular resonance in Guatemalan society (it even brought the conservative business sector on board). The extent of public reaction which the corruption charges triggered in summer 2015, with mass mobilization and public demonstrations calling for the president's resignation, surprised many political observers. CICIG and its activities featured prominently in the slogans deployed at these events. Some fear, however, that this focus on corruption fosters the widespread Guatemalan 'anti-politics' stance, with its general scepticism of state institutions and fiscal practices. Symptomatic of this tendency, some observers believe, was the election of a political outsider – the former comedian Jimmy Morales – to the Guatemalan presidency in 2015 (see debates in International Crisis Group 2016: 10).

In the period up to 2010, the resistance frame had become less widespread and its focus had shifted to CICIG's lack of accountability and neutrality.[100] After this date, by contrast, the commission's strategies and political statements began once again to elicit criticism, even amongst domestic allies.[101] Prior to 2010 also, the 'constructive criticism' frame had largely disappeared – although former partners from the support group who were dissatisfied with the way the commission had been reshaped did express concern, notably about the close cooperation with state institutions:

It also silences the voices of people who, because of the history of terror associated with the internal armed conflict, have a right to object to the actions of the state. The lesson delivered by international bodies, by countries interested in clarifying some deed or other is a brutal and negative one, because (...) resolving the case will strengthen the country's political power set-up.[102]

These groups also expressed disappointment when the close cooperation they hoped for between the commission and civil-society

[99] See 'Cicig, institución mejor valorada' (2015).
[100] See e.g. Zapeta (2010), Minondo Ayau (2010).
[101] See e.g. Bargent (2013).   [102] Argueta (2010).

groups did not materialize (int. 40 2010; International Crisis Group 2011a: 10).

As a reaction to the commission's rapid growth and complex political role, the third phase of implementation saw UN headquarters and international donors lay greater stress on capacity-building and local ownership (int. 63 2011) and the international donor community began to promote the 'assistive' set-up as the most appropriate for rule-of-law commissions in general. The commission's reshaped mandate thus became the new model for commissions of this kind. UN member states were introduced to it in both New York and Vienna, after which a number of them expressed interest in establishing a mechanism of this kind.[103] In 2010 or thereabouts, several other Central American countries publicly mooted the idea of local or regional versions of the commission.[104] Ultimately, however, practical experiences with the CICIG's institutional model demonstrated the many conflicts it triggered with domestic elites,[105] making it less attractive to Guatemala's neighbours.

The debate regained momentum after the events of 2015, when, as explained previously, President Otto Pérez Molina and Vice President Roxana Baldetti were forced to step down in the wake of public protest at their involvement in a tax racket. The United States now declared CICIG to be an important institutional model for the Central American region in the fight against corruption.[106] El Salvador, for its part, rejected US suggestions that it implement a similar measure. The Honduran government, by contrast, was forced to give in to pressure at home and abroad following the uncovering of a major corruption scandal. In concert with the OAS, it established the Misión de Apoyo contra la Corrupción y la Impunidad en Honduras (MIACCIH).[107] Rather than replicating the CICIG's institutional set-up, however, this body relies on the 'old' template of an external investigative commission mandated to make recommendations and engage in capacity-building.

---

[103] See WOLA (2015a: fn. 171).
[104] Guatemala, El Salvador and Honduras considered a regional commission based on CICIG. Use of the model for individual countries was also discussed. See e.g. Valladares (2010) and Schünemann (2010b).
[105] See e.g. International Crisis Group (2011b); WOLA (2015).
[106] See Renteria (2015); Tabory (2015).
[107] See OAS (2016). Also Flores/Magallanes (2016).

The upshot is that, although the model has not yet been directly applied anywhere else, its local incarnation has influenced international discourse on further applications and on scripts and best practices for rule-of-law commissions overall. The idea of this kind of 'locally owned' commission, exercising an assistive function and embedded within domestic structures, resonated widely within more general UN discourse. In addition, the Guatemalan commission's stronger focus on corruption, organized crime and clandestine networks as entities independent of civil war has been welcomed as a valuable contribution to developments in this area.[108]

Implementation of the CICIG agreement ultimately brought with it a great many problems. Although the commission's investigative work was moderately successful, achievements in terms of final sentencing in the Guatemalan courts, legislative reform and capacity-building – considered the commission's most important task – were meagre. In public discourse, emphasis on the demonstrative effects of CICIG's work, coupled with a shift of focus to emblematic corruption cases, fostered some positive responses amongst the population, but despite its framing as an assistive body, the commission came to be seen by supporters as a potential substitute for the state in this area. This shift was paralleled in changes to the format, orientation and practices of the commission as originally envisaged: from a small-scale body taking on a modest number of cases for demonstrative purposes and engaging mostly in capacity-building, CICIG ballooned in size and multiplied its activities. To counter this trend, international discourse shifted to much greater stress on local ownership. The assistive framework, together with the new focus on corruption and organized crime, was now presented as the way to success for rule-of-law commissions. What CICIG's long-term impact will be on state institutions, in terms of capacity-building, remains to be seen.

## 6.3 Reshaping a Rule-of-Law Commission in Guatemala

This chapter has explored the evolution and translation of scripts for rule-of-law commissions in post-conflict states. During the 2000s, these

---

[108] See the UN's own description of CICIG: 'Road to Justice: A Novel Approach to Fight Crime and Impunity', www.un.org/en/events/tenstories/08/justice.shtml, accessed 20 June 2015. Also: Schünemann (2010b: 18).

scripts underwent considerable change: whereas external information-gathering bodies working in the area of transitional justice and human rights had been the norm in 1990s, the 2000s saw the emergence of hybrid commissions which, whilst retaining the focus on human rights violations, worked from within the domestic legal system exercising some combination of investigative and prosecutorial functions.

The first model for a commission – CICIACS 1.0 – was developed *from below* by the human rights community and was based on a 1990s' script for regional human rights commissions. It took the form of an independent fact-finding and information-gathering body charged with investigating the so-called CIACS – networks left over from the civil war who perpetrated crimes against human rights activists. Rather than conforming to the models of norm diffusion currently posited, developments here took the form of a learning process in which local actors drew on global scripts and fed their proposed modifications back into the international debate via their requests to the UN for backing. Within the resistance frame, meanwhile, the proposed commission was portrayed as generating parallel institutional structures, breaching sovereignty and damaging Guatemalan pride.

In 2003, the UN remodelled CICIACS 1.0 in line with the 'hybrid' script for rule-of-law commissions that was then evolving at the global level. In its new incarnation, the commission was to be an autonomous investigative and prosecutorial body that would work on a small number of high-impact cases from within the Guatemalan legal system. It would still concern itself with CIACS and human rights violations but would not limit its focus to crimes against human rights defenders (Step 1). Following the application of considerable direct pressure behind closed doors – primarily by the United States but also by European countries – the government lent rhetorical support to the new model. However, CICIACS 2.0 provoked strong opposition from a number of elite groups and went on first to be rejected by Congress and ultimately, in 2004, to be declared unconstitutional by the Guatemalan Constitutional Court (Step 2).

Rejection of the second model by the Guatemalan political system prompted a more deliberative process between the UN, the Guatemalan government and the relevant sectors (Step 3). This process, directed by the Guatemalan government, led to substantial reshaping of the 'hybrid' script. The commission was remodelled into an assistive body with functions intended to help strengthen the state. The autonomous prosecutorial powers were removed and although the mandate retained its focus on CIACS, it did so mostly to ensure continued cooperation with UN headquarters, which required that the commission have a human rights framing. As the negotiating actors envisaged it, the commission would not just take on human rights cases but also look into organized crime, drug trafficking and corruption. In this substantially reshaped form, the proposal for the newly named CICIG made it successfully through Congress. In parallel with these developments, a process of reinterpretation and reframing was going on in the pro-commission media discourse. Although officially its mandate still centred on CIACS, CICIG was presented in public discourse as a body fighting the whole of organized crime for the whole of the population.

In terms of policy-making and institutional cooperation, translation into implementation was only partially successful. Investigation produced some good results, but the 'embedded prosecution' design met with little success. CICIG then underwent further reshaping of an informal kind: instead of focusing on capacity-building and taking on a small number of cases for purely demonstrative purposes, it sought to tackle impunity across the board and as a consequence ballooned in size and took on many more cases than envisaged. This was also done in response to expectations that had arisen within the domestic support frame, where demonstrative activity and the pursuit of corrupt high-ranking politicians had worked all too well and CICIG, in reality an assistive body, was now regarded by some as a potential replacement for Guatemalan institutions. Strong expressions of dissent in the media became less common, but elites who felt under threat continued, at regular intervals, to call the commission into question. Doubt was increasingly cast on CICIG's accountability and neutrality and this led to efforts – by the UN and others – to emphasize CICIG's original objectives of capacity-building and capacity transfer.

The mode of interaction between the international community and the support coalition in Guatemala gradually changed as political discussions about the possibility of a rule-of-law commission progressed. During the first phase, the international community worked behind the scenes, using tactics of shaming and conditionality to get government actors onside. This first strategy was a failure. However, thanks to the institution of a prompter, more inclusive process of deliberation and negotiation – this time directed by the government – support was garnered for a new version of the commission. The UN allowed scope for

Table 6.5 *Stages in the translation of rule-of-law commissions in Guatemala*

| Translation | Resistance | Localization | Full adoption |
|---|---|---|---|
| Into discourse | Proposed activities condemned as illegal interference in state affairs (during translation into law) Criticized for lack of neutrality/ accountability (during translation into implementation) | Demand for mandate to be opened up and reshaped to suit Guatemalan system | Focus on protection of human rights defenders (phase 1) Emphasis on security for all and on role as assistant to/ substitute for the state (phase 3) |
| Into law | | Shift from international prosecutorial body to assistive commission with a focus on organized crime | |
| Into implementation | | Shift to tackling corruption in general | |

a body that was more in line with Guatemalan conceptions, and the activities of conditionality and persuasion used in this round were aimed less at the government but at potential veto players in the Guatemalan Congress. This mode of interaction remained in place during implementation – though the international community had to maintain a high level of persuasion and lobbying to ensure that CICIG continued to function, and diplomatic circles in particular had to mediate between CICIG and domestic political actors.

In sum, then, the reshaping process that transformed CICIACS into CICIG was the direct result of a shift in the mode of interaction towards dialogue and the provision of substantial scope for reshaping. The reshaping was possible because of the low precision of the global script and the considerable potential for adaptation offered by the 'hybrid' format. In contrast to the line of action adopted in the other cases under investigation in this study, the approach here was essentially one of 'trial and error'. The rethinking process resulted in a reshaped commission that moved away from the general human rights mandate and, rather than operating independently within the domestic legal system, had assistive status only. However, when implementation began, CICIG expanded rapidly and assumed far more responsibilities within the Guatemalan judicial system than had been envisaged when the commission was reshaped. To counter this trend in some measure, the original vision of CICIG – as a body that would engage in capacity-building and perform an ancillary role inside the domestic legal system – was lauded as the new international paradigm for rule-of-law promotion, based on local ownership and assistive function. The shift of emphasis onto organized crime and corruption, which decoupled the commission from an explicitly human rights–based agenda, was, likewise, hailed as a positive development (see Table 6.5). This, then, is the only one of the three cases examined here in which domestic translation had an impact (so far only discursive) in international diplomatic circles and the NGO domain.

# 7 | Towards an Interactive Perspective on Norm Translation

How do international rule-of-law promoters deal with the dilemma of balance between global norms and their local faces? And how do they react to specific domestic norm translations? Although there is apparent consensus that external actors have a notion as to what constitutes good or bad context-sensitive norm translation, systematic evidence here has so far been in short supply. There are certainly cases in which the international donors are critical of domestic translations – for example, where legislative bodies that have been reformed according to standards of liberal democracy are penetrated by patronage networks. On the other hand, there are times when external promoters of democracy appear to approve of and encourage adaptation to local context – the use of local ('traditional') mediation mechanisms in externally funded processes of transitional justice is a case in point. With these variations in mind, the core questions which this study has posed is: how does external rule-of-law promotion affect norm translation in post-conflict states and how does interaction over global norms and their local faces actually take place? These questions are of fundamental practical and theoretical relevance.

The study has looked at the translation of three rule-of-law norm sets of varying precision in post-conflict Guatemala. These related to children's rights, access to public information and scripts for post-conflict rule-of-law commissions. The findings clearly showed that the effect of external rule-of-law promotion on norm translation is not unidirectional. Rather, the process of interaction can prompt the norm promoters to change their approach, thus influencing the final outcome of translation. The overall pattern here is that of a 'feedback loop': international promoters begin by pressing for full adoption of global standards using a conditionality-oriented mode of interaction; in response to local interpretation and contestation, they shift to a more persuasion-oriented (and less transparent) style of interaction and allow more scope for discussion about local translation – the extent of that scope being determined by the degree of precision of the global norm set in question. Surprisingly, this approach is not, as the paradigm of 'context sensitivity' would lead one to assume, a consciously elaborated policy on the part of the external actors.

The present chapter summarizes the study's findings and draws out their implications for IR theory. It argues that a new type of norm research is called for – one that takes interaction seriously and examines the norm-translation process in the context of contested global orders.

## 7.1 Moving Norm-Translation Research Forward

This study has demonstrated the need for more interaction-based accounts of norm translation, of a kind that are currently lacking in norm research. The framework it posits offers a more comprehensive account than has existed previously of what happens to global norms in new contexts and it proposes a dynamic model of interaction and norm translation. This contrasts with the 'outside-in' perspective of the widespread norm-socialization approach, in which international norm promotion is generally seen as an independent variable influencing a dependent norm-diffusion outcome. Here, interaction between domestic context and international actors may occur, and the latter may adapt their strategies to the domestic situation, but only as a means to achieving full norm adoption. Localization research, meanwhile, fixes its attention on the dynamic between norm promotion and creative translation in the new context but tends to see localization primarily as a product of domestic agency. It too fails to take adequate account of the interactive nature of norm promotion. Moreover, neither approach has a systematic model for interpreting the results of norm translation.

Interaction has recently become a focus of research into peacebuilding and norm change, but accounts either mostly conceptualize it as a rational bargaining process or they largely disregard domestic translation in their studies on the cyclic contestation of norms, focusing instead on norm change at the international level.

Having highlighted the limits of these approaches (see Chapter 2), the present study has shown that the political discourse and political processes that take place in post-conflict countries in relation to norm translation influence the modes of interaction employed by external actors, resulting in joint translation of a kind that goes beyond mere rational bargaining with domestic elites. The case studies presented here have illustrated the way in which international actors become enmeshed, ad hoc, in domestic discourse, domestic frames and domestic contestation. They have shown how, in reaction, these actors shift to a more persuasion-oriented mode of interaction but at the same time seek both to retain control over the direction of domestic translation and to restrict the space allowed for it in line with the precision – that is to say, specificity and formality – of the international norm set in question. In other words, norm translation in post-conflict states does not begin with a *tabula rasa* and does not involve only local actors.

By analysing the pattern followed by interactive norm translation in all three cases under review – the 'feedback loop' – we can gain a number of valuable insights in terms of the theoretical debate about norm diffusion. These concern: (1) the role of domestic framing contests; (2) changes in the modes of interaction used by external rule-of-law promoters; (3) the non-formalized shift of such promoters to joint norm translation; (4) the part played by precision as a scope condition in determining the space available for joint norm translation; (5) the often neglected trend to informalization in the style of interaction used by external rule-of-law promoters; (6) the link between translation into discourse and law and translation into implementation; and (7) the re-translation of reshaped norms into international contexts.

## Frame Contests and Norm Translation

Translation of norms into discourse is an aspect often neglected in IR research, but the present study has shown that it plays a key role in shaping subsequent translation into law and into implementation (for a categorization of norm translation, see Chapter 2). This conclusion was reached chiefly by means of frame analysis. IR norm research makes frequent use of the concept of frames, which it has adopted from social-movement research.[1] In norm research, however, the focus is generally on how norm entrepreneurs frame norms in order to achieve their diffusion (Keck/Sikkink 1998; Price 1998) or on how international actors perceive domestic contexts and react to them (Autesserre 2010). Although there has recently been increased interest

---

[1]  For an overview, see Klotz/Lynch (2007: 51–6).

in polarized framing contests at the transnational level (Bob 2012; Payne 2001), no research has so far been done into conflicts between norm-related domestic frames and the effects of such conflicts on further translation.

In the cases under scrutiny here, *translation into discourse* was accompanied by the formation of frames centred respectively on rejection, constructive criticism and support of an externally promoted norm set (see Chapter 2). From analysis of these processes, a number of points emerged that may serve as a useful basis for further research in this field. First, frames were not stable but shifted over time and this influenced the direction of subsequent translation into law and into implementation. The framing of children's rights, for example, underwent fundamental change over the period of the study, loosening its ties with the overall democratization of the country and linking into a discourse of impunity. This resulted in considerable differences between the translation into law and the translation into implementation. The same correlation was observable in regard to the rule-of-law commission examined in the study. Second, although domestic frames always corresponded to some extent with themes in existing transnational frames, they never replicated them completely. Even in supportive frames, the domestic interpretations and meanings attached to specific global standards differed from those at global level. For example, the way in which domestic support groups in Guatemala initially interpreted children's rights and translated them into law – namely, as a right of children to protection against their own families – can only be understood against the background of Guatemala's experience of civil war and authoritarian government. Third, differences in the constellations of the various frames and the groups supporting them resulted in differences in the dynamics of interaction and of translation into law and implementation. The constellation of frames in the case of the right to access to information differed from that in the other two cases, in that two support groups were promoting a single norm set via different frames. This led to significant framing contests between the two groups but, perhaps surprisingly, to a lesser degree of reshaping during translation into law, because each set of frame supporters had its own priorities in regard to which standards could be reshaped.

There were some points on which the case-study findings tallied with existing research on framing and others where it did not. Consistent with previous studies, framing was found to be both a strategic device wielded by specific groups of actors and also a product of the broader discursive constellation in Guatemalan society. Its value as a *strategic tool* stemmed from its dynamic, adaptive character, which allowed it to evolve as debates about a particular norm proceeded and in reaction to opposing frames. In the discourse on the creation of a rule-of-law commission, for example, supporters of the commission acted in response to the arguments of the rejectionist frame – which presented the proposed body as seeking to supplant state institutions – and adjusted their own framing to make it more persuasive. In contrast to other studies, meanwhile, where a transnational element is identified in frame producers and promoters on both the rejectionist and supportive side (Bob 2012), analysis of the Guatemalan cases found this element to be confined largely to the supporting frames.

Framing contests in the Guatemalan cases were also influenced by *broader structural and discursive constellations* and by what might be termed meta-discourses, which shaped the specific debates about the norm sets. Translation into discourse, for example, was strongly dominated by elite frames – even where actor groups were involved who would regard themselves as progressive. In the case of children's rights frames, for example, there was virtually no mention of the situation of the indigenous population or of socio-economic issues (such as poverty or child labour) more generally. The main entry point to the debate was the issue of authoritarian family structures, and the discourse focused on the situation of middle- and upper-class children in the Guatemalan capital.

Translation into discourse in all three cases was also shaped by a broader meta-frame then dominating the Guatemalan public and media – that of impunity, crime and corruption. Linking norms to this meta-frame ensured greater prominence and in many cases prompted the government to act. A case in point was the debate on access to information, which only gained real attention when the norm set was framed more directly as a tool for improving transparency and fighting corruption. Again, in the case of the rule-of-law commission, a shift from a frame that stressed the latter's human rights responsibilities to one that stressed its role in protecting society as a whole from organized crime resulted in increased media support for the commission. With this meta-frame at work, certain standpoints became taboo. For example, whereas it was possible for politicians publicly to oppose access to information as a transitional-justice issue, public opposition to it as a transparency issue was more difficult.

## Feedback Loops: International Reaction to Contestation

Existing research on norm socialization on the one hand stresses the central role of conditionality in norm diffusion (Kelley 2004; Schimmelfennig et al. 2006) and on the other asserts that conditionality can achieve very little beyond the adoption of norms into law (Morlino/ Magen 2009b: 237, 42–43). Meanwhile, in the paradigm of 'context sensitivity' that currently dominates promotion of democracy and the rule of law, orientation to conditionality is frowned upon and the generation of local ownership is lauded as a means of securing lasting normative change (see Chapter 1). The empirical evidence presented in this study suggests that where norm promoters adopt a conditionality-oriented approach in order to secure full adoption of a norm, this in fact blocks further adoption into law. And yet, in contravention of the prevailing paradigm of context sensitivity, this is still the first strategy opted for by international norm promoters. In the situations described here, it was only after experiencing domestic rejection that the external rule-of-law promoters shifted to more persuasion-oriented modes of interaction.

This was the case in all three contexts studied here. Defying the prevailing paradigm of context sensitivity, international rule-of-law promoters began by attempting to secure full adoption of a set of global standards through conditionality-oriented interaction. On the one hand, they built coalitions with those elements in the country that supported a framing of the norm set similar to their own, thereby teaming up with existing domestic groups and supporting the creation of domestic partner organizations. At the same time, however, they applied more conditionality-oriented strategies against presumed veto players, including the domestic government. Congressional movement on ATI legislation, for example, was only achieved after a bout of alternate praising and shaming by the OAS Rapporteur and after threats of cuts in aid by the main donor forum in Guatemala. Again, in the case of the creation of a rule-of-law commission, the government was brought to the negotiating table through a mix of informal shaming and conditionality. In the case of children's rights, UNICEF and the donor forum employed a strategy of shaming and threatened aid cuts to move the legislative discussion forward. Besides all this, international actors supported the lobbying activities and media campaigns conducted by their domestic coalition partners and, crucially, exerted a major influence on the drafting process, which often took place in informal working groups. The Guatemalan Congress and government were rarely the real locus of political discussion or re-discussion.

Where the government saw rhetorical promotion of a norm set as an opportunity to 'look good' in the eyes of the international community, these strategies succeeded in moving legislation forward. They did not, however, succeed in ensuring its definitive adoption. The result, rather, was intense opposition – both to the substance of the norm sets in question and to the methods being used by the international actors and their domestic partners to get those norms adopted. In the case of children's rights, for example, approval of the relevant legislation by Congress sparked massive opposition in the religious and private sectors and the law became the focus of a polarized conflict over past events and future values in Guatemalan society. Again, the initial blueprint for a rule-of-law commission, which provided for the possibility of prosecution before domestic courts, was regarded with great suspicion by both the oligarchic and industrial elites of Guatemala. Opposition to legislation on access to information was less vocal, but the legislation itself was blocked by the military and the private sector.

In response to resistance of this kind, international actors changed their mode of interaction: in the case of children's rights, UNICEF shifted to a more inclusive dialogue process in its dealings with opposing groups; in the case of the rule-of-law commission, the support coalition opened a dialogue with the government about a new incarnation of the commission and made moves to win the support of sceptical sections of society and Congress; and in the case of access to information, the conflict between different support coalitions over the focus of ATI legislation led to new and more inclusive discussion and negotiation that also encompassed critical groups. In all three cases, conditionality and shaming continued to be used by international actors and their domestic partners as a means of getting Congress to adopt the reshaped versions of the legislation. However, interaction with many of those formerly regarded as veto players underwent a change – from being based on conditionality and shaming to being geared more to dialogue. Whether this new, persuasion-oriented mode of interaction constituted a form of arguing, or whether it was a type of 'vertical' teaching (on this distinction, see Chapter 2), is difficult to determine. Those involved in the interaction often differed on this point: former opponents of the children's rights proposals, for example, insisted that what they had taken part in was a process of arguing between equals, whereas members of the support coalition contended that the main approach was one of teaching. A similar constellation is observable in ATI promotion. By contrast, in the case of interaction on the rule of law, both norm promoters and former opponents described the nature of the interaction as that of a dialogue founded on mutual recognition.

## Joint Translation but No Formal Policy

In all three cases under review, the changes in modes of interaction resulted in the creation of spaces in which it was possible, through dialogue and negotiation between the agents of the major frames, to reshape the norm set in question – by omitting or modifying certain elements of it as it was translated into law.

Interaction went beyond mere 'rational bargaining' (for such a model, see Barnett/Zürcher 2009). According to this model, although acquisition of outside resources is of interest to elites in post-conflict states, the reforms expected in return are costly to them and present a threat to their interests and power base. In order to maintain local support and stability, peacebuilders therefore compromise on the extent of liberal reform demanded. In this model, domestic political processes and dis-courses around norm promotion have no dynamic influence on the negotiations between domestic elites and international actors. They do figure, but abstractly, as part of the costs which adoption occasions to domestic elites. This study too has shown that norm promoters make pragmatic decisions about the extent to which they can get global stan-dards translated into domestic law. However, as indicated in the preced-ing section, in the cases described, these decisions took place in a dynamic context of reaction to specific domestic discourse. The matter of which standards were translated and how can only be understood from the perspective of interaction of norm promotion and norm translation. By way of example: the debate on children's rights legislation had to address Guatemalan 'family values' – vigorously championed by the Guatemalan Churches – and subject this issue to serious discussion. Again, although the debate about a Guatemalan rule-of-law commission was dominated by specific elite concerns regarding independent interna-tional prosecution, the renewed negotiations on the commission were also shaped by broader public interpretations of the security threats facing the country.

Surprisingly, that there was, over and above this interaction, any formal policy for ensuring global norms with local faces – an aspiration to which all sorts of rule-of-law promoters lend at least rhetorical support – was not demonstrated in this study. In their rhetoric on outcomes, meaning essentially the reshaped global norms, external norm promoters at no point acknowledged that a translation had taken place and made no use of the 'global norms with local faces' metaphor. If a modification fell within their tolerances, it was described as 'full adoption' according to the international labelling; if it did not, it was condemned as an unacceptable deviation (a case in point is the specific regulation of confidential information in the ATI legislation). The results of the more dialogue-oriented re-drafting processes always fell within the tolerances, whereas later cuts made by Congress were mostly described as deviations. Two conclusions may be drawn from this: first, the approach of external actors to domestic translation was an ad hoc one, prompted by contestation and rejection; second, translation outcomes were never described as such by these actors.

## The Role of Precision

Another factor which a simple 'bargaining' account fails to take into consideration is the degree of precision of the norms in question and the part this plays in determining how much space for reshaping is accorded by external actors or found to be acceptable domestically. By taking this factor on board, the present study offers a basis for a more systematic definition of scope conditions for the outcomes of norm translation.

It is a central tenet of classical norm research that the more precise a norm set, the greater the chance of its being fully adopted and complied with (Finnemore/Sikkink 1998: 906–7; Legro 1997: 34) – though there are some who argue that the reverse is the case (Van Kersbergen/Verbeek 2007). This study has shown that the precision of a norm does indeed affect the degree to which it is modified during translation; but in the cases described, even high-precision norm sets underwent some modification and were thus not fully adopted.

Precision made itself felt in two ways during translation into law. The more specific the content of the norm set, the more rigid the 'text' on which discussions about reshaping were based. In addition, the level of normativity varied according to the formality of the source involved – international treaty, soft law or script – another criterion by which precision is defined. Thus, whilst a deviation from the CRC seemed difficult to justify, the space allowed for 'innovations' in the case of the rule-of-law commission was considerable.

The support coalition in the children's rights case spent a lot of time trying to win over former detractors of the global standards and, time and again, emphasized the normativity and obligation of the CRC. As a result, in the case of these high-precision legal norms, although there were some changes in overall rhetoric and in minor aspects regarding freedoms, the great majority of CRC standards were retained. When it came to the soft-law standards on access to information, meanwhile, deviations were accepted – provided there were legal precedents for them in the region. In the case of the standards for rule-of-law commissions, the level of precision was very low and – as this would suggest – the degree of reshaping that was possible in regard to the proposed commission's tasks and institutional set-up was considerable: both the external rule-of-law promoters and their domestic partners were negotiating with the Guatemalan government to secure a version that would 'work' for the specific context. Even here, however, reshaping remained within the scope of existing global practices and models: the work of designing a rule-of-law commission for Guatemala did not start from scratch.

### Giving the Appearance of Ownership: Informalizing Interaction

To date, research on the promotion of democracy has focused largely on the effects of different strategies of promotion and has shown little interest in other dimensions of interaction. Analysis of the cases under scrutiny here showed a shift by external actors to a more persuasion-oriented mode of interaction. But in the wake of contestation there was also a shift from a more public to a more informal style of interaction.

Following the surge of opposition triggered by the proposals on children's rights, UNICEF moderated its public profile in order to avoid exacerbating the controversy. It abandoned open praising and shaming and retreated into the background. From this position, it continued to operate as the main instigator of political discussion on children's rights but ceded the role of protagonist to domestic groups. Likewise, the United States, given its historical and continuing role in

Guatemala, took care to avoid creating a public impression that it was meddling in domestic affairs. In the case of access to information, for example, use of the USAID logo in campaigns was eschewed in order to ward off a public backlash. Again, when it came to the establishment of the rule-of-law commission, the United States, having become the main butt of the criticisms directed at the international donor community and its strategies, refrained from any public attempt to influence the outcome – and this despite the fact that it had quite firm views on the form such a commission should take.

External actors often also responded to contestation by presenting draft legislation as the product of internal endeavours, even though this was far from the truth – as illustrated by the cases of ATI and children's rights. The role played here by, respectively, international experts and UNICEF was not publicly acknowledged. And where contestation arose, international bodies cast their domestic coalition partners in the leading role. Together with their national counterparts they sought to portray political debates as 'bottom-up' processes triggered by internal demand, though this seldom reflected the reality.

In summary: strong domestic contestation not only led to the adoption of more dialogue-oriented strategies by external actors; it also caused these actors to shift to a less public mode of interaction. Along with their domestic partners, the outside actors framed the relevant processes as internally driven and as enjoying domestic ownership – a factor which may also have hindered public debate by rendering internal political processes less transparent.

## All Law and No Practice? The Extent of Decoupling

A concept commonly employed in norm-socialization research in order to understand the results of norm diffusion is that of decoupling (see Chapter 2). This is defined as a situation in which particular norms and ideas are adopted rhetorically by a government, and written into law, but are then detached or 'decoupled' from further implementation and local practice. This, many argue, is a feature particularly characteristic of developing states with weak state capacities.[2] Besides resulting from problems of capacity (Börzel/Risse 2013), however, decoupling may be

---

[2] For the theoretical background to this concept in sociology, see Drori et al. (2003) and Meyer et al. (1997).

the product of strategic considerations, as domestic elites seek to appease external actors by adopting a measure into law but then take it no further (Barnett/Zürcher 2009; Levitsky/Murillo 2009).

The findings of the present study to some extent chime with this interpretation. Strategic considerations of the government and other implementing actors, and the state's lack of capacity, did lead to major reshaping during implementation. In addition, external actors often accommodated to this situation. Even so, there was no true decoupling from previous interaction over translation.

The course of translation into implementation can only be understood in the context of the other dimensions of translation, particularly translation into discourse. During the implementation phase, frames shifted, either because new groups became part of the political discussion[3] or because the overall situation in the country had changed. In the case of children's rights, for example, child-related policy became part of a new 'impunity' frame and was therefore securitized. Protection of children against crime was strongly supported; protection of children in conflict with the law won little backing – thus decisively shaping the omissions that fed through to implementation. Translation into implementation in the area of ATI highlighted the country's problems of capacity and the different economic interests that were at work. Implementation varied greatly even within government institutions but was at its weakest and most contested in the autonomous municipalities, which had not been included in the political negotiations on ATI. What occurred here was therefore not so much a decoupling of law from practice, but a decoupling of practice from initial expectations – the expectation, for example, that corruption would be defeated, that there would be greater citizen participation, that the marginalized would be emancipated, and that measures for transitional justice would be put in place. When it came to the rule-of-law provisions, implementation was largely overseen by the external commissioners of the new institution – and interestingly even here further reshaping was observable, in line with and in response to domestic discourse. As domestic frames shifted and supporters began to perceive CICIG as a potential replacement for Guatemalan institutions, informal reshaping – in the sense of rapid institutional

---

[3] On implementation and the empowerment of new actors, see Van Kersbergen/ Verbeek (2007).

expansion – took place and the spotlight was turned from human rights issues to general corruption.

The approach of external actors during implementation differed from that during translation into law in that they tended to be less prominent in shaping frames and more willing to accommodate to those proposed by domestic actors. UNICEF, for example, presented its activities as part of the overall securitized impunity frame then dominating Guatemalan discourse; and in the case of the rule-of-law commission, international actors supported a framing in which the commission figured as a tool for combating organized crime as a whole. The implementation phase also saw no major shifts in the mode of interaction, though the degree of politicization in two of the cases (children's rights and access to information) began to decline once the law had been passed and domestic and international attention waned. Only in the case of the rule-of-law commission did politicization continue to be strong, on account of the international activities associated with the commission's operations – which also implied a stronger recourse to conditionality if the overall operation of CICIG came under threat. In all three areas, the dominant mode of interaction adopted by international norm promoters was that of teaching, in a wide variety of permutations – though a degree of shaming and conditionality was kept up as a way of ensuring the continued cooperation of specific actors.

## Norm Cycles of a New Kind?

The research presented here points the way to a recalibrated research agenda that shifts its sights beyond the norm-diffusion perspective and focuses on the dynamic changes undergone by norms. In future, scholarly attention should turn to a greater extent not only to the patterns of interaction that occur in relation to norm translation but also to processes of re-translation – the ways in which 'localized' norms are made sense of in international contexts.

In their highly influential article of 1998, Martha Finnemore and Kathryn Sikkink propose a cyclical model of norm diffusion (1998). In this model, however, movement ends with full norm adoption. By contrast, the findings of the present study prompt us to ask to what extent norm translation brings about a more comprehensive kind of circularity – in other words, to what extent domestic translations affect the dynamics and meaning, and perhaps even the robustness, of international norms themselves.[4]

The case studies presented here show that, although norm translation in other Latin American states served to some extent as a model in Guatemala, domestic translation of children's rights and of the right of access to information elicited little discussion outside the field offices of international organizations or embassies. The Guatemalan translation in these cases had no impact on either the meaning or the validity of the relevant global norm sets. Only in the case of the script for a rule-of-law commission did the Guatemalan translation figure more prominently in the international debate, helping to shape 'best practice' in the field and inspiring discussion on rule-of-law tools, both in neighbouring Central American states and in other states grappling with the effects of organized crime and corruption. Only here, because of the considerable reshapings involved, did the Guatemalan example offer an interesting 'test case' for potential use in similar contexts.

The general lack of international impact of Guatemala's norm translations seems to be due to its status as a small, post-conflict state with negligible foreign-policy clout. This is borne out by a number of other studies – such as those on the translation of intellectual property norms – which have shown, conversely, that where the state that is translating a global norm is an internationally influential one, the translation is likely to be emulated more widely and, thanks to this increased support, may even lead to changes in the meaning and content of the norm at the international level (Chorev 2012). One conclusion is therefore that post-conflict countries like Guatemala remain in the position of 'norm takers' rather than 'norm shapers' for more formalized and specific global standards, despite the fact that norm-taking involves the translation and appropriation of norms. Only if small countries such as this become part of a more general pattern of translation will norm circularity also lead to changes in global norm sets.

## 7.2 A Research Agenda for Norm Translation

The aim of this study has been to explain the interactive process by which external rule-of-law promotion impacts on domestic norm

---

[4] On the first, see Acharya (2013), Chorev (2012) and Halliday (2009); on the second, see Deitelhoff and Zimmermann (2013b).

translation. Its detailed examination of the interaction patterns observed in the cases under scrutiny have theoretical import and open up a new path for norm-diffusion research – one involving more systematic study of translation processes and the dynamic contestation of global norms. Still, a theory-generating study such as this, based on case studies in a single country, prompts questions regarding generalizability and the applicability of an interactive model of norm translation beyond the post-conflict context.

Norm translations are, of course, fluid processes and their outcomes should therefore not be viewed either as stable or complete: analytically speaking, they can only serve as 'snapshots'. However, whilst specific translations are context-dependent (in both content and meaning), they can nonetheless – this study contends – be grouped into subtypes. The subtypes proposed are based not on the content of the translation but on the degree and nature of norm contestation evoked and the way in which the norms in question are translated into law and into implementation. Contestation may be either non-existent, focused on the meaning and application of a norm, or concerned with a norm's validity; translation into law and into implementation, meanwhile, may take the form of full adoption, modification or non-adoption. A scheme such as this offers a basis for an improved explanation of how and why particular conditions lead to particular types of translation – a field of enquiry that has so far remained largely unexplored.

Focusing on the three stages of translation – into discourse, into law and into implementation – is, moreover, an approach that has application far beyond the post-conflict context. It can be used to analyse translation to new contexts in a general sense: from one international organization or context to another (global–global); within or into a domestic context (local–local or global–local); and from the domestic to the international, either where domestic norms are translated into international standards or where reshaped norms are re-translated in an international context (local–global). The concept of translation is thus inherently more comprehensive than that of localization or socialization, in which norm translation is assumed to proceed in one direction only.

The analytical sections of this study suggest that interactive translation processes are at work during norm diffusion. Although the constellations of actors and norms that figure in the present study vary, the overall pattern of interaction on norm translation – the feedback loop – is surprisingly consistent across all three of the cases studied. This inductive inference naturally requires further empirical testing, but it is highly likely that the interactive pattern identified here – that is to say, the feedback loop – will emerge more generally where norms are translated, not just in post-conflict contexts but in any situation where there is marked dependency on external norm promoters. By contrast, the specific constellations of actors and discursive emphases involved in the loop, and the scope and space available for translation, will undoubtedly differ. One important factor here will be the general status and range of influence of promoters and, allied to this, their current and historical roles in the context concerned; another will be the 'ability' of targeted actors to resist norm promoters; and yet another will be the specific structural conditions prevailing in the domestic context. In addition, every norm is made sense of in a specific socio-political context. While it might therefore be possible to identify specific conditions as resulting in certain *types* of interactive patterns and *types* of norm-translation outcomes, the actual *content* of the translation remains context-specific.

Clearly, interactive patterns may not always take the form of a feedback loop as in this study: the initial reaction of translating actors will not always be one of outright rejection; nor will promoting actors always have a role like that of the international donor community, with the structural capacity this implies to guide dialogue-oriented renegotiation of global norms. This is particularly true in relation to translation in other constellations – from one international context to another, for example. Even where the configurations differ, however, the focus on interaction over translation which this study advocates is likely to prove a key analytical tool. Although the specific patterns of interaction will need to be identified, the overall approach will ensure that senders and recipients are not considered from a unidirectional perspective. A norm is something that has to be brought to life in its new context by a process of discursive interaction, negotiation and contestation.

## 7.3 Shifting Coordinates

This study has argued for a shift of analytical focus from norm diffusion to interaction between norm promotion and norm translation. The relationship between patterns of interaction and the outcomes of norm translation is a promising field of enquiry for future research, not least because it links into key areas of interest in IR theory and IR norm research – the contestedness of international orders, for example, or the effects which contestation and resistance to global norms have on the latter's overall dynamic and resilience.

These issues are not just of interest when dealing with post-conflict states. In a new 'world time' (Risse/Sikkink 1999: 19) that is no longer defined, as it was in the 1990s, by a consensus on the desirability of liberal global governance, such matters are of crucial political relevance. Global politics today is shaped by dissension over formerly stable global norms as rising powers, religious groups and new social movements assert themselves. Not least, many Western states are less focused on outward projections of democracy and rule-of-law, but struggle internally with right-wing and populist movements. At a time of generalized 'backlash' against the promotion of democracy and the rule of law (including in Europe), and in the aftermath of an 'Arab spring' which, rather than bringing renewal, seems to have plunged the region into conflict and triggered an escalation in Islamist radicalization, evocations of 'context sensitivity' by promoters of democracy appear hollow.

A more general questioning of the liberal consensus and of the activities of international organizations (Maiguashca 2003; Rajagopal 2007; Richmond 2010; Zürn et al. 2012) has in turn raised the question of the effects of contestation on the international liberal order. A shift of focus to translation and contestation thus brings with it a renewal of emphasis on the controversial nature of global norms, in the sense not only of conflict over the mode of their implementation but also, more fundamentally, of dissension over their validity. This is an issue that IR research had lost sight of in its eagerness to explore new (liberal) forms of global governance during the 1990s and 2000s.

The present study has offered analytical insights into the ways in which interactive processes shape the translation of liberal rule-of-law norms in post-conflict states, but it has not so far commented on whether translation itself is a 'good thing' or what its implications might be in terms of current practices of rule-of-law promotion. This will be the focus of the final chapter.

# 8 | Balancing Global Norms and Local Faces

This study began by observing that a rhetoric of context sensitivity and local ownership has come to dominate promotion of democracy and the rule of law. Many of the organizations active in these areas – from the United Nations through the European Union to state development agencies and independent foundations – have begun to revise their strategies accordingly, encouraged in this trend by the failure of previous approaches and what is regarded as a 'backlash' against the promotion of democracy and the rule of law (see Chapter 1). Nowadays, adapting global norms and institutional models to the local context – but not completely overhauling them – is viewed as the best strategy to improve the effectiveness of democracy promotion. How this works in practice is a question that has so far been neglected by researchers. The present study, however, shows that 'context sensitivity' as currently practised on the ground takes the form not of a systematic policy approach but of an ad hoc reaction by norm promoters to local norm-translation processes.

Given the empirical findings of this study, what normative judgements can we make about the approach of those promoting democracy and the rule of law, and about the ways in which norms are translated? How far can and should the translation and localization of global norms go? And how far can and should these processes be supported by external actors? Should the translation of global norms be seen as a mere 'watering down' or as a valuable 'appropriation' with its own democratic qualities? The promotion of democracy, and likewise peacebuilding in the aftermath of civil war and other internal conflict, are central aspects of global governance. The normative implications of this study are therefore of particular relevance when it comes to formulating international policy on post-conflict and emergent democratizing states.

In this chapter, I argue that the current paradigm of 'context sensitivity' is too narrow. Norm translation should be understood as appropriation and needs to be incorporated into norm-promotion strategies. The appropriation must, however, aspire to be democratic, and the dilemma of choice between global norms and their local faces must be viewed as an ongoing and productive source of tension.

## 8.1 Global Norms with a Local Face: Is Translation 'a Good Thing'?

Whether the promotion of democracy in general, and the particular strategies used to achieve this, are normatively appropriate is the subject of wide discussion.[1] By contrast, the normative desirability of norm translation has – so far – attracted little attention. As yet, the question of whether norm promotion should aim at a maximum adoption of global standards on human rights, democracy and the rule of law, or whether it should create even greater scope for contestation and appropriation, has elicited little comment.

Currently, when operating on the international stage, external actors make rhetorical claims about promoting 'global norms with a local face'. A glance at their policies and deliberations reveals a limited interpretation of this notion. What they mean by it in practice is essentially avoiding 'copy and paste' laws, ensuring that invited experts hail from the regions in question rather than from the United States or Europe and redoubling the rhetorical emphasis on 'ownership' and domestic protagonists. To quote Mac Ginty's summation: 'While projects may have a local face, and be enacted by local personnel in local communities, the real power may come from donors and administrators in New York, London, Geneva or elsewhere' (2015: 846).

Domestic translation on the ground has, however, gone considerably further than this account suggests: as an ad hoc reaction to contestation, interactive processes of translation have taken place in which varying degrees of reshaping have occurred depending on the precision of the norm in question. External norm promoters have continued to try to influence proceedings, endeavouring to determine the direction, scope and content of the reshaping. In consequence, domestic translations bear the stamp of the particular interpretation of democracy and the rule of law which these external actors have pushed for. As shown

---

[1]  See e.g. Fabry (2009), Gädeke (2014), Kurki (2013), Pangle (2009), Walzer (2008), and for a general discussion: Poppe/Wolff (2013).

in this study, the translation of the Convention on the Rights of the Child into Guatemalan law took place amidst intensive domestic debate and elicited the interest of a wide range of civil-society organizations, all keen to be involved in formulating the new code. This was considered a positive participatory process by the Code's support coalition and this created ownership. Had the outcome of this inclusive process of dialogue been not a law securing children's rights but legislation that did not recognize children as rights-holders, UNICEF would probably not have supported it (see Chapter 4). The line between what rule-of-law promoters regard as good *appropriation* and what they regard as 'watering down' seems to be a fine one.

As indicated in Chapter 2, IR's two main theoretical perspectives on norm diffusion – centred respectively on norm socialization and norm localization – make normative claims about the (democratic) value of translation processes.

Scholars of socialization often focus on norms which they themselves deem to be 'right' and which they consider should be disseminated. They expect norms to be adopted into law, implemented and also internalized. Anything short of this is tantamount to a 'watering down'. By contrast, there are many students of norm interpretation and translation for whom localization is more than simply a failure to achieve complete norm adoption. These scholars emphasize the creative nature of the process of appropriation and argue that such a process produces greater norm stability at local level because it offers a better 'fit' with the domestic political and cultural context. In addition, they say, local political discussion and deliberation over norms and the conduct of dialogue with norm promoters during the translation process can lend a norm more lasting legitimacy in the eyes of the domestic population.

However, both approaches are normatively problematic. The first is open to the charge that, where an outcome is doubtful, the logical response must be recourse to interventionist strategies, conditionality or actual sanctions in order to secure full adoption of the international standards in question. The principle of self-determination as the cornerstone of a democracy (or aspiring democracy) carries little weight here. Within this framework, the standards promoted are simply regarded as the basis on which a functioning liberal democracy can be built in the future.

The second approach brings with it the danger that domestic culture and differing normative orders will be reified and essentialized as constraints on democracy and the rule of law. Appropriation and resistance are depicted as inherently positive simply by virtue of being local and despite the fact that outcomes may merely be the expression of structures of socio-economic inequality and repression (see also Chandler 2013). In addition, data on the positive long-term effects of local translation in post-conflict states – higher legitimacy, for example, or greater compliance – remains thin on the ground, and no substantial evidence of this has been uncovered in the present study. Translation in Guatemala did indeed lead to moments of societal contention and debate, and to a kind of symbolic occupation or appropriation of the norms in question,[2] but it cannot be said to have produced medium- or long-term stability and legitimacy of the norms in their new context. There were many reasons for this: translation was often the product of polarized conflict, the attention span for political issues was limited and a multitude of capacity problems continued to afflict the process. Where translation was based on a more inclusive and deliberative process, consensus was achieved but quickly faded. A change to a more dialogue-oriented format for repeat discussions produced moments of procedural legitimacy, but these did not translate into longer-term legitimacy for the norm set that was appropriated. In addition, the political discourse continued to be characterized by marginalization and exclusion. Basing normative desirability solely on increased 'effectiveness', or on the potential participatory component of a translation process, remains at the least questionable.

The second approach also raises the question of the extent to which a norm can be moulded for local translation. To what extent can norms be translated and still maintain a relation to standards agreed at international level? Three points of view are distinguishable here, none of them completely satisfactory.

Most scholars opt for the easy way out: there is no need to establish a 'limit' for norm translation since the latter is an interim step on the way to full adoption. Goodman and Jinks (2008), for example, try to allay the fear of a 'watering down' by arguing that translation (in their terms: 'acculturation') prepares the ground for further progress in the area of human rights. For Acharya (2004: 253) too, norm localization can lead, in the long run, to full norm adoption. That norm translation can give rise to this kind of linear route to norm adoption is doubtful, as this study has also demonstrated.

---

[2]  On such symbolic occupation in the global context, see Deitelhoff (2012).

The second point of view is the one advanced by Merry and Levitt in their anthropological studies on human rights localization. Norms can indeed be translated and appropriated, they say, but the 'core concern', the core of the norm, must remain untouched if we are to continue to speak of the same norm (Merry 2006: 137). This, they argue, leads to a resonance dilemma: a norm needs to be adapted to fit a local context but at the same time needs to link back to a 'universal norm'. In their case study on the diffusion of women's rights, for example, they contend that local translations still need to question existing power relations (Levitt/Merry 2009). Here again the question remains of how such a normative 'core' can be identified from outside. Should states perhaps agree what constitutes the 'core' of the Convention on the Rights of the Child and what parts of it can be localized? In addition, as demonstrated by the present study, the empirical evidence indicates that different international coalitions interpret norms differently (at global, regional, national and local levels) and promote them via different types of framings. This can result in disagreement as to what constitutes the core of a norm and where there might be scope for interpretation and modification – as was the case with access to information in Guatemala (see Chapter 4).

The third point of view defines the limits of acceptable localization by reference to substantive and procedural criteria. Thus Oliver Richmond argues that a distinction can be made between 'malevolent hybridity' and 'good hybridity': 'malevolent hybridity' is a process of translation 'in which liberal peacebuilders make deals with rights-deniers, corrupt politicians and warlords' (Richmond 2011: 184–5); 'good hybridity', by contrast, has an emancipatory thrust (Richmond 2011: 149). But Richmond remains vague on just how the 'rights deniers' in question might be identified and what criteria we might use to determine which localizations are emancipatory.

None of these 'localizing' standpoints has so far produced a satisfactory answer to the question of how norm translations should be evaluated normatively and where the limits of translation should be set. Does this mean we should revert to the norm-socialization stance of full adoption and minimal reshaping?

Democratic theory suggests that appropriation is still the more desirable option normatively. However, a graduation of the translation-process is possible here, based on procedural criteria – an aspect virtually ignored in IR debates. On this view, democracy is seen primarily in terms of deliberation and contestation and it is argued that appropriation processes need to be enabled and have their democratic quality enhanced. Two analytical dimensions need to be distinguished here: that of norm translation and contestation in the (democratic) domestic context; and that of international or transnational interaction over global norms.

## Democratic Iterations, Contestation and Collective Self-Determination

Regarding the domestic context: amongst debaters of democratic theory, Benhabib in particular has focused on the problem of norm translation, asking how the dilemma that pits cosmopolitan norms (human rights) against collective self-determination (in domestic democracies) can be resolved. Benhabib's specific area of interest is the link between the interpretation of citizenship rights in Western democracies and the role of migrants – in other words, the participation and recognition of 'the other' in established democracies. She locates herself within a deliberative model of democracy – that is to say, a model of democracy in which legitimacy is created in accessible and open processes of deliberation, in the course of which actors present each other with 'good reasons' for their positions.[3]

As a way out of the dilemma, Benhabib offers the notion of 'democratic iteration'. According to this, cosmopolitan norms are subject to continual, repetitive negotiation and opinion formation in democratic domestic contexts – either within institutionalized settings or in civil society more generally. Iteration thus closely parallels the notion of norm translation in IR research: '[E]very iteration transforms meaning, adds to it, enriches it in ever-so-subtle ways' (Benhabib 2006: 47). In the language of norm research, iterations are translation processes in which the interpretations and meanings of rights change as the public discourse proceeds. People, says Benhabib (2006: 49; also 2009: 698), 'make these rights their own by democratically deploying them' – a process she calls 'jurisgenerative politics' because it creates meanings beyond formal legal texts and enables new actors to participate in contestation.

---

[3] Jürgen Habermas (1992) has played a major role in shaping this paradigm. It differs from traditional liberal models of democracy, in which interests are located outside the discourse and can be aggregated in majority decisions.

Contestation, conflict and rejection are key elements of these processes. As Benhabib points out (2006: 50), iteration does not always lead to 'normative learning' or produce normatively 'good' results, but it does at least open up public spaces for re-discussion and reinterpretation.

Benhabib believes that global norms must be subject to democratic, participative, deliberation-oriented decision-making processes in which it is possible for their meanings to change. On this view, prevention of democratic iteration would constitute an undemocratic act. The appropriation of norms and their translation into law are central to democracy because they 'mediate between universal norms and the will of democratic majorities' (Benhabib 2006: 49). In addition, when norms are appropriated in this way, 'they lose their parochialism as well as the suspicion of Western paternalism often associated with them' (Benhabib 2013: 98).

Unsurprisingly, the notion of democratic iteration has prompted widespread debate.[4] Bonnie Honig, for example, charges Benhabib with assuming that 'universal human rights will win out over democratic particularity in the end' (Honig 2006: 112). As in the case of some of the sections of norm research discussed earlier, norm translation in Benhabib's model would merely be the first step on the way to a more comprehensive adoption of global standards. Moreover, according to Honig (2006: 110–11), democratic iteration would preclude radical critique: the validity and claim to universality of global (human rights) norms cannot be questioned; the only aspect of them open to debate is their interpretation and application.[5]

According to those of agonistic or republican persuasion, this latter criticism in particular points up a fundamental problem of deliberative democratic theory. In the view of such commentators, the ability radically to challenge orders of any kind – as being inherently exclusionary (Rancière 1999) – constitutes the essence of democracy. Crucially, Mouffe has also highlighted the normative role played by conflict and passion in politics, contrasting it with the rational discourse and dialogue that define deliberative concepts of democracy. Mouffe believes that irreconcilable ethical differences exist within society and that, as a result, conflict is a central element of democratic

---

[4] This not being a work of political theory, I do not claim to give a comprehensive account of the debate evolving around Benhabib's work in these pages.

[5] On this point, see also Benhabib (2007: 454).

practice (Mouffe 2000, 2005). On this view, processing difference by institutional means is impossible. The only thing this can achieve, according to Lefort (1988: 19), is moments of legitimacy with symbolic import.

Speaking from a more republican standpoint, Tully contends that 'there will always be disagreement ... over the interpretation, procedures, application, institutionalization and review in accordance with the orienting principles of constitutionalism and democracy in any instance' (Tully 2002: 207). In Tully's view, contestation and dissent in regard to norms are inevitable, and 'ongoing disagreement, negotiation, amendment, implementation and review' (Tully 2002: 209) are part and parcel of democratic constitutionalism. Even the most fundamental rules are up for contestation and change, according to Tully, but in contrast to more radical approaches, the position he advances allows for more institutionalized ways of dealing with dissent.

If we follow the arguments advanced by Benhabib and Tully, we can assume that the fundamental norms of society – and, in the case of the present study, the norms underlying the international system – are open to contestation and reinterpretation. We can further assume that such contestation and reinterpretation are essential because they can bring about a democratic appropriation of norms – though the two authors would differ as to the extent to which these features can be institutionalized. If we apply this reasoning to the present study, we must conclude that where external actors hinder processes of appropriation they are thereby hindering democratic practice. Appropriation has to be part of any kind of democracy promotion.

That said, it should be noted that both authors are talking about contestation and democratic iteration within more or less stable democratic systems. Benhabib's democratic iteration, for example, entails adherence to some quite demanding principles of discourse ethics – amongst them the inclusive participation of all affected parties. Without this, it cannot produce legitimacy (Benhabib 2007: 455; 2009: 699). As indicated in the present study, post-conflict states fall far short of this ideal – as undoubtedly do many real-life Western democracies.[6] Should the absence of these (democratic) preconditions for contestation and deliberation elicit even more robust intervention from the international donor community in

---

[6]  A point made by postcolonial critics. See e.g. Kapoor (2005: 1208–9).

order to make good this deficit? Examination of the second of the analytical dimensions distinguished above – namely, relations between those promoting democracy and the rule of law and their addressees – suggests not.

## The Role of Power and Postcolonial Dependency in Norm Diffusion

The present study has also shown that interactive translation processes are strongly shaped by relations of dependency between external norm promoters and domestic actors. In the case of Guatemala, the former group saw rule-of-law promoters as 'teaching good norms' and locals as often simply refusing to try to understand these. 'The patient refuses to take the medicine' is a well-known remark made by the head of CICIG, Carlos Castresana, summing up Guatemala's response to the rule-of-law commission's recommendations.[7] It reflects a more general perception of external actors in Guatemala.

The problem of dependency is one discussed in particular in postcolonial literature and in recent research on imperialism, the focus most often being on development aid. Scholars in this field describe how 'wrong solidarity' and the idea of 'help' enshrined in Western development cooperation have reinforced rather than reduced relationships of dependency (see, for example, Kapoor 2008; Spivak 2008). They question the basic notion of universal human rights norms and criticize the practices currently used to promote them. In their view, aid-based relationships and practices such as the promotion of democracy are founded on structural dependencies; they disempower local institutions by inappropriately empowering donors; and they are often tied to economic interests.[8]

Mutua, for example, views the Western interpretation and application of human rights standards as simplistic and based on a reductionist 'savages–victims–saviours' metaphor, according to which local victims in exotic places are rescued from savage elites by Western saviours (Mutua 2001). Mutua interprets norm entrepreneurship in this field as part of 'the historical continuum of the Eurocentric colonial project' resulting in 'an "othering" process that imagines the creation of inferior clones, in effect dumb copies of the original' (2001: 205).

---

[7] 'Castresana, un Eliot Ness' (2010).    [8] For an overview, see Gädeke (2014).

In his view, democracy promoters do not expect the 'Global South' actually to attain the Western ideal of liberal democracy.[9]

But the normative impetus of nom-diffusion activities is not the only questionable factor here: IR norm research itself is called upon to consider whether international norms do not inevitably come with a 'darker side' rooted in colonialism and imperialism (see Inayatullah/ Blaney 2012).

Exactly what would follow from such critical self-reflection, with its deconstruction both of democracy promotion and of the academic attempts to explore it, remains an open question. Again, once we have acknowledged that the diffusion of 'good' norms and the existence of relations of dependency are co-constituent in practices of democracy promotion, what then?[10] Is all such activity normatively doomed? Do we need to do more than simply engage in ongoing reflection about such co-constitution as we practice or investigate the promotion of democracy?

In his most recent work, Tully has also looked at the issue of inter-action and global norm promotion and, rather than completely dis-missing the notion of norm appropriation, has put in a plea for it. His critique of the international system essentially tallies with that of the postcolonial scholars. He views international norms as a component part of a liberal model of citizenship rights which Western states have promoted across the globe – but only in a selective, self-interested fashion, concentrating on norms designed to foster electoral democracy and neo-liberal economic policies and excluding, or neglecting, eco-nomic, social and cultural rights (Tully 2008b, 2008c). In Tully's view, the diffusion of liberal democracy and the rule of law in post-conflict states is thus part and parcel of an imperial system.[11]

As an alternative to such dependency, Tully proposes that interac-tion be democratized in ways that would allow citizenship rights to be contested and negotiated and would create space for dialogue and creative appropriation: '[T]he laws must always be open to the criti-cism, negotiation, and modification of those who are the subjects of

---

[9]  Adler-Nissen (2014: 150) likewise points to socialization activities as constructions of 'others' designed to stabilize notions of the 'normal'; also Epstein (2014).

[10]  On this debate, see also Engelkamp et al. (2012, 2013), Deitelhoff and Zimmermann (2013a).

[11]  What he understands by imperialism is detailed in Tully (2008b: ch. 5). Cf. Ayers (2009).

them as they follow them' (Tully 2008b: 217). The ultimate aim, according to Tully, must be to establish joint authority in the relationship between norm promoters and their addressees and to create space for alternative organizations and institutions (2008a: 489, 92; 2008b: 217). Progress in democratization, he believes, is a function of such interaction, and the spaces set aside for this interplay should therefore be used to create preconditions for appropriation that are normatively acceptable to *all* the parties involved.[12]

Both Tully and his postcolonial counterparts highlight the relations of dependency created by seemingly positive norm diffusion. Tully goes on to argue for their democratization as a prerequisite to appropriation.

## Democratizing Norm Translation

Taking into account both of the dimensions just outlined – namely, the context of domestic translation and the interaction between norm promoters and their addressees – new strategies need to be developed for the promotion of democracy and the rule of law. Rather than merely coping with contestation and translation in the kind of ad hoc, spur-of-the-moment way observed in this study, these strategies should aim at real democratization.

As Benhabib and Tully's account suggests, argument as to whether a particular translation is normatively desirable or not should consider the quality of political discourse (deliberation) and the scope available for contesting and critiquing the results of that discourse. Indicators of the quality of discourse will include, as a minimum: access to plural spaces of discourse, equitable distribution of the power and resources required to participate in discourse, inclusion of the marginalized and rules of deliberation that are not necessarily predetermined by promoters of democracy (on deliberation, see Mainsbridge 1996; Young 1996). Indicators of scope for contestation, meanwhile, will include – at the least – outward transparency of discourse, accountability and the existence of possibilities for changing the rules of deliberation. If appropriation is to become more democratic, these elements need

---

[12] In similar vein, Gädeke, reflecting on democracy promotion, proposes understanding such practices as 'domination' (a concept drawn from the political theory of Philip Pettit) and proposes transnational and international institutionalization, based on mutual recognition, accountability and opportunities for contestation (2014: 245).

to be improved, both within post-conflict societies and between external and domestic actors. In terms of strategy, this means that external norm promoters must support the inclusion of marginalized groups and allow for a greater plurality of voices in post-conflict spaces. At the same time, they must devise better, more institutionalized mechanisms for dialogue between external and domestic actors – mechanisms that are more transparent and that foster mutual recognition.

The aim cannot be either to champion translation that results from completely undemocratic processes or to impose global standards in disregard of the right of (aspiring) democracies to self-determination. Instead, we have to tackle the dilemma inherent in translation by assessing both dimensions of appropriation and, where possible, democratizing them.

How might these insights into ways of coping with the tension between global norms and their local faces inform the promotion of democracy and the rule of law in practice? As mentioned previously, the central paradigm guiding democracy promotion at present is context sensitivity. However, this paradigm is all about effectiveness – essentially it asks why the promotion of democracy has not been as successful as expected. Absent from these deliberations is any attempt to address the depth of the normative dilemma currently facing promoters of democracy. Reflection on norm translation therefore has to reach beyond the paradigm of context sensitivity, to encompass the problems associated with ad hoc response to contestation, including the informalization of international activities. Its outcome should be a process of context-bound balancing in which questions about interaction – for example, how far international standards or the basic norms pursued by organizations promoting democracy are compromised by a translation process, or to what extent access to deliberation and contestation has been denied to groups – are considered alongside domestic issues such as the degree of space made available for contestation and deliberation or the possibility of such contestation and deliberation lending legitimacy to final outcomes.

International organizations, development agencies, transnational NGOs and foundations need to develop a more systematic approach to dealing with the dilemma inherent in translation. At a practical level, their reflections might take shape around questions of the following kind: although Bolivia and Ecuador do not fully comply with the model of a liberal democracy, should promoters of democracy nevertheless support constitutional reforms in these countries because such reforms give indigenous groups a voice and thus empower them? Should promoters of democracy include moderate Islamists in processes of dialogue in the Middle East? And where is the dividing line between moderate and non-moderate Islamists? Specific adaptations resulting from such practical considerations cannot be used as a basis for general rules: such a move would run counter to the context specificity of democratization processes. As an alternative, this study has suggested the use of a number of basic indicators to clarify the normative considerations associated with the translation of global norms and help strike a balance between them. Only on the basis of this kind of balance can a new, more democratic paradigm of appropriation, and a policy of interaction 'between equals', be successful. Appropriation is necessary and democracy promoters need to provide space for it on the basis of even-handed negotiation, thus ensuring that the over-arching objective of real democratization is achieved.

## 8.2 Making Appropriation (More) Democratic

Is norm translation, and the reinterpretation and modification it entails, normatively desirable – particularly in relation to the norms of liberal democracy and the rule of law in post-conflict states? Or should democracy promotion aim at the fullest possible adoption of existing global standards? In this chapter, I have argued that a new paradigm of democratic appropriation is needed – one that moves beyond 'context sensitivity' and seeks to enhance the democratic quality of deliberation and contestation in processes of norm appropriation. However, a balance needs to be struck here in which appropriation in post-conflict states becomes more democratic and input from external norm promoters becomes less patronizing. If there is any doubt about which way to go here, the fact that appropriation processes help to create a more inclusive political discourse and wider access to contestation may carry more weight than does the necessity for all international standards to be adopted in their entirety. This leaves us with the question of whether some kind of minimal standard needs to be obtained before we can even consider the institution of practices of appropriation which we think may be democratic or democracy-enhancing. That minimal standard is the absence of an authoritarian regime: the purpose of an appropriation approach is not to help repressive regimes continue with their repression; it is to give societies a chance to discover their own path to (perhaps) greater democracy rather than following one predetermined by external actors.

# Annex 1  List of Interview Partners

The interviews listed below were conducted during the following research stays:

| November 2009: | Guatemala City |
| 18 to 31 January 2010: | Washington, D.C. |
| February to April 2010: | Guatemala City |
| July 2011: | Guatemala City |

Int. 1 (2009, November 5). Head, development agency in Guatemala, Guatemala City. Personal interview.

Int. 2 (2009, November 9). Local staff, German foundation, Guatemala City. Personal interview.

Int. 3 (2009, November 12). Staff, office of European Union in Guatemala (2 people), Guatemala City. Personal interview.

Int. 4 (2009, November 13). Staff, development agency in Guatemala, Guatemala City. Personal interview.

Int. 5 (2009, November 17). Government staff, Segeplan, Guatemala City. Personal interview.

Int. 6 (2009, November 18). Local staff, German foundation, Guatemala City. Personal interview.

Int. 7 (2009, November 25). Staff, development agency in Guatemala, Guatemala City. Personal interview.

Int. 8 (2009, November 26). Staff, German embassy, Guatemala City. Personal interview.

Int. 9 (2010, January 19). Staff, USAID, Washington, D.C. Personal Interview.

Int. 10 (2010, January 20). Guatemalan diplomat, Washington, D.C. Personal Interview.

Int. 11 (2010, January 21). Staff, US State Department, Washington, D.C. Personal Interview.

Int. 12 (2010, January 25). Staff, US House of Representatives Washington, D.C. Personal Interview.

Int. 13 (2010, January 26). Staff, US NGO, Washington, D.C. Personal Interview.

Int. 14 (2010, January 27). Staff, US Senate, Washington, D.C. Personal Interview.

Int. 15 (2010, February 2). Staff, Guatemalan think tank, Guatemala City. Personal Interview.

Int. 16 (2010, February 10). Staff, development agency in Guatemala, Guatemala City. Personal Interview.

Int. 17 (2010, February 15). Staff, UNDP office in Guatemala, Guatemala City. Personal Interview.

Int. 18 (2010, February 16). Staff, office of human rights ombudsman, Guatemala City. Personal Interview.

Int. 19 (2010, February 17). Staff, development agency in Guatemala, Guatemala City. Personal Interview.

Int. 20 (2010, February 17). Former government employee, Guatemala City. Personal Interview.

Int. 21 (2010, February 17). Staff, office of human rights ombudsman, Guatemala City. Personal Interview.

Int. 22 (2010, February 23). Staff, Guatemalan NGO, Guatemala City. Personal Interview.

Int. 23 (2010, February 24). Head, Guatemalan NGO, Guatemala City. Personal Interview.

Int. 24 (2010, February 24). Staff, Guatemalan NGO, Guatemala City. Personal Interview.

Int. 25 (2010, February 24). Staff, Guatemalan NGO, Guatemala City. Personal Interview.

Int. 26 (2010, February 24). Professor, Universidad Rafael Landívar/former member of government, Guatemala City. Personal Interview.

Int. 27 (2010, February 26). Staff, Guatemalan foundation (2 people), Guatemala City. Personal Interview.

Int. 28 (2010, February 26). Staff, Dutch foundation (one local employee, one Dutch), Guatemala City. Personal Interview.

Int. 29 (2010, February 26). Staff, Guatemalan Catholic human rights organization, Guatemala City. Personal Interview.

Int. 30 (2010, March 1). Local staff, embassy, Guatemala City. Personal Interview.

Int. 31 (2010, March 1). Guatemalan consultant, formerly government member, Guatemala City. Personal Interview.

Int. 32 (2010, March 2). Head, Guatemalan NGO, Guatemala City. Personal Interview.

Int. 33 (2010, March 2). Head, Guatemalan think tank, Guatemala City. Personal Interview.

Int. 34 (2010, March 3). Head, Guatemalan NGO, Guatemala City. Personal Interview.

Int. 35 (2010, March 5). Local staff, international foundation, Guatemala City. Personal Interview.

Int. 36 (2010, March 8). Board of Guatemalan NGO (several people), Cobán. Personal Interview.

Int. 37 (2010, March 8). Professor, activist, Cobán. Personal Interview.

Int. 38 (2010, March 23). Staff, Guatemalan foundation, Guatemala City. Personal Interview.

Int. 39 (2010, March 26 and 31). Head, office of German foundation, Guatemala City. Personal Interview.

Int. 40 (2010, March 29). Staff, office of human rights ombudsman, formerly government employee, Guatemala City. Personal Interview.

Int. 41 (2010, March 30). Staff, Guatemalan Foreign Ministry, Guatemala City. Personal Interview.

Int. 42 (2010, March 30). Staff, Swedish embassy, Guatemala City. Personal Interview.

Int. 43 (2010, April 6). Staff, Guatemalan think tank (2 people), Guatemala City. Personal Interview.

Int. 44 (2010, April 9). Staff, CICIG (2 people), Guatemala City. Personal Interview.

Int. 45 (2011, July 6). Head, office of German foundation, Guatemala City. Personal Interview.

Int. 46 (2011, July 8). Head, development agency in Guatemala, Guatemala City. Personal Interview.

Int. 47 (2011, July 8). Staff, office of human rights ombudsman, Guatemala City. Personal Interview.

Int. 48 (2011, July 11). Staff, development agency, Guatemala City. Personal Interview.

Int. 49 (2011, July 13). Head and staff, Guatemalan NGO (2 people), Guatemala City. Personal Interview.

Int. 50 (2011, July 15). Staff, Guatemalan Ministry of Finance, Guatemala City. Personal Interview.

Int. 51 (2011, July 15). Staff, Guatemalan NGO, Guatemala City. Personal Interview.

Int. 52 (2011, July 18). Head and staff, Guatemalan NGO (2 people), Guatemala City. Personal Interview.

Int. 53 (2011, July 19). Local staff, embassy, Guatemala City. Personal Interview.

Int. 54 (2011, July 19). Local staff, UNICEF, Guatemala City. Personal Interview.

Int. 55 (2011, July 19). Staff, Guatemalan Vice-Presidency, Guatemala City. Personal Interview.

Int. 56 (2011, July 21). Guatemalan Lawyer, Guatemala City. Personal Interview.

Int. 57 (2011, July 21). Representative, Anglican Church, Guatemala City. Personal Interview.

Int. 58 (2011, July 22 and July 26). Former government member, Guatemala City. Personal Interview.

Int. 59 (2011, July 25). Head, national adoption agency, formerly government employee, Guatemala City. Personal Interview.

Int. 60 (2011, July 25). Staff, Guatemalan NGO, Guatemala City. Personal Interview.

Int. 61 (2011, July 26). Representative, Evangelical Alliance, Guatemala City. Personal Interview.

Int. 62 (2011, July 27). Staff, contractor of development agency, Guatemala City. Personal Interview.

Int. 63 (2011, November 11). Staff, UN Political Affairs. Telephone Interview.

# Annex 2  Presidential Administrations since Democratization in Guatemala

| Time frame | President | Party |
| --- | --- | --- |
| 1986–91 | Vinicio Cerezo | Guatemalan Christian Democracy |
| 1991–3 | Jorge Serrano Elías | Solidarity Action Movement |
| 1993–3 (Interim) | Gustavo Adolfo Espina Salguero | Solidarity Action Movement |
| 1993–6 | Ramiro de León Carpio | None |
| 1996–2000 | Álvaro Arzú | National Advancement Party/ Unionist Party |
| 2000–4 | Alfonso Portillo | Guatemalan Republican Front |
| 2004–8 | Óscar Berger | National Solidarity Party; election alliance: Grand National Alliance |
| 2008–12 | Álvaro Colom | National Unity for Hope |
| 2012–15 | Otto Pérez Molina | Patriotic Party, election alliance: Grand National Alliance |
| 2015–16 (Acting President) | Alejandro Maldonado | None |
| 2016- | Jimmy Morales | National Convergence Front |

# Annex 3 Data Selection Media Discourses

A detailed overview of data selection strategies, the complete corpus of newspaper editorials and op-eds as well as a complete coding scheme can be found in Zimmermann (2012). Editorials and op-eds were collected cluster-fashion around major discussion points (such as the proposal, passing or entry into force of a law), as these moments of contention were representative of the more general political discourse.

## Discourse on Children's Rights

### Search Strategy

Op-eds or editorials were selected if they contained one of the following key words in at least one paragraph:

- Código de la Niñez (y Juventud)
- Código del Niño
- Niñez + derechos
- Familia + ley + niño
- Código + niñez
- Código de la familia
- Derechos humanos + niñez
- Convención sobre los Derechos del Niño
- Convención Internacional de Adopciones
- Adopción + ley/convención

Major discussion points were:

- 25 March 1998: Extension of non-entering into force of CNJ;[1]
- 24 February 2000: Extension of non-entering into force of CNJ;
- 16 May 2002: Extension of non-entering into force of CNJ;

---

[1] No media discourse on children's rights before that date, see also Chapter 4.

- 2003: Ley PINA passed (4 June 2003); accession to The Hague Convention (1 August 2003):
- July and September 2005 (discussion of draft adoption law)
- 16 December 2007: law on inter-country adoption passed

## Discourse on Right to Access Information

### *Search strategy*

Op-eds or editorials were selected if they contained one of the following key words in at least one paragraph:

- acceso de/a la información
- derecho de saber
- derecho de conocer
- derecho de informarse
- secreto de Estado/militar
- derecho de ser informado
- conocer información

Major discussion points were:

- before 2005: discussion in newspaper scattered (see Chapter 5)
- 29 October 2005: government passes decree on ATI
- 24 September 2008: law on ATI passed
- 22 April 2009: law on ATI enters into force

## Discourse on Scripts for Rule-of-Law Commission

### *Search Strategy*

Op-eds or editorials were selected if they contained one of the following key words:

- CICIACS
- CICIG
- Castresana
- organismo internacional

Major discussion points were:

- 13 March 2003: Agreement on CICIACS between government, ombudsman and human rights groups
- 7 January 2004: Agreement on CICIACS between Guatemalan government and UN
- 6 August 2004: Decision of Guatemalan Constitutional Court on CICIACS
- 12 December 2006: Agreement on CICIG between Guatemalan government and UN
- 1 August 2007: Congress decides on CICIG
- 21 April 2009: First prolongation of CICIG mandate
- 12 January 2010: Public presentation of investigations on Rosenberg case
- 7 June 2010: Resignation of Commissioner Castresana

# References

Abbott, Kenneth W./Keohane, Robert O./Moravcsik, Andrew/Slaughter, Anne-Marie/Snidal, Duncan (2000). The Concept of Legalization. *International Organization* 54(3), 401–19.

Acción Ciudadana (2010). *Índice de acceso a la información pública del organismo ejecutivo del 2010*. Guatemala: Magna Terre Editores.

Acción Ciudadana/Promudel/USAID (n.d.). *Guía Ciudadana para el Acceso a la Información Pública*, Guatemala City.

Acharya, Amitav (2004). How Ideas Spread: Whose Norms Matter? Norm Localization and Institutional Change in Asian Regionalism. *International Organization* 58(2), 239–75.

Acharya, Amitav (2009). *Whose Ideas Matter? Agency and Power in Asian Regionalism*. Ithaca, NY: Cornell University Press.

Acharya, Amitav (2013). The R2P and Norm Diffusion: Towards a Framework of Norm Circulation. *Global Responsibility to Protect* 5(4), 466–79.

Ackerman, John M./Sandoval-Ballestreros, Irma E. (2006). The Global Explosion of Freedom of Information Laws. *Administrative Law Review* 58(1), 85–130.

Ackermann, Alice (2003). The Idea and Practice of Conflict Prevention. *Journal of Conflict Resolution* 40(3), 339–47.

Adler-Nissen, Rebecca (2014). Stigma Management in International Relations: Transgressive Identities, Norms, and Order in International Society. *International Organization* 68(01), 143–76.

African Commission on Human and Peoples' Rights (2013). *Model Law on Access to Information*. www.achpr.org/files/news/2013/04/d84/model _law.pdf, accessed 6 November 2014.

Agenda de leyes: Ley de Libre Acceso a la Información quedó burlada (2004). *Prensa Libre*, 25 April 2004. www.prensalibre.com/noticias/Agenda-leye s_0_72593760.html, accessed 1 March 2016.[1]

Aharoni, Sarai B. (2014). Internal Variation in Norm Localization: Implementing Security Council Resolution 1325 in Israel. *Social Politics* 21(1), 1–25.

---

[1] The website of the Guatemalan newspaper *Prensa Libre* was relaunched in 2015. Since that time its newspaper archive is no longer accessible. For that reason links to articles from *Prensa Libre* are not active any more

231

Ajanel, Carlos (2009). Inacceso a la información. *Siglo Veintiuno*, 30 April 2009, p. 1.

Albizures, Miguel Ángel (1998). ¿Por qué les causa pánico el Código? *El Periódico*, 18 March 1998, p. 10.

Albizures, Miguel Ángel (2004). CICIACS, golpe a la impunidad. *El Periódico*, 12 January 2004, p. 15.

Alderson, Kai (2001). Making Sense of State Socialization. *Review of International Studies* 27(3), 415–33.

Alianza Regional por la Libertad de Expresión e Información (2010). *Saber mas II: Informe regional sobre el acceso a la información como herramienta para acceder a otros derechos*. www.cainfo.org.uy/images/Informes/sabermasii.pdf, accessed 1 March 2016.

Alonso, Conrado (2004). El guirigay de las adopciones. *Prensa Libre*, 27 October 2004. www.prensalibre.com/opinion/CONTRASTESbrEl-guiri gay-adopciones_0_95391869.html, accessed 5 October 2014.

Alvarado, Hugo (2008). Otra iniciativa para información. *Prensa Libre*, 1 January 2008. www.prensalibre.com/noticias/iniciativa-informacion_0 _163186112.html 2008, accessed 28 June 2014.

Álvarez, Alejandra (2009). ONG incumplen Ley de Acceso a Información. *Prensa Libre*, 18 May 2009. www.prensalibre.com/noticias/ONG-incum plen-Ley-Acceso-Informacion_0_44995576.html, accessed 28 June 2014.

Álvarez, Carlos (2015). PDH ve ilegalidad en norma de Ministerio de Gobernación. *Prensa Libre*, 29 January 2015. www.prensalibre.com/noti cias/justicia/Acceso-informacion-publica-Ministerio-Gobernacion-ilegali dad-PDH_0_1294070582.html, accessed 28 February 2016.

Amnesty International (2011). *Annual Report: Guatemala 2011*. www.am nestyusa.org/research/reports/annual-report-guatemala-2011, accessed 26 May 2014.

Anam/Promudel (2010). *Guía para la implementación de la Ley de Acceso a la Información Pública en las Municipalidades*, Guatemala City. http://ide .segeplan.gob.gt/ranking/ranking_portal/documentos/IndiceInformacion Ciudadania/GuiaLAIP.pdf, accessed 6 November 2014.

Ángel, Otto (2005). Prevén sanción penal por negar información. *Siglo Veintiuno*, 30 October 2005, p. 4.

Ante la Farsa del Secreto Militar (2004). [Editorial] *Siglo Veintiuno*, 18 November 2004, p. 12.

Argueta, Otto (2013). *Private Security in Guatemala: Pathway to Its Proliferation*. Baden-Baden: Nomos.

Arellano, Pavel (1998a). Obispos rechazan Código de la Niñez. *Prensa Libre*, 17 March 1998, p. 3.

Arellano, Pavel (1998b). Opositores protestarán frente al Congreso. *Prensa Libre*, 17 March 1998, p. 3.

Arellano, Pavel (2000). Apoyo para hábeas data. *Prensa Libre*, 15 April 2000. www.prensalibre.com/noticias/Apoyo-habeas-data_0_292776893 .html, accessed 28 June 2014.

Arévalo, Karl Yván (2006). El precio de la impunidad. *Siglo Veintiuno*, 15 December 2006, p. 22.

Arévalo, Karl Yván (2009). Un freno a la arbitrariedad. *Siglo Veintiuno*, 24 April 2009, p. 16.

Argueta, José Miguel (2010). Reflexione, Señor Presidente. *Prensa Libre*, 15 January 2010, p. 18.

Article 19 (1999). *The Public's Right to Know. Principles on Freedom of Information Legislation*, London. www.article19.org/data/files/pdfs/stan dards/righttoknow.pdf, accessed 6 November 2014.

Article 19 (2000). *Memorandum on the Guatemalan Draft Law on Access to Public Information*, London. www.article19.org/data/files/pdfs/analysis/ guatemala-freedom-of-information-2003-draft.pdf, accessed 1 March 2016.

Article 19 (2001). *A Model Freedom of Information Law*. London. www .article19.org/data/files/pdfs/standards/modelfoilaw.pdf, accessed 6 November 2014.

Article 19 (2003). *Memorandum on the Republic of Guatemala's Draft Law on Free Access to Information*, 1 February, London. www.refworld.org/ cgi-bin/texis/vtx/rwmain?docid=475409120, accessed 6 November 2014.

Arzú monta falso show para defender fideicomisos (2008). *Prensa Libre*, 7 July 2008. www.prensalibre.com/noticias/Arzu-monta-falso-defender-fid eicomisos_0_166784034.html, accessed 28 June 2014.

Associated Press (2012). New Guatemala Pres Wants to Regain US Military Aid. *NewsOK*, 12 January 2012. newsok.com/new-guatemala-pres-wants -to-regain-us-military-aid/article/feed/335015, accessed 28 February 2016.

Autesserre, Séverine (2009). Hobbes and the Congo: Frames, Local Violence, and International Intervention. *International Organization* 63(2), 249–80.

Autesserre, Séverine (2010). *The Trouble with the Congo: Local Violence and the Failure of International Peacebuilding*. Cambridge: Cambride University Press.

Axelrod, Robert (1985). Achieving Cooperation under Anarchy: Strategies and Institutions. *World Politics* 38(1), 226–54.

Axelrod, Robert (1986). An Evolutionary Approach to Norms. *The American Political Science Review* 80(4), 1095–111.

Ayers, Alison J. (2009). Imperial Liberties: Democratisation and Governance in the 'New' Imperial Order. *Political Studies* 57(1), 1–27.

Azpuru, Dinorah (1999). Peace and Democratization in Guatemala: Two Parallel Processes. In Arnson, Cynthia J., (ed.), *Comparative Peace*

*Processes in Latin America*. Washington, D.C.: Woodrow Wilson Center Press/Stanford University Press, pp. 97–128.

Azpuru, Dinorah (2006a). La opinión pública y el estado de derecho en Guatemala. *Revista ASIES(1)*.

Azpuru, Dinorah (2006b). Strengthening Human Rights in Guatemala. In de Zeeuw, Jeroen/Kumar, Krishna, (eds.), *Promoting Democracy in Postconflict Societies*. Boulder, CO: Lynne Rienner, pp. 99–126.

Azpuru, Dinorah/Finkel, Steven E./Pérez-Liñán, Aníbal/Seligson, Mitchell A. (2008). Trends in Democracy Assistance. What Has the United States Been Doing? *Journal of Democracy* 19(2), 150–9.

Azpuru, Dinorah/Mendoza, Carlos/Blanck, Evelyn/Blanco, Ligia (2004). *Democracy Assistance to Post-Conflict Guatemala. Finding a Balance between Details and Determinants*, Netherlands Institute of International Relations Clingendael, The Hague.

Bad apples everywhere: Corruption in Guatemala (2016). The Economist, 11 June 2016. http://www.economist.com/news/americas/21700418-ousted-president-accused-masterminding-kleptocracy-bad-apples-everywhere, accessed 15 February 2017.

Badescu, Cristina G./Weiss, Thomas G. (2010). Misrepresenting R2P and Advancing Norms: An Alternative Spiral? *International Studies Perspectives* 11(4), 354–74.

Baldwin, Maria T. (2009). *Amnesty International and U.S. Foreign Policy: Human Rights Campaigns in Guatemala, United States, and China*. El Paso: LFB Scholarly Publishing.

Banisar, David (2002). Freedom of Information and Access to Government Records around the World, *Privacy International*. www.forum.mn/res_mat/Freedom%20of%20Information%20records%20around%20world.pdf, accessed 12 March 2014.

Banisar, David (2006). Freedom of Information around the World 2006: A Global Survey of Access to Government Information Laws, *Privacy International*. http://dx.doi.org/10.2139/ssrn.1707336, accessed 2 March 2016.

Bargent, James (2013). Last Rites for Guatemala's Anti-Impunity Crusaders CICIG? *Insight Crime*, 16 September 2013. www.insightcrime.org/news-analysis/last-rites-for-guatemalas-anti-impunity-warriors, accessed 1 March 2016.

Barnett, Michael (1999). Culture, Strategy and Foreign Policy Change: Israel's Road to Oslo. *European Journal of International Relations* 5(1), 5–36.

Barnett, Michael (2006). Building a Republican Peace. Stabilizing States after War. *International Security* 30(4), 87–112.

Barnett, Michael/Fang, Songying/Zürcher, Christoph (2014). Compromised Peacebuilding. *International Studies Quarterly* 58(3), 608–20.

Barnett, Michael/Finnemore, Martha (2004). *Rules for the World: International Organizations in Global Politics.* Ithaca, NY: Cornell University Press.

Barnett, Michael/Zürcher, Christoph (2009). The Peacebuilder's Contract: How External Statebuilding Reinforces Weak Statehood. In Paris, Roland/Sisk, Timothy D., (eds.), *The Dilemmas of Statebuilding: Confronting the Contradictions of Postwar Peace Operations.* London: Routledge, pp. 23–52.

Barrera, Byron (2008). Posponen dictamen a ley de información. *Prensa Libre*, 10 June 2008, p. 8.

Barrios Peña, Ricardo (2000). No al Código de la Niñez. *Prensa Libre*, 17 February 2000, p. 14.

Bauer, Michael W./Knill, Christoph/Pitschel, Diana (2007). Differential Europeanization in Eastern Europe: The Impact of Diverse EU Regulatory Governance Patterns. *Journal of European Integration* 29(4), 405–23.

Bauer Rodríguez, Federico (1998). Acerca del neonazismo. *Siglo Veintiuno*, 26 March 1998, p. 15.

Benavente, Claudia (2003). Modificaciones para aprobar ley de protección a los menores. *El Periódico*, 4 June 2003, p. 8.

Benford, Robert D./Snow, David A. (2000). Framing Processes and Social Movements: An Overview and Assessment. *Annual Review of Sociology* 26, 611–39.

Benhabib, Seyla (2006) *Another Cosmopolitanism.* Oxford: Oxford University Press.

Benhabib, Seyla (2007). Democratic Exclusions and Democratic Iterations: Dilemmas of 'Just Membership' and Prospects of Cosmoplitan Federalism. *European Journal of Political Theory* 6(4), 445–62.

Benhabib, Seyla (2009). Claiming Rights across Borders. *American Political Science Review* 103(4), 691–704.

Benhabib, Seyla (2013). Human Rights, International Law and the Transatlantic Rift. In Transatlantic Academy, (ed.), *The Democratic Disconnect: Citizenship and Accountability in the Transatlantic Community.* Washington, D.C.: The German Marshall Fund of the United States, pp. 89–100.

Berliner, Daniel (2014). The Political Origins of Transparency. *The Journal of Politics* 76(2), 479–91.

Berliner, Daniel (2016). Transnational Advocacy and Domestic Law: International NGOs and the Design of Freedom of Information Laws. *The Review of International Organizations* 11(1), 121–44.

Bermeo, Nancy (2009). Conclusion: Is Democracy Exportable? In Barany, Zoltan/Moser, Robert G., (eds.), *Is Democracy Exportable?* Cambridge: Cambridge University Press, pp. 242–63.

Bhabha, Homi (1994). Of Mimikry and Man: The Ambivalence of Colonial Discourse. In Bhabha, Homi, (ed.), *The Location of Culture*. London: Routledge, pp. 85–92.

Bhabha, Homi K. (1985). Signs Taken for Wonders: Questions of Ambivalence and Authority under a Tree outside Delhi, May 1817. *Critical Inquiry* 12(1), 144–65.

Bicchi, Federica (2006). 'Our Size Fits All': Normative Power Europe and the Mediterranean. *Journal of European Public Policy* 13(2), 286–313.

Biekart, Kees (2009). Civil-Society Participation in Donor-Driven Governance Programmes. Experiences from Central America. In Hout, Wil/Robison, Richard, (eds.), *Governance and the Depoliticisation of Development*. London: Routledge, pp. 152–66.

Bishop, Cheryl Ann (2009) *Internationalizing the Right to Know: Conceptualizations of Access to Information in Human Rights Law*. Unpublished dissertation, University of North Carolina, Chapel Hill.

Björkdahl, Annika/Chaban, Natalia/Leslie, John/Masselot, Annick (2015). Introduction: To Take or Not to Take EU Norms? Adoption, Adaptation, Resistance and Rejection. In Björkdahl, Annika/Chaban, Natalia/Leslie, John/Masselot, Annick, (eds.), *Importing EU Norms: Conceptual Framework and Empirical Findings*. Cham: Springer International Publishing, pp. 1–9.

Björkdahl, Annika/Höglund, Kristine (2013). Precarious Peacebuilding: Friction in Global–Local Encounters. *Peacebuilding* 1(3), 289–99.

Blanco, Ligia/Zapata, Adrián (2007). La contribución del proceso de paz a la construcción de la democracia en Guatemala. In Azpuru, Dinorah/Blanco, Ligia/Córdova Macías, Ricardo/Loya Marín, Nayelly/Ramos, Carlo G./Zapata, Adrián, (eds.), *Construyendo la democracia en sociedades posconflictos. Guatemala y El Salvador, un enfoque comparada*. Guatemala City: F&G editores, pp. 289–509.

Blanton, Thomas (2002). The World's Right to Know. *Foreign Policy* 131, 50–58.

Blas, Ana Lucía (2008a). Acceso a información será posible en enero. *Prensa Libre*, 24 September 2008, p. 3.

Blas, Ana Lucía (2008b). Álvaro Arzú desconoce la ley. *Prensa Libre*, 3 July 2008. www.prensalibre.com/noticias/Alvaro-Arzu-desconoce-ley_0_1667 83592.html, accessed 28 June 2014.

Blas, Ana Lucía (2009). Datos en línea para municipalidades. *Prensa Libre*, 1 May 2009. www.prensalibre.com/noticias/Datos-linea-municipali dades_0_34798013.html, accessed 28 June 2014.

Blas, León (2008). Que se evidencie a quienes se oponen a ley para libre acceso a información. *Prensa Libre*, 25 June 2008. www.prensalibre.com/noticias/evidencie-oponen-libre-acceso-informacion_0_166186050.html, accessed 28 June 2014.

Bob, Clifford (2012). *The Global Right Wing and the Clash of World Politics*. Cambridge: Cambridge University Press.

Boesenecker, Aaron P./Vinjamuri, Leslie (2011). Lost in Translation? Civil Society, Faith-Based Organizations and the Negotiation of International Norms. *International Journal of Transitional Justice* 5(3), 345–65.

Bonilla, María Isabel (2002). Democracia también es información. *Prensa Libre*, 30 October 2002. www.prensalibre.com/opinion/CONCIENCIA brDemocracia-informacion_0_58795643.html, accessed 28 June 2014.

Bonillo, Cristina (2009). Comunas son las más denunciadas; no respetan ley de acceso a información. *Prensa Libre*, 18 August 2009. www.prensalibre .com/noticias/Comunas-denunciadas-respetan-acceso-informacion_0_1001 90059.html, accessed 28 June 2014.

Bonillo, Cristina (2010a). Critican trabas de Ley de Libre Acceso a la Información. *Prensa Libre*, 10 March 2010. www.prensalibre.com/noti cias/politica/Critican-trasbas-Ley-Libre-Informacion_0_222577843.html, accessed 28 June 2014.

Bonillo, Cristina (2010b). Pocos entregan informe de LAIP. *Prensa Libre*, 31 January 2010. www.prensalibre.com/noticias/Pocos-entregan-informe -LAIP_0_199780090.html, accessed 28 June 2014.

Börzel, Tanja A./Risse, Thomas (2000). When Europe Hits Home: Europeanization and Domestic Change. *European Integration Online Papers (EIoP)* 4(15).

Börzel, Tanja A./Risse, Thomas (2009). *The Transformative Power of Europe. The European Union and the Diffusion of Ideas*. KFG The Transformative Power of Europe Working Paper No. 1, May 2009. FU Berlin.

Börzel, Tanja A./Risse, Thomas (2012). From Europeanisation to Diffusion: Introduction. *West European Politics* 35(1), 1–19.

Börzel, Tanja A./Risse, Thomas (2013). Human Rights in Areas of Limited Statehood: The New Agenda. In Risse, Thomas/Ropp, Stephan/Sikkink, Kathryn, (eds.), *The Persistent Power of Human Rights: From Commitment to Compliance*. Cambridge: Cambridge University Press, pp. 63–84.

Boswell, Christina (2008). Evasion, Reinterpretation and Decoupling: European Commission Responses to the 'External Dimension' of Immigration and Asylum. *West European Politics* 31(3), 491–512.

Brake, Benjamin/Katzenstein, Peter J. (2013). Lost in Translation? Nonstate Actors and the Transnational Movement of Procedural Law. *International Organization* 67(4), 725–57.

Brands, Hal (2011). Crime, Irregular Warfare, and Institutional Failure in Latin America: Guatemala as a Case Study. *Studies in Conflict and Terrorism* 34(3), 228–47.

Briscoe, Ivan/Pellecer, Martín Rodríguez (2010). *A State under Siege: Elites, Criminal Networks and Institutional Reform in Guatemala.* Clingendael, The Hague. www.clingendael.nl/publications/2010/20100913_cru_publi cation_ibriscoe.pdf, accessed 10 January 2015.

Brown, Stephen (2005). Foreign Aid and Democracy Promotion: Lessons from Africa. *European Journal of Development Research* 17(2), 179–98.

Brunnée, Jutta/Toope, Stephen J. (2010). *Legitimacy and Legality in International Law: An Interactional Account.* Cambridge: Cambridge University Press.

Brysk, Alison (1995). 'Hearts and Minds': Bringing Symbolic Politics Back In. *Polity* 27(4), 559–85.

Brysk, Alison (2008). Communicative Action and Human Rights in Colombia. *Colombia Internacional* 69(1), 36–49.

Burnell, Peter (2007). *Does International Democracy Promotion Work?*, Discussion Paper 17/2007, DIE, Bonn. www.die-gdi.de/CMS-Homepage/ openwebcms3.nsf/%28ynDK_contentByKey%29/ADMR-7BRF46/$FIL E/BurnellPromotionWork.pdf, accessed 12 March 2012.

Burnell, Peter/Youngs, Richard (eds.) (2010). *New Challenges to Democratization.* London: Routledge.

Busby, Joshua William (2007). Bono Made Jesse Helms Cry: Jubilee 2000, Debt Relief, and Moral Action in International Politics. *International Studies Quarterly* 51(2), 247–75.

Call, Charles T./Cook, Susan E. (2003). On Democratization and Peacebuilding. *Global Governance* 9(2), 233–46.

Callamard, Agnes (2008). *Towards a Third Generation of Activism for the Right to Freedom of Information*, 3 May 2008, Article 19. www.article19 .org/data/files/pdfs/publications/mozambique-unesco-world-press-free dom-day.pdf, accessed 1 March 2016.

Calvario de CICIG (2007). [Editorial] *El Periódico*, 25 July 2007, p. 16.

Camacho, José Joaquín (1998). El Código: cómo arreglar un error. *Siglo Veintiuno*, 21 March 1998, p. 16.

Camacho, José Joaquín (2002). Cumbre de la Infancia: ¿Derechos o protección? *Siglo Veintiuno*, 25 May 2002, p. 12.

Camilleri, Michael J. (2005). Age of Enlightenment? Contemporary U.S. Policy in Guatemala. *ReVista, Harvard Review of Latin America* (Spring/Summer), 25–27.

Canciller pidió a Europa 'apoyo político' (2003). *Prensa Libre*, 20 January 2003, p. 2.

Canteo, Carlo (2000). Los niños, la batalla ideológica. *Siglo Veintiuno*, 27 February 2000, p. 14.

Capie, David (2008). Localization as Resistance: The Contested Diffusion of Small Arms Norms in Southeast Asia. *Security Dialogue* 39(6), 637–58.

Cardona, Karen (2009). Anam sugiere secretividad sobre sueldos de alcaldes. *Prensa Libre*, 5 May 2009. www.prensalibre.com/noticias/Anam-sugiere -secretividad-sueldos-alcaldes_0_37197785.html, accessed 28 June 2014.

Cardona, Karen (2010a). El Ministerio de Economía restringe acceso a la información. *Prensa Libre*, 15 March 2010. www.prensalibre.com/noti cias/politica/Ministerio-Economia-restringe-acceso-informacion_0_22557 7644.html, accessed 28 June 2014.

Cardona, Karen (2010b). Secreto protege datos de pymes, mineras y maquila. *Prensa Libre*, 16 March 2010. www.prensalibre.com/noticias/ Secreto-protege-datos-mineras-maquila_0_226177417.html, accessed 28 June 2014.

Carey, David, Jr. (2004). Maya Perspectives on the 1999 Referendum in Guatemala: Ethnic Equality Rejected? *Latin American Perspectives* 31(6), 69–95.

Carothers, Thomas (1998). The Rule of Law Revival. *Foreign Affairs* 77(2), 95–106.

Carothers, Thomas (1999). *Aiding Democracy Abroad: The Learning Curve*. Carnegie Endowment for International Peace, Washington, D.C.

Carothers, Thomas (2003). *Promoting the Rule of Law Abroad: The Problem of Knowledge*. Working Papers Rule of Law Series No. 34, Washington, D.C., January 2003.

Carothers, Thomas (2006). The Backlash against Democracy Promotion. *Foreign Affairs* 85(2), 55–68.

Carothers, Thomas (2007). How Democracies Emerge. The 'Sequencing' Fallacy. *Journal of Democracy* 18(1), 12–27.

Carothers, Thomas (2009a). Democracy Assistance: Political vs. Developmental? *Journal of Democracy* 20(1), 5–19.

Carothers, Thomas (2009b). *Revitalizing U.S. Democracy Assistance. The Challenge of USAID*. Carnegie Endowment for International Peace, Washington, D.C.

Carothers, Thomas/Brechenmacher, Saskia (2014). *Closing Space: Democracy and Human Rights Support under Fire*. Washington, D.C.: Carnegie Endowment for International Peace.

Carrera, Margareta (2000). El silencio impuesto. *Prensa Libre*, 18 March 2000, p. 14.

Carrera, Mario Alberto (1998). El Código de la Niñez y un análisis del poder. *Siglo Veintiuno*, 19 March 1998, p. 15.

Carvill, Courtney (2009). Guatemala: Another Democracy Hangs in the Balance. *SperoNews* (21 November 2009). www.speroforum.com/a/1977 0/Guatemala-another-democracy-hangs-in-the-balance, accessed 1 March 2016.

Casals and Associates, Inc. (2004). *Anti-Corruption and Transparency Program.* *Guatemala Technical Assistance for Anti-Corruption Activities, Final Report,* Task Order Number AEP-I-00–00–00010–00, December, USAID, Guatemala. http://pdf.usaid.gov/pdf_docs/Pdacd338 .pdf, accessed 6 November 2014.

Casasola, Suseth (2010). 90% no conoce LAIP en seis municipios. *Siglo Veintiuno,* 18 August 2010. www.s21.com.gt/node/17454, accessed 28 February 2016.

Castellanos, Amafredo (2006). EE.UU. sugiere controles. *Prensa Libre,* 15 March 2006. www.prensalibre.com/noticias/EEUU-sugiere-controles_0 _127787288.html, accessed 15 November 2014.

Castresana, Carlos (2004). La ONU en la lucha contra la impunidad en Guatemala. *Papeles* 87, 105–12.

Castresana, un Eliot Ness moderno que motiva aplausos y críticas (2010). *Prensa Libre,* 4 May 2010. www.prensalibre.com/noticias/justicia/Castres ana-Eliot-Ness-aplausos-criticas_0_255574560.html, accessed 5 October 2014.

CEJIL (2006). Los derechos de los niños y las niñas: avances y desafíos del sistema interamericano. *CEJIL Gaceta* 26. www.cejil.org/sites/default/fil es/legacy_files/Gaceta_26_sp_0.pdf, accessed 1 March 2016.

CEJIL/Save the Children Sweden (2005). *Construyendo los derechos del niño en las Américas,* Buenos Aires. https://viejaweb.cejil.org/sites/default/files/ construyendo_los_derechos_del_nino_en_las_americas_0.pdf, accessed 12 March 2012.

Cereser, L. (2009). Se pierde interés por ley de acceso a información. *Prensa Libre,* 28 August 2009. www.prensalibre.com/noticias/pierde-interes-ley -acceso-informacion_0_103789692.html, accessed 28 June 2014.

Cerigua (2014). *PDH presentó Informe de Situación del Derecho Humano de Acceso a la Información Pública.* http://cerigua-org.cyclope.ws/article/pdh -presento-informe-de-situacion-del-derecho-huma/, accessed 6 November 2015.

Chandler, David (2010). The Uncritical Critique of 'Liberal Peace'. *Review of International Studies* 36(S1), 137–55.

Chandler, David (2013). Promoting Democratic Norms? Social Constructivism and the 'Subjective' Limits to Liberalism. *Democratization* 20(2), 215–39.

Channell, Wade (2006). Lessons Not Learned about Legal Reform. In Carothers, Thomas, (ed.), *Promoting the Rule of Law Abroad: In Search of Knowledge.* Washington, D.C.: Carnegie Endowment for International Peace, pp. 137–60.

Charnysh, Volha/Lloyd, Paulette/Simmons, Beth A. (2015). Frames and Consensus Formation in International Relations: The Case of Trafficking in Persons. *European Journal of International Relations* 21(2), 323–51.

Chay, Lucy (2003a). Aprueban nuevo Código de menores. *El Periódico*, 5 June 2003, p. 8.

Chay, Lucy (2003b). Congreso se compromete a aprobar leyes priorizadas para la paz. *El Periódico*, 13 March 2003, p. 3.

Checkel, Jeffrey T. (1999). Norms, Institutions, and National Identity in Contemporary Europe. *International Studies Quarterly* 43(1), 83–114.

Checkel, Jeffrey T. (2001). Why Comply? Social Learning and European Identity Change. *International Organization* 55(3), 553–88.

Checkel, Jeffrey T. (2005). International Institutions and Socialization in Europe: Introduction and Framework. *International Organization* 59(4), 801–26.

Cheng, Sealing (2011). The Paradox of Vernacularization: Women's Human Rights and the Gendering of Nationhood. *Anthropological Quarterly* 84(2), 475–505.

Chorev, Nitsan (2012). Changing Global Norms through Reactive Diffusion: The Case of Intellectual Property Protection of AIDS Drugs. *American Sociological Review* 77(5), 831–53.

Chwieroth, Jeffrey M. (2015). Managing and Transforming Policy Stigmas in International Finance: Emerging Markets and Controlling Capital Inflows after the Crisis. *Review of International Political Economy* 22(1), 44–76.

Ciciacs, a discusión (2005). *Prensa Libre*, 7 July 2005. www.prensalibre.com/noticias/Ciciacs-discusion_0_112189596.html, accessed 15 November 2014.

CICIACS Agreement (2004). *Agreement between the United Nations and the Government of Guatemala for the Establishment of a Commission for the Investigation of Illegal Groups and Clandestine Security Organizations in Guatemala ('CICIACS')*, New York City. www.un.org/News/dh/guatemala/ciciacs-eng.pdf, accessed 6 November 2014.

CICIG (2010). *Tercer año de labores*, Guatemala City. http://cicig.org/uploads/documents/tercer_anio_de_labores.pdf, accessed 12 November 2014.

CICIG (2012). *Report on the Fifth Year of Activities*, COM-067–20120911-DOC02-EN, Guatemala City. http://www.cicig.org/uploads/documents/2012/COM-067–20120911-DOC02-EN.pdf, accessed 12 November 2014.

CICIG (2013). *Sixth Report of Activities of the International Commission against Impunity in Guatemala (CICIG)*, COM-045–20130822-DOC01-EN, Guatemala City. www.cicig.org/uploads/documents/2013/COM-045–20130822-DOC01-EN.pdf, accessed 12 November 2014.

CICIG (2015). *Informe de la Comisión Internacional contra la Impunidad en Guatemala con ocasión de su octvao año de labores*, Guatemala Ciudad. www.cicig.org/uploads/documents/2015/COM_085_20151113_VIII.pdf, accessed 16 February, 2016.

CICIG Agreement (2006). *Agreement between the United Nations and the State of Guatemala on the Establishment of an International Commission Against Impunity in Guatemala ('CICIG')*, New York City. http://www .cicig.org/uploads/documents/mandato/cicig_acuerdo_en.pdf, accessed 6 November 2014.

Cicig, institución mejor valorada por guatemaltecos; Presidencia, la peor (2015). *Estrategia y negocios*, 2 August 2015. www.estrategiaynegocios .net/lasclavesdeldia/868160–330/cicig-instituci%C3%B3n-mejor-valor ada-por-guatemaltecos-presidencia-la-peor, accessed 1 March 2016.

Cicig, un debate que apenas principia (2007). [Editorial] *Prensa Libre*, 30 July 2007, p. 14.

Collier, David/Levitsky, Steven (1997). Democracy with Adjectives: Conceptual Innovation in Comparative Research. *World Politics* 49(3), 430–51.

Colop, Sam (2004). Desnudez del Sistema. *Prensa Libre*, 24 January 2004. www.prensalibre.com/opinion/UCHAXIKbrDesnudez-sistema_0_899920 96.html, accessed 12 November 2014.

Commission for Historical Clarification (1999). *Guatemala. Memory of Silence*. www.aaas.org/sites/default/files/migrate/uploads/mos_en.pdf, accessed 26 May 2014.

Commonwealth (2003). *Freedom to Information*. www.humanrightsinitia tive.org/programs/ai/rti/international/cw_standards/Cth%20model%20l aw%20-%20FOI%20Act.pdf, accessed 6 November 2014.

Congreso de la República de Guatemala (1996). *Código de la Niñez y la Juventud*, Decreto número 78–1996.

Congreso de la República de Guatemala (2001). *Iniciativa de Ley 2594*.

Congreso de la República de Guatemala (2002). *Iniciativa que aprueba la Ley de Protección Integral de la Niñez y Adolecencia*. Iniciativa 2767.

Congreso de la República de Guatemala (2004). *Reformas a la Ley de Protección Integral de la Niñez y Adolescencia*, Decreto número 02–2004.

Congreso de la República de Guatemala (2008). *Acceso a la información pública*, Decreto 57–2008.

Conrad, Sebastian/Randeria, Shalini (2002). *Jenseits des Eurozentrismus: Postkoloniale Perspektiven in den Geschichts- und Kulturwissenschaften*. Frankfurt/Main: Campus.

Corte de Constitucionalidad (2004). *Opinión consultiva*, Expediente No. 1250–2004.

Cortell, Andrew P./Davis, James W. (1996). How Do International Institutions Matter? The Domestic Impact of International Rules and Norms. *International Studies Quarterly* 40(4), 451–78.

Cortell, Andrew P./Davis, James W. (2000). Understanding the Domestic Impact of International Norms: A Research Agenda. *International Studies Review* 2(1), 65–87.

Cortell, Andrew P./Davis, James W. (2005). When Norms Clash: International Norms, Domestic Practices, and Japan's Internalisation of the GATT/WTO. *Review of International Studies* 31(1), 3–25.

Cowles, Maria Green/Carproso, James/Risse, Thomas (eds.) (2001). *Transforming Europe: Europeanization and Domestic Change*. Ithaca, NY: Cornell University Press.

Crawford, Gordon (2002). Evaluating European Union Promotion of Human Rights, Democracy and Good Governance: Towards a Participatory Approach. *Journal of International Development* 14, 911–26.

Crawford, Neta (2002). *Argument and Change in World Politics*. Cambridge: Cambridge University Press.

Darch, Colin/Underwood, Peter G. (2010). *Freedom of Information and the Developing World: The Citizen, the State and Models of Openness*. Oxford: Chandos Publishing.

de Zeeuw, Jeroen (2005). Projects Do Not Create Institutions: The Record of Democracy Assistance in Post-Conflict Societies. *Democratization* 12(4), 481–504.

Debe romperse cultura del secreto (2004). [Editorial] *Siglo Veintiuno*, 20 October 2004, p. 12.

Debiel, Tobias (2002). Do Crisis Regions Have a Chance of Lasting Peace? The Difficult Transformation from Structures of Violence. In Debiel, Tobias/Klein, Axel, (eds.), *Fragile Peace: State Failure, Violence and Development in Crisis Regions*. London: Zed Books in association with The Development and Peace Foundation, pp. 1–30.

Deere, Carolyn (2009). *The Implementation Game: the TRIPS Agreement and the Global Politics of Intellectual Property Reform in Developing Countries*. Oxford: Oxford University Press.

Deitelhoff, Nicole (2006). *Überzeugung in der Politik*. Frankfurt/Main: Suhrkamp.

Deitelhoff, Nicole (2009). The Discursive Process of Legalization: Charting Islands of Persuasion in the ICC Case. *International Organization* 63(1), 33–65.

Deitelhoff, Nicole (2012). Leere Versprechungen? Deliberation und Opposition im Kontext transnationaler Legitimitätspolitik. In Daase, Christopher/Geis, Anna/Nullmeier, Frank, (eds.), *Leviathan-Sonderheft*

27: *Der Aufstieg der Legitimitätspolitik. Rechtfertigung und Kritik politisch-ökonomischer Ordnungen.* Baden-Baden: Nomos, pp. 63–80.

Deitelhoff, Nicole/Müller, Harald (2005). Theoretical Paradise – Empirically Lost? Arguing with Habermas. *Review of International Studies* 31(1), 167–79.

Deitelhoff, Nicole/Zimmermann, Lisbeth (2013a). Aus dem Herzen der Finsternis: Kritisches Lesen und wirkliches Zuhören der konstruktivistischen Normenforschung. *Zeitschrift für Internationale Beziehungen* 20(1), 61–74.

Deitelhoff, Nicole/Zimmermann, Lisbeth (2013b). *Things We Lost in the Fire. How Different Types of Contestation Affect the Validity of International Norms,* PRIF Working Paper No 18 Frankfurt, PRIF, Frankfurt. http://hsfk .de/fileadmin/downloads/PRIF_WP_18.pdf, accessed 12 November 2014.

Del Cid, Marvin (2002). A discución Ley de Libre Accesso a la Información. *El Periódico,* 17 October 2002, p. 4.

Del Cid, Marvin (2003a). FRG busca el control de información official. *Prensa Libre,* 23 April 2003. www.prensalibre.com/noticias/FRG-busca-control-informacion-oficial_0_73192797.html, accessed 28 June 2014.

Del Cid, Marvin (2003b). Quieren ley de libre accesso a información. *Prensa Libre,* 22 April 2003. www.prensalibre.com/noticias/Quieren-ley-libre-acceso-informacion_0_73192866.html, accessed 28 June 2014.

Del Cid, Marvin (2004). Otto Reich: 'Deben combater corrupción y pobreza'. *Prensa Libre,* 4 May 2004. www.prensalibre.com/noticias/Otto-Reich-De ben-combatir-corrupcion_0_92391522.html, accessed 12 November 2014.

Delegación va de nuevo a México por Ley de Acceso a la Información (2009). *Prensa Libre,* 16 February 2009. www.prensalibre.com/noticias/Delegaci on-Mexico-Ley-Acceso-Informacion_0_7201310.html, accessed 28 June 2014.

Diamond, Larry (2002). Thinking about Hybrid Regimes. *Journal of Democracy* 13(2), 21–35.

Diamond, Larry (2008a). The Democratic Rollback. *Foreign Affairs* 87(2), 36–48.

Diamond, Larry (2008b). *The Spirit of Democracy: The Struggle to Build Free Societies throughout the World.* New York, NY: Holt.

Dickinson, Laura A. (2003). The Promise of Hybrid Courts. *The American Journal of International Law* 97(2), 295–310.

Diputados urgidos de ilustración (2003). [Editorial] *Siglo Veintiuno,* 3 September 2003, p. 12.

Donais, Timothy (2009). Empowerment or Imposition? Dilemmas of Local Ownership in Post-Conflict Peacebuilding Processes. *Peace & Change* 34(1), 3–26.

Donati, Paolo R. (2001). Die Rahmenanalyse politischer Diskurse. In Keller, Reiner/Hirseland, Andreas/Schneider, Werner/Viehöver, Willy, (eds.), *Handbuch Sozialwissenschaftliche Diskursanalyse. Band 1: Theorien und Methoden*. Opladen: Leske + Budrich, pp. 145–76.

Dosal, Paul J. (1993). *Doing Business with the Dictators: A Political History of United Fruit in Guatemala, 1899–1944*. Lanham, MD: Scholarly Resources.

Drori, Gili S./Meyer, John W./Ramirez, Francisco O./Schofer, Evan (2003). Loose Coupling in National Science: Policy versus Practice. In Drori, Gili S./Meyer, John W./Ramirez, Francisco O./Schofer, Evan, (eds.), *Science in the Modern World Polity: Institutionalization and Globalization*. Stanford, CA: Stanford University Press, pp. 155–73.

Dubón, Lucía (1998). Código del Niño: 300 mil firmas lo adversan. *Prensa Libre*, 18 March 1998, p. 6.

Duffield, Mark (2007). *Development, Security and Unending War. Governing the World of Peoples*. Cambridge: Polity Press.

Eisenstadt, Shmuel N. (2000). Multiple Modernities. *Daedalus* 129(1), 1–29.

Ejército, obligado a la transparencia (2003). [Editorial] *Siglo Veintiuno*, 27 September 2003, p. 10.

Elaboran proyecto contra acciones al protador y secreto bancario (2010). *Prensa Libre*, 18 October 2010. www.prensalibre.com/noticias/politica/acciones_portador_secreto_bancario_0_361764021.html, accessed 28 June 2014.

Elbasani, Arolda (2004). Albania in Transition: Manipulation or Appropriation of International Norms? *Southeast European Politics* 5(1), 24–44.

Elgström, Ole (2000). Norm Negotiations. The Construction of New Norms Regarding Gender and Development in EU Foreign Aid Policy. *Journal of European Public Policy* 7(3), 457–76.

El mensaje del Grupo Consultivo (2003). [Editorial] *Prensa Libre*, 15 May 2003. www.prensalibre.com/opinion/EDITORIALbrEl-mensaje-Grupo -Consultivo_0_73792657.html, accessed 28 June 2014.

Engelkamp, Stephan/Glaab, Katharina/Renner, Judith (2012). In der Sprechstunde. Wie (kritische) Normenforschung ihre Stimme wiederfinden kann. *Zeitschrift für Internationale Beziehungen* 19(2), 101–28.

Engelkamp, Stephan/Glaab, Katharina/Renner, Judith (2013). Ein Schritt vor, zwei Schritte zurück? *Zeitschrift für Internationale Beziehungen* 20(2), 105–18.

En torno a las reformas al Código de la Niñez y la Juventud (1998). [Editorial] *El Periódico*, 21 March 1998, p. 10.

Epstein, Charlotte (2012). Stop Telling Us How to Behave: Socialization or Infantilization? *International Studies Perspectives* 13(2), 135–45.

Epstein, Charlotte (2014). The Postcolonial Perspective: An Introduction. *International Theory* 6(2), 294–311.

Escaler, Karin (2005). La cultura de la adopción. *Siglo Veintiuno*, 26 September 2005, p. 20.

Escobar Sarti, Carolina (1998). La Iglesia, la niñez y la juventud. *Prensa Libre*, 19 March 1998, p. 12.

Espada, Rafael (2009). Hay lineamientos mínimos. *Prensa Libre*, 26 April 2009. www.prensalibre.com/opinion/COLABORACION-lineamientos -minimos_0_31796826.html, accessed 28 June 2014.

European Parliament (2007). *Resolution*, P6_TA(2007)0084, 15 March 2007. www.europarl.europa.eu/sides/getDoc.do?pubRef=-//EP//TEXT+T A+P6-TA-2007-0084+0+DOC+XML+V0//EN, accessed 6 November 2014.

Fabry, Mikulas (2009). The Right to Democracy in International Law: A Classical Liberal Reassessment. *Millennium – Journal of International Studies* 37(3), 721–41.

Falcoff, Mark (1991). Desdibujando las zonas de influencia: los Estados Unidos, Europa, y America Central. In Roy, Joaquín, (ed.), *La reconstrucción de Centroamérica: el papel de la Comunidad Europea*. Coral Gables: University of Miami, pp. 365–76.

Falta de voluntad política (2009). [Editorial] *El Periódico*, 18 April 2009. www.elperiodico.com.gt/es/20090418/opinion/97986/, accessed 28 June 2014.

Faundez, Julio (2005). The Rule of Law Enterprise: Promoting a Dialogue between Practitioners and Academics. *Democratization* 12(4), 567–86.

Fernández, Dina (2010). Nueva etapa. *El Periódico*, 9 June 2010. www.elp eriodico.com.gt/es/20100609/opinion/156526/, accessed 10 June 2012.

Figueroa, Luis (2004). No a la Ciciacs. *Prensa Libre*, 24 January 2004. www .prensalibre.com/opinion/CARPE-DIEMbrNo-Ciciacs_0_89992097.html, accessed 12 November 2014.

Figueroa, Luis (2006). En clandestinidad. *Prensa Libre*, 16 December 2006. http://luisfi61.com/2006/12/16/en-clandestinidad/, accessed 5 October 2014.

Finkel, Steven E./Pérez, Aníbal S/Seligson, Mitchell A. (2007). The Effects of U.S. Foreign Assistance on Democracy Building, 1990–2003. *World Politics* 59(3), 404–40.

Finnemore, Martha (1996). *National Interests in International Society*. Ithaca, NY: Cornell University Press.

Finnemore, Martha (2008). Paradoxes in Humanitarian Intervention. In Price, Richard, (ed.), *Moral Limit and Possibility in World Politics*. Cambridge: Cambridge University Press, pp. 197–224.

Finnemore, Martha/Sikkink, Kathryn (1998). International Norm Dynamics and Political Change. *International Organization* 52(4), 887–917.

Fischer, Edward (2004). Beyond Victimization: Maya Movements in Post-War Guatemala. In Grey Postero, Nancy/Zamsoc, Leon, (eds.), *The Struggle for Indigenous Rights in Latin America*. Eastbourne: Sussex Academic Press, pp. 81–104.

Flockhart, Trine (2005a). Complex Socialization and the Transfer of Democratic Norms. In Flockhart, Trine, (ed.), *Socializing Democratic Norms. The Role of International Organizations for the Construction of Europe*. Basingstoke: Palgrave Macmillan, pp. 43–62.

Flockhart, Trine (2005b). Socialization and Democratization: A Tenuous but Intriguing Link. In Flockhart, Trine, (ed.), *Socializing Democratic Norms. The Role of International Organizations for the Construction of Europe*. Basingstoke: Palgrave Macmillan, pp. 1–20.

Flores, Alex/Magallanes, Johnny (2016). Honduras y OEA firmaron este martes la Maccih. *El Heraldo*, 19 January 2016. www.elheraldo.hn/pais/921110–466/honduras-y-oea-firmaron-este-martes-la-maccih, accessed 1 March 2016.

Florini, Ann (1996). The Evolution of International Norms. *International Studies Quarterly* 40(3), 363–89.

Florini, Ann (1999). *Does the Invisible Hand Need a Transparent Glove? The Politics of Transparency*, Annual World Bank Conference on Development Economics, 28–30 April 1999, Washington, D.C.

Florini, Ann (ed.) (2007). *The Right to Know: Transparency for an Open World*. New York: Columbia University Press.

Francisco Dall'Anese renunciará a la Cicig (2013). *Prensa Libre*, 28 May 2013. www.prensalibre.com/noticias/politica/Francisco-DallAnese-renuncia-Cicig_0_927507498.html, accessed 2 June 2014.

Franck, Thomas M. (1990). *The Power of Legitimacy among Nations*, Oxford: Oxford University Press.

Franco, Leonardo/Kotler, Jared (1998). Combining Institution Building and Human Rights Verification in Guatemala: The Challenge of Buying In without Selling Out. In Henkin, Alice H., (ed.), *Honoring Human Rights Form Peace to Justice*. Washington, D.C.: The Aspen Institute, pp. 39–70.

Fuentes Destarac, Mario (2004). Acceso a la información pública. *El Periódico*, 25 October 2004. www.elperiodico.com.gt/es/20041025/opinion/8689/, accessed 5 October 2014.

Fukuyama, Francis (2005). 'Stateness' First. *Journal of Democracy* 16(1), 84–88.

Fulmer, Amanda M./Godoy, Angelina Snodgrass/Neff, Philip (2008). Indigenous Rights, Resistance, and the Law: Lessons from a Guatemalan Mine. *Latin American Politics and Society* 50(4), 91–121.

Funcionarios aprenden acerca de Ley Federal de Acceso a la Información Pública en México (2009). *Prensa Libre*, 1 January 2009. www.prensalibre .com/noticias/Funcionarios-Federal-Informacion-Publica-Mexico_0_66028 67.html, accessed 28 June 2014.

Gädeke, Dorothea (2014). Externe Demokratieförderung und kollektive Selbstbestimmung: Zu normativen Grundlagen und Grenzen einer umstrittenen Praxis. In Kadelbach, Stefan, (ed.), *Effektiv oder gerecht? Die normativen Grundlagen der Entwicklungspolitik*. Frankfurt/Main: Campus, pp. 214–51.

Galvan, Dennis/Sil, Rudra (2007). The Dilemma of Institutional Adaptation and the Role of Syncretism. In Galvan, Dennis/Sil, Rudra, (eds.), *Reconfiguring Institutions across Time and Space: Syncretic Responses to Challenges of Political and Economic Transformation*. New York, NY: Palgrave Macmillan, pp. 3–29.

Gálvez Borrell, Víctor (2007) ¿Quién le teme a la CICIG? *Siglo Veintiuno*, 6 August 2007, p. 18.

GAM (2011). *Informe de resultados de talleres de ley de acceso a la información pública impartidos en cinco departamentos de Guatemala*. Guatemala City. http://areadetransparencia.blogspot.de/2011/07/informe -de-resultados-de-talleres-de.html, accessed 6 November 2014.

Ganovsky-Larsen, Simon (2007). *La CICIACS: Defensores de Derechos Humanos y el Estado de Derecho en la Pos-Guerra*, GAM, Guatemala City.

García, Mario David (1998). Mos maiorum. *Siglo Veintiuno*, 28 March 1998, p. 14.

García Molina, J. Fernando (1998). Guatemala inmortal. *Siglo Veintiuno*, 19 March 1998, p. 14.

Garmendia, Maite (2004a). Abogarán por Hábeas Data. *Prensa Libre*, 15 April 2004. www.prensalibre.com/noticias/Abogaran-Habeas-Data_0_91 790853.html, accessed 28 June 2014.

Garmendia, Maite (2004b). Cabildeo en Congreso por Ley Hábeas Data. *Prensa Libre*, 29 April 2004. www.prensalibre.com/noticias/Cabildeo -Congreso-Ley-Habeas-Data_0_91791413.html, 28 June 2014.

Garrard-Burnett, Virginia (1998). *Protestantism in Guatemala: Living in the New Jerusalem*. Austin, Tx: University of Texas Press.

Gerhards, Jürgen/Rucht, Dieter (1992). Mesomobilization: Organizing and Framing in Two Protest Campaigns in West Germany. *American Journal of Sociology* 98(3), 555–96.

Gerrits, André (2007). Is there a Distinct European Democratic Model to Promote? In Van Doorn, Marieke/Meijenfeldt, Roel von, (eds.), *Democracy: Europe's Core Value? On the European Profile in World-wide Democracy Assistance*. Delf: Eburon, pp. 51–63.

Gershman, Carl/Allen, Michael (2006). The Assault on Democracy Assistance. *Journal of Democracy* 17(2), 36–52.

Gheciu, Alexandra (2005). Security Institutions as Agents of Socialization? NATO and the 'New Europe'. *International Organization* 59(4), 973–1012.

Giddens, Anthony (1979). *Central Problems in Social Theory: Action, Structure and Contradicion in Social Analysis*, Berkeley/Los Angeles, CA: University of California Press.

Gobierno de Guatemala (2007). *Reglamento Interno de la Comisión Nacional de la Niñez y de la Adolescencia*, Acuerdo gubernativo No. 512–2007. www.oj.gob.gt/es/QueEsOJ/EstructuraOJ/UnidadesAdministra tivas/CentroAnalisisDocumentacionJudicial/cds/CDs%20leyes/2007/pdfs/ normativa/N006%20Reglamento%20interno.pdf, accessed 2 June 2014.

Goetschel, Laurent/Hagmann, Tobias (2009). Civilian Peacebuilding: Peace by Bureaucratic Means? *Conflict, Security & Development* 9(1), 55–73.

Goffman, Erving (1986). *Frame Analysis: An Essay on the Organization of Experience*. Boston, MA: Northeast University Press.

Golub, Stephen (2006). A House without Foundation. In Carothers, Thomas, (ed.) *Promoting the Rule of Law Abroad: In Search of Knowledge*. Washington, D.C.: Carnegie Endowment for International Peace, pp. 105–36.

González, Miguel/Jiménez, Vivian/del Cid, Victor (2014). Indigenous and Afro-Descendant Social Movements in Central America. In Sánchez-Ancochea, Diego/Martí, Salvador, (eds.), *Handbook of Central American Governance*. Abingdon: Routledge, pp. 287–306.

González Merlo, José (1998). Si pero no . . . aunque siempre sí. *Prensa Libre*, 13 March 1998, p. 11.

González Merlo, José (2007). Expectativas y la Cicig. *Prensa Libre*, 7 August 2007. www.prensalibre.com/opinion/HOMO-ECONOMICUSbrExpect ativas-Cicig_0_149385842.html, accessed 5 October 2014.

González Moraga, Miguel/Arellano, Pavel (2000). Intensada jornade ayer. *Prensa Libre*, 13 April 2000. www.prensalibre.com/noticias/Intensa-jor nada-ayer_0_292777369.html, accessed 20 April 2012.

Goodman, Ryan/Jinks, Derek (2008). Incomplete Internalization and Compliance with Human Rights Law. *European Journal of International Law* 19(4), 725–48.

Goodman, Ryan/Jinks, Derek (2013). *Socializing States: Promoting Human Rights through International Law*. New York, NY: Oxford University Press.

Grabbe, Heather (2006). *The EU's Transformative Power: Europeanization through Conditionality in Eastern Europe*. Basingstoke: Palgrave Macmillan.

Gramajo Valdés, Silvio René (2003). El derecho de acceso a la información: análisis del proceso de discusión y gestión en Guatemala. Guatemala Ciudad: SEDEM-DOSES.

Gramajo Valdés, Silvio René (2005). *Acceso a la información en Guatemala: La experiencia de un proyecto desde la sociedad civil*, Diálogo Internacional de Comisionados de Acceso a la Información, 20–23 February, Cancún.

Gramajo Valdés, Silvio René (2009). *Un pasado que aún pesa. Los legados autoritarios imprimen su huella en la ley de Acceso a la Información Pública en Guatemala*. Unpublished dissertation. FLACSO México, México City.

Grigorescu, Alexandru (2003). International Organizations and Government Transparency: Linking the International and Domestic Realms. *International Studies Quarterly* 47(4), 643–67.

Grimes, Marcia (2011). *Multilevel Mobilization: Civil Society Efforts to Promote Access to Information Laws in Central America*. ECPR General Conference, 25–27 August 2011, Reykjavik.

Groß, Lisa/Grimm, Sonja (2014). The External-Domestic Interplay in Democracy Promotion: A Case Study on Public Administration Reform in Croatia. *Democratization* 21(5), 912–36.

Großklaus, Mathias (2015). Appropriation and the Dualism of Human Rights: Understanding the Contradictory Impact of Gender Norms in Nigeria. *Third World Quarterly* 36(6), 1253–67.

Grugel, Jean (2005). The 'International' in Democratization: Norms and the Middle Ground. In Flockhart, Trine, (ed.), *Socializing Democratic Norms. The Role of International Organizations for the Construction of Europe*. Basingstoke: Palgrave Macmillan, pp. 23–42.

Grugel, Jean (2007). Democratization and Ideational Diffusion: Europe, Mercosur and Social Citizenship. *Journal of Common Market Studies* 45(1), 43–68.

Grugel, Jean/Peruzzotti, Enrique (2010). Grounding Global Norms in Domestic Politics: Advocacy Coalitions and the Convention on the Rights of the Child in Argentina. *Journal of Latin American Studies* 42(1), 29–57.

Guoz, Abner (2003a). Ésta tiene mayor mandato. Entrevista con Reed Brody, Human Rights Watch. *El Periódico*, 17 March 2003, p. 6.

Guoz, Abner (2003b). Guatemala pide a ONU y OEA participar en la CICIACS. *El Periódico*, 8 March 2003, p. 3.

Guoz, Abner (2003c). Gutiérrez: anteproyecto sobre CICIACS antes de abril. *El Periódico*, 5 March 2003, p. 8.

Guoz, Abner (2003d). Minugua presentará informe 'amargo' ante Grupo Consultivo. *El Periódico*, 24 April 2003, p. 3.

Guoz, Abner (2003e). Proponen delimitar mandato de la CICIACS. *El Periódico*, 11 March 2003, p. 3.

Guoz, Abner/Herrera, Ó. (2003). Gobierno y sociedad civil acuerdan instalar la CICIACS. *El Periódico*, 14 March 2003, p. 3.

Gutiérrez, Edgar (1998). Lecciones del IUSI. *El Periódico*, 23 March 1998, p. 9.

Hábeas Data (2002). *El Periódico*, 24 Oct. 2002, p. 4.

Habermas, Jürgen (1981). *Theorie des kommunikativen Handelns*. Frankfurt/Main: Suhrkamp.

Habermas, Jürgen (1992). *Faktizität und Geltung: Beiträge zur Diskurstheorie des Rechts und des demokratischen Rechtsstaats*, 4th edn. Frankfurt/Main: Suhrkamp.

Hafner-Burton, Emilie M./Tsutsui, Kiyoteru (2005). Human Rights in a Globalizing World: The Paradox of Empty Promises. *American Journal of Sociology* 110(5), 1373–411.

Halliday, Terence C. (2009). Recursivity of Global Normmaking: A Sociolegal Agenda. *Annual Review of Law and Social Science* 5(1), 263–89.

Handy, Jim (1984). *Gift of the Devil: A History of Guatemala*. Boston, MA: South End Press.

Handy, Jim (1994). *Revolution in the Countryside: Rural Conflict & Agrarian Reform in Guatemala, 1944–1954*. Chapel Hill, NC: University of North Carolina Press.

Handy, Jim (2004). Chicken Thieves, Witches, and Judges: Vigilante Justice and Customary Law in Guatemala. *Journal of Latin American Studies* 36(3), 533–61.

Hannerz, Ulf (1996). *Transnational Connections: Culture, People, Places*. London: Routledge.

Harris-Short, Sonia (2001). Listening to 'the Other'? The Convention on the Rights of the Child. *Melbourne Journal of International Law* 2, 304–50.

Harrison, Graham (2001). Post-Conditionality Politics and Administrative Reform: Reflections on the Cases of Uganda and Tanzania. *Development and Change* 32(4), 657–79.

Haughton, Tim (2007). When Does the EU Make a Difference? Conditionality and the Accession Process in Central and Eastern Europe. *Political Studies Review* 5(2), 233–46.

Hawkins, Darren (2004). Explaining Costly International Institutions: Persuasion and Enforceable Human Rights Norms. *International Studies Quarterly* 48(4), 779–804.

Hellmüller, Sara (2014). A Story of Mutual Adaptation? The Interaction between Local and International Peacebuilding Actors in Ituri. *Peacebuilding* 2(2), 188–201.

Hemisphere Conference on Free Speech (1994). *Chapultepec Declaration*, 28 June 2014. www.oas.org/en/iachr/expression/showarticle.asp?artID=60, accessed 6 November 2015.

Henderson, Sarah L. (2002). Selling Civil Society: Western Aid and the Nongovernmental Organization Sector in Russia. *Comparative Political Studies* 35(2), 139–67.

Hernández, Manuel (2009). Promueven reformas a LAI. *Siglo Veintiuno*, 7 July 2009, p. 4.

Hill, Matthew Alan (2010). Exploring USAID's Democracy Promotion in Bosnia and Afghanistan: a 'Cookie-Cutter Approach'? *Democratization* 17(1), 98–124.

Hobson, Christopher (2009). The Limits of Liberal-Democracy Promotion. *Alternatives: Global, Local, Political* 34(4), 383–405.

Hobson, Christopher/Kurki, Milja (2012). Introduction: The Conceptual Politics of Democracy Promotion. In Hobson, Christopher/Kurki, Milja, (eds.), *The Conceptual Politics of Democracy Promotion*. London: Routledge, pp. 1–16.

Holiday, David (2000). Guatemala's Precarious Peace. *Current History* 99(634), 78–84.

Holzscheiter, Anna (2010). *Children's Rights in International Politics*. Basingstoke: Palgrave Macmillan.

Honig, Bonnie (2006). Another Cosmopolitanism? Law and Politics in New Europe. In Post, Robert, (ed.), *Another Cosmopolitanism*. Oxford: Oxford University Press, pp. 102–27.

Howse, Robert/Teitel, Ruti (2010). Beyond Compliance: Rethinking Why International Law Really Matters. *Global Policy* 1(2), 127–36.

Hudson, Andrew/Taylor, Alexandra W. (2010). The International Commission against Impunity in Guatemala. A New Model for International Criminal Justice Mechanisms. *Journal of International Criminal Justice* 8, 1–22.

Hughes, Caroline/Öjendal, Joakim/Schierenbeck, Isabell (2015). The Struggle versus the Song – the Local Turn in Peacebuilding: An Introduction. *Third World Quarterly* 36(5), 817–24.

Hüllen, Vera van/Stahn, Andreas (2009). Comparing EU and US Democracy: Promotion in the Mediterranean and the Newly Independent States. In Magen, Amichai/Risse, Thomas/McFaul, Michael, (eds.), *Promoting Democracy and the Rule of Law: American and European Strategies*. Basingstoke: Palgrave Macmillan, pp. 118–49.

Human Rights Committee (2011). *General Comment No. 34*, CCPR /C/GC/ 34. 102nd Session, 11–29 July. www2.ohchr.org/english/bodies/hrc/docs/ gc34.pdf, accessed 6 November 2014.

Hurrell, Andrew (2002). Norms and Ethics in International Relations. In Carlsnaes, Walter/Risse, Thomas/Simmons, Beth, (eds.), *Handbook of International Relations*. London: Sage, pp. 137–54.

Inayatullah, Naeem/Blaney, David L. (2012). The Dark Heart of Kindness: The Social Construction of Deflection. *International Studies Perspectives* 13(2), 164–75.

Informarse es derecho básico (2005). [Editorial] *Prensa Libre*, 29 October 2005. www.prensalibre.com/opinion/EDITORIALbrInformarse-derecho -basico_0_113989219.html, accessed 28 June 2014.

Inter-American Commission on Human Rights (2000). *Inter-American Declaration of Principles on Freedom of Expression*, 108th Regular Session, 19 October. www.iachr.org/declaration.htm, accessed 6 November 2014.

International Crisis Group (2010). *Guatemala: Squeezed between Crime and Impunity*, Latin America Report No 33. www.crisisgroup.org/~/media/Fi les/latin-america/33%20Guatemala%20–%20Squeezed%20Between%2 0Crime%20and%20Impunity.pdf, accessed 12 November 2014.

International Crisis Group (2011a). *Guatemala: Drug Trafficking and Violence,* Latin America Report No 39. www.crisisgroup.org/~/media/Fil es/latin-america/39%20Guatemala%20–%20Drug%20Trafficking%20 and%20Violence.pdf, accessed 12 November 2014.

International Crisis Group (2011b). *Learning to Walk without a Crutch: An Assessment of the International Commission against Impunity in Guatemala*, Latin America Report No 36. www.crisisgroup.org/~/media/ Files/latin-america/36%20Learning%20to%20Walk%20without%20a %20Crutch%20–%20The%20International%20Commission%20Again st%20Impunity%20in%20Guatemala.pdf, accessed 12 November 2014.

International Crisis Group (2013). *Justice on Trial in Guatemala: The Ríos Montt Case*, Latin America Report No 50. www.crisisgroup.org/ ~/media/Files/latin-america/Guatemala/050-justice-on-trial-in-guate mala-the-rios-montt-case.pdf, accessed 12 November 2014.

International Crisis Group (2016). *Crutch to Catalyst? The International Commission against Impunity in Guatemala*, Latin America Report No 56. www.crisisgroup.org/en/regions/latin-america-caribbean/guate mala/056-crutch-to-catalyst-the-international-commission-against-imp unity-in-guatemala.aspx, accessed 16 February 2016.

International Mechanism for Promoting Freedom of Expression (1999). *Joint Declaration.* www.article19.org/pdfs/igo-documents/three-man dates-dec-1999.pdf, accessed 6 November 2014.

Isaacs, Anita (2010). At War with the Past? The Politics of Truth Seeking in Guatemala. *International Journal of Transitional Justice* 4(2), 251–74.

Jackson, Jean E./Warren, Kay B. (2005). Indigenous Movements in Latin America, 1992–2004: Controversies, Ironies, New Directions. *Annual Review of Anthropology* 34(1), 549–73.

Jacobs, Jorge (1998). La renuncia a la libertad. *Prensa Libre*, 1998, 28 March p. 12.

Jacobs, Jorge (2007). Condenados. *Prensa Libre*, 20 December 2007. www.prensalibre.com/opinion/IDEASbrCondenados_0_151786234.html, accessed 5 October 2014.

Jacobs, Jorge (2007). La carabina. *Prensa Libre*, 26 July 2007, p. 16.

Jawad, Pamela (2008). Conflict Resolution through Democracy Promotion? The Role of the OSCE in Georgia. *Democratization* 15(3), 611–29.

Jetschke, Anja/Liese, Andrea (2013). The Power of Human Rights a Decade After: From Euphoria to Contestation? In Risse, Thomas/Ropp, Stephan/Sikkink, Kathryn, (eds.), *The Persistent Power of Human Rights: From Commitment to Compliance*. Cambridge: Cambridge University Press, pp. 26–42.

Jetschke, Anja/Murray, Philomena (2012). Diffusing Regional Integration: The EU and Southeast Asia. *West European Politics* 35(1), 174–91.

Jetschke, Anja/Rüland, Jürgen (2009). Decoupling Rhetoric and Practice: the Cultural Limits of ASEAN Cooperation. *The Pacific Review* 22(2), 179–203.

Joachim, Jutta (2003). Framing Issues and Seizing Opportunities: The UN, NGOs, and Women's Rights. *International Studies Quarterly* 47(2), 247–74.

Joachim, Jutta/Schneiker, Andrea (2012). Changing Discourses, Changing Practices? Gender Mainstreaming and Security. *Comparative European Politics* 10(5), 528–63.

Job, Brian L./Shesterinina, Anastasia (2014). China as a Global Norm-Shaper: Instutionalization and Implementation of the Responsibility to Protect. In Betts, Alexander/Orchard, Phil, (eds.), *Implementation & World Politics*. Oxford: Oxford University Press, pp. 144–59.

Johnson, David (1992). Cultural and Regional Pluralism in the Drafting of the UN Convention on the Rights of the Child. In Freeman, Michael/Veerman, Philip, (eds.), *The Ideologies of Children's Rights*. Dordrecht: Martinus Nijhoff, pp. 95–114.

Jolly, Richard (2014). *UNICEF (United Nations Children's Fund): Global Governance that Works*. London: Routledge.

Jonas, Susanne (1991). *The Battle for Guatemala: Rebels, Death Squads, and U.S. Power*. Boulder, CO: Westview Press.

Jonas, Susanne (1995). Electoral Problems and the Democratic Project in Guatemala. In Seligson, Mitchell A., (ed.), *Elections and Democracy in*

*Central America, Revisited*. Chapel Hill, NC: University of North Carolina Press, pp. 25–44.

Jonas, Susanne (1996). Dangerous Liaisons: The U.S. in Guatemala. *Foreign Policy* (103), 144–60.

Jonas, Susanne (2000). *Of Centaurs and Doves: Guatemala's Peace Process*. Boulder, CO: Westview Press.

Kapoor, Ilan (2005). Participatory Development, Complicity and Desire. *Third World Quarterly* 26(8), 1203–20.

Kapoor, Ilan (2008). *The Postcolonial Politics of Development*. London: Routledge.

Karl, Terry Lynn (1995). The Hybrid Regimes of Central America. *Journal of Democracy* 6(3), 72–86.

Keck, Margaret E./Sikkink, Kathryn (1998). *Activists beyond Borders: Advocacy Networks in International Politics*. Ithaca, NY: Cornell University Press.

Kelley, Judith (2004). International Actors on the Domestic Scene: Membership Conditionality and Socialization by International Institutions. *International Organization* 58(3), 425–57.

Keohane, Robert O. (1984). *After Hegemony: Cooperation and Discord in the World Political Economy*. Princeton, NJ: Princeton University Press.

Kincaid, A. Douglas (2000). Demilitarization and Security in El Salvador and Guatemala: Convergences of Success and Crisis. *Journal of Interamerican Studies and World Affairs* 42(4), 39–58.

Klotz, Audie (1995). Norms Reconstituting Interests: Global Racial Equality and U.S. Sanctions against South Africa. *International Organization* 49(3), 451–78.

Klotz, Audie/Lynch, Cecilia (2007). *Strategies for Research in Constructivist International Relations*. Armonk, NY: M.E. Sharpe.

Knack, Stephen (2004). Does Foreign Aid Promote Democracy? *International Studies Quarterly* 48(1), 251–66.

Knill, Christoph/Lenschow, Andrea (2005). Compliance, Competition and Communication: Different Approaches of European Governance and Their Impact on National Institutions. *Journal of Common Market Studies* 43(3), 583–606.

Koh, Harold Hongju (1996). *Transnational Legal Process*, Faculty Scholarship Series Paper 2096. http://digitalcommons.law.yale.edu/fss_pa pers/2096, accessed 1 March 2016.

Koh, Harold Hongju (1997). Why Do States Obey International Law? *The Yale Law Journal* 106(8), 2599–659.

Koh, Harold Hongju (1998). The 1998 Frankel Lecture: Bringing International Law Home. *Houston Law Review* 35, 623–81.

Kolbay, Brendan (2005). Guatemala's Ley de Proteccion Integral de la Niñez y Adolescencia: One Year On, School of International and Public Affairs, Columbia University/Associación Nuestros Derechos Guatemala, New York/Guatemala City.

Kopstein, Jeffrey (2006). The Transatlantic Divide over Democracy Promotion. *The Washington Quarterly* 29(2), 85–98.

Kowert, Paul/Legro, Jeffrey W. (1996). Norms, Identity, and Their Limits: A Theoretical Reprise. In Katzenstein, Peter J., (ed.), *The Culture of National Security: Norms and Identity in World Politics*. New York, NY: Columbia University Press, pp. 451–97.

Krappmann, Lothar (2006). Über die Schwierigkeit, die Kinderrechte zu verwirklichen. Die Arbeit des Ausschusses der Vereinten Nationen für die Rechte des Kindes. *Die Friedens-Warte* 81(1), 145–62.

Kratochwil, Friedrich (1989). *Rules, Norms and Decisions: On the Conditions of Practical and Legal Reasoning in International Relations and Domestic Affairs*. Cambridge: Cambridge University Press.

Kratochwil, Friedrich/Ruggie, John Gerard (1986). International Organization: A State of the Art on an Art of the State. *International Organization* 40(4), 753–75.

Krook, Mona Lena/True, Jacqui (2012). Rethinking the Life Cycles of International Norms: The United Nations and the Global Promotion of Gender Equality. *European Journal of International Relations* 18(1), 103–27.

Kumar, Chetan/Lodge, Sara (2002). *Sustainable Peace through Democratization: The Experiences of Haiti and Guatemala*, IPA Policy Paper, International Peace Academy, New York.

Kumar, Krishna/de Zeeuw, Jeroen (2006). Democracy Assistance to Postconflict Societies. In de Zeeuw, Jeroen/Kumar, Krishna, (eds.), *Promoting Democracy in Postconflict Societies*. Boulder, CO: Lynne Rienner, pp. 1–21.

Kurki, Milja (2010). Democracy and Conceptual Contestability: Reconsidering Conceptions of Democracy in Democracy Promotion. *International Studies Review* 12(3), 362–86.

Kurki, Milja (2011a). Governmentality and EU Democracy Promotion: The European Instrument for Democracy and Human Rights and the Construction of Democratic Civil Societies. *International Political Sociology* 5(4), 349–66.

Kurki, Milja (2011b). Human Rights and Democracy Promotion: Reflections on the Contestation in, and the Politico-Economic Dynamics of, Rights Promotion. *Third World Quarterly* 32(9), 1573–87.

Kurki, Milja (2013). *Democratic Futures: Revisioning Democracy Promotion*. New York, NY: Routledge.

Kurtenbach, Sabine (2008). *Guatemala's Post-War Development. The Structural Failure of Low Intensity Peace*, Working Paper No 3, INEF, Duisburg.

La CICIG debe continuar (2009). [Editorial] *El Periódico*, 24 April 2009, p. 4.

Laffey, Mark/Nadarajah, Suthaharan (2012). The Hybridity of Liberal Peace: States, Diasporas and Insecurity. *Security Dialogue* 43(5), 403–20.

Larra, Myriam (1996). Diputados aprueban por unanimidad el Código de la Niñez y la Juventud. *Prensa Libre*, 12. September 1996, p. 6.

Larra, Myriam (1998). Planta 83 reformas al Código de Niñez. *Prensa Libre*, 19 March 1998, p. 4.

Larra, Myriam (2000a). De la niñez a la familia. *Prensa Libre*, 2 February 2000, p. 6.

Larra, Myriam (2000b). Golpe al Código. *Prensa Libre*, 24 February 2000, p. 4.

Larra, Myriam/Maldonado, Nuria/Sandoval, Juliet (2000). PAN pide postergar Código del Niño. *Prensa Libre*, 24 March 2000, p. 2.

La Rue, Frank (2007). Una victoria para la justicia. *Prensa Libre*, 5 August 2007, p. 28.

La Rue, Frank/Taylor, Harvey/Salazar Volkmann, Christian (1998). *Can Human Rights Be Denied to Children? Opposition and Defence of the Code for Children and Youth in Guatemala*, UNICEF, European Union, Radda Barnen, CALDH, GTZ, Guatemala City.

Lefort, Claude (1988). *Democracy and Political Theory*. Cambridge: Polity.

Legro, Jeffrey W. (1997). Which Norms Matter? Revisiting the 'Failure' of Internationalism. *International Organization* 51(1), 31–63.

Leininger, Julia (2010). 'Bringing the Outside In': Illustrations from Haiti and Mali for the Re-conceptualization of Democracy Promotion. *Contemporary Politics* 16(1), 63–80.

Lemay-Hébert, Nicolas (2012). Coerced Transitions in Timor-Leste and Kosovo: Managing Competing Objectives of Institution-Building and Local Empowerment. *Democratization* 19(3), 465–85.

Levitsky, Steven/Murillo, María Victoria (2009). Variation in Institutional Strength. *Annual Review of Political Science* 12(1), 115–33.

Levitt, Peggy/Merry, Sally (2009). Vernacularization on the Ground: Local Uses of Global Women's Rights in Peru, China, India and the United States. *Global Networks* 9(4), 441–61.

Lewin, Elisabeth (2000). *Supporting the Change of National Frameworks to Meet the Demands of the CRC: The Role of UNICEF*, TARCO, UNICEF. www.unicef.org/evaldatabase/files/TACRO_2000_Supporting_the_Change_part_1.pdf, accessed 1 March 2016.

Lidén, Kristoffer (2011). Peace, Self-Governance and International Engagement: From Neo-Colonial to Post-Colonial Peacebuilding. In

Tadjbakhsh, Shahrbanou, (ed.), *Rethinking the Liberal Peace: External Models and Local Alternatives*. London: Routledge, pp. 57–74.

Liese, Andrea (2009). Exceptional Necessity: How Liberal Democracies Contest the Prohibition of Torture and Ill-Treatment When Countering Terrorism. *Journal of International Law and International Relations* 5(17), 17–47.

Lijphart, Arend (1971). Comparative Politics and the Comparative Method. *The American Political Science Review* 65(3), 682–93.

Linde, Robyn (2014). The Globalization of Childhood: The International Diffusion of Norms and Law against the Child Death Penalty. *European Journal of International Relations* 20(2), 544–68.

Linden, Ronald H. (2002). Conclusion: International Organizations and East Europe – Bringing Parallel Tracks Together. In Linden, Ronald H., (ed.), *Norms and Nannies: The Impact of International Organizations on the Central and Eastern European States*. Lanham: Rowman & Littlefield, pp. 369–82.

Lineares Beltranena, Fernando (2000). ¿Qué hacer con los niños tragafuegos y mendigos? *Prensa Libre*, 18 March 2000, p. 14.

López, Olga (2002). Código de la Niñez entrará en vigencia. *Prensa Libre*, 17 May 2002. www.prensalibre.com/noticias/Codigo-Ninez-entrara-vigen cia_0_55795223.html, accessed 2 June 2014.

López, Olga (2006). La Ciciacs será CICIG. *Prensa Libre*, 12 December 2006. www.prensalibre.com/noticias/Ciciacs-Cicig_0_133187386.html, accessed 15 November 2014.

Lutz, Ellen L./Sikkink, Kathryn (2000). International Human Rights Law and Practice in Latin America. *International Organization* 54(3), 633–59.

MacCreery, David (1994). *Rural Guatemala, 1760–1940*. Stanford, CA: Stanford University Press.

Mac Ginty, Roger (2008). Indigenous Peace-Making versus the Liberal Peace. *Cooperation and Conflict* 43(2), 139–63.

Mac Ginty, Roger (2010). Hybrid Peace: The Interaction between Top-Down and Bottom-Up Peace. *Security Dialogue* 41(4), 391–412.

Mac Ginty, Roger (2011). *International Peacebuilding and Local Resistance: Hybrid Forms of Peace*. Basingstoke: Palgrave Macmillan.

Mac Ginty, Roger (2015). Where Is the Local? Critical Localism and Peacebuilding. *Third World Quarterly* 36(5), 840–56.

Mac Ginty, Roger/Richmond, Oliver P. (2013). The Local Turn in Peace Building: A Critical Agenda for Peace. *Third World Quarterly* 34(5), 763–83.

Mac Ginty, Roger/Richmond, Oliver P. (2015). The Fallacy of Constructing Hybrid Political Orders: A Reappraisal of the Hybrid Turn in Peacebuilding. *International Peacekeeping*, 1–21.

Mac Ginty, Roger/Sanghera, Gurchathen (2012). Hybridity in Peacebuilding and Development: An Introduction. *Journal of Peacebuilding & Development* 7(2), 3–8.

Maclure, Richard/Sotelo, Melvin (2004). Children's Rights and the Tenuousness of Local Coalitions: A Case Study in Nicaragua. *Journal of Latin American Studies* 36(1), 85–108.

Magen, Amichai/McFaul, Michael (2009). Introduction: American and European Strategies to Promote Democracy – Shared Values, Common Challenges, Divergent Tools? In Magen, Amichai/Risse, Thomas/ McFaul, Michael, (eds.), *Promoting Democracy and the Rule of Law: American and European Strategies*. Basingstoke: Palgrave Macmillan, pp. 1–33.

Magen, Amichai A./Morlino, Leonardo (eds.) (2009a). *International Actors, Democratization and the Rule of Law: Anchoring Democracy?*, Abingdon: Routledge.

Magen, Amichai/Morlino, Leonardo (2009b). Hybrid Regimes, the Rule of Law, and External Influence on Domestic Change. In Magen, Amichai/ Morlino, Leonardo, (eds.), *International Actors, Democratization and the Rule of Law: Anchoring Democracy?* Abingdon: Routledge, pp. 1–25.

Magen, Amichai/Risse, Thomas/McFaul, Michael (eds.) (2009). *Promoting Democracy and the Rule of Law: American and European Strategies*, Basingstoke: Palgrave Macmillan.

Maiguashca, Bice (2003). Governance and Resistance in World Politics. *Review of International Studies* 29(S1), 3–28.

Mainsbridge, Jane (1996). Using Power/Fighting Power: The Polity. In Benhabib, Seyla, (ed.), *Democracy and Difference*. Princeton, NJ: Princeton University Press, pp. 47–66.

Maldonado, Nuria/Larra, Myriam (1998). Con 300 mil firmas pieden derogar Código del Niño. *Prensa Libre*, 18 March 1998, p. 4.

Mandaville, Alicia Phillips/Mandaville, Peter P. (2007). Introduction: Rethinking Democratization and Democracy Assistance. *Development* 50(1), 5–13.

Mani, Rama (1998). Conflict Resolution, Justice and the Law: Rebuilding the Rule of Law in the Aftermath of Complex Political Emergencies. *International Peacekeeping* 5(3), 1–25.

Mani, Rama (2008). Exploring the Rule of Law in Theory and Practice. In Hurwitz, Agnès/Huang, Reyko, (eds.), *Civil War and the Rule of Law*. Boulder, CO: Lynne Rienner, pp. 21–45.

Marks, Frederick W. (1990). The CIA and Castillo Armas in Guatemala, 1954: New Clues to an Old Puzzle. *Diplomatic History* 14(1), 67–86.

Martínez, Francisco Mauricio (1998). Modificarán 73 articulos del Código de la Niñez. *Prensa Libre*, 22 March 1998, p. 8.

Mayora Alvarado, Eduardo (2007). Apruébese o no la CICIG. *Siglo Veintiuno*, 2 August 2007, p. 15.

McCreery Bunkers, Kelley/Groza, Victor/Lauer, Daniel P. (2009). International Adoption and Child Protection in Guatemala. *International Social Work* 52(5), 649–60.

McFaul, Michael (2002). The Fourth Wave of Democracy and Dictatorship: Noncooperative Transitions in the Postcommunist World. *World Politics* 54(2), 212–44.

Mearsheimer, John J. (1994/95). The False Promise of International Institutions. *International Security* 19(3), 5–49.

Mechanism for Follow-up on the Implementation of the Inter-American Convention against Corruption (2005). *Republic of Guatemala: Final Report*, SG/MESICIC/doc.155/05 rev. 4, 30 September. www.oas.org/juridico/english/mec_rep_gtm.pdf, accessed 6 November 2014.

Mechanism for Follow-up on the Implementation of the Inter-American Convention against Corruption (2008). *Republic of Guatemala: Final Report*, OEA/Ser.L, SG/MESICIC/doc.217/08 rev. 4, 27 June 27. www.oas.org/juridico/english/mesicic_II_inf_gtm_en.pdf, accessed 6 November 2014.

Mehan, Hugh/Nathanson, Charles E./Skelly, James M. (1990). Nuclear Discourse in the 1980s: The Unravelling Conventions of the Cold War. *Discourse and Society* 1(2), 133–65.

Mendel, Tobias (2009). *The Right to Information in Latin America. A Comparative Legal Survey*, UNESCO, Quito. http://unesdoc.unesco.org/images/0018/001832/183273e.pdf, accessed 5 January 2012.

Mendel, Toby (2006). Access to Information: The Existing State of Affairs around the World. *Comparative Media Law Journal* 8(3), 3–12.

Mendelson, Sarah E. (2015). *Why Governments Target Civil Society and What Can Be Done in Response: A New Agenda*, CSIS Human Rights Initiative, Washington, D.C.

Méndez Villaseñor, Claudia (2003a). Califican de ilegal plan de la ONU sobre Ciciacs. *Prensa Libre*, 24 October 2003. www.prensalibre.com/noticias/Califican-ilegal-plan-ONU-Ciciacs_0_76793432.html, accessed 12 November 2014.

Méndez Villaseñor, Claudia (2003b). Creación de Ciciacs va a paso lento. *Prensa Libre*, 16 September 2003. www.prensalibre.com/noticias/Creacion-Ciciacs-va-paso-lento_0_76192460.html, accessed 12 November 2014.

Méndez Villaseñor, Claudia (2003c). Piden investigar a grupos represores. *Prensa Libre*, 17 January 2003, p. 6.

Méndez Villaseñor, Claudia (2010). Organismos apoyan acceso a información. *Prensa Libre*, 13 May 2010. www.prensalibre.com/noticias/Organismos-a poyan-acceso-informacion_0_260973951.html, accessed 28 June 2014.

Mendoza, Carlos Aldana (1998). Más allá del Código. *Prensa Libre*, 26 March 1998, p. 12.

Mérida, Mario (2007). Ni a favor, ni en contra de la CICIG. *El Periódico*, 31 July 2007, p. 14.

Merry, Sally Engle (2006). *Human Rights & Gender Violence: Translating International Law into Local Justice*. Chicago, IL: University of Chicago Press.

Meyer, John W./Boli, John/Thomas, George M./Ramirez, Francisco O. (1997). World Society and the Nation-State. *American Journal of Sociology* 103(1), 144–81.

Meyer, John W./Rowan, Brian (1977). Institutionalized Organizations: Formal Structure as Myth and Ceremony. *American Journal of Sociology* 83(2), 340–63.

Meyer, Peter J./Ribando Seelke, Clare (2012). *Central America Regional Security Initiative: Background and Policy Issues for Congress*, Congressional Research Service. www.fas.org/sgp/crs/row/R41731.pdf, accessed 6 November 2014.

Michener, Greg (2011). FOI Laws around the World. *Journal of Democracy* 22(2), 145–59.

Michener, Gregory (2015a). Assessing Freedom of Information in Latin America a Decade Later: Illuminating a Transparency Causal Mechanism. *Latin American Politics and Society* 57(3), 77–99.

Michener, Gregory (2015b). How Cabinet Size and Legislative Control Shape the Strength of Transparency Laws. *Governance* 28(1), 77–94.

Millar, Gearoid (2013). Expectations and Experiences of Peacebuilding in Sierra Leone: Parallel Peacebuilding Processes and Compound Friction. *International Peacekeeping* 20(2), 189–203.

Millar, Gearoid/van der Lijn, Jaïr/Verkoren, Willemijn (2013). Peacebuilding Plans and Local Reconfigurations: Frictions between Imported Processes and Indigenous Practices. *International Peacekeeping* 20(2), 137–43.

Minondo Ayau, Raúl (2004a). Avalancha contra los DD.HH. *El Periódico*, 13 September 2004, p. 19.

Minondo Ayau, Raúl (2004b). Comentarios. *El Periódico*, 11 August 2004, p. 16.

Minondo Ayau, Raúl (2007a). Comentarios. *El Periódico*, 1 August 2007, p. 14.

Minondo Ayau, Raúl (2007b). Comentarios. *El Periódico*, 8 August 2007. www.elperiodico.com.gt/es/20070808/opinion/42339/, accessed 5 October 2014.

Minondo Ayau, Raúl (2010). El glorioso encabeza los esfuerzos en el lugar de la tragedia. *El Periódico*, 2 June 2010. www.elperiodico.com.gt/es/2010 0602/opinion/155144/, accessed 5 October 2014.

Minority Rights Group International (2015). *State of the World's Minorities and Indigenous Peoples 2015*. www.refworld.org/country,GTM,55a4f a5631,0.html, accessed 26 January 2015.

MINUGUA (2001). *Duodécimo informe sobre Derechos Humanos de la Misión de Verificación de las Naciones Unidas en Guatemala*. www.acn ur.org/t3/uploads/media/550.pdf?view=1, accessed 6 November 2014.

Molenares, Nadia/Renard, Robrecht (2003). The World Bank, Participation and PRSP: The Bolivian Case Revisited. *The European Journal of Development Research* 15(2), 133–161.

Montenegro, Nineth (2009). Transparencia en proceso. *Prensa Libre*, 26 April 2009. www.prensalibre.com/opinion/COLABORACION-Transpar encia-procesos_0_31796825.html, accessed 5 October 2014.

Monzón, Marielos (2003). Impunidad: ¿el comienzo del fin? *Prensa Libre*, 18 March 2003, p. 16.

Moody, Zoe (2014). Transnational Treaties on Children's Rights: Norm Building and Circulation in the Twentieth Century. *Paedagogica Historica* 50(1–2), 151–64.

Morales López, Henry (2007). *¿Por que tanta frustración? La cooperación internacional en la década de la Agenda de la Paz en Guatemala*, Movimiento Tzuk Kim-Pop, Guatemala Cuidad. http://biblioteca.hegoa.ehu .es/system/ebooks/17838/original/Por_que_tanta_frustracion.pdf, accessed 15 December 2011.

Morlino, Leonardo/Magen, Amichai (2009a). Methods of Influence, Layers of Impact, Cycles of Change. In Magen, Amichai/Morlino, Leonardo, (eds.), *International Actors, Democratization and the Rule of Law: Anchoring Democracy?* Abingdon: Routledge, pp. 26–52.

Morlino, Leonardo/Magen, Amichai (2009b). Scope, Depth and Limits of External Influence. In Magen, Amichai/Morlino, Leonardo, (eds.), *International Actors, Democratization and the Rule of Law: Anchoring Democracy?* Abingdon: Routledge, pp. 224–58.

Morroquín, Ericka (2008). UNE impulsa restricciones a Ley de Acceso. *Siglo Veintiuno*, 2 September 2008, p. 4.

Mouffe, Chantal (2000). *The Democratic Paradox*. London: Verso.

Mouffe, Chantal (2005). *On the Political*. London: Routledge.

Müller, Harald/Wunderlich, Carmen (eds.) (2013). *Norm Dynamics in Multilateral Arms Control: Interests, Conflicts, and Justice*. Athens, GA: University of Georgia Press.

Munck, Gerardo L. (2004). Tools for Qualitative Research. In Brady, Henry E./Collier, David, (eds.), *Rethinking Social Inquiry: Diverse Tools, Shared Standards*. Lanham, MD: Rowman & Littlefield, pp. 105–22.

Mutua, Makau (2001). Savages, Victims, and Saviors: The Metaphor of Human Rights. *Harvard International Law Journal* 42(1), 201–45.

Naciones Unidas, Comisión de Derechos Humanos (2000). *Informe del Relator Especial sobre la independencia de magistrados y abgoados, Sr. Param Coomaraswamy, presentado de conformidad con la resolución 1999/31 de la Comisión*, E/CN. 4/2000/61/Add.1. www.derechos.org/nizkor/guatemala/doc/param1.html, accessed 1 March 2016.

Nadarajah, Suthaharan/Rampton, David (2015). The Limits of Hybridity and the Crisis of Liberal Peace. *Review of International Studies* 41(1), 49–72.

Nadelmann, Ethan A. (1990). Global Prohibition Regimes: The Evolution of Norms in International Society. *International Organization* 44(4), 479–526.

Nájera, Walter/Barrilas, Byron (2004). Ejecutivo negociará una nueva CICIACS. *Siglo Veintiuno*, 7 August 2004, p. 8.

National Security Archive (n.d.). *Guatemala Project*. www.gwu.edu/~nsarchiv/guatemala/index.htm, accessed 13 November 2014.

Nieuwenhuys, Olga (1998). Global Childhood and the Politics of Contempt. *Alternatives: Global, Local, Political* 23(3), 267–89.

No hay mejora en la situación de la libertad de información, dice la SIP (2008). *Prensa Libre*, 20 March 2008. www.prensalibre.com/noticias/mejora-situacion-libertad-informacion-SIP_0_164386399.html, accessed 28 June 2014.

Noutcheva, Gergana (2009). Fake, Partial and Imposed Compliance: The Limits of the EU's Normative Power in the Western Balkans. *Journal of European Public Policy* 16(7), 1065–84.

Nuevo golpe a la Libertad de Prensa (2000). [Editorial] *Prensa Libre*, 4 February 2000, p. 12.

O'Connor, Vivienne (2006). Rule of Law and Human Rights Protections through Criminal Law Reform: Model Codes for Post-Conflict Criminal Justice. *International Peacekeeping* 13(4), 517–30.

O'Donnell, Guillermo (1996). Illusions about Consolidation. *Journal of Democracy* 7(2), 34–51.

O'Neill, William G. (2008). UN Peacekeeping Operations and Rule of Law Programs. In Hurwitz, Agnès/Huang, Reyko, (eds.), *Civil War and the Rule of Law: Security, Development, Human Rights*. Boulder, CO: Lynne Rienner, pp. 91–114.

OAS (1969). *American Declaration of the Rights and Duties of Man*. www.oas.org/en/iachr/mandate/Basics/declaration.asp, accessed 2 June 2014.

OAS (2001). *Inter-American Commission on Human Rights: Fifth Report on the Situation of Human Rights in Guatemala*, OEA/Ser.L/V/II.111. http://cidh.org/countryrep/Guate01eng/chap.12.htm, accessed 2 June 2014.

OAS (2003a). *Access to Public Information: Strengthening Democracy*, AG/Res. 1932 (XXXIII-O/03), 10 June, OAS fourth plenary session,. www.oas.org/juridico/english/ga03/agres_1932.htm, accessed 6 November 2014.

OAS (2003b). *Inter-American Commission on Human Rights: Justicia e inclusión social: los desafíos de la democracia en Guatemala*, OEA/Ser.L/V/II.118, 29 December. www.cidh.org/countryrep/Guatemala2003sp/indice.htm, accessed 2 June 2014.

OAS (2011). *Convention and MESICIC*. www.oas.org/juridico/english/corr_bg.htm, accessed 6 November 2014.

OAS (2016). *Misión de Apoyo contra la Corrupción y la Impunidad en Honduras (MACCIH)*. www.oas.org/documents/spa/press/Mision-Apoyo-contra-Corrupcion-Impunidad-Honduras-MACCIH.pdf, accessed 1 March 2016.

OAS Plenary Session (2010). *Model Inter-American Law on Access to Public Information*, AG/RES. 2607 (XL/O/10), 8 June. www.oas.org/dil/AG RES_2607–2010_eng.pdf, accessed 6 November 2014.

Ochaeta, Ronalth (2003). CICIACS, instrumento contra el oscurantismo. *El Periódico*, 28 March 2003, p. 16.

OECD (2005/2008). *The Paris Declaration on Aid Effectiveness and the Accra Agenda for Action*. www.oecd.org/dac/effectiveness/34428351.pdf, accessed 22 October 2013.

Oestreich, Joel E. (1998). UNICEF and the Implementation of the Convention on the Rights of the Child. *Global Governance* 4(2), 183–98.

Oestreich, Joel E. (2007). *Power and Principle: Human Rights Programming in International Organizations*. Washington, D.C.: Georgetown University Press.

Office of the Special Rapporteur for Freedom of Expression (1999). *Annual Report*, OEA/Ser.L/V/II.102, Doc. 6 rev., 16 April.

Office of the United States Trade Representative (n.d.). *CAFTA-DR (Dominican Republic-Central America FTA)*. www.ustr.gov/trade-agreements/free-trade-agreements/cafta-dr-dominican-republic-central-america-fta/final-text, accessed 6 November 2014.

Onuf, Nicholas Greenwood (1989). *World of Our Making: Rules and Rule in Social Theory and International Relations*. Columbia, SC: University of South Carolina Press.

Orantes Troccoli, Carlos (1998). Los códigos ocultos del Código. *Siglo Veintiuno*, 19 March 1998, p. 16.

Orr, Zvika (2012). The Adaptation of Human Rights Norms in Local Settings: Intersections of Local and Bureaucratic Knowledge in an Israeli NGO. *Journal of Human Rights* 11(2), 243–62.

Osorio, Jéssica (2008). En pie compromiso para ley de acceso. *Prensa Libre*, 20 September 2008, p. 5.

Ottaway, Marina (2003). Promoting Democracy after Conflict: The Difficult Choices. *International Studies Perspectives* 4(3), 314–22.

Palencia, Gema (2004). Gobierno apoyará ley de Hábeas Data. *Prensa Libre*, 2 April 2004. www.prensalibre.com/noticias/Gobierno-apoyara-ley-Hab eas-Data_0_91791987.html, accessed 28 June 2014.

Palma, Claudia (2004). La recomendación de Naciones Unidas de detener adopciones. *El Periódico*, 16 October 2004, p. 6.

Palmieri, Jorge (1998). Oportuno testimonio. *El Periódico*, 23 March 1998, p. 9.

Pangle, Thomas L. (2009). The Morality of Exporting Democracy: A Historical-Philosophical Perspective. In Barany, Zoltan/Moser, Robert G., (eds.), *Is Democracy Exportable?* Cambridge: Cambridge University Press, pp. 15–34.

Panke, Diana/Petersohn, Ulrich (2012). Why International Norms Disappear Sometimes. *European Journal of International Relations* 18(4), 719–42.

Pape-Yalibat, Edgar (2003). *Citizen Initiative for Freedom of Information in Guatemala*. Latin America and Caribbean Regional Workshop on Accountability, Participation and Poverty Reduction, June 2003, Punta Cana.

Paredes, Jennyffer/Rodríguez, Martín P. (2006). Dialogan sobre Ciciacs. *Prensa Libre*, 19 January 2006. www.prensalibre.com/noticias/Dialogan -Ciciacs_0_126587939.html, accessed 15 November 2014.

Paris, Roland (2004). *At War's End: Building Peace after Civil Conflict*. Cambridge: Cambridge University Press.

Paris, Roland/Sisk, Timothy D. (2009). Introduction: Understanding the Contradictions of Postwar Statebuilding. In Paris, Roland/Sisk, Timothy D., (eds.), *The Dilemmas of Statebuilding: Confronting the Contradictions of Postwar Peace Operations*. London: Routledge, pp. 1–20.

Park, Susan/Vetterlein, Antje (2010). Owning Development: Creating Policy Norms in the IMF and the World Bank. In Park, Susan/Vetterlein, Antje, (eds.), *Owning Development: Creating Policy Norms in the IMF and the World Bank*. Cambridge: Cambridge University Press, pp. 3–26.

Pásara, Luis (2001). *The Guatemalan Peace Process: The Accords and Their Accomplishments*, Kroc Institute Occasional Paper No 21, University of Notre Dame.

Payne, Rodger A. (2001). Persuasion, Frames and Norm Construction. *European Journal of International Relations* 7(1), 37–61.

PDH manejará archivo military (2008). *Prensa Libre*, 5 March 2008. www
.prensalibre.com/noticias/PDH-manejara-archivo-militar_0_164384119
.html, accessed 28 June 2014.

Peacock, Susan C./Beltrán, Adriana (2003). *Hidden Powers in Post-Conflict Guatemala. Illegal Armed Groups and the Forces behind Them.* Washington Office on Latin America, Washington, D.C.

Pearce, Jenny (2005). The International Community and Peacebuilding. *Development* 48(3), 41–49.

Pérez, Luis Enrique (2004). Semántica de la CICIACS. *Siglo Veintiuno*, 9 January 2004, p. 13.

Pérez, Mynor Enrique (2005). Sugieren replantear proyecto para Ciciacs. *Prensa Libre*, 17 May 2005. www.prensalibre.com/noticias/Sugieren-repla ntear-proyecto-Ciciacs_0_110989988.html, accessed 15 November 2014.

Pérez, Sina/Rodríguez, Luisa (2004). Seguirán luchando por creación de la Ciciacs. *Prensa Libre*, 7 August 2004, p. 3.

Pérez, Sonia (2005). Preocupan escollos a libertad de expression. *Prensa Libre*, 11 November 2005, p. 3.

Pérez, Sonia (2006). Encuesta: Desconfianza en las autoridades. *Prensa Libre*, 20 September 2006. www.prensalibre.com/noticias/Encuesta-Desc onfianza-autoridades_0_131388520.html, accessed 2 June 2014.

Peshkopia, Ridvan/Imami, Arben (2008). Between Elite Compliance and State Socialisation: The Abolition of the Death Penalty in Eastern Europe. *The International Journal of Human Rights* 12(3), 353–72.

Peterson, Jenny H. (2010). 'Rule of Law' Initiatives and the Liberal Peace: The Impact of Politicised Reform in Post-Conflict States. *Disasters* 34(S1), 15–39.

Peterson, Jenny H. (2012). A Conceptual Unpacking of Hybridity: Accounting for Notions of Power, Politics and Progress in Analyses of Aid-Driven Interfaces. *Journal of Peacebuilding & Development* 7(2), 9–22.

Piden cambios en Ley de Accesso a la Información (2002). *El Periódico*, 18 October 2002, p. 6.

Piden ley que no restrinja acceso a la información (2008). *Prensa Libre*, 30 January 2008. www.prensalibre.com/noticias/Piden-ley-restrinja-acceso-i nformacion_0_163188091.html, accessed 28 June 2014.

Pimentel, David (2010). Can Indigenous Justice Survive? Legal Pluralism and the Rule of Law. *Harvard International Review* 32(2), 32–36.

Plausible apoyo contra impunidad (2006). [Editorial] *Prensa Libre*, 13 December 2006, p. 14.

Poppe, Annika E./Wolff, Jonas (2013). The Normative Challenge of Interaction: Justice Conflicts in Democracy Promotion. *Global Constitutionalism* 2(3), 373–406.

Porras, Gustavo (2007). La CICIG hoy, ¿y mañana qué? *Siglo Veintiuno*, 8 August 2007, p. 15.

Portillo, F. (2003). Berger se compromete con la prensa. *Siglo Veintiuno*, 20 September 2003, p. 6.

Pouligny, Béatrice (2003). UN Peace Operations, INGOs, NGOs, and Promoting the Rule of Law: Exploring the Intersection of International and Local Norms in Different Postwar Contexts. *Journal of Human Rights* 2(3), 359–77.

Prantl, Jochen/Nakano, Ryoko (2011). Global Norm Diffusion in East Asia: How China and Japan Implement the Responsibility to Protect. *International Relations* 25(2), 204–23.

Presidencia de la República Guatemala (2005). *Acuerdo gobernamental para transparencia y acceso a la información*, Acuerdo gubernativo 645–2005, 6 December.

Presidente Colom suscribirá la declaración de Chapultepec ante directives de la SIP (2008). *Prensa Libre*, 30 March 2008. www.prensalibre.com/noti cias/Presidente-Colom-Declaracion-Chapultepec-SIP_0_164386400.html, accessed 28 June 2014.

Preti, Humberto (1998). Ojalá no quemen las naves. *Prensa Libre*, 21 March 1998, p. 11.

Preti, Humberto (2006). Con toda claridad. *Prensa Libre*, 16 December 2006. www.prensalibre.com/opinion/MACROSCOPIObrCon-toda-clari dad_0_133186828.html, accessed 5 October 2014.

Preti, Humberto (2007a). Mal necesario. *Prensa Libre*, 4 August 2007, p. 15.

Preti, Humberto (2007b). Mala herencia. *Prensa Libre*, 28 July 2007, p. 15.

Price, Richard (1998). Reversing the Gun Sights: Transnational Civil Society Targets Land Mines. *International Organization* 52(3), 613–44.

Price, Richard (ed.) (2008a). *Moral Limit and Possibility in World Politics*. Cambridge: Cambridge University Press.

Price, Richard (2008b). Moral Limit and Possibility in World Politics. *International Organization* 62(2), 191–220.

Privacidad: Luces y sombras (2003). [Editorial] *Siglo Veintiuno*, 22 April 2003, p. 8.

Pupavac, Vanessa (2001). Misanthropy Without Borders: The International Children's Rights Regime. *Disasters* 25(2), 95–112.

Pupavac, Vanessa (2011). Punishing Childhoods: Contradictions in Children's Rights and Global Governance. *Journal of Intervention and Statebuilding* 5(3), 285–312.

Q38 millones costar poner en marcha nuevo Código de la Niñez y la Juventud (1996). *Prensa Libre*, 13 September 1996, p. 6.

Rajagopal, Balakrishnan (2007). *International Law from Below: Development, Social Movements, and Third World Resistance.* Cambridge: Cambridge University Press.

Rajagopal, Balakrishnan (2008). Invoking the Rule of Law: International Discourses. In Hurwitz, Agnès/Huang, Reyko, (eds.), *Civil War and the Rule of Law: Security, Development, Human Rights.* Boulder, CO: Lynne Rienner, pp. 49–67.

Ramírez, Alberto E. (2002). Promueven el libre acceso a información. *Prensa Libre,* 29 August 2002, p. 8.

Ramírez, Gladys/Marroquín, Ericka (2007). Aprueban Ley de Adopciones. *Siglo Veintiuno,* 12 December 2007, pp. 2–9.

Rancière, Jacques (1999). *Disagreement: Politics and Philosophy.* Minneapolis, MN: University of Minnesota Press.

Randeria, Shalini (2005). Verwobene Moderne: Zivilgesellschaft, Kastenbindungen und nicht-staatliches Familienrecht im (post) kolonialen Indien. In Brunkhorst, Hauke/Costa, Sérgio, (eds.), *Jenseits von Zentrum und Peripherie: Zur Verfassung der fragmentierten Weltgesellschaft.* München: Hampp, pp. 169–96.

Randeria, Shalini (2007). Civil Society and Legal Pluralism in the Shadow of Caste: Entangled Modernities in Post-Colonial India. In Schirmer, Dominique/Saalmann, Gernot/Kessler, Christl, (eds.), *Hybridising East and West: Tales beyond Westernisation. Empirical Contributions to the Debates on Hybridity.* Münster: LIT, pp. 97–124.

Raustiala, Kal/Slaughter, Anne-Marie (2002). International Law, International Relations and Compliance. In Carlsnaes, Walter/Risse, Thomas/Simmons, Beth, (eds.), *Handbook of International Relations.* London: Sage, pp. 538–58.

Relly, Jeannine E. (2008) *The Global Diffusion of Access to Information Laws in Developing Countries: A Contextual Interpretation.* Unpublished dissertation, Arizona State University.

Renteria, Nelson (2015). El Salvador Rejects U.N.–backed Anti-Graft Body, Backs Milder Plan, *Reuters,* 22 October 2015. http://uk.reuters.com/arti cle/uk-el-salvador-corruption-idUKKCN0SG2E620151022, accessed 1 March 2016.

Retomará la Ciciacs (2005). *Prensa Libre,* 13 September 2005. www.prensa libre.com/noticias/Retomara-Ciciacs_0_113389084.html, accessed 15 November 2014.

Reus-Smit, Christian (2001). Human Rights and the Social Construction of Sovereignty. *Review of International Studies* 27(4), 519–38.

Rey Marcos, Francisco (2000). La Unión Europea y la rehabilitación posbélica. El caso de Guatemala. In Osorio, Tamara/Aguirre, Mariano, (eds.), *Después de la guerra. Un manual para la reconstrucción posbélica.* Barcelona: Icaria, pp. 165–82.

Reynolds, Luisa (2015). President Pérez Molina Refuses to Renew CICIG's Mandate, 16 March 2015, *Americas Quarterly.* www.americasquarterly .org/content/president-perez-molina-refuses-renew-cicig-mandate, accessed 1 March 2016.

Richmond, Oliver P. (2009). Becoming Liberal, Unbecoming Liberalism: Liberal-Local Hybridity via the Everyday as a Response to the Paradoxes of Liberal Peacebuilding. *Journal of Intervention and Statebuilding* 3(3), 324–44.

Richmond, Oliver P. (2010). Resistance and the Post-Liberal Peace. *Millennium – Journal of International Studies* 38(3), 665–92.

Richmond, Oliver P. (2011). *A Post-Liberal Peace.* London: Routledge.

Richmond, Oliver P./Franks, Jason (2009). *Liberal Peace Transitions: Between Statebuilding and Peacebuilding.* Edinburgh: Edinburgh University Press.

Richmond, Oliver P./Mitchell, Audra (eds.) (2012a). *Hybrid Forms of Peace: From Everyday Agency to Post-Liberalism.* Basingstoke: Palgrave Macmillan.

Richmond, Oliver P./Mitchell, Audra (2012b). Introduction – Towards a Post-Liberal Peace: Exploring Hybridity via Everyday Forms of Resistance, Agency and Autonomy. In Richmond, Oliver P./Mitchell, Audra, (eds.), *Hybrid Forms of Peace: From Everyday Agency to Post-Liberalism.* Basingstoke: Palgrave Macmillan, pp. 1–38.

Ríos de Rodríguez, Carroll (1998). El Código es centralizante. *Siglo Veintiuno,* 26 March 1998, p. 14.

Ríos de Rodríguez, Carroll (2000). ¿Confundido por el debate sobre el Código? *Siglo Vientiuno,* 20 February 2000, p. 12.

Ríos de Rodríguez, Carroll (2006). Sobre la soberanía nacional. *Siglo Veintiuno,* 14 December 2006, p. 18.

Ríos Montt se reunió con funcionarios de Unicef (2000). *Siglo Veintiuno,* 2 February 2000, p. 5.

Risse, Thomas (2000). 'Let's Argue!': Communicative Action in World Politics. *International Organization* 54(1), 1–39.

Risse, Thomas (2002). Transnational Actors and World Politics. In Carlsnaes, Walter/Risse, Thomas/Simmons, Beth, (eds.), *Handbook of International Relations.* London: Sage, pp. 255–74.

Risse, Thomas (2004). Global Governance and Communicative Action. *Government and Opposition* 39(2), 288–313.

Risse, Thomas/Ropp, Stephan (1999). International Human Rights Norms and Domestic Change: Conclusions. In Risse, Thomas/Ropp, Stephan/ Sikkink, Kathryn, (eds.), *The Power of Human Rights: International*

*Norms and Domestic Change*. Cambridge: Cambridge University Press, pp. 234–78.

Risse, Thomas/Ropp, Stephan C. (2013). Introduction and Overview. In Risse, Thomas/Ropp, Stephan C./Sikkink, Kathryn, (eds.), *The Persistent Power of Human Rights: From Commitment to Compliance*. Cambridge: Cambridge University Press, pp. 3–25.

Risse, Thomas/Ropp, Stephan C./Sikkink, Kathryn (eds.) (2013). *The Persistent Power of Human Rights: From Commitment to Compliance*. Cambridge: Cambridge University Press.

Risse, Thomas/Ropp, Stephen/Sikkink, Kathryn (eds.) (1999). *The Power of Human Rights: International Norms and Domestic Change*. Cambridge: Cambridge University Press.

Risse, Thomas/Sikkink, Kathryn (1999). The Socialization of International Human Rights Norms into Domestic Practices: Introduction. In Risse, Thomas/Ropp, Stephen C./Sikkink, Kathryn, (eds.), *The Power of Human Rights: International Norms and Domestic Change*. Cambridge: Cambridge University Press, pp. 1–38.

Risse-Kappen, Thomas (1994). Ideas do not Float Freely: Transnational Coalitions, Domestic Structures, and the End of the Cold War. *International Organization* 48(2), 185–214.

Roberts, David (2008). Hybrid Polities and Indigenous Pluralities: Advanced Lessons in Statebuilding from Cambodia. *Journal of Intervention and Statebuilding* 2(1), 63–86.

Robertson, Roland (1995). Glocalization: Time-Space and Homogeneity-Heterogeneity. In Featherstone, Mike/Lash, Scott/Robertson, Roland, (eds.), *Global Modernities*. London: Sage, pp. 25–44.

Robinson, William I. (1996) *Promoting Polyarchy: Globalization, US Intervention and Hegemony*. Cambridge: Cambridge University Press.

Rodríguez, Luisa (2000). Portillo apoya Código. *Prensa Libre*, 5 February 2000, p. 3.

Rodríguez, Luisa (2004). El peor país en adopciones. *Prensa Libre*, 16 October 2004. www.prensalibre.com/noticias/peor-pais-adopciones_0_95 390546.html, accessed 2 June 2014.

Rodríguez, Luisa F. (2006). Creación de la Ciciacs está en evaluación. *Prensa Libre*, 7 September 2006. www.prensalibre.com/noticias/Creacion-Cicia cs-evaluacion_0_131387626.html, accessed 15 November 2014.

Rodríguez, Martín P. (2004). ONU dice que no apoyará un CICIACS débil. *Prensa Libre*, 28 July 2004. www.prensalibre.com/noticias/ONU-dice-ap oyara-CICIACS-debil_0_93591119.html, accessed 12 November 2014.

Rodríguez, Martín P. (2006a). Continúa diálogo por Ciciacs. *Prensa Libre*, 30 January 2006. www.prensalibre.com/noticias/Continua-dialogo-Cicia cs_0_126589485.html, accessed 15 November 2014.

Rodríguez, Martín P. (2006b). Plan Mesoamericano contra las drogas. *Prensa Libre*, 2 January 2006. www.prensalibre.com/noticias/Plan-Meso americano-drogas_0_126589061.html, accessed 15 November 2014.

Rodríguez Fernández, Silvia (2001). *Report concerning the Application of the Convention on the Rights of the Child by Guatemala*, ED 458 014, World Organization against Torture (OMCT), Geneva.

Roesch, Rita María (2004). Vencer lo imposible. *Prensa Libre*, 26. November 2004. www.prensalibre.com/opinion/VENTANAbrVencer -imposible_0_95990951.html, accessed 5 October 2014.

Roht-Arriaza, Naomi (2008–2009). Making the State Do Justice: Transnational Prosecutions and International Support for Criminal Investigations in Post-Armed Conflict Guatemala. *Chicago Journal of International Law* 9(1), 79–105.

Ropp, Stephan C./Sikkink, Kathryn (1999). International Norms and Domestic Politics in Chile and Guatemala. In Risse, Thomas/Ropp, Stephan C./Sikkink, Kathryn, (eds.), *The Power of Human Rights: International Norms and Domestic Change*. Cambridge: Cambridge University Press, pp. 172–204.

Rosales, Edgar (2004). ¿Un estado paralelo? *Siglo Veintiuno*, 9 January 2004, p. 13.

Rosert, Elvira/Schirmbeck, Sonja (2007). Zur Erosion internationaler Normen: Folterverbot und nukleares Tabu in der Diskussion. *Zeitschrift für Internationale Beziehungen* 14(2), 253–87.

Ruano, Victor (2010). La Cicig y las mafias. *Prensa Libre*, 13 June 2010, p. 22.

Ruiz, Juan Carlos (2000). Pilar democrático. Creación de 'habeas data' representa un paso adelante. *Prensa Libre*, 1 June 2000. www.prensali bre.com/noticias/Pilar-democratico_0_292780199.html, accessed 28 June 2014.

Rüland, Jürgen/Bechle, Karsten (2014). Defending State-Centric Regionalism through Mimicry and Localisation: Regional Parliamentary Bodies in the Association of Southeast Asian Nations (ASEAN) and Mercosur. *Journal of International Relations and Development* 17(1), 61–88.

Sabaratnam, Meera (2013). Avatars of Eurocentrism in the Critique of the Liberal Peace. *Security Dialogue* 44(3), 259–78.

Samayoa, Claudia (2004). *El rostro del terror. Análisis de los ataques en contra de Defensores de Derechos Humanos del 2000 al 2003*, Coalición para la CICIACS, Guatemala Ciudad.

Sánchez, Omar (2008). Guatemala's Party Universe: A Case Study in Underinstitutionalization. *Latin American Politics and Society* 50(1), 123–51.

Sandholtz, Wayne (2008). Dynamics of International Norm Change: Rules against Wartime Plunder. *European Journal of International Relations* 14(1), 101–31.

Sandholtz, Wayne/Stiles, Kendall W. (2009). *International Norms and Cycles of Change*. Oxford: Oxford University Press.

Sandoval, Julietta (2000a). En marcha suspensión de Código. *Prensa Libre*, 23 February 2000, p. 4.

Sandoval, Julietta (2000b). Entre rechazo y aprobación. *Prensa Libre*, 13 February 2000, p. 2.

Sandoval, Julietta (2000c). Llaman a consenso. *Prensa Libre*, 5 February 2000, p. 3.

Sandoval, Julietta (2002). Nueva propuesta de Código de la Niñez. *Prensa Libre*, 16 October 2002. www.prensalibre.com/noticias/Nueva-pro puesta-Codigo-Ninez_0_58794197.html, accessed 2 June 2014.

Schaefer, Christoph Daniel (2010). Local Practices and Normative Frameworks in Peacebuilding. *International Peacekeeping* 17(4), 499–514.

Schia, Niels Nagelhus/Karlsrud, John (2013). 'Where the Rubber Meets the Road': Friction Sites and Local-Level Peacebuilding in Haiti, Liberia and South Sudan. *International Peacekeeping* 20(2), 233–48.

Schimmelfennig, Frank (2002). Introduction: The Impact of International Organizations on the Central and Eastern European States – Conceptual and Theoretical Issues. In Linden, Ronald, (ed.), *Norms and Nannies: The Impact of International Organizations on the Central and East European States*. Lanham: Rownman & Littlefield, pp. 1–32.

Schimmelfennig, Frank (2003). Internationale Sozialisation: Von einem 'erschöpften' zu einem produktiven Forschungsprogramm? In Hellmann, Gunther/Wolf, Klaus Dieter/Zürn, Michael, (eds.), *Die neuen Internationalen Beziehungen. Forschungsstand und Perspektiven in Deutschland*. Baden-Baden: Nomos, pp. 401–27.

Schimmelfennig, Frank/Engert, Stefan/Knobel, Heiko (2006). *International Socialization in Europe: European Organizations, Political Conditionality and Democratic Change*. Basingstoke: Palgrave Macmillan.

Schimmelfennig, Frank/Schwellnus, Guido (2007). Politiktransfer durch politische Konditionalität. Der Einfluss der EU auf die Nichtdiskriminierungs- und Minderheitenschutzgesetzgebung in Mittel- und Osteuropa. In Holzinger, Katharina/Jörgens, Helge/Knill, Christoph, (eds.), *Transfer, Diffusion und Konvergenz von Politiken*. Wiesbaden: VS Verlag für Sozialwissenschaften, pp. 271–96.

Schimmelfennig, Frank/Sedelmeier, Ulrich (2004). Governance by Conditionality: EU Rule Transfer to the Candidate Countries of Central and Eastern Europe. *Journal of European Public Policy* 11(4), 661–79.

Schimmelfennig, Frank/Sedelmeier, Ulrich (eds.) (2005). *The Europeanization of Central and Eastern Europe*. New York, NY: Cornell University Press.

Schlesinger, Stephen (2015). This Is One of the Most Innovative Programs in the UN's Toolbox, *The Nation*, 5 October 2015. www.thenation.com/article/this-is-one-of-the-most-innovative-programs-in-the-uns-toolbox/, accessed 1 March 2015.

Schmitter, Philippe C. (1996). The Influence of the International Context upon the Choice of National Institutions and Policies in Neo-Democracies. In Whitehead, Laurence, (ed.), *The International Dimensions of Democratization. Europe and the Americas*. Oxford: Oxford University Press, pp. 26–54.

Schmitz, Hans Peter (2004). Domestic and Transnational Perspective on Democratization. *International Studies Review* 6(3), 403–26.

Schmitz, Hans Peter/Sikkink, Kathryn (2013). International Human Rights. In Carlsnaes, Walter/Risse, Thomas/Simmons, Beth, (eds.), *Handbook of International Relations*. London: Sage, pp. 827–53.

Schraeder, Peter (2002). Promoting an International Community of Democracies. In Schraeder, Peter, (ed.) *Exporting Democracy. Rhetoric vs. Reality*. Boulder, CO: Lynne Rienner, pp. 1–11.

Schultze-Kraft, Markus (2012). Security and the Rule of Law in Colombia and Guatemala: Priorities, Trade-Offs and Interdependencies. *Hague Journal on the Rule of Law* 4(S1), 135–57.

Schünemann, Julia (2010a). 'Looking the Monster in the Face': The *International Commission against Impunity in Guatemala and the 'Rule of Law-builders Contract'*, FRIDE, Madrid.

Schünemann, Julia (2010b). *Reform without Ownership? Dilemmas in Supporting Security and Justice Sector Reform in Honduras*, Fride, Madrid.

Sectores aplauden paso en pro de transparencia (2008). *Prensa Libre*, 24 September 2008. www.prensalibre.com/noticias/Sectores-aplauden-paso-pro-transparencia_0_167985819.html, accessed 28 June 2014.

SEDEM (2004). CICIACS: Sistematización de un proceso. Guatemala City.

Shamsie, Yasmine (2007). The International Political Economy of Democracy Promotion: Lessons from Haiti and Guatemala. In Legler, Thomas/Lean, Sharon F./Boniface, Dexter S., (eds.), *Promoting Democracy in the Americas*. Baltimore, MD: Johns Hopkins University Press, pp. 249–69.

Shaw, Rosalind/Waldorf, Lars (2010a). Introduction: Localizing Transitional Justice. In Shaw, Rosalind/Waldorf, Lars with Hazan, Pierre, (eds.), *Localizing Transitional Justice: Interventions and Priorities after Mass Violence*. Stanford, CA: Stanford University Press, pp. 3–26.

Shaw, Rosalind/Waldorf, Lars with Hazan, Pierre (eds.) (2010b). *Localizing Transitional Justice: Interventions and Priorities After Mass Violence.* Stanford, CA: Stanford University Press.

Short, Nicola (2007). *The International Politics of Post-Conflict Reconstruction in Guatemala.* Basingstoke: Palgrave Macmillan.

Sieder, Rachel (2001). War, Peace, and Memory Politics in Central America. In Barahona de Brito, Alexandra/González-Enríquez, Carmen/Aguilar, Paloma, (eds.), *The Politics of Memory: Transitional Justice in Democratizing Societies.* Oxford: Oxford University Press, pp. 161–89.

Sieder, Rachel (2002). Recognising Indigenous Law and the Politics of State Formation. In Sieder, Rachel, (ed.), *Multiculturalism in Latin America: Indigenous Rights, Diversity and Democracy.* Basingstoke: Palgrave Macmillan, pp. 184–207.

Sieder, Rachel (2011). Contested Sovereignties: Indigenous Law, Violence and State Effects in Postwar Guatemala. *Critique of Anthropology* 31(3), 161–84.

Sieder, Rachel/Thomas, Megan/Vickers, Jack (2002). *Who Governs? Guatemala Five Years after the Peace Accords,* Hemisphere Initiatives, Cambridge, MA. http://lanic.utexas.edu/project/hemisphereinitiatives/wh ogoverns.pdf, accessed 1 March 2016.

Sikkink, Kathryn (2008). The Role of Consequences, Comparison and Counterfactuals in Constructivist Ethical Thought. In Price, Richard, (ed.), *Moral Limit and Possibility in World Politics.* Cambridge: Cambridge University Press, pp. 83–111.

Sikkink, Kathryn (2013). The United States and Torture: Does the Spiral Model Work? In Risse, Thomas/Ropp, Stephan C./Sikkink, Kathryn, (eds.), *The Persistent Power of Human Rights: From Commitment to Compliance.* Cambridge: Cambridge University Press, pp. 145–63.

Siu, Vivian (2014). In Guatemala, a Child's Abduction and Death Inspires Stronger Child Protection Law. www.unicef.org/infobycountry/guate mala_61693.html, accessed 1 March 2016.

Snodgrass Godoy, Angelina (2002). Lynchings and the Democratization of Terror in Postwar Guatemala: Implications for Human Rights. *Human Rights Quarterly* 24(3), 640–61.

Snow, David A./Benford, Robert D. (1988). Ideology, Frame Resonance, and Participant Mobilization. *International Social Movement Research* 1, 197–218.

Snow, David A./Rochford, E. Burke, Jr./Worden, Steven K./Benford, Robert D. (1986). Frame Alignment Processes, Micromobilization, and Movement Participation. *American Sociological Review* 51(4), 464–81.

Special Rapporteur for Freedom of Expression (2000). *Annual Report 2000.* http://cidh.org/relatoria/showarticle.asp?artID=136&lID=1, accessed 6 November 2014.

Special Rapporteur for Freedom of Expression (2001). *Annual Report 2001.* www.oas.org/en/iachr/expression/showarticle.asp?artID=137&llD=1, accessed 13 November 2014.

Special Rapporteur for Freedom of Expression (2002). *Annual Report 2002.* www.oas.org/en/iachr/expression/showarticle.asp?artID=138&llD=1, accessed 13 November 2014.

Special Rapporteur for Freedom of Expression (2003). *Annual Report 2003.* http://cidh.org/relatoria/showarticle.asp?artID=139&lID=1, accessed 6 November 2014.

Special Rapporteur for Freedom of Expression (2004). *Annual Report 2004.* www.oas.org/en/iachr/expression/showarticle.asp?artID=459&llD=1, accessed 13 November 2014.

Spence, Jack (2004). *War and Peace in Central America: Comparing Transitions toward Democracy and Social Equity in Guatemala, El Salvador, and Nicaragua,* Hemisphere Initiatives, Brookline, MA. http://lanic.utexas.edu/project/hemisphereinitiatives/warpeace.pdf, accessed 14 March 2012.

Spivak, Gayatri Chakravorty (2008). *Other Asias.* Malden, MA: Blackwell.

Sriram, Chandra Lekha (2008). Prevention and the Rule of Law: Rhetoric and Reality. In Hurwitz, Agnès/Huang, Reyko, (eds.), *Civil War and the Rule of Law: Security, Development, Human Rights.* Boulder, CO: Lynne Rienner, pp. 71–90.

Sriram, Chandra Lekha (2012). Post-Conflict Justice and Hybridity in Peacebuilding: Resistance or Cooptation? In Richmond, Oliver P./Mitchell, Audra, (eds.), *Hybrid Forms of Peace: From Everyday Agency to Post-Liberalism.* Basingstoke: Palgrave Macmillan, pp. 58–72.

Stanley, William (2013). *Enabling Peace in Guatemala: The Story of MINUGUA.* Boulder, CO: Lynne Rienner.

Stanley, William/Holiday, David (2002). Broad Participation, Diffuse Responsibility: Peace Implementation in Guatemala. In Stedman, Stephen John/Rothchild, Donald/Cousens, Elizabeth M., (eds.), *Ending Civil Wars: The Implementation of Peace Agreements.* Boulder, CO: Lynne Rienner, pp. 421–62.

Stewart, Charles (2006). *Creolization: History, Ethnography, Theory.* Walnut Creek, CA: Left Coast.

Stromseth, Jane/Wippman, David/Brooks, Rosa (2006). *Can Might Make Rights? Building the Rule of Law after Military Interventions.* Cambridge: Cambridge University Press.

Surge primera queja contra Ley de Acceso a la Información (2009). *Prensa Libre*, 21 April 2009. www.prensalibre.com/noticias/Surge-primera-Ley -Acceso-Informacion_0_28797159.html, accessed 28 June 2014.

Swidler, Ann (1986). Culture in Action: Symbols and Strategies. *American Sociological Review* 51(2), 273–86.

Swiss, Liam (2009). Decoupling Values from Action. *International Journal of Comparative Sociology* 50(1), 69–95.

Tabory, Sam (2015). El Salvador Should Consider 'CICIG'-Like Body: US Official, *Insight Crime*, 9 July 2015. www.insightcrime.org/news-briefs/el -salvador-cicig-impunity-thomas-shannon, accessed 1 March 2016.

Taft-Morales, Maureen (2004). *Guatemala: Political Conditions, Elections, and Human Rights*, RL32124, Congressional Research Service, Washington, D.C.

Taft-Morales, Maureen (2013). *Guatemala: Political, Security, and Socio-Economic Conditions and U.S. Relations*, R42580, Congressional Research Service, Washington, D.C.

Tostensen, Arne/Stokke, Hugo/Trygged, Sven/Halvorsen, Kate (2011). *Supporting Child Rights: Synthesis of Lessons Learned in Four Countries*, Sida. www.oecd.org/dataoecd/43/43/48350333.pdf, accessed 20 October 2011.

Transparencia Internacional urge a aprobar ley de acceso a la información (2008). *Prensa Libre*, 19 August 2008. www.prensalibre.com/noticias/Tra nsparencia-Internacional-aprobar-acceso-informacion_0_167385506.html, accessed 28 June 2014.

Trenkov-Wermuth, Calin (2010). *United Nations Justice: Legal and Judicial Reform in Governance Operations*. Tokyo: United Nations University Press.

Triunfo del estado de derecho (2004). [Editorial] *Siglo Veintiuno*, 6 Aug. 2004, p. 12.

Tully, James (2002). The Unfreedom of the Moderns in Comparison to Their Ideals of Constitutional Democracy. *The Modern Law Review* 65 (2), 204–28.

Tully, James (2008a). Modern Constitutional Democracy and Imperialism. *Osgoode Hall Law Journal* 46, 461–93.

Tully, James (2008b). *Public Philosophy in a New Key. Volume II: Imperialism and Civic Freedom*. Cambridge: Cambridge University Press.

Tully, James (2008c). Two Meanings of Global Citizenship: Modern and Diverse. In Peters, Michael A./Blee, Harry/Britton, Alan, (eds.), *Global Citizenship Education: Philosophy, Theory and Pedagogy*. Rotterdam: Sense Publications, pp. 15–41.

UN General Assembly (2000). *Eleventh Report on Human Rights of the United Nations Verification Mission in Guatemala*, A/55/174. www.un .org/documents/ga/docs/55/a55174.pdf, accessed 6 November 2014.

UN General Assembly (2001). *Twelfth Report on Human Rights of the United Nations Verification Mission in Guatemala*, A/56/273. www.un .org/documents/ga/docs/56/a56273.pdf, accessed 6 November 2014.

UN General Assembly (2008). *Report of the Secretary-General: The Rule of Law at the National and International Levels*, A/63/64. https://documents -dds-ny.un.org/doc/UNDOC/GEN/N08/268/76/PDF/N0826876.pdf?Ope nElement, accessed 1 March 2016.

UN General Assembly (2009). *GA/10877*, October 28. www.un.org/press/ en/2009/ga10877.doc.htm, accessed 6 November 2014.

Una campaña para despertar conciencias. (2011). *Prensa Libre*, 6 September 2011, p. 14.

UNDP (2009). *Assessment of Development Results: Evaluation of UNDP Contribution, Guatemala*. http://web.undp.org/execbrd/pdf/ADR-Guate mala.pdf, accessed 26 May 2014.

UNICEF (2007). *UNICEF's Position on Inter-Country Adoption*. www.uni cef.org/media/media_41118.html, accessed 2 June 2014.

UNICEF (2010a). *Annual Report 2010*. www.unicef.org/about/annualre port/files/Guatemala_COAR_2010.pdf, accessed 1 March 2016.

UNICEF (2010b). *The Congress of Guatemala Passed the Law on Early Alert System to Locate and Protect Missing or Abducted*. www.unicef.org/ lac/media_18628.htm, accessed 2 June 2014.

UNICEF (2010c). *Guatemala: Country Programme Document 2010–2014*. www.unicef.org/about/execboard/files/Guatemala_final_approved_CP D12_Jan_2010.pdf, accessed 2 June 2014.

UNICEF (2011). *Going North: Violence, Insecurity and Impunity in the Phenomenon of Migration in Guatemala*, Guatemala Ciudad.

United Nations (1948–2006). *United Nations Treaty Collection: Chapter IV – Human Rights*. https://treaties.un.org/Pages/Treaties.aspx?id=4&subid= A&lang=en, accessed 2 June 2014.

United Nations (1989). *United Nations Treaty Collection: Convention on the Rights of the Child*. https://treaties.un.org/Pages/ViewDetails.aspx?src=TR EATY&mtdsg_no=IV-11&chapter=4&lang=en, accessed 2 June 2014.

United Nations (1998). *Report of the Special Rapporteur: Promotion and Protection of the Right to Freedom of Opinion and Expression*, UN Doc. E/CN.4/1998/40. http://daccess-ods.un.org/access.nsf/Get?Open&DS=E/ CN.4/1998/40&Lang=E, accessed 28 June 2014.

United Nations (2004). *United Nations Convention against Corruption*. http:// www.unodc.org/documents/treaties/UNCAC/Publications/Convention/08 –50026_E.pdf, accessed 6 November 2014.

United Nations Committee on the Rights of the Child (2001). *Concluding Observations: Guatemala*, CRC/C/15/Add.154, 9 July. http://tbinternet

.ohchr.org/_layouts/treatybodyexternal/Download.aspx?symbolno=CRC
%2fC%2f15%2fAdd.154&Lang=en, accessed 2 October 2014.

United Nations Committee on the Rights of the Child (2008). *Third and
Fourth Periodic Report, Guatemala*, CRC/C/GTM/3–4, 25 April. http://
tbinternet.ohchr.org/_layouts/treatybodyexternal/Download.aspx?symb
olno=CRC%2fC%2fGTM%2f3-4&Lang=en, accessed 2 June 2014.

United Nations Committee on the Rights of the Child (2010a). *Concluding
Observations: Guatemala*, CRC/C/GTM/CO/3–4, 25 October. http://tbin
ternet.ohchr.org/_layouts/treatybodyexternal/Download.aspx?symboln
o=CRC%2fC%2fGTM%2fCO%2f3-4&Lang=en, accessed 2 June 2014.

United Nations Committee on the Rights of the Child (2010b). *Summary
Record of the 1544th (Chamber A) Meeting*, CRC/C/SR.1544, 22
September. http://tbinternet.ohchr.org/_layouts/treatybodyexternal/Do
wnload.aspx?symbolno=CRC%2fC%2fSR.1544&Lang=en, accessed 2
June 2014.

United Nations Committee on the Rights of the Child (2010c). *Summary
Record of the 1546th (Chamber A) Meeting*, CRC/C/SR.1546, 27
September. http://tbinternet.ohchr.org/_layouts/treatybodyexternal/Dow
nload.aspx?symbolno=CRC%2fC%2fSR.1546&Lang=en, accessed 2
June 2014.

United Nations Office of the High Commissioner for Human Rights (2013).
*Committee on the Rights of the Child – Membership (as of 1 March 2013)*.
www.ohchr.org/EN/HRBodies/CRC/Pages/Membership.aspx, accessed 2
June 2014.

United Nations Office of the High Commissioner for Human Rights (2017).
*Committee on the Rights of the Child – General Comments*. http://tbinter
net.ohchr.org/_layouts/treatybodyexternal/TBSearch.aspx?Lang=en&Tr
eatyID=5&DocTypeID=11, accessed 14 February 2017.

United Nations Security Council (1992). *Report of the Secretary-General:
An Agenda for Peace: Preventive Diplomacy, Peacemaking and Peace-
Keeping*, A/47/277 – S/24111. www.un-documents.net/a47-277.htm,
accessed 23 May 2013.

United Nations Security Council (1994). *Report of the Joint Group for the
Investigation of Politically Motivated Illegal Armed Groups in El
Salvador*, S/1994/090.

United Nations Security Council (2004). *Report of the Secretary-General:
The Rule of Law and Transitional Justice in Conflict and Post-Conflict
Societies*, S/2004/616. www.un.org/en/ga/search/view_doc.asp?symbol=
S/2004/616, accessed 1 March 2016.

United States Institute of Peace (1996). *Peace Agreement Digital Collection:
Guatemala, Agreement on the Strengthening of Civilian Power and on the
Role of Armed Forces in a Democratic Society*. www.usip.org/files/file/resour

ces/collections/peace_agreements/guat_960919.pdf, accessed 6 November 2014.

United States Institute of Peace (2011). *Truth Commission: Guatemala*. www .usip.org/publications/truth-commission-guatemala, accessed 26 May 2014.

Upham, Frank (2002). *Mythmaking in the Rule of Law Orthodoxy*, Working Papers Rule of Law Series No 30, Carnegie Endowment for International Peace, Washington, D.C.

US State Department/USAID (2009). *Guatemala. U.S. Foreign Assistance Performance Publication, Fiscal Year 2009*. www.state.gov/documents/o rganization/159248.pdf, accessed 6 November 2014.

USAID Guatemala (2012). *Transparency and Integrity Project, Quarterly Report (Jan 1–March 31, 2012), ARD*. https://dec.usaid.gov/dec/content/ Detail.aspx?ctID=ODVhZjk4NWQtM2YyMi00YjRmLTkxNjktZTcxM jM2NDBmY2Uy&rID=MzMzNzIy, accessed 6 November 2014.

Vachudová, Milada Anna (2005). *Europe Undivided: Democracy, Leverage, and Integration after Communism*. Oxford: Oxford University Press.

Valenzuela, Felipe (2007). Cicigimos así . . . *Siglo Veintiuno*, 6 August 2007, p.18.

Valladares, Danilo (2003). Ley para proteger niñez. *Prensa Libre*, 5 May 2003. www.prensalibre.com/noticias/Ley-proteger-ninez_0_73792647.html, accessed 15 November 2014.

Valladares, Danilo (2010). Regional Commission against Impunity in Central America. *Inter Press Service*, 14 May 2010. www.ipsnews.net/2010/05/reg ional-commission-against-impunity-in-central-america/, accessed 1 March 2016.

Van Kersbergen, Kees/Verbeek, Bertjan (2007). The Politics of International Norms: Subsidiarity and the Imperfect Competence Regime of the European Union. *European Journal of International Relations* 13(2), 217–38.

Vásquez Araya, Carolina (2004). Secreto de Estado. *Prensa Libre*, 18 October 2004. www.prensalibre.com/opinion/QUINTO-PATIObrSecret os_0_95391337.html, accessed 28 June 2014.

Vaughn, Jocelyn/Dunne, Tim (2015). Leading from the Front: America, Libya and the Localisation of R2P. *Cooperation and Conflict* 50(1), 29–49.

Véliz, Lesly (2009). Quieren jugarnos la vuelta. *Siglo Veintiuno*, 24 April 2009, p. 15.

Ventajas y riesgos de la CICIACS (2003). [Editorial] *Prensa Libre*, 17 March 2003, p. 14.

Vera Martínez, Martín Cutberto/Rocha Romero, David/Martínez Rodríguez, María Concepción (2015). El modelo de Gobierno Abierto en América Latina. Paralelismo de las políticas públicas de transparencia y la corrupción. *Revista de Ciencias Sociales* 53, 85–103.

Vetterlein, Antje/Wiener, Antje (2013). Gemeinschaft Revisited: Die sozialen Grundlagen internationaler Ordnung. *Leviathan: Berliner Zeitschrift für Sozialwissenschaft* 41(S28), 78–103.

Villagrán, Wendy (2015). Un fracaso Ley de Acceso a la Información Pública. *La Nación*, 25 January 2015. www.lanacion.com.gt/un-fracaso-ley-de-acceso-a-la-informacion-publica, accessed 1 March 2016.

Viscidi, Lisa (2004). *A History of Land in Guatemala: Conflict and Hope for Reform*. www.nisgua.org/themes_campaigns/land_rights/Background/A%20History%20of%20Land%20in%20Guatemala%20091704.pdf, accessed 26 May 2014.

Walzer, Michael (2008). On Promoting Democracy. *Ethics & International Affairs* 22(4), 351–55.

Warren, Kay B. (1998). *Indigenous Movements and Their Critics: Pan-Maya Activism in Guatemala*. Princeton, NJ: Princeton University Press.

Weldes, Jutta (1998). Bureaucratic Politics: A Critical Constructivist Assessment. *Mershon International Studies Review* 42(2), 216–25.

Wendt, Alexander E. (1987). The Agent-Structure Problem in International Relations Theory. *International Organization* 41(3), 335–70.

Werle, Gerhard/Jeßberger, Florian (2014). *Principles of International Criminal Law*, 3rd edn. Oxford: Oxford University Press.

Werner, Michael/Zimmermann, Bénédicte (2006). Beyond Comparison: Histoire Croisée and the Challenge of Reflexivity. *History and Theory* 45, 30–50.

Wetzel, Anne/Orbie, Jan/Bossuyt, Fabienne (2015). One of What Kind? Comparative Perspectives on the Substance of EU Democracy Promotion. *Cambridge Review of International Affairs* 28(1), 21–34.

Whitehead, Laurence (1996). Three International Dimensions of Democratization. In Whitehead, Laurence, (ed.), *The International Dimensions of Democratization. Europe and the Americas*. Oxford: Oxford University Press, pp. 3–26.

Whitfield, Teresa (2007). *Friends Indeed? The United Nations, Groups of Friends, and the Resolution of Conflict*, United States Institute for Peace, Washington, D.C.

Wiener, Antje (2004). Contested Compliance: Interventions on the Normative Structure of World Politics. *European Journal of International Relations* 10(2), 189–234.

Wiener, Antje (2007). The Dual Quality of Norms and Governance beyond the State: Sociological and Normative Approaches to 'Interaction'. *Critical Review of International Social and Political Philosophy* 10(1), 47–69.

Wiener, Antje (2008). *The Invisible Constitution of Politics: Contested Norms and International Encounters*. Cambridge: Cambridge University Press.

Wiener, Antje (2014). *A Theory of Contestation*. Heidelberg: Springer.

Wiener, Antje/Puetter, Uwe (2009). The Quality of Norms Is What Actors Make of It: Critical Constructivist Research on Norms. *Journal of International Law and International Relations* 5(1), 1–16.

Williams, Paul D. (2009). The 'Responsibility to Protect', Norm Localisation, and African International Society. *Global Responsibility to Protect* 1(3), 392–416.

Williams, Robert Glynne (1994). *States and Social Evolution: Coffee and the Rise of National Governments in Central America*. Chapel Hill, NC: University of North Carolina Press.

Williams, Sarah (2012). *Hybrid and Internationalised Criminal Tribunals: Selected Jurisdictional Issues*. Oxford: Hart.

Wojkowska, Ewa (2006). *Doing Justice: How Informal Justice Systems Can Contribute*, UNDP: Democratic Governance Fellowship Programme. http://siteresources.worldbank.org/INTLAWJUSTINST/Res ources/EwaWojkowska.pdf, accessed 1 March 2016.

WOLA (2008). *Advocates against Impunity. A Case Study on Human Rights Organizing in Guatemala*, Washington, D.C. www.wola.org/sites/default/ files/downloadable/Citizen%20Security/past/cicig_advocates_against_im punity.pdf, accessed 12 November 2011.

WOLA (2015). *The CICIG: An Innovative Instrument for Fighting Criminal Organizations and Strengthening the Rule of Law*, Washington, D.C. www .wola.org/sites/default/files/Citizen%20Security/2015/WOLA_CICIG_EN G_FNL_extra%20page.pdf, accessed 15 February 2016.

Wolff, Jonas (2011). *Challenges to Democracy Promotion. The Case of Bolivia*, March 2011, The Carnegie Papers. Democracy and the Rule of Law, Washington, D.C. http://carnegieendowment.org/files/democracy_ bolivia.pdf, accessed 1 March 2016.

Wolff, Jonas (2012). Democracy Promotion, Empowerment, and Self-Determination: Conflicting Objectives in US and German Policies towards Bolivia. *Democratization* 19(3), 415–37.

Wolff, Jonas/Poppe, Annika E. (2015). *From Closing Space to Contested Spaces: Re-assessing Current Conflicts over International Civil Society Support*, PRIF-Report No 137, Frankfurt. http://www.hsfk.de/fileadmin/ downloads/prif137.pdf, accessed 1 March 2016.

Wolff, Jonas/Spanger, Hans-Joachim/Puhle, Hans-Jürgen (2014). *The Comparative International Politics of Democracy Promotion*, London: Routledge.

Wolff, Jonas/Zimmermann, Lisbeth (2016). Between Banyans and Battle Scenes: Liberal Norms, Contestation, and the Limits of Critique. *Review of International Studies* 24(3), 513–534.

World Bank (2007). *World Development Indicators: 6.11 – 'Aid Dependency'*. http://siteresources.worldbank.org/DATASTATISTICS/Re sources/table6_11.pdf, accessed 26 May 2014.

Young, Andrea (2015). Comment: Advances in Children's Rights over the Past Decade: The Inter-American Court of Human Rights and the European Court of Human Rights' Progressive Incorporation of the Convention on the Rights of Children. *Journal of the American Academy of Matrimonial Lawyers* 28(1), 285–307.

Young, Iris Marion (1996). Communication and the Other: Beyond Deliberative Democracy. In Benhabib, Seyla, (ed.), *Democracy and Difference*. Princeton, NJ: Princeton University Press, pp. 121–35.

Youngs, Richard (2001). *Democracy Promotion: The Case of European Union Strategy*, CEPS Working Document No. 167, Centre for European Policy Studies.

Youngs, Richard (2002). The European Union and Democracy in Latin America. *Latin American Politics and Society* 44(3), 111–39.

Youngs, Richard (2004). *International Democracy and the West: The Roles of Governments, Civil Society, and Multinational Business*. Oxford: Oxford University Press.

Youngs, Richard (2008). Trends in Democracy Assistance: What Has Europe Been Doing? *Journal of Democracy* 19(3), 160–69.

Youngs, Richard (2012). Misunderstanding the Maladies of Liberal Democracy Promotion. In Hobson, Christopher/Kurki, Milja, (eds.), *The Conceptual Politics of Democracy Promotion*. London: Routledge, pp. 100–16.

Zapeta, Estuardo (2005a). ¿CICIACS, o No-CIACS, o fuero especial? *Siglo Veintiuno*, 9 January 2005, p. 13.

Zapeta, Estuardo (2005b). Guatemala infeliz que tu maras. *Siglo Veintiuno*, 5 July 2005, p. 13.

Zapeta, Estuardo (2007a). CICIG: la cobardía Berger-Stein. *Siglo Veintiuno*, 27 July 2007, p. 21.

Zapeta, Estuardo (2007b). Minugua reloaded. *Siglo Veintiuno*, 3 August 2007, p.17.

Zapeta, Estuardo (2010). 'Castre-sarna': ¿Renunció o le pidieron la renuncia? *Siglo Veintiuno*, 7 June 2010. www.s21.com.gt/opinion/2010/06/07/ucas tre-sarna-renuncio-le-pidieron-renuncia, accessed 1 March 2016.

Zarakol, Ayşe (2014). What Made the Modern World Hang Together: Socialisation or Stigmatisation? *International Theory* 6(2), 311–32.

Zimmermann, Lisbeth (2012). *Global Norms with a Local Face? The Interaction of Rule of Law Promotion and Norm Translation in Guatemala*, Unpublished dissertation TU Darmstadt, Darmstadt.

Zimmermann, Lisbeth (2016). Same Same or Different? Norm Diffusion Between Resistance, Compliance, and Localization in Post-Conflict States. *International Studies Perspectives* 17(1), 98–115.

Zinecker, Heidrun (2009). Regime-Hybridity in Developing Countries: Achievements and Limitations of New Research on Transitions. *International Studies Review* 11(2), 302–31.

Zuercher, Christoph/Roehner, Nora/Riese, Sarah (2009). External Democracy Promotion in Post-Conflict Zones: A Comparative-Analytical Framework. *Taiwan Journal of Democracy* 5(1), 1–26.

Zürn, Michael/Binder, Martin/Ecker-Ehrhardt, Matthias (2012). International Authority and Its Politicization. *International Theory* 4(1), 69–106.

Zürn, Michael/Checkel, Jeffrey T. (2005). Getting Socialized to Build Bridges: Constructivism and Rationalism, Europe and the Nation-State. *International Organization* 59(4), 1045–79.

Zwingel, Susanne (2012). How Do Norms Travel? Theorizing International Women's Rights in Transnational Perspective. *International Studies Quarterly* 56(1), 115–29.

# Index

# CAMBRIDGE STUDIES IN INTERNATIONAL RELATIONS